Becoming a Reader

THIRD EDITION

Becoming a Reader

A Developmental Approach to Reading Instruction

Michael P. O'Donnell

University of Southern Maine

Margo Wood

University of Southern Maine

PEARSON

Boston ▪ New York ▪ San Francisco
Mexico City ▪ Montreal ▪ Toronto ▪ London ▪ Madrid ▪ Munich ▪ Paris
Hong Kong ▪ Singapore ▪ Tokyo ▪ Cape Town ▪ Sydney

Series Editor: Aurora Martínez Ramos
Editorial Assistant: Katie Freddoso
Senior Marketing Manager: Elizabeth Fogarty
Senior Editorial Production Administrator: Deborah Brown
Composition Buyer: Linda Cox
Manufacturing Buyer: Andrew Turso
Cover Administrator: Kristina Mose-Libon
Editorial Production Service: Susan McNally
Text Design/Electronic Composition: Denise Hoffman

For related titles and support materials, visit our online catalog at www.ablongman.com.

Library of Congress Cataloging-in-Publication Data

O'Donnell, Michael P.
    Becoming a reader : a developmental approach to reading instruction /
Michael P. O'Donnell, Margo Wood. — 3rd ed.
      p. cm.
    Includes bibliographical references and index.
    ISBN 0-205-33293-5
    1. Developmental reading.   2. Individualized reading instruction.   3. Reading
comprehension.   4. Reading—Remedial teaching.   I. Wood, Margo, 1939–   II. Title

LB1050.53.035   2004
428.4'3—dc21

    2003041812

Printed in the United States of America

6 7 8 9 10 V036 15 16 14 13 12 11

Contents

2 Initial Reading Stage: The Process of Learning to Read   53

3 **Initial Reading Stage:**
Instructional Approaches and Programs **73**

■ **PART TWO** **Becoming Fluent** **103**

4 **Transitional Stage** **107**

APPENDIXES

Preface

Becoming a Reader: A Developmental Approach to Reading Instruction, Third Edition, is intended as a basic developmental reading text for preservice and in-service teachers. It has been our experience in teaching undergraduate and graduate students in education that a developmental perspective of literacy learning provides a helpful framework for understanding the process. We have found that most textbooks on reading methods are organized topically, with chapters on word identification, comprehension, study strategies, use of basal readers, literature, and classroom organization. *Becoming a Reader* is organized differently. We use a stage model of reading development to describe how children become skilled readers. Specific topics (such as word identification and comprehension) are discussed within this broader framework.

The text represents a synthesis of current thinking about how literacy is acquired. We have endeavored to produce a reader-friendly text by providing concise descriptions of the various aspects of literacy learning and instruction, supplemented by examples and case studies. To avoid overburdening the reader with lengthy literature reviews, we have cited only the most current and relevant sources to document and support the viewpoints presented.

As you read the text, bear in mind that we regard literacy learning as a constructivist process that is best acquired through the functional, purposeful use of print. The instructional methods we advocate reflect this basic premise.

Features of the Third Edition

The third edition of *Becoming a Reader: A Developmental Approach to Reading Instruction* continues to stress relevant, balanced approaches to teaching reading, but pays additional attention to diverse learners. Since the publication of the second edition, the research base pertaining to early literacy development and instruction has expanded greatly. Moreover, early literacy increasingly is the focus of political and academic debate. In response, we have added a chapter and reorganized material within Part I, *The Beginning Reader.* There are now two chapters on the Initial Reading Stage: "The Process of Learning to Read," and "Instructional Approaches and Programs." As in the second edition, throughout the text we emphasize the importance of teachers' knowledge of literacy development for assessing the needs of children, planning appropriate instruction, and fostering true enjoyment of reading. New features of the third edition include:

- New information on phonological and phonemic awareness, teaching of phonics, and fostering independent application of word identification strategies (Chapters 1 and 2).

- Expanded discussion of word study and teaching functional decoding skills within a well-balanced beginning reading program (Chapters 2 and 3).
- New sections on the use of leveled texts and on interactive writing (Chapter 3).
- Added emphasis on promoting literacy growth for second-language learners (Chapters 3 through 15).
- Expanded discussion of ways to help students acquire lasting knowledge of new concepts and words, as well as more suggestions for teaching **meaning vocabulary** (Chapter 6).
- Major outcomes outlined in **IRA/NCTE Standards** (2002) that are identified throughout the text.
- Thorough coverage of **how to assess the reading process** through actual case studies and related specific practices. Examples of assessment materials such as portfolios and teacher records can be found in the Appendix for easy access.
- How mandated state and federal standards can be related to the reading stage assessment and how schools are using the developmental stages to plan and assess reading instruction in relation to local, state, and national standards.
- **Case studies** that describe three children found in most classrooms (special needs, average, and gifted) and present what kind of assessment and accommodation is needed for these children, preparing students for a variety of challenges (Chapters 1, 2, 4, 7, and 9).
- Case studies related to student "portfolios" giving students the opportunity to practice assessment (Chapter 11).
- Reading development as a process that integrates supporting professional literature in literacy development, offering practical examples and classroom applications.

ACKNOWLEDGMENTS

We would like to thank the many practicing teachers and graduate students who have contributed to the development of this text. Their thoughtful reviews and suggestions have kept us firmly grounded in classroom practice. In particular, we would like to thank those individuals who reviewed this third edition and offered useful comments: Linda Conrad, Baldwin Wallace College; Janet Sue Rohner, Mount Mercy College; Michele Southerd, Illinois State University; and Joan Livingston Prouty, Sam Houston State University. The following Maine teachers offered invaluable suggestions for expanding our discussions: Judy Kennedy, reading consultant, Breakwater School, Portland; Shelly McNeil Moody, third-grade teacher, Oakland Schools; Kimberly O'Donnell, multiage teacher, Blue Point School, Scarborough; Tracy Warren, reading consultant, Riverton School, Portland; Peter Lancia, second-grade teacher, Westbrook, and Maine's 2001 Teacher of the Year.

Finally, we extend special thanks to Aurora Martínez Ramos, our editor at Allyn and Bacon, and Katie Freddoso, editorial assistant.

Prologue

*A*s we begin this prologue to the third edition of *Becoming a Reader*, written fewer than ten years after our first edition, much of what we know about reading and teaching reading has remained fairly constant. However, we never anticipated a decade ago the intensity of the debates that would take place regarding the teaching of reading, specifically the revival of the debate over the efficacy of skills-based (phonics) vs. meaning-based (whole-language) instruction. This debate has been fueled by the publication of several government-funded "scientific" research reports (Coles, 2000).

Although literacy researchers have been very critical of the conclusions drawn by the National Reading Panel (NICHD, 2001) to support skills-based reading instruction, the panel's report is being used to attack whole-language instruction and to mandate the explicit teaching of phonics in many states (Coles, 2000; Garan, 2001; Yatvin, 2002). The reviewers of the report stress that while such skills as phonemic awareness and phonics indeed correlate to reading development, there is no direct causal relationship between mastery of these skills and becoming an accomplished reader. They emphasize that the research has failed to show that direct phonics instruction has a statistically significant impact on tasks requiring the authentic application of reading in context (Garan, 2001), and that the research has not demonstrated the superiority of skills-based over whole-language instruction (Coles, 2000).

According to the media, Americans are engaged in a "reading war" (Vacca, 1996). Strident voices, both within and outside the education profession, are arguing about what and how to teach. According to Richard Vacca, a professor of education, "Newspaper coverage . . . has characterized the wars as a bloody conflagration between the proponents of phonics and whole language" (Vacca, 1996, p. 3). Teachers and students of education are frequently baffled by this controversy. Is there a real dichotomy? Whom should they believe? What is really best for children? How can teachers decide? Where has all this come from, and where is the teaching of reading headed? In the years since Vacca made his statement, politicization of the issue has further complicated the debate. The U.S. government has sponsored research of a particular type and restricted federal grants to programs having a "scientific" base according to a narrow definition of "scientific."

In fact, the controversies of today are not new. From 1950 to 1980, reading instruction was dominated by the use of basal readers and accompanying skill-building activities. Students were grouped by ability and teachers were expected to adhere to teachers' manuals written by so-called experts. This view of reading instruction held that children learn best when they are taught the component skills, in particular how to take apart sounds within words, connect sounds to make words, and recognize high-frequency "sight" words. In most classrooms, instruction was entirely teacher driven during this period, and opportunities for extended silent reading of "real books" were limited.

In the 1980s, due to the increasingly rich mix of research contributions from the fields of cognition, linguistics, and child development, as well as education, the process of literacy acquisition became better understood. Two major understandings that evolved were 1) that reading is an active, meaning-building process and 2) that literacy acquisition is an extension of language acquisition governed by many principles that apply to language learning. In the 1980s, instruction therefore shifted toward using meaningful literature instead of relying on basals. Teachers became more empowered to design instruction and to acknowledge children's needs and preferences. Strategies for processing texts were likely to be taught in context.

Proponents of instruction based on these ideas identified themselves as whole-language teachers. The whole-language movement assumed that children's motivation for learning to read was an extension of the desire to make meaning in order to communicate with a community of language users. Underlying premises of this movement were that reading is learned through immersion in meaningful, age-appropriate literature and that the process is modeled with whole texts. Systematic instruction and decoding skills were deemphasized and taught in meaningful literacy contexts.

In some classrooms, an imbalance in the direction of the child-centered curriculum and apparent rejection of systematic instruction in the skills and strategies of reading and writing sometimes resulted in lack of progress by students. The media and the public latched on to the problems these students were encountering and blamed whole-language instruction. Whole-language became the scapegoat for an array of literacy problems, regardless of circumstances or actual teaching practices. The fact that many children were benefiting from instruction based on whole-language philosophy was largely ignored.

A countermovement developed that heavily emphasized phonics instruction and the literal interpretation of texts (Weaver, 1994). This group was very vocal and politically active in support of its agenda: to give phonics instruction the central role in the teaching of reading. Purist proponents of phonics-based instruction went so far as to claim that the use of meaningful stories in early reading instruction actually impaired students' progress. They proposed that students should, instead, practice reading only decodable texts that are contrived to include only phonic elements that have been explicitly taught. Because this view reduces the complexity of literacy acquisition to a simplistic explanation, it has attracted many followers.

It should be noted that this controversy is focused primarily on decoding and literal comprehension—the most rudimentary beginnings of reading. What is our goal, as teachers? What is literacy? In her book *Transitions from Literature to Literacy* (1988), Regie Routman described genuine literacy as "using reading, writing, thinking, and speaking daily in the real world, with options, appreciation, and meaningful purposes in various settings and with other people. An actively literate person is constantly thinking, learning, and reflecting, and is assuming the responsibility for continued growth in personal literacy" (Routman, 1988, p. 15). She went on to say that the way we teach reading and writing in school is critical to the development of genuine, active literacy.

In fact, national tests show that from 1950 to the present, standardized test scores in reading have actually increased, based on the National Assessment of Educational Progress, which is administered regularly to fourth-, eighth-, and eleventh-graders across the country. The scores indicate gains in decoding and literal comprehension. However, U.S. students do not fare well at integrating and applying knowledge (Routman, 1996). Society is moving toward an increasing need for critical and analytical literacy; therefore, the data point to the following critical instructional needs:

- An increase in total reading instruction for all students
- More experience with challenging texts
- More opportunities to critically analyze and synthesize information from multiple sources
- Attention to increasing meaning vocabulary at all grade levels (Routman, 1996)

The answers to questions about effective teaching of reading are not to be found in the extremes, because effective teachers do not embrace fads or extreme positions. Rather, they recognize the need for balance between the study of the structure of printed language and meaningful encounters with whole texts. They also recognize the need for instruction to extend beyond decoding and literal comprehension. In David Pearson's words, teachers need to "reclaim the center" (Pearson, 1996). This book is intended to present a balanced perspective of how children become readers and to focus on practices that contribute to real literacy.

As always, the challenge facing educators is to translate theoretical knowledge into viable classroom practice. What qualities characterize teachers who have succeeded in designing effective literacy programs? They have usually participated in high-quality in-service programs, courses, and workshops. They have developed a knowledge base that enables them to make sound instructional decisions. They are astute observers, always watching, listening, and responding to their students. There is a pervasive atmosphere of enthusiasm and excitement about reading and writing in their classrooms, and both they and their students have high expectations for success. Their perspective of the literacy process transcends age and grade-level considerations and frees them from dependence on the rigid prescriptions of teachers' manuals. How do teachers acquire such a perspective?

A basic principle of comprehension is that information must be organized and classified by the learner if it is to be understood, remembered, and used. Our goal in writing this text is to organize the current body of knowledge about readers' development and reading instruction in an understandable and coherent manner. We have found in our work with both prospective and experienced teachers that establishing a framework for understanding the reading process helps them greatly in using the information they acquire to plan appropriate instruction. The framework we will present is based on the fact that learning to read is a developmental process.

Stages of Literacy Development

Literacy acquisition is continuous; however, distinct stages of reading growth can be discerned as students gradually become proficient readers. Initially, children must acquire an understanding of the nature and purpose of print. As they progress from generic understandings and rough approximations to more conventional uses of print, they begin to identify words in their printed form. Extensive reading practice leads to automatic recognition of a sizable number of words. Readers begin to encounter more concepts and ideas that transcend their experience. Further growth involves relating what is new to what is known in order to understand and use what is read.

This pattern has been described by various writers (Betts, 1957; Chall, 1983; Hill, 2001; O'Donnell, 1979; Powell, 1977) as consisting of a sequence of developmental stages. There is considerable similarity among these descriptions. Our particular designation of stages of reading progress is based on our own observations and many teachers' reports of children's reading growth, as well as the literature and research relating to literacy acquisition. We present five discernible stages of reading development; these stages form the basis for the organization of the text. It should be noted that these stages do not necessarily correlate with age or grade levels. However, general grade-level equivalents are cited in the following stage descriptions to give a sense of typical literacy development.

Stage I: Emergent Reading

Recent studies of young children indicate that a basic skills "set" for literacy must be acquired before they can begin to accurately match speech to print. Concepts relating to printed language—what it is for, how it is used, how it relates to speech—must be promoted through extensive modeling and meaningful experiences with the printed word. Emergent readers are extending their concepts of the world around them. Other significant features of this stage are extension of oral language facility and expansion of concepts and classification ability. As a consequence of appropriate literacy experiences, children will acquire those characteristics that form the foundations of further literacy development: They will seek and enjoy experiences with print, they will become familiar with the language of literature, they will understand and follow the sequence of stories read to them and will imitate reading on their own, and they will develop some specific understandings of the nature and purpose of print. Most preschoolers and kindergartners are in the emergent reading stage.

Stage II: Initial Reading

Students enter the initial stage as they begin to identify specific words in their printed form. These first *sight words* characteristically are frequently encountered and personally meaningful to the student: names, labels (*McDonald's, STOP, Cheerios*), and other high-meaning words (*love, ghost*). During this stage, students increase the number of words they can identify easily and learn to use word identification strategies to figure out words that they do not recognize at sight. They use language patterns and meaning cues, as well as knowledge of letter-sound correspondences to construct meaning from the printed text. If appropriate methods and materials are used at this stage, the readers will expect print to be meaningful. They will predict what the print says and will confirm their predictions by monitoring for meaning as they read. The majority of children pass through the initial reading stage during their first- and second-grade years.

Stage III: Transitional Reading

Students who have begun to decode print but are not yet fluent independent readers are in the transitional stage of reading. They recognize many words at sight and use word identification strategies successfully to decode many others; however, their reading tends to be slow and laborious since they have to consciously figure out words they do not yet recognize instantly. The major task of students at this stage is to increase reading fluency through extensive reading practice with interesting, easy-to-read materials that will maintain focus on meaning making. As a consequence of extended reading practice, students learn to recognize more and more words automatically. They literally learn to read by reading. Most children pass through the transitional stage between second and fourth grades.

Stage IV: Basic Literacy

This stage begins when students have acquired enough word identification proficiency to be able to concentrate more on the content of reading material than on the act of reading. They are able to read an increasing variety of materials independently and to use their reading competencies for different purposes. Word meanings and concepts that are outside readers' repertoires of experiences (i.e., words that are not part of readers' listening/speaking vocabularies) are now encountered more often in both narrative and informational reading. Major tasks of the stage include expanding the breadth of reading experiences, increasing meaning vocabulary, understanding material of increasing complexity, and developing awareness and use of productive study strategies. The basic literacy stage characteristics fit many of the students in fourth, fifth, and sixth grades. During passage through this stage, students' literacy becomes permanently established; even if reading instruction and practice are discontinued, basic reading competency will not deteriorate appreciably (Powell, 1977). For this reason the attainment of approximately a sixth-grade reading level, which marks entry into the next stage, is generally considered to be a benchmark of minimal, or *functional*, literacy. The reader is capable of performing most reading tasks required for day-to-day living.

Stage V: Refinement

This final stage of reading progress involves refining the competencies of the preceding stage. Vocabulary continues to expand, reading rate and flexibility increase, and higher-level reading and thinking competencies develop. The refinement stage is extremely important since it is during this time that students become able to deal with specialized subjects and technical information as well as to use reading for personal growth and enjoyment. Most students who have had appropriate literacy experiences through elementary school enter this stage in sixth or seventh grade and continue to refine their reading throughout their lives. Students who do not progress to this stage are unlikely to realize their full potential as critical readers and writers.

Generic Goals for All Reading Stages

While the delineation of stages is helpful in organizing the study of reading and in planning reading instruction, it should be noted that some instructional goals are not stage-specific; that is, they are applicable to students at every stage of reading. Helping students to develop positive attitudes toward reading, for example, should be a major goal at every stage. Leading children to experience pleasure in reading and confidence in their ability to read creates voluntary readers. At every grade level, effective teachers plan their instructional programs with this goal in mind. Another instructional goal that transcends stages or levels is the promotion of extensive and varied reading experiences. Teachers who read aloud frequently from a wide variety of literary genres are helping to achieve this goal. So are teachers who make good books available and provide their students with time and incentives to read them.

A third goal of reading instruction that runs through all stages of development is fostering reading for meaning. From the earliest imitative reading of preschoolers to the reading of a complex novel by a college student, the successful reader's focus is on meaning. In discussing each stage, we will show how teachers can promote this focus at every level.

Table P.1 summarizes the five stages of reading progress, including student entry characteristics, major goals, and instructional approaches for each stage. The text will elaborate on each stage; readers may find it helpful to refer frequently to the chart to maintain a perspective on how various topics in the text relate to the framework of literacy development.

The five-stage organization is intended primarily as a way to structure the study and discussion of the reading process. There will, of course, be variations in the rate of children's reading development. Instructional approaches and materials will be influenced by children's ages and experiences as well as by their designated stages. Occasionally, variations in the pattern of their development may also be observed. However, the majority of readers of all ages pass through these general stages in the sequence presented. When reading instruction is related to this framework, the pattern of reading development assumes clear organization, and teachers can see where various proficiencies fit into the overall picture. More importantly, a thorough knowledge of the development of the reading process provides teachers with a sound basis for making informed instructional decisions. When developmental continuums are combined with benchmarks or standards, teachers can then apply assessment information knowledgeably and usefully (Hill, 2001).

TABLE P.1   *Development of Literacy*

Stage of Reading	Student Entry Characteristics	Major Goals	Instructional Approaches to Be Used
I. Emergent Reading Typical of preschool, K	▪ Has oral language facility ▪ Shows interest in print	▪ Seek out and enjoy experiences with books and print ▪ Become familiar with the language of literature and patterns of stories ▪ Understand and follow the sequence of stories read to them ▪ Begin to acquire specific understandings about the nature, purpose, and function of print ▪ Experiment with reading and writing independently, through approximation ▪ See themselves as developing readers and writers	▪ Reading aloud to children ▪ Retelling stories ▪ Experimenting with writing ▪ Language experience approach ▪ Shared reading
II. Initial Reading Typical of grades 1–2	▪ Reads some words ▪ Has developed some specific print concepts ▪ Matches some speech sounds with letters	▪ Understand that reading is a meaning-making process ▪ Acquire sight vocabulary ▪ Make balanced use of the cueing systems in written language (syntax, semantics, and graphophonemics) to identify words not known at sight ▪ See themselves as readers and writers	▪ Continued immersion in children's literature ▪ Language experience approach ▪ Shared reading ▪ Follow-up activities focusing on sight vocabulary, storytelling, and word identification strategies ▪ Writing process
III. Transitional Typical of grades 2–4	▪ Recognizes many words at sight ▪ Successfully applies word identification strategies ▪ Reads independently	▪ Increase fluency in reading and writing ▪ Increase motivation to read and write ▪ Focus on meaning in reading and writing	▪ Extensive independent reading of self-selected materials ▪ Sharing reactions to reading with peers and teacher ▪ Directed reading at appropriate level ▪ Writing process
IV. Basic Literacy Typical of grades 4–6	▪ Reads a variety of materials independently ▪ Has an extensive sight vocabulary (reads fluently)	▪ Expand breadth of experience in reading ▪ Comprehend increasingly complex reading material ▪ Extend meaning vocabulary ▪ Develop awareness and use of study strategies	▪ Self-selected independent reading ▪ Sharing reactions to reading ▪ Directed reading at appropriate level ▪ Activities designed to promote comprehension ▪ Concept-building activities for vocabulary expansion ▪ Metacognitive strategies for coping with content area materials ▪ Writing process
V. Refinement Typical of grade 6 on	▪ Has acquired functional literacy ▪ Reads for a variety of purposes	▪ Extend goals undertaken at preceding stage with increasingly advanced and abstract materials	▪ Same as basic literacy

Content and Features of the Text

The purpose of this text is to provide prospective teachers and practitioners who have not had recent courses in reading with a concise overview of the process of literacy acquisition and an introduction to instructional approaches that acknowledge current thinking in the field. The sheer amount of recent research and literature on literacy is overwhelming. For this reason, we have attempted to synthesize and summarize in narrative form the major findings and recommendations from this body of work. Extensive elaborations of theory, technical discussions, and references to specific works have been kept to a minimum. The text is intended to provide a basic, organized framework of knowledge, the background for understanding more extensive and theoretical studies. While the text includes only what we consider the most essential information about reading development and teaching, it is intended to provide a sufficient knowledge base to facilitate the design and implementation of effective reading programs.

In order to foster the literacy development of their students, teachers need to systematically promote writing as well as reading. Reading and writing development are closely intertwined; for this reason, we have included limited discussions of aspects of writing development and writing process that are particularly appropriate to each reading stage. A full treatment of the writing process is beyond the scope of this text. We recommend that our readers pursue coursework and readings that will provide the necessary knowledge base to integrate reading and writing in their literacy instruction.

The text is divided into five major parts. Part I deals with the beginning reader and includes chapters on the emergent and initial reading stages. Part II is devoted to the transitional stage, which is unique in that readers move from dependence to independence in reading during this stage. Part III covers a wide range of topics relating to the instruction of readers who have become fluent. Chapters on the basic literacy stage include description of the stage, development of meaning vocabulary, the effective reading of increasingly difficult texts, and study strategies. Chapters on the refinement stage include the characteristics and instruction of middle school students and the special requirements of reading in the content areas. Part IV discusses the assessment of reading through standardized and informal measures and the relationship between assessment and instruction. Part V describes the organization and management of classroom reading instruction, including descriptions of two elementary classrooms.

Each of Parts I through V begins with an introduction to the content covered in that section. Each chapter begins with a structured overview, a visual representation of the content to be covered, which is designed to help you in two ways. First, it will show you what content to expect and how the major ideas are organized. Thinking about this before reading will help you comprehend the chapter. Second, you may find the overview helpful in guiding later review of the chapter.

Key terms in each chapter have been italicized and explained or defined within the text. Each chapter ends with a summary.

Case studies of three children with different developmental rates help you apply the information contained in the text. Each child's reading development is traced from kindergarten through seventh grade. At the end of the discussion of each stage of reading, these children are profiled, and you are invited to design appropriate instruction for them and to compare your recommendations with ours.

Kim's reading development lags behind that of most children her age.

John is a typical reader whose rate of development is average.

Theresa is a candidate for a program for gifted and talented children. Already reading when she enters school, she makes rapid progress in her subsequent literacy development.

Variations of Kim, John, and Theresa can be found in virtually any classroom at any grade level. Two of the three (Kim and Theresa) would be classified in most school systems as students with special needs. Although they might well benefit from extra help or attention, you will find that their reading instruction can be designed and managed appropriately by classroom teachers who have a good understanding of the literacy acquisition process. Our recommendations are based on the belief that while rates of development differ from child to child, the conditions and experiences that are necessary for literacy learning are the same for all children.

BIBLIOGRAPHY

Betts, E. (1957). *Foundations of reading instruction*. New York: American Book Company.

Chall, J. S. (1983). *Stages of reading development*. New York: McGraw-Hill.

Coles, G. (2000). *Misreading reading: The bad science that hurts children*. Portsmouth, NH: Heinemann.

Garan, E. (March 2001). Beyond the smoke and mirrors: A critique of the National Reading Panel report on phonics. *Phi Delta Kappan, 82*(7), 500–506.

Hill, B. C. (2001). *Developmental continuums: A framework for literacy instruction and assessment K–8*. Norwood, MA: Christopher-Gordon Publishers.

O'Donnell, M. P. (1979). *Teaching the stages of reading progress*. Dubuque, IA: Kendall-Hunt.

Pearson, D. (1996). Reclaiming the center. In M. F. Graves, P. Van der Broek, & B. M. Taylor (Eds.), *The first r: Every child's right to read*. New York: Teachers College Press.

Powell, W. (1977). Levels of literacy. *Journal of Reading, 20*(6), 488–492.

Routman, R. (1988). *Transitions from literature to literacy*. Portsmouth, NH: Heinemann.

Routman, R. (1996). *Literacy at the crossroads*. Portsmouth, NH: Heinemann.

Vacca, R. (1996). The reading wars: Who will be the winners? Who will be the losers? *Reading Today, 14*(2), 3.

Weaver, C. (1994). *Reading process and practices*. Portsmouth, NH: Heinemann.

Yatvin, Joanne (January 2002). Babes in the woods: The wanderings of the National Reading Panel. *Phi Delta Kappan, 83*(5), 364–369.

The Beginning Reader

*L*iteracy development begins in infancy. Babies and preschoolers are surrounded by language. During this period, they acquire more and more knowledge about oral language and about reading and writing, as well. In the past, preschoolers were not viewed as readers and writers by parents and teachers. It was thought that preparation for reading and writing should wait until oral language was well developed and children were ready for literacy instruction. Recent research has changed this perspective; we are now aware of the literacy learning evidenced by very young children. The 3-year-old who has been read to since infancy knows a great deal about stories and how they are read. The 2-year-old who delights in scribbling on paper knows something about writing. It is now recognized that children's developing understanding about literacy must be acknowledged and incorporated into early school experiences (Morrow, 2001).

The discussion of the theory and practice in beginning reading instruction in Part I is based on assumptions derived from research. These assumptions were summarized by the International Reading Association and the National Association for the Education of Young Children (NAEYC) in 1998. Young children need developmentally appropriate experiences and teaching to support literacy learning. These include, but are not limited to:

- Positive, nurturing relationships with adults who engage in responsive conversations with individual children, model reading and writing behavior, and foster children's interest in and enjoyment of reading and writing;
- Print-rich environments that provide opportunities and tools for children to see and use written language for a variety of purposes, with teachers drawing children's attention to specific letters and words;
- Daily reading by adults of high quality books to individual children or small groups, including books that positively reflect children's identities, home languages, and cultures;
- Opportunities for children to talk about what is read and to focus on the sounds and parts of language as well as the meaning of the text;
- Teaching strategies and experiences that develop phonemic awareness, such as songs, fingerplays, games, poems, and stories in which phonemic patterns such as rhyme and alliteration are salient;
- Daily experiences of being read to and independently reading meaningful and engaging stories and informational texts;
- A balanced instructional program that includes systematic code instruction along with meaningful reading and writing activities; and
- Writing experiences that allow children the flexibility to use nonconventional forms of writing at first (invented or phonic spelling) and over time move to conventional forms.

We consider children in the first two stages of reading progress (emergent reading and initial reading) to be beginning readers. The very beginning reader, in the emergent reading stage, is primarily engaged in discovering the "whole" of reading, the nature and purpose of printed language and the way it relates to speech or signing. This is the stage during which children notice signs and labels and use the surrounding context to guess what they mean. They imitate reading behaviors, paging through books and making up texts or reciting those that have been memorized. They attempt to write using scribble, letterlike marks, or (later) strings of familiar letters. This stage is characterized by developing awareness of what reading and writing are all about.

As children progress into the initial reading stage, they focus increasingly on the accurate mapping of speech to print. They recognize and read certain words, and they learn to use various cues in the printed language in conjunction with their experience to figure out the printed message. This stage is characterized by the development of strategies for determining the author's intended message.

Beginning readers progress through these two stages as a result of many meaningful and functional literacy experiences. Children's early reading experiences occur in social and cultural contexts and involve much interaction with other children and adults. The three chapters that make up Part I describe in more detail children's early literacy development. In Chapter 1, "Emergent Reading Stage," readers will find discussion of learning goals, supporting theories, and related instructional practices. The first set of case studies introduces Kim, John, and Theresa in kindergarten. The section on the initial reading stage is divided into two chapters (see Prologue). Chapter 2, "Initial Reading Stage: The Process of Learning to Read," elaborates on goals and general instructional content, while Chapter 3, "Initial Reading Stage: Instructional Approaches," discusses the theory and specifics of beginning reading methods, programs, and techniques.

BIBLIOGRAPHY

Morrow, L. M. (2001). *Literacy development in the early years* (4th ed.). Boston: Allyn and Bacon.

Neuman, S. B., Copple, C., & Bredekamp, S. (2000). *Learning to Read and Write: Developmentally Appropriate Practices for Young Children* (Position Statement). Newark, DE: International Reading Association.

1 Emergent Reading Stage

■ *Overview*

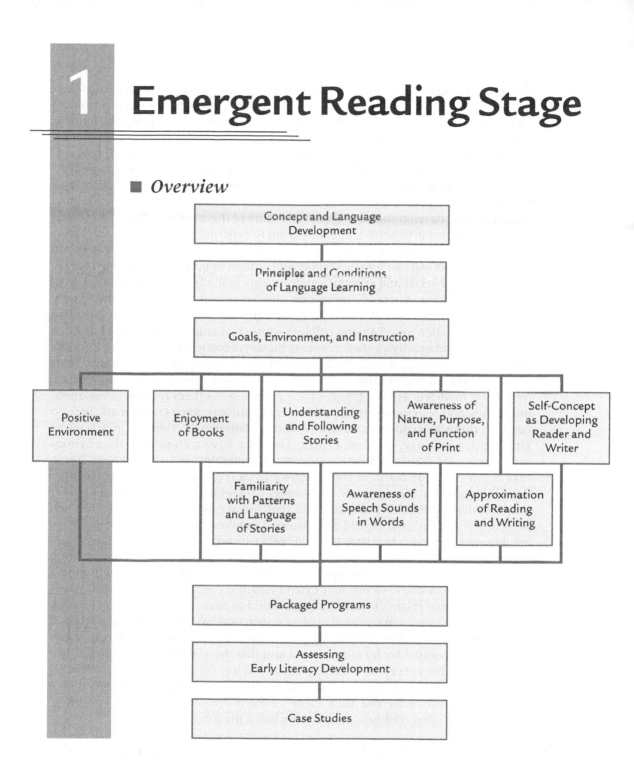

Concept and Language Development

Principles and Conditions of Language Learning

Goals, Environment, and Instruction

Positive Environment

Enjoyment of Books

Understanding and Following Stories

Awareness of Nature, Purpose, and Function of Print

Self-Concept as Developing Reader and Writer

Familiarity with Patterns and Language of Stories

Awareness of Speech Sounds in Words

Approximation of Reading and Writing

Packaged Programs

Assessing Early Literacy Development

Case Studies

*L*iteracy development begins in infancy and continues as children accumulate experiences and encounters with language in their environments. Children from all socioeconomic groups and all ethnic and cultural backgrounds develop the foundations for literacy in their early years (Sulzby & Barnhart, 1992). Emergent literacy includes increasing awareness of reading and writing and is an ongoing process.

Preschoolers and most kindergartners are at the emergent reading stage. They have mastered the basic grammatical structures of their native language; most have extensive listening and speaking vocabularies. As children are exposed to printed language, they develop curiosity about the nature of this medium. They come to see print as a problem to be solved, and they begin to experiment with reading and writing. Children who come from literate environments know the difference between pictures and text and can imitate reading and writing in inventive ways.

Children's social and cultural environments will affect the extent and use of their oral language. A steadily increasing number of children in the United States come from homes in which English is not the primary language spoken. The most significant variation found among children whose first language is English will be in the amount and quality of their previous literacy experiences. Some children will have been read to regularly and will be familiar with many books and stories. Their homes are literate environments in which reading and writing occur daily and are frequently modeled, as they observe their parents and others reading newspapers, magazines, and books and writing letters, notes, and lists. Such children are likely to emulate these behaviors. In contrast, other children will come to preschool or kindergarten with very different experiences. They have seen print in the environment (on street signs and food containers, for example) and on television. There may be no children's books in their homes and their parents may not have read to them. However, studies in inner-city settings by Taylor and Dorsey-Gaines (1988) and Gadsden (1994) have documented that literacy resources and practices are present in even the poorest and most stressed families' home environments. They are different and less varied than those in higher-income families where adults have had more formal education; nevertheless it is a mistake to assume that children growing up in poverty have no exposure to literacy outside of school. Effective early literacy programs acknowledge and extend children's previous experiences, whatever they are, and relate them to the larger world of print.

The beginning component of reading instruction has historically been referred to as *reading readiness*. The underlying premise was that a set of skills or competencies were prerequisite for learning to read and that these skills must be taught. The concept of readiness became widely accepted when publishers of commercial reading series developed materials for kindergarten and first grade that were intended to build prerequisite skills and thus make children "ready" for reading (Morrow, 2001). Most reading readiness programs included the following skills:

- *Gross-motor abilities* such as skipping, hopping, and walking across a balance beam
- *Fine-motor skills* such as coloring within lines, using a pencil, and cutting with scissors

16

- *Visual discrimination skills* such as identifying like and different pictures and geometric shapes, matching and naming letters, and matching words
- *Auditory discrimination abilities* such as identifying environmental sounds, hearing rhyming sounds in words, and hearing similarities and differences in letter sounds within words

The reading readiness model assumes that all children need to practice and master a specified set of skills before they can benefit from work with whole texts. The model fails to take into account the literacy experiences that children have had and the varying degrees of knowledge about reading and writing that they have acquired in natural, nonschool settings. The readiness model has fallen out of favor since we now know that children are not all at the same level of literacy development when they enter school and that literacy acquisition occurs along a continuum and in the context of real reading and writing experiences. The newer paradigm of emergent literacy is based on premises that derive from a large and expanding base of knowledge about cognition and language development. The following discussion of concept and language development and of the conditions of language learning are designed to provide the background for understanding literacy development, goals, and instructional practices at the emergent stage.

Concept and Language Development

The human brain has a unique capability for detecting patterns. This enables us to organize, to classify, to impose order on the world as we perceive it. *Concept attainment* can be simply defined as placing things, events, or ideas into categories. Children instinctively categorize, beginning at birth. This process occurs as a consequence of comparing, noting similarities and differences, and can be seen in the way children learn—first about the world around them, later as they achieve mastery of spoken language, and finally as they make sense of the world of print. Each of these instances of learning involves active problem solving as the learner attempts to impose order on the environment.

Can concepts be taught? We may be born with the ability to construct a coherent theory of the world; however, the specific contents of this theory depend on our experience and the way in which we organize it. Very little of the content and order of our theory is the result of direct instruction. Children themselves are responsible for most of their learning. For example, consider the following: A 2-year-old, out for a walk with his mother, points to a squirrel and says, "Kitty." His mother replies, "No, that's a squirrel." She does not necessarily elaborate on this or call attention to the differences between cats and squirrels. Naming the squirrel does not teach the child anything about it; it simply alerts him to the existence of a new category. The mother has created a problem; the child is left to discover the differences between cats and squirrels on his own. He will eventually differentiate between the two as a result of repeated exposure to them, assisted by adults' labeling ("Look at the squirrel" or "You can pat the kitty"). This process of assigning things and events to categories applies to everything we learn to distinguish: houses, cars, animals, letters of the alphabet, words (Smith, 1988).

While concepts are not directly taught, teachers can greatly facilitate the process of concept attainment by providing and structuring experiences. Children can be led to label, to compare, to explain, and to classify in many varied situations. Any activity that involves these processes will enhance concept attainment and add to the store of knowledge on which reading comprehension (as well as other learning) will eventually be based. For example, one kindergarten teacher introduced a new class pet—a guinea pig. Few of the children in the class had ever seen a guinea pig. The teacher encouraged the children to look closely at the animal and describe it. She then asked them to compare it to animals with which they were more familiar: a rabbit, a kitten, a rat. The children generated similarities and differences and talked about them.

Language development parallels, reflects, and shapes concept acquisition. Together they provide the raw materials for literacy development. It is widely agreed among linguists that the human linguistic system is largely innate (Chomsky, 1965; Pinker, 1994). Learning to understand and speak the language of the surrounding culture occurs naturally with maturation, provided the child is not isolated or deprived of language stimuli. It is plausible that an innate linguistic system provides the child with the complex grammatical structure that is shared by all languages. This same system could guide the learning process of the parts of language that need to be learned, such as vocabulary and certain kinds of grammatical rules. Reading and writing, on the other hand, are not innate, but must be consciously taught and learned (more easily by some than by others). Nevertheless, the writing system is based on language, and there are many significant similarities between the way children acquire aspects of their language and the way they develop literacy in that language. Children draw upon their oral language experiences in learning to read. Therefore, it is imperative that teachers of reading have a general understanding of the pattern of oral language development.

Children acquire their oral language in an environment that is rich with its purposeful use and in the context of social interaction. Their understanding and use of oral language proceed, in general, from whole to part. During the first several months of life, babies appear to randomly produce a wide range of vocalizations. The first evidence of awareness of the communicative nature of language can be seen when a child begins to visibly respond to such utterances as "Where's Daddy?" or "Wave bye-bye" by looking at Daddy or waving. The first apparently conscious attempts at speech production typically consist of global imitations of language (the whole), complete with varied intonations and social conventions such as turn taking, but including no identifiable words or phrases (the parts). Such babbling indicates that the child has acquired a gestalt for language—a general understanding of its nature and purpose.

This behavior has clear parallels in literacy development. Young children literally babble with print. Early attempts to write, for example, involve scribbling and production of letterlike marks that are distinct from drawings. Children who have been read to often sit and "read" books, turning the pages and telling the stories in their own words. Both of these behaviors reflect a general understanding of the way print looks and how it is used by readers and writers.

The most heralded event in a child's language development (from the parents' perspective, at least) is the spontaneous production of the first identifiable word. It is noteworthy that children's early attempts at producing words are usually greeted by adults with delight and encouragement and are referred to as talking even though the pronunciations are far from accurate. Adults focus on the meaning of the child's utterance, guessing it from the context and from cues that the child gives, such as pointing. Children's first attempts to read sometimes do not receive the same kind of acceptance and encouragement. Traditionally, first-grade teachers have treated inaccuracies in children's early attempts at reading as serious mistakes that must be corrected and worked on. If accuracy is prematurely stressed, children are deprived of an environment that supports their natural tendency to learn through experimentation and approximation.

J curve

As oral language development continues, single-word utterances are followed by combinations of two or three words, often referred to as *telegraphic speech*. The meaning of a whole sentence is condensed into a short phrase ("Allgone juice"). Two important observations can be made about telegraphic speech: One is that the utterances are not imitations of adult speech (parents do not say "Allgone juice"). The second is that the constructions are not random; the child is consistent in the ordering of words to express meaning according to rules he or she has constructed. The formation of rules for structuring language assumes a larger role in language development as the child's utterances become longer and more complex.

A period of extremely rapid language growth occurs during the preschool years. Speaking and listening vocabularies increase dramatically. Children's growth in understanding and use of the grammar of their language is even more phenomenal. During the preschool years, they master most of the basic grammatical forms and conventions of their native language, simply through functional interaction with others. This accomplishment is not the result of direct instruction or imitation. One hypothesis is that while language development may arise from an innate linguistic system, it also reflects a problem-solving process (Lindfors, 1987). Immersed in a language-rich environment, children may form implicit hypotheses about language structures on the basis of their experiences, test them in new situations, and revise them according to feedback from other language users. For example, many children produce incorrect past-tense forms that they have certainly never heard used by adults: "We goed to the circus." Having intuited that past tense is indicated by adding *ed* to verbs, they apply this rule in all situations. While linguists are not in agreement about the true frequency and cause of such overgeneralizations, it does seem evident that with further language experience and feedback, children qualify their use of the rule to include irregular past-tense forms: "We went to the circus."

This sort of problem solving can also be observed in children's early attempts to spell. Children who have learned that letters represent speech sounds and whose spelling reflects this knowledge often use letter names to represent sounds in words. For example, they come up with such spellings as *nhr* (nature) or *lft* (elephant). The use of letter names to represent portions of words is a logical and efficient way to spell them; however, it is not part of standard English orthography. As children gain experience with standard spellings (generally through reading activities), letter-name spellings disappear. The strategy has not been reinforced by the printed language environment.

Principles and Conditions of Language Learning

Approximations ↓ Structures

Language production appears to begin with gross approximations and to proceed gradually toward the conventional structures and forms of adult users (Lindfors, 1987; Wells, 1986; Wood, 1999). This same sequence of development can be seen in the acquisition of literacy by young children who are exposed to an abundance of appropriate literacy experiences. They first come to understand the general nature and purpose of print, as revealed in their gross approximations of the reading and writing acts. With additional reading and writing experiences, children proceed with solving the puzzle of print and how it works. They appear to form hypotheses and test them, revising them according to feedback from the environment and gradually moving toward more standard forms of reading and writing.

Brian Cambourne, an Australian researcher, added another dimension to our understanding of language and literacy development through his studies of the conditions under which language is learned. After hundreds of hours of observations of very young children interacting with their caregivers, Cambourne identified seven conditions that were present in all natural, social environments in which children's language develops. According to Cambourne, "In order to talk one must not only be human, but certain conditions must operate to permit that learning to occur" (Cambourne, 1987, p. 6). *Cambourne's Conditions*, as they have come to be known, are *immersion, demonstration, expectation, responsibility, approximation, use,* and *response* (Cambourne, 1987). An eighth factor, *engagement*, interacts in crucial ways with all the others (Cambourne, 1988, 2001). These conditions appear to be important in all kinds of language-based learning including learning to read and write and learning a second language. Therefore, it is important for teachers to become familiar with them. Let us look briefly at each one.

Immersion

Children are immersed in language from birth. It is an integral part of their environment; language flows around them constantly during their waking hours. They are surrounded by expert users of the language they will eventually acquire. The sounds, rhythms, and meanings of this language are all around them. Children learn to talk in an environment in which the language that is being used around them is meaningful, functional, and whole. Similarly, to acquire literacy, children need immersion in printed language that is meaningful, functional, and whole. They must be surrounded by print in many forms: books, newspapers, magazines, and mail in their homes. Environmental print, such as signs, ads, and labels, provides added exposure to print.

Demonstration

Language users in a child's environment constantly demonstrate functional, meaningful uses of the spoken form of the language. A toddler sitting on the couch with her father, for example, hears a stream of sounds issue from his mouth and sees her mother, in response, pass him the newspaper. Frequent demonstrations of this type occur in many different situations. Some demonstrations are repeated in similar contexts over and over, modeling the connection between language and meaning. The learner is thus provided with a great deal of data to use in incorporating these conventions as she learns to comprehend and produce language.

Speech is constantly modeled for children as they learn to talk. Similarly, reading and writing must be demonstrated on a daily basis by literate people in the children's environment as they learn about print. Just as the modeling of speech consists of real, functional talking, the modeling of reading and writing should occur in the context of real literacy activities. These might include reading for pleasure and information, writing to organize and manage (making lists, for example), or writing to communicate (writing a letter). Children from literacy-rich environments, where reading and writing materials are abundant and literate activities are an integral part of the everyday lives of the adults around them, generally are at an advantage in learning to read and write. The conditions of immersion and demonstration have been fully present in their lives. Regardless of the home settings children come from, teachers must make sure that their school classrooms are literacy-rich environments and that their students encounter frequent modeling and demonstration of every aspect of the reading and writing processes.

Expectation

Everyone expects children to learn to walk, feed themselves, and talk, unless they are born with severe disabilities. Cambourne believes that these expectations, which amount to assumptions, are subtly conveyed to children and positively influence their learning. When expectations for success are not present, there can be an adverse effect on learning. All parents expect their toddlers to learn to talk. They tend to be more equivocal about whether their children will learn to read and write and are often worried about whether their children will have difficulty learning to read.

We immerse our children in spoken language and enjoy every stage of their language acquisition without conveying to them the fear that they might not succeed or that we are worried about their lack of progress. Even children who learn to talk later than average are seldom hampered in their learning by adults' anxiety. (No one argues about the best methods for teaching children to talk!) Parents fully expect that all their children will eventually master spoken language, and they do.

In spite of the fact that learning to talk is based on innate capabilities while learning to read is not, all children except those who have major disabilities are capable of eventually becoming functionally literate, given the necessary conditions for literacy learning. Teachers must not only believe but convey their belief to parents and children alike that all students will learn to read and write. Too many adults doubt the truth of this and convey their anxiety if a child is not learning to read and write on a predetermined schedule. Within critical periods of time, children learn to talk at different rates; they also acquire literacy at different rates. Special concern and concerted interventions are called for only when children lag far behind the norms in developing literacy.

Responsibility

The order and pace of language learning are self-determined. We do not plan a sequential curriculum to teach preschoolers how to talk—responsibility for the individual route to language acquisition lies within each child. The order and rate of learning language are internally determined but of course not conscious. It is hard to imagine a mother saying "Sasha is still making mistakes in using past-tense forms of verbs. So that is what we'll be drilling her on for the next few weeks, until she masters it." You probably find this example silly. The age at which children master specific grammatical constructions varies; however, by the time they enter school, the majority have reached the same general level of language mastery and use. If adults were to assume responsibility for their children's speech development and design a sequential curriculum for teaching them to talk, learning to talk would become far more difficult for them.

All children pass through predictable developmental stages as they become literate; however, there is no prescribed sequence in which they master the various specific print conventions. Case studies of young children consistently demonstrate that they take somewhat individual routes to reach the same destination, in terms of literacy. Effective teachers take cues from their students regarding the pace and order of learning and are sensitive to what individuals know and seem ready to learn. Based on their observations, they help children extend their learning through guidance and practice. However, responsibility for learning ultimately resides in the learner.

Approximation

Language does not suddenly appear in its conventional, adult form. Rather, children's speech begins with gross approximations of language that become more and more refined over time. Adults respond to children's early attempts at speech with pleasure and encouragement. When a toddler points to his ball and says, "Bah!" his parents respond with delight. They do not expect him to produce precise, correct pronunciation. Their response is to the meaning of his utterance, not the form. Since they have the expectation that their child will learn to talk, they trust that his approximations will become more and more like adult speech as he hears and uses language. Approximation is expected and therefore accepted and encouraged.

Unfortunately, this is often not the case in the context of literacy learning. Although approximation is readily accepted as a matter of course in speech development, it is considered problematic in learning to read and write. In the past, children were often expected to read and write conventionally from the very beginning. It is now increasingly recognized by early childhood educators that children begin their literacy acquisition by imitating reading and writing acts. With lots of modeling, purposeful practice, and acceptance of their attempts, they gradually move toward accuracy. If approximation is frowned upon, and early attempts are consistently criticized and corrected, novice readers and writers are likely to lose their confidence and become reluctant to take risks for fear of making mistakes. If they stop experimenting with print, their literacy development will be hampered.

Use

One of the conditions for acquiring oral language is using speech repeatedly for real purposes. Children are not restricted in their opportunities to talk: They talk throughout their waking hours, accompanying nearly everything they do with speech. They have unlimited opportunities to practice the conventions of spoken language as they spontaneously generate speech. Suppose children were given only 20 or 30 minutes of "talk time" every day. This would not provide for nearly enough use of language to acquire proficiency and master the conventions. Moreover, it would be highly unnatural!

Just as young children have constant opportunities to use speech when they are learning to talk, school-age children need to be provided with frequent occasions for real reading and writing. The amount of reading and writing students do correlates highly with their achievement, not only in reading and writing, but in other school subjects as well. U.S. schools have been criticized for not allowing students enough time for sustained reading and writing practice (Anderson, Hiebert, Scott, & Wilkinson, 1985; Foertsch, 1992). In effective schools, literacy activities assume prominence in the curriculum at every grade level and across the content areas (Allington, 2001; Allington & Cunningham, 1996; Pressley et al., 2000).

Response

Another important condition of language learning is response to the language learner's intended meaning. When caregivers respond to young children's speech, they always respond to the meaning of the child's utterance rather than its form. In addition, they usually expand upon the child's language, modeling the adult use of conventions and pronunciation. These exchanges are natural; the intention is to communicate, not to correct or directly teach. For example, if a toddler says, "Daddy goed to work," her mother might reply, "Yes, Daddy went to work. He'll be home at supper time."

This type of response and modeling continues over a long period of time. Adults know that immature forms of speech will gradually disappear as children accumulate experience with adult conventions of language. Parents do not respond to children's speech with corrections of form: "The past tense of 'go' is 'went.' Now try that sentence again, and do it right!" Instead of drawing attention to differences between the child's speech and our own, we always respond to their meaning, and in doing so, we model correct forms again and again.

In the area of literacy development, teachers support beginning readers and writers by responding to meaning first and foremost, while continually modeling conventional forms. A good example of this type of feedback is the teacher who responds to a child's piece of writing by writing back, commenting on the child's message. In doing so, she uses some of the same words the child spelled unconventionally, thus modeling their conventional spellings. Teachers of young children expect to model in this way repeatedly before children's spelling becomes conventional.

Engagement

In addition to the seven conditions, Cambourne also writes about the child's willing *engagement* in learning to read and write. According to Cambourne, the main factor that leads to engagement is immersion in a print-rich environment in which adults are frequently writing and reading, demonstrating how texts are constructed and used. Engagement is fostered by adults' expectation—in fact their conviction—that children will succeed in learning to read and write. In environments that foster engagement, children will have opportunities to use written language frequently and for authentic purposes and to take responsibility for what they will learn from each literacy event. Acceptance of their approximations and appropriate, meaning-based response to their efforts are important as well.

It is important to note that Cambourne's use of the term *engagement* implies mental and emotional commitment (Weaver, 1994). Engagement will occur only if the child considers herself a potential writer and reader with her own real, immediate purposes for reading and writing. Furthermore, literacy events must not be associated with fear of criticism when attempts to write and read are not fully correct. If the learning environment subtly or explicitly conveys the message that learning to read and write is too difficult, complicated, and/or not relevant for learners like them, children will not fully engage in the task, even when instruction is exemplary (Cambourne, 2001). In other words, if engagement is lacking, literacy development can be delayed or derailed, even if all other conditions of literacy learning are present. For this reason, it is extremely important for teachers to be aware of the effect of their instructional approaches and curriculum on the self-concepts, interests, and motivations of their young students.

Goals, Environment, and Instruction in the Emergent Literacy Stage

The role of concept and language development and the conditions of language learning provide us with a background for understanding literacy acquisition. In instructional settings, goals must be specified. In an era of increasing attention to standards, attention must also be paid to assessment that demonstrates achievement of outcomes. The major goals for all children during the emergent reading stage are to:

- Seek out and enjoy experiences with books and print
- Become familiar with the patterns of stories and the language of literature
- Understand and follow the stories read to them
- Become aware of separate speech sounds in words
- Begin to understand the nature and purpose of print
- Experiment with reading and writing independently, through approximation
- See themselves as developing readers and writers

In the course of daily teaching practice, these goals are seen to encompass both competencies (what students can do) and dispositions (student's expectations and attitudes). Our discussion of the emergent literacy stage focuses on the nature and development of these competencies and dispositions as well as (later in the chapter) their assessment. The competencies and dispositions are closely interrelated and develop simultaneously as a result of meaningful language and literacy experiences and instruction. We will begin by examining the environmental factors that foster all of the goals, and will then discuss each goal and related instruction separately. Bear in mind that we view literacy acquisition as building on the child's language development and extending it into the medium of print, and we view the act of reading as the active process of constructing meaning from text (Farstrup & Myers, 1996).

Creating a Positive Environment for Literacy Learning

Developing solutions to the national problems of illiteracy and aliteracy begins with examination of the kind of school environments children encounter as emergent readers. If these environments nurture a positive attitude toward reading—that is, that reading is pleasurable, accessible to the children, and relevant to their lives— then they are well on their way to becoming adults who value and use the skill of reading. While this goal of nurturing positive attitudes toward reading is of the utmost importance at every stage of reading progress, it is particularly crucial at the emergent reading stage; during this period we can do a great deal to help children get off to the right start.

In addition to promoting positive attitudes, effective literacy environments also foster the goals of the emergent reading stage in an integrated manner. For example, when a teacher reads a new story to the children, they may acquire new concepts and discuss them, they will add to their experience with story structure and language, and they will reinforce their understanding of how print is used. When teachers write with children, encouraging "word stretching" (slow, drawn-out pronunciation) and spelling-by-sound, they simultaneously promote phonemic awareness and understanding of letter–sound relationships.

Establishing a Print-Rich Environment

The materials the teacher provides and the way they are arranged in the classroom invite children to explore the uses and pleasures of reading. Print is everywhere. It is used to define and organize the environment: Labels (used discriminately and with clear functions) designate where materials are kept; name tags identify children's personal coat hooks, cubbies, or work tubs; simple instructions are posted in interest centers; and sign-up sheets are used to keep track of children's activities and use of materials. These all demonstrate to children the functional uses of print.

Books are a featured attraction in the classroom. The way they are displayed and arranged conveys the teacher's high regard for reading and invites children to enter the world of books. The classroom library is an essential component of a print-rich environment. Studies have shown that children who have access to literature collections in their classrooms read and look at books significantly more often than children who do not have immediate access to such collections (Hickman, 1995). Moreover, Lesley Morrow's research showed that when classroom library corners were well designed, children chose to use them frequently during free-choice time.

Poorly designed library corners, on the other hand, were among the least popular areas during free-choice time (Morrow, 1982, 2001).

What are the characteristics of a well-designed classroom library area? First, the space is well defined. Separated from the rest of the room by partitions on two or three sides, the library area is large enough to accommodate several children comfortably, yet offers a certain amount of privacy. A piano, bulletin boards, and bookcases can serve as boundaries. Furnished with rugs, pillows, or bean-bag chairs and decorated with posters, book covers, and displays of children's responses to books and authors they have enjoyed, the library area attracts attention when children enter the classroom. Rather than simply housing books, it is a place where children can comfortably browse and explore books—becoming a favorite place for reading.

Books and other reading materials are prominently displayed in the classroom library, many in open-faced racks or shelves that allow the covers—not just the spines—to be seen. Books should be arranged according to categories. They may also be color-coded according to genre or topic. For example, alphabet books might be clustered together on the shelf, each with a label on its spine, marked with a green dot. Other colors could be used to designate holiday books, poetry, animal books, and so on. Categorizing books in this way introduces children to the concept that books in libraries are arranged topically to make them easier to find (Morrow, 2001). A recommended number of books for a classroom collection is at least five to eight books per child, with various genres of children's literature represented. Although the classroom library is the focal point of a print-rich environment, books should be displayed in other areas of the classroom as well.

Fostering an Atmosphere for Literacy Learning

There is convincing evidence that early literacy learning occurs as a result of extensive modeling, emulation, self-motivated practice, and direct instruction (Graves, Juel, and Graves, 2001; Morrow, 2001; Teale, 1982). When children observe the adults in their environment using and sharing reading and writing, their desire to engage in these activities is stimulated. A child who is encouraged to participate in literacy events with an adult and whose efforts are supported will independently imitate reading and writing behaviors. First attempts will represent gross approximations of the activities he has observed. When these efforts are accepted and applauded, when modeling and participation are continued, and when direct instruction is provided as needed, the child's independent attempts will gradually approach adult standards.

Natural, developmental learning can occur only in environments in which adults understand the importance of inducting children into literacy through authentic reading experiences. Adults must also realize that a long period of approximation precedes attainment of adult standards and that movement toward conventional reading and writing ("correctness") is incremental. The teacher knows that the vast majority of children will eventually become successful readers and writers provided they are immersed in a print-rich environment, that reading is modeled for them, that they participate in reading with others, and that their approximations of reading are accepted and encouraged. Because of this, the teacher creates a class-

Kindergartners' approximations of reading should be accepted and encouraged.

room atmosphere that is stimulating, supportive of risk taking, and free from threat of failure. Ideally, the climate of an early childhood classroom should be relaxed and accepting but also well organized and predictably structured to gradually increase children's reading and writing skills while at the same time fostering positive dispositions toward reading. Let us now examine each emergent reading goal and related instruction.

Enjoyment of Books

Children who have not had generous amounts of exposure to print and who have not seen reading for pleasure and information demonstrated by adults in their environment are not likely to seek out and enjoy experiences with books. When asked why read aloud to children in this age of electronic information, noted author Jim Trelease responds:

> The initial reasons are the same reasons you talk to a child: to reassure, to entertain, to inform or explain, to arouse curiosity, and to inspire—and to do it all personally, not impersonally with a machine. All those experiences create or strengthen a positive attitude about reading, and attitude is the foundation stone upon which you build appetites. (Trelease, 1985, p. 1)

Reading Aloud

Helping children to discover, over and over again, that reading is enjoyable begins with the sharing of good children's literature. Reading aloud to and with children is unquestionably the heart of effective early reading programs. Usually there are several opportunities each day to engage children in this activity. In one kindergarten classroom where we spent a morning, the teacher began the day by gathering the children around her on the rug to listen to a favorite story, *Alexander and the Terrible, Horrible, No Good, Very Bad Day* (Viorst, 1972). During snack time, she read aloud *The Three Billy Goats Gruff* (Brown, 1957) in preparation for a shared reading of an enlarged, simpler version. She ended the morning by reading aloud *Where the Wild Things Are* (Sendak, 1963), brought in by one of the children. In this classroom, reading aloud occurred frequently, every day.

Reading aloud to children must be accompanied by opportunities for the children to participate in the reading and in extension activities. Interactions between adult readers and children during and after the sharing of stories contribute greatly to children's orientation to literacy. For example, the teacher can stop reading from time to time and encourage children to react to a part of the story, predict what may occur next, and relate story characters and events to the children's real-life experiences. Such conversations encourage the kinds of thinking found to be most important in comprehending and fully appreciating stories (Morrow, 2001; Wood, 2001).

Familiarity with Patterns and Language of Stories

Research has consistently shown that children who have been read to a great deal are far more likely to be successful in learning to read than children who have not had this experience. One reason is that when children are exposed repeatedly to stories, they develop a sense of narrative. In other words, they gain familiarity with story patterns and story language. This enables them to predict the language and content of new stories and facilitates their comprehension and recall of stories.

Well-constructed stories have a common form and clearly identifiable parts. Story structures and their effect on readers have been extensively studied (Golden, 1984; Mandler & Johnson, 1977; Whaley, 1981). Scholars often use the term *story grammar* because it specifies the elements of a story and their relationships in the same way that sentence grammar portrays elements of the sentence and their relationships. A simple story grammar includes the following elements: introduction of character and setting, initiating event, internal responses (including goal setting), attempt, consequence, and reactions.

There are variations in scholars' descriptions of story structures and in the terminology they use. All, however, attempt to specify the common features of stories. When reading narratives, readers make use of story grammar, although not consciously. As we read, we anticipate the parts of stories, and our knowledge of the parts and their ordering helps us understand and remember the stories. Preschoolers who are read to a great deal acquire an implicit knowledge of story patterns and elements that enables them to enjoy and respond to a wide variety of stories. Teachers need to have a more explicit knowledge of story grammar, including awareness of specific story elements, in order to select appropriate stories, guide children's discussions, and assess their comprehension and ability to retell stories (Morrow, 1997; Schmitt & O'Brien, 1986). Story grammars will be discussed in greater detail in Chapter 7.

The best books to read aloud to young children are those with a well-developed structure and clearly defined, interesting characters. Such stories may have traditional narrative structure (story grammar) with each element well developed. Examples of children's favorites are *Goldilocks and the Three Bears, Blueberries for Sal* (McCloskey, 1948), and *Bread and Jam for Frances* (Hoban, 1964). Other stories do not follow a typical narrative pattern; rather, their appeal lies in repetition, catchy phrases, and high predictability. *Brown Bear, Brown Bear, What Do You See?* (Martin, 1982) and *I Know an Old Lady* (Bonne, 1985) are examples of books of this type that children love.

Reading good literature to children allows them to experience story language, as well as story structure. Story language differs considerably from the language of everyday conversation. Many whole phrases are unique to literature: *Once upon a time, he went off to seek his fortune.* The vocabulary is much richer than that of conversation: *Oh! exclaimed the king.* Or, *They dined on mince and slices of quince.* Word order is often changed in literature to achieve a rhythmic effect: *Over the hill the three birds flew.* Through frequent opportunities to hear good stories read aloud, children develop familiarity with the unique language of literature. This exposure to literature language presented orally adds immeasurably to children's overall knowledge of written language forms. Experiences with story patterns and language, then, provide a foundation for further literacy development.

Understanding and Following Stories

The ability to follow and recall the features of stories is essential for both listening and (later) reading comprehension and should receive a great deal of attention at the emergent reading stage (Gambrell, Pfeiffer, & Wilson, 1985). This goal, like goal 2, is addressed through listening and retelling stories. Retelling helps children develop awareness of story structure and sequence. Through practice in retelling stories, children learn to begin with an introduction of characters and setting, specify the central problem or theme, recount the episodes in sequence, and describe the resolution. They demonstrate their ability to organize the story coherently.

Teachers can facilitate and direct such practice in structured ways. For example, teacher-led discussion of stories helps to improve children's retelling ability (Morrow, 2001). The teacher's knowledge of story grammar helps him to lead children through a retelling that includes all essential story elements. The following series of prompts might be used:

- Who was the story about?
- How did the story begin?
- What was _____'s problem? Or what did _____ want to do?
- What happened?
- What happened next?
- Was _____ able to solve his problem?
- How did the story end?

Such a series of questions would lead to a simple reconstruction of the story. Certainly story discussion should not be limited to this purpose; children should also be encouraged to interpret, give opinions, compare characters, and pursue other lines of inquiry linking the story to their own experiences. Recapitulation of the story is useful, however, in helping children learn to follow and retell stories more completely.

Story Retelling

After a story has been read several times, children are encouraged to engage in activities that lead them to retell or extend the content of the story. Preschool and kindergarten teachers find that their students love to dramatize familiar stories, illustrate them, and retell them in their own words, using simple props. *Storyboards*, for example, are easy to make and stimulate children's retellings of favorite stories. A storyboard is a piece of oaktag on which key elements of the story setting are illustrated. A storyboard for *The Three Billy Goats Gruff* might include a bridge, grass, hills, and water under the bridge, all cut from colored construction paper and glued onto the oaktag. Once children have seen how the teacher constructs a simple storyboard, they enjoy making their own. Cutouts of the story characters, made by the teacher or the children, are kept in a construction paper pocket stapled to the back of the storyboard. Children use such boards frequently, alone or with other children, to repeatedly recreate the stories.

Puppets are also excellent props for retelling stories that contain a lot of dialogue. Many kinds of puppets can be simply made, including stick puppets and finger puppets. Stuffed animals and dolls can also be used to represent characters. The use of puppets enables shy children to feel more comfortable retelling stories.

Many other techniques for creating and using props help stimulate story retelling. Regardless of what sort of props are used, the value of these activities is the involvement of the children in repeated retellings of the stories. Story retelling leads to internalization of story structure and story language as well as increased recall of stories and interpretation of characters. Opportunities for these kinds of activities can be maximized in the classroom by providing art, drama, and storytelling centers that children can use independently. The involvement of parents creates still more outlets for sharing stories.

Awareness of Speech Sounds in Words

An increasing focus of research in recent years has been *phonemic awareness*, the understanding that spoken words are made up of separate speech sounds, or *phonemes*. A young child does not naturally distinguish sounds within words; becoming aware of phonemes requires focusing on the structure of language rather than its meaning. This critical awareness develops gradually during the emergent and initial stages of reading, and influences the child's ability to use letter–sound correspondences (phonics) in decoding and encoding print.

Phonemic awareness is part of an important aspect of language development known as *metalinguistic awareness*, the awareness of the structure of language apart from its meaning. As preschoolers, children learn to think about language itself, play with it, talk about it, and analyze it. Metalinguistic skills continue to be refined throughout the school years. The areas of metalinguistic development that are most closely related to beginning reading are those that relate to words and their makeup. During the preschool years, children advance beyond the concept that things have "names"; gradually they attain the understanding of words as linguistic units whose sounds are arbitrarily related to their meanings. Additionally, they begin to attend to the internal phonological (sound) structure of spoken words.

Phonological awareness is awareness of the sound features (both general and specific) of spoken words as distinct from their meaning. Phonological awareness develops on many levels in preschoolers, including the ability to identify and create rhyming words, and to manipulate, add, and take away initial phonemes to form different words (*Batman, Ratman, Satman*). Phonological awareness can be developed through repeated exposure to nursery rhymes, chants, poems, and stories that play on the sounds of words, such as the classic Dr. Seuss books (*The Cat in the Hat, Green Eggs and Ham*) and other popular children's books such as *There's a Wocket in my Pocket* (Cunningham, 1992). These experiences lead participants to listen closely to a text and to focus on its sound structure. (True phonemic awareness—the ability to separate words into all component sounds and manipulate them—typically does not develop until students are well into the initial stage of reading, and will be further discussed in Chapter 2.)

Typically teachers engage preschool, kindergarten, and first-grade students in read-alouds, games, and exercises that focus their attention on component sounds in words. At the same time, they provide many activities that involve recognizing and forming letters. Children in the emergent stage of reading simultaneously develop phonological awareness at increasingly refined levels and knowledge of the alphabet. These developing understandings come together in the teaching and use of *phonics*, the matching of letters with the phonemes they represent. Work with letter–sound correspondences aids phonemic awareness. For this reason, one of the most effective practices for helping young children simultaneously develop phonemic awareness, letter knowledge, and letter–sound knowledge is to encourage their approximations of writing.

When young children attempt to write, they are actively engaged in representing phonemes in print. This is perhaps the most important activity of all for enhancing phonemic awareness. Lesley Morrow explains the value of writing at the emergent literacy stage:

> When children write, they have to transform the spoken word into written language. This fosters understanding of the structure of spoken language and how it is related to written language. The more children write, the better they become at segmenting words into sounds, which not only develops their ability to write, but also their ability to read independently. (Morrow, 2001, p. 293)

Awareness of the Nature, Purpose, and Function of Print

The most crucial prerequisite for learning to read is an awareness of the existence, nature, and purpose of print. In order for children to understand the uses of print and purposes of literacy, they must have role models in their everyday environment—

people who draw upon both spoken and written language for a variety of purposes and who share these activities with children. An understanding of the exact nature of printed language and its relationship to spoken language can only be gained through direct experiences with print, mediated by a literate model. It is often assumed that these conditions are present only in homes where parents are well educated and have at least a middle-class level of income. Studies of early readers show, however, that many of the children who learn to read before entering school are not from traditional or high-income families. Although their circumstances vary widely, they all have had family members (often older siblings) who introduced them to literacy concepts, arousing their curiosity and building positive associations with reading and writing (Durkin, 1966; Taylor, 1988). Poverty is likely to contribute to lack of success in reading only if it is coupled with absence of literacy events, materials, and models in the child's environment.

Children who are immersed in a print-rich environment develop awareness of the existence, nature, and purpose of print as they see it used functionally every day. Their experiences lead to insights about what print is, how it is used, and, later, how it relates to speech. These insights are referred to as *print concepts*. Examples of print concepts children typically acquire during the emergent reading stage include: Words are made up of letters, print is read from left to right, letters stand for speech sounds. Such understandings are implicit; that is, children internalize these concepts and use them, but they cannot verbalize them.

Print concepts are interrelated and overlapping; some are learned simultaneously rather than sequentially. For example, as the child observes an adult following the print with a finger while reading aloud, the child may notice the left-to-right direction followed and also that letters are clustered together with spaces in between. In general, however, children's understanding of print concepts follows the principle that language learning proceeds from whole to part. The most global understandings are likely to be acquired first, and the more specific ones follow, though not necessarily in any particular order. The major print concepts, listed in order of most general to most specific, are as follows:

■ *Print is meaningful.* Unlike patterns on wallpaper or decorations on packaging material, print carries a specific message. A child who understands this concept distinguishes print from other graphic symbols. When asked to show where the name of the book is on the cover, the child will point to print rather than to a picture or border design.

■ *Print is recorded language.* As children observe the reading and writing processes or dictate to an adult who records their message, they come to realize that printed symbols represent language. Moreover, print captures language permanently. The label, name, or story will be read the same way by everyone who can read, every time they read it.

■ *Reading progresses from left to right, top to bottom (in English).* This concept develops as children repeatedly observe reading and writing modeled. Left-to-right progression is a sense that is acquired as children watch readers demonstrate (through pointing) the reading pattern and observe writers constructing print from left to right.

■ *Printed language is divided into words. Each written word represents one spoken word.* The concept of *word* develops slowly, as children observe and work with print. Speech occurs in streams; there are usually no discernible boundaries between words. In printed language, however, words are separated from each other by spaces. As children gain experience with reading and writing, they gradually become able to distinguish words from letters, syllables, or phrases.

■ *Words are made up of letters.* Most preschoolers encounter isolated letters in a variety of contexts, including alphabet books, toy letters, and *Sesame Street.* Until children have had a great deal of experience with functional print, however, they tend to confuse the terms *letter, word,* and *sentence.*

■ *Letters represent speech sounds.* Linguists refer to this concept as the *alphabetic principle.* Children learn first that the letters that make up texts are not randomly chosen. Letters stand for speech sounds. Once children have acquired this general understanding and have developed the ability to segment words into component sounds, they can begin to associate specific letters with the sounds they represent.

Many additional concepts related to the nature and purpose of print have been enumerated. All are interrelated and develop through extensive interactions with print. In addition, the social contexts in which literacy experiences occur are very important in shaping children's understandings and expectations of print. A well-known study by Shirley Brice Heath (1982) showed that cultural differences in parents' own use of print and in the way they interacted with their children about print had significant effects on their children's literacy development and success in school. She studied three socioeconomic groups within the same geographic area. She observed dialogues between mothers and their children, noting particularly how the mothers directed children's attention to books and the kinds of reading-related questions that were raised. The differences she observed were striking and highly predictive of later school achievement.

The expectations of the school most closely paralleled the kinds of literacy events that occurred in the high socioeconomic group. Heath found that when teachers were sensitized to the cultural and linguistic backgrounds of their students, they were able to relate some of their instruction to the children's experiences, which were thus acknowledged and valued. The children who fared best in school had teachers who understood and appreciated the unique ways in which their cultures had introduced them to literacy (Heath, 1982; Taylor & Dorsey-Gaines, 1988). Two important implications can be drawn from this research. First, it is clear that situations in which caregivers read to children frequently, encourage elaboration of texts, and help children relate the content of stories to real-life experiences are most conducive to success in learning to read. Second, teachers need to provide these experiences to young children in the school setting, using the children's previous literacy experiences and cultural expectations as a starting point (Wood, 2001).

Use of Enlarged Print

Children's understanding of the relationship between speech and print increases significantly if they can see the print as it is read aloud. For this reason, enlarged print ("big books," teacher-made charts, overhead transparencies) should be used extensively to demonstrate this association. Virtually any activity in which the teacher models reading as the children follow the lines of print will develop and reinforce specific understandings about printed language. For example, when the teacher points to each word as it is read, the children are learning that reading is recorded speech, each written word represents one spoken word, and reading progresses from left to right. Only after children are very familiar with a selection should the teacher call attention to features of print, such as words, letters, and letter–sound correspondences. Two specific methodologies that involve the use of enlarged print are the language experience approach and shared reading with big books. These will be treated in detail in Chapter 3.

In recent years the use of enlarged texts, or "big books," has become so popular that many teachers of young children end up substituting the sharing of big books for the reading aloud of rich children's literature. To avoid this pitfall, one must be fully aware of the differences in purpose between the two activities and in the kinds of books that are appropriate for each. Big books tend to be short, highly predictable, and lacking in literary elements. These materials are tailored for teaching and reinforcing print concepts and for facilitating speech–print matching and are entirely appropriate for these purposes. However, they should not replace well-crafted children's literature in the curriculum. Characteristics of high-quality children's literature include: elaborated settings, well-developed characters, a clearly defined plot, and rich language, as well as artistically powerful illustrations. When children hear *Peter Rabbit* (Potter, 1902) or *Blueberries for Sal* (McCloskey, 1948), they are acquiring a sense of story structure and language. They are responding to meaning, experiencing all that good literature (and therefore reading) has to offer. It is important for teachers to include excellent children's literature, read aloud on a regular basis for children's listening enjoyment in early childhood curricula. Reading of "big books" should be used in addition to—not instead of—literature reading.

Approximation of Reading and Writing

As Brian Cambourne explained, children learn through approximation. With practice, they move from gross approximations of reading and writing to more and more conventional forms. For this reason, it is important for teachers to encourage approximation and provide many opportunities for children to experiment with reading and writing. In order to monitor children's progress, teachers must be conversant with the developmental literacy behaviors they are likely to observe. What happens when kindergarten children sit down to look at books on their own? Billy sits by himself in a corner of the classroom library paging through *Where the Wild Things Are* (Sendak, 1963). He examines each illustration carefully before turning to the next one but says nothing. Nearby on the rug, Sovan is equally absorbed in his book, *The Lonely Firefly* (Carle, 1995), but as he turns the pages, he makes up a story to go with the illustrations. He speaks softly to himself in a conversational style. Rachel has *There's a Nightmare in My Closet* (Mayer, 1968), a favorite she has heard many times. As she turns the pages, paying close attention to the pictures, she recites the story, using much of the actual language from the book. Her friend Maria "reads" her book, *Mrs. Wishy-Washy* (Cowley, 1980), pointing to the words as she recites the text from memory.

These four examples represent various forms of story reading described by Sulzby, Barnhart, and Heishima (1989):

- Attending to pictures, not forming stories (Billy looks at pictures without verbalizing.)
- Attending to pictures, forming oral stories (Sovan explains each picture in his own words.)
- Attending to pictures, combining oral and written storytelling (Child explains pictures; includes some story language.)
- Attending to pictures, forming written stories (Rachel uses literature-like narrative to tell the story from the pictures. She includes some language from the book.)
- Attending to print, "reading" or reading (María tracks the print as she tells the story. She remembers and uses a lot of language from the book.)

Children may combine two of these forms of emergent reading (mixing conversational and literature-like narrative, for example). As they accumulate experiences with literature, they move toward the last form, attending to print while retelling the story.

Sulzby, Barnhart, & Heishima (1989) also described the various ways in which young children attempt to write. Within kindergarten classrooms, she noted the following writing behaviors:

- *Writing by drawing:* When children write by drawing, they use drawing to communicate a message and "read" their drawings as though they were accompanied by print.
- *Writing by scribbling:* Young children who use scribbling to represent writing have some idea of what conventional writing looks like (cursive, particularly) and how it is formed. They often move across the page from left to right and appear to have a general understanding of the nature and purpose of writing.
- *Writing by making letterlike forms:* When using this form of writing, children show their awareness that writing consists of strings of separate marks. The marks made by the child are not poorly formed letters; they are original creations that resemble letters.
- *Writing by reproducing memorized units:* Recognizable letters appear in this form of writing. Children who have learned to write their names or isolated letters reproduce these well-known units in random order to represent writing.
- *Writing by invented spelling:* There are many varieties and levels of invented spelling, but all represent attempts to use the alphabetic principle (letters stand for speech sounds). At first, whole words may be represented by single letters, usually the first letter sound heard in the word (*b* for *boy*, for example). As children develop more knowledge about letter–sound relationships, more speech sounds are represented in their spellings.
- *Writing using conventional spelling:* The child's writing consists mostly of standard spellings.

Sulzby et al. (1989) notes that these categories of writing are not always sequential in their use. Young children sometimes switch from one form to another depending on the length and complexity of the message. For example, a 5-year-old might use invented spelling to write a caption for her picture but revert to letter strings or scribble to represent a story. The effort required to identify the letters needed to record words phonetically is far too laborious for this child to use when recording a long text. Even though children switch from one form to another, the categories of writing are still helpful in structuring teachers' observations about children's writing development (Sulzby, Barnhart, & Heishima, 1989).

Promoting Writing

In the past, parents and teachers tended to view children's earliest attempts at writing with amusement. The general feeling about learning to write was that children couldn't communicate through writing until they knew how to read and had mastered the conventional spellings of many words. Writing is viewed very differently today. Over the past 20 years, early writing has been the focus of much research and observation. Today, children's early writing is recognized as an integral part of their literacy development and is encouraged, in all its many forms, in early childhood classrooms. In the emergent reading stage, children teach themselves to write, to some extent, in the same way they teach themselves to talk and later to read—through experimentation. Reading and writing are closely linked in the emergent reading stage. Through their experiments with writing, children construct and refine the knowledge about print that is necessary for both reading and writing (Teale & Sulzby, 1989).

Writing, like reading, develops in an environment where children see its use modeled by adults, where inviting materials are plentiful and accessible, and where approximations are expected and accepted. Current understanding of literacy development dictates that teachers respond to all of children's efforts at writing, even the most primitive, as meaningful messages. It is also important to accept the different kinds of writing undertaken by young children as equally valuable. Lists of words, strings of letters, and copied book titles are no less important than attempts to create stories. Emergent readers are focused more on the process of writing than on the form or content. Therefore, while modeling by the teacher is highly appropriate, excessive direction to children is not. Help and correction should be given only in response to children's individual requests and expressed needs (Morrow, 2001).

Self-Concept as Developing Reader and Writer

Years ago when the role of approximation in language development was not recognized, children were not considered to be reading and writing until they could read and write conventionally. When children are encouraged to experiment with print, and when adults respond to their attempts positively, with a focus on meaning, even very young children perceive their attempts as valid, age-appropriate products.

Although young children recognize that their forms differ from those of adults, they consider themselves to be reading and writing. In a print-rich environment, they continually elaborate and refine their concepts of how one reads and writes. The role of adults is to celebrate and encourage young children's approximations and to model the processes and conventions of reading and writing.

Packaged Programs

Surveys of reading instructional practices show that many kindergartens use commercial materials designed to promote reading "readiness." Because many kindergarten teachers have their pupils for only half of each school day, contact time is limited and should therefore be carefully planned. Literacy acquisition is a high priority in early childhood education and should receive primary emphasis. Commercial programs, however, tend to provide an indiscriminate coverage of so-called readiness skills, many of which are not relevant to the goals of the emergent reading stage. Most of the commercial materials used in kindergartens are part of the sequence of basal reader programs. At the kindergarten level, there are generally two or three workbooks and a teacher's manual. In many schools, teachers are required to use basal materials. If this is the case, kindergarten teachers should choose these materials critically and selectively, bearing in mind that they do not constitute a complete literacy program. At best they serve a supplementary function. It is up to each teacher to decide which materials are appropriate for her children and how these materials should be used. The following questions may be helpful in making such choices:

- Do the objectives of the program or activity reflect the instructional goals of the emergent reading stage?
- Is the content appropriate for the children in your class? In other words, do the activities and illustrations reflect the cultural backgrounds of the children?
- Does the teacher's manual encourage decision making by the teacher and flexible use of the materials, rather than giving rigid prescriptions?

Those materials deemed appropriate are probably best used independently by children to reinforce concepts when the teacher needs to work with individuals or small groups. In classrooms in which teachers use commercial materials effectively, the materials are integrated into a comprehensive literacy program that includes many meaningful experiences with print.

Assessing Early Literacy Development

Assessment of emergent literacy has changed significantly, from reliance on formal, standardized testing to an emphasis on informal, ongoing teacher observations. In the past, standardized "reading readiness" tests were used to place children and to measure their achievement in kindergarten and first grade. These measures traditionally included vocabulary knowledge, letter knowledge, visual discrimination of shapes and words, auditory discrimination, letter–sound correspondences, and copying. The usefulness of standardized readiness tests was often questioned, since the scores they provided did not correlate highly with success in beginning reading (Dykstra, 1967). This is not surprising in view of the fact that crucial factors in reading success—familiarity with books, understanding of the nature and purpose of print, and phonological awareness—were not tested. As standardized tests have largely been replaced by informal or structured observations, teachers have assumed greater responsibility for assessment (Ruddell & Ruddell, 1995). This requires them to know a great deal about both early literacy development and about assessment.

Before considering more appropriate assessments of emergent reading, the role of assessment in general, and at this level in particular, must be examined. There are two purposes for which assessments are used: to obtain information that will help the teacher plan appropriate instruction and to measure students' progress. Since all children profit greatly from immersion in a print-rich environment, the usefulness of assessment of individuals' placement on the literacy continuum may be questioned. For example, a kindergarten teacher who is planning to use an enlarged version of *The Three Billy Goats Gruff* for a shared reading lesson will base his plans on a sound knowledge of what is appropriate for all children: modeling the reading act; encouraging children to predict, read along, and discuss the story; and providing opportunities for retelling and extension of the story. The teacher knows that the children will respond differently and acquire different insights from the lesson based on their varying levels of literacy development and experience. Since all the children's differences can be accommodated appropriately within such functional reading and writing activities, assessment of individual children is often not necessary for the purpose of instructional planning.

The use of assessment instruments to measure student growth is also problematic at the emergent reading stage. Schools are legitimately concerned with the documentation of student progress. But what, exactly, constitutes progress toward beginning reading and writing? As we have seen, progress toward literacy is a complex process involving concept building, language development, and experiences with print. None of these areas can be broken into isolated, measurable components without risking artificiality and loss of meaning in activities. Growth can be observed and documented, however, through structured observations of situations in which children demonstrate their understanding of language and interact with print.

The most useful assessments of early literacy, then, are informal and observational in nature and focus on children's experiences with language and print. A review of the instructional goals for the emergent reading stage would indicate that assessment should focus on three areas: familiarity with books and stories, awareness of the phonological components of speech, and concepts about print.

Familiarity with Books

Children who have had extensive exposure to books will spontaneously turn a storybook right side up, open it with the spine on the left, and distinguish between pictures and print (which "tells the story"). In addition, children who have been read to extensively will be able to retell a story in sequence and with considerable detail, using some of the language from the story. By observing children's interactions with books and reactions to stories, the teacher can learn a great deal about the extent of their literacy experiences (Morrow, 2001).

Phonological Awareness

Children demonstrate phonological awareness when they manipulate words. There are many levels of phonological awareness, and children develop some before others. Perhaps the best way to informally assess the development of awareness of speech sounds and of the ability to manipulate them is to observe individual children's participation in group activities that require them to detect and produce rhymes and alliteration, as well as to clap or count syllables.

Print Concepts

Children's understandings about print can be assessed by asking them questions about the print, following the reading aloud of a story. For example, can they point to a letter? Can they point out a word and indicate where it begins and ends? Can they identify any letters or words?

One of the best ways to assess children's knowledge of specific print concepts is through analysis of writing samples. To be useful for assessment, the writing sample must include an attempt by the child to compose a printed message without help. Through analysis of this sample, the teacher can make inferences about the child's knowledge of the form and function of print. Although Sulzby (1992) cautions against a sequential interpretation of the forms of writing used by young children, Gentry (1987, 1997) and others have documented and described four distinct stages of invented spelling that early writers pass through before becoming proficient with standard spelling. In the *precommunicative* stage, spellings consist of random orderings of whatever letter and letterlike marks the child is able to produce from recall. No awareness of letter–sound correspondence is evidenced. The writer appears to be experimenting with writing and with the alphabet. The second stage is labeled *semiphonetic*. The child in this stage produces one-, two-, or three-letter spellings that reflect a primitive concept of the alphabetic principle, or linking of letter to sound. Children in the *phonetic* stage, which follows, show a far more complete understanding of letter–sound correspondences. All sound features in each word are represented according to the way the child hears and pronounces them. In the fourth, or *transitional*, stage, vowels are usually included in every syllable and familiar spelling patterns are used, although often inappropriately. Invented words are interspersed with sight words, correctly spelled, for the child has had considerable reading experience and has been systematically exposed to standard spelling. The child is moving from spelling "by ear" to spelling "by eye" (Gentry, 1997).

Samples of young children's writings should be of particular interest to teachers, as they provide clear evidence of print concepts that have been acquired (Wood, 1999). The stages of invented spelling, with characteristics, examples, and implicit understandings shown, are summarized in Table 1.1. By using the invented spelling chart the teacher can establish which print concepts have been attained. For example, does the child understand that language is recorded with graphic symbols? Does he know that letters stand for speech sounds and use this knowledge to spell phonetically? What other observations can be gleaned from the child's writing?

TABLE 1.1   *Invented Spelling Development*

Stage	Characteristics	Examples	Implicit Understandings Shown
Precommunicative	Random ordering of letters and other symbols known by child, sometimes interspersed with letterlike marks.	*b + B p A* = monster *7 PAHI* = giant	▪ Language can be recorded by means of graphic symbols.
Semiphonetic	One-, two-, and three-letter representations of discrete words. Letters used represent some speech sounds.	*P* = pie *D G* = dog	▪ Language is composed of words. Recorded language consists of written words.
Phonetic	Spellings include all sound features of words, as child hears and articulates them.	*P P L* = people *Spashle* = especially	▪ Every sound feature of a word is represented by a letter or combination of letters. ▪ The written form of a word contains every speech sound, recorded in the same sequence in which sounds are articulated when the word is spoken.
Transitional	Vowels are included in every recorded syllable, familiar spelling patterns are used, standard spelling is interspersed with "incorrect" phonetic spelling.	*highcked* = hiked *tode* = toad *come* = come	▪ It is necessary to spell words in such a way that they may be read easily by oneself and others. ▪ Every word has a conventional spelling that is used in printed materials. ▪ There are various ways to spell many of the same speech sounds. ▪ Many words are not spelled entirely phonetically.

A simplified format for assessment of early literacy that has been successfully by many teachers is included in Table 1.2. While this assessment is extremely informal, it could be administered at the beginning and end of the school year. Comparison of noted results would document progress in a slightly more structured way than day-to-day or month-to-month teacher observations. For more detailed discussion and guides for analyzing emergent readers' behaviors, see *Literacy Development in the Early Years* by Lesley M. Morrow (2001).

TABLE 1.2 *Early Literacy Assessment: Understanding the Nature and Purpose of Print*

Part I: Familiarity with Books

- Select an age-appropriate book that is new to the child. Hand the book to the child and invite her to look at it. Note whether she turns the book *right side up, opens it with the spine on the left,* and so on.

- Try to discover whether the child *distinguishes print from pictures.* (Ask, "What part tells the story? What part do I have to look at when I read?")

- Read the story aloud; ask the child to retell the story without referring to the book. Create an authentic reason for this. For example, "Suppose you are going to tell your Mom (brother or friend, etc.) what this story was about. Let's practice. Tell everything you can remember." Prompt as little as possible. If the child is unable to retell the story from memory, let him or her use the book as a prop. Observe the following: Was the retelling complete and in sequence? Did it include many details? Did the child use complete sentences? Did she or he include any "story language"?

Part II: Phonological Awareness

- Give the child several words that rhyme (*fat, cat, bat*). Ask her to tell you another word that would "fit" with those, i.e., that would rhyme with them. If the child cannot think of any, suggest several words and ask whether or not each one rhymes with *fat* and *cat* (*rat, jump, hat*). Go through the same process with alliteration (Peter packed purple pants) and see whether the child can either generate (supply) or designate (choices supplied by you) words that begin with the same sound as those in your sentence.

Part III: Print Concepts

- See if the child can point to a word, a letter, a sentence in the book. (The task is not to read words or name letters, but rather to demonstrate understanding of these concepts.) Does the child know names of any letters? Does he recognize any words?

- Encourage the child to "write something" (or to draw and label the drawing). Analyze the writing sample according to Table 1.1. Specify what print concepts the child has acquired and which ones are not yet developed. (A word of caution is in order here. Emergent writers may use different forms of writing in different situations. To ensure that the sample you get is typical for the child, you may want to get others from the child's parent or teacher for comparison.)

If teachers are required by their school systems to use a standardized assessment, they are advised to choose an instrument that reflects the instructional goals of the emergent reading stage. Perhaps the most widely used assessment that conforms to this criterion continues to be Marie Clay's Concepts about Print test. Instructions for use and follow-up procedures can be found in Clay's book *The Early Detection of Reading Difficulties: A Diagnostic Survey with Recovery Procedures* (1979).

■ CASE STUDIES

As noted in the prologue, case studies of three children—Kim, John, and Theresa—will be used to show variations in literacy development and to illustrate the characteristics of each stage manifested in real children. In this chapter, we introduce Kim, John, and Theresa as they begin kindergarten. As you read each child's profile, think about what experiences would be particularly appropriate for that child.

■ Kim

When Kim entered kindergarten, her teacher described her as a very active, social child. She moved quickly from one activity to another and obviously enjoyed the company of other children. She communicated spontaneously with the teacher and other children, but her language was less mature than that of most of her classmates. She mispronounced many words, often used phrases rather than complete sentences, and seemed to have a somewhat limited vocabulary. She could not recognize or provide rhyming words (spoken) without help from the teacher or other children.

After the first few weeks of school, Kim was beginning to enjoy story time but could attend to the reading for only a short period of time without becoming restless. She could not retell a complete story. She could respond to specific questions but did not elaborate. Kim was able to recognize only a few letters of the alphabet and had difficulty with fine-motor tasks such as drawing. On the basis of her behaviors, her teacher speculated that Kim had not had extensive experiences with print. The teacher used the early literacy assessment shown in Table 1.2 to discover more about Kim's familiarity with books and stories and about her knowledge of the nature and purpose of print. The results were as follows:

PART I: Familiarity with Books

The teacher handed Kim a copy of *Where the Wild Things Are* (Sendak, 1963) and invited her to look at it. Kim turned the book right side up with spine on the left, opened it, and paged through it. She was intrigued with the monsters, which she referred to as "funny animals." When asked to look at a page and tell "What part do I have to look at to read the story?", Kim moved her hand over the whole page. She did not point to the print.

The teacher read the story aloud to Kim, who appeared to attend with interest. Then the teacher closed the book and said, "When you get home today, you might want to tell your mom about this story. What will you say to her? Try to tell me all you can remember about the story."

Kim: It was a boy and his dog.

Teacher: Can you tell me any more? What happened?

Kim: They went to the woods. (Pause) An' they seed some aminals.

Teacher: Can you remember any more? (Kim shook her head, no.)

Teacher: Would you like to use the book to help you? (She offered Kim the book, but Kim waved it away. She had lost interest and asked if she could go play.)

After following the directions for eliciting a retelling of a story, the teacher considered the questions outlined in the early literacy assessment: Was the retelling complete and in sequence? Did it include many details? Did the child use complete sentences? Did she include any story language? In Kim's case, the answer to each of these questions is no.

PART II: Phonological Awareness

Since Kim showed little phonological awareness during rhyming activities and games with names of children in the class, her teacher did not attempt to assess her phonological awareness further.

PART III: Print Concepts

The next day the teacher took Kim aside and looked at the book with her again. Kim was unable to distinguish between a word, a letter, and a sentence when she was asked to point to them. In each case, she swept her hand across a whole line of print. When asked to point to any letters she knew, she pointed to a *k* and named it but did not identify any other letters. She did not recognize any words, either.

When asked to write something, Kim produced the writing sample shown in Figure 1.1. According to Gentry's (1987) and Gentry and Gillet's (1993) classification of the forms of early writing, Kim is best described as precommunicative.

FIGURE 1.1 *Kim's Writing Sample*

Her writing consisted entirely of letterlike marks (no recognizable letters), sprinkled randomly over the paper. When asked to "read" what she had written, Kim said (without pointing), "Kim play with blocks." Kim showed that she knows that print conveys a message and that it consists of graphic symbols. Although she cannot make any actual letters, she knows what letters look like.

Interpretation of Kim's Assessment

On the basis of Kim's responses to the assessment tasks, her teacher drew the following conclusions:

> Kim has not had extensive experiences with stories. She lacks awareness of story structure and language. Her understanding of the nature and purpose of print is still very global. She understands that print conveys meaning, but she does not yet have a sense of the specific structure and function of print.

On the basis of the information presented, speculate on the components of an appropriate instructional program for Kim. Then read on to compare your ideas with our suggestions.

Kim's Instructional Program

Most important, Kim needs to be in a print-rich environment where she will encounter books, labels, signs, charts, and a variety of reading and writing materials. Within this setting, the following activities would be particularly appropriate:

- Listening to stories read aloud by the teacher (and frequently repeated)
- Discussing those stories and comparing them to other stories and to real-life events
- Retelling familiar stories by means of dramatization, storyboards, puppets, and artwork
- Opportunities to look at books independently or with other children and to "play at reading"
- Listening to nursery rhymes and chants, and playing games that involve rhymes or alliteration
- Activities involving letter identification
- Frequent opportunities to compose, through drawing, "writing," and dictation

In all of these activities, Kim's teacher can best promote her literacy development by accepting her approximations, encouraging her efforts to communicate, and constantly modeling both oral and written language in use. She can also help Kim by drawing attention to the characteristics of words ("Kite. Hear? It begins just like Kim!") and the names of letters. ("They both start with *K* when we write them.")

■ John

John's kindergarten teacher noted that he got along well with other children but often chose solitary activities such as looking at books, doing puzzles, and drawing. His oral language seemed to be similar to that of the majority of 5-year-olds.

Story time was a favorite with John. He was engrossed in listening and sustained interest throughout every story that was read aloud. He made many spontaneous comments about characters and events and was able to retell stories in considerable detail when prompted. When he entered kindergarten, he recognized most letters of the alphabet and showed beginning awareness of letter–sound correspondences. (He remarked to his teacher that "Jam begins like John, so it has a *j*.")

Following are the results of John's early literacy assessment, which was administered early in the school year.

PART I: Familiarity with Books

When John was handed a copy of *Where the Wild Things Are,* he turned the book right side up and said, "Hey! This book is about monsters!" He paged through it, commenting on the monsters and speculating about Max: "What's he doing here?" "The boy is going in a boat." "Why does he have on a crown? He must be a king!" When the teacher asked what part of the page she had to look at in order to read the story, John pointed to the print and said, "All these words." John listened with great interest as the teacher read the story to him. Afterward, the teacher asked John to retell everything he could remember about the story.

> *John:* Well, Max got in trouble because he chased his dog. And he yelled at his mother. So he had to go to his room. And then all kinds of trees started growing in his room. (John paused, and looked at the teacher.)
>
> *Teacher:* Yes, they did. What happened then?
>
> *John:* He got in a boat and sailed far away. Then he found the wild things. (Another pause.)
>
> *Teacher:* What did they do?
>
> *John:* They roared at him. And they had terrible teeth and claws. So he had a wild rumpus with them. (John chuckled.)
>
> *Teacher:* And then what happened?
>
> *John:* He sent them to bed and went home in his boat. And they didn't want him to go, but he went anyway.
>
> *Teacher:* Do you remember what he found when he got back to his room?
>
> *John:* Oh yeah, his supper was there.

The teacher noted that when he was prompted, John was able to remember most of the story and retell it in sequence. He supplied some details and spoke in complete sentences. He used some language from the story, but tended to incorporate specific words (*teeth, claws, rumpus, sailed*) rather than complete descriptive phrases.

Part II: Phonological Awareness

Teacher: Remember how his mother called Max a "wild thing"? *Thing* is an interesting sounding word. It rhymes with *sing*. *Thing, sing.* Can you think of another word that rhymes with *thing* and *sing*?

John (after thinking for a moment): "*Ring.* Or how about *ring ding*?" He grinned.

Teacher: Yes, those rhyme. The author uses some words that begin the same, too, like *terrible teeth*. Can you think of another word that begins like terrible and teeth?

John: Um . . . terrible tail?

Teacher: Yes, absolutely!

PART III: Print Concepts

The teacher showed John the book again, and asked him if he could point to a word (he pointed to *Max*), a letter (he pointed to an *a*), and a sentence (he pointed to the word *and*). She asked him to point to letters he knew. He correctly named several letters. He was not able to identify any words, however.

When asked to write, John produced the writing sample shown in Figure 1.2. Using Gentry and Gillet's (1993) classification of early writing forms, the teacher established that John's writing was precommunicative. Unlike Kim's writing, however, John's consisted of recognizable letters, written from left to right across the page. John appeared to use letters he knew how to write, with no regard to letter–sound correspondences. When asked to read back what he had written, John replied, "It says, 'My dad and me went fishing.'" John evidently understood that print conveys a message and that it consists of letters.

FIGURE 1.2   *John's Writing Sample*

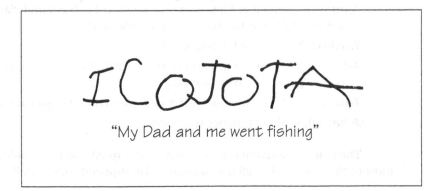

"My Dad and me went fishing"

Interpretation of John's Assessment

John's teacher drew the following conclusions, based on his responses during the assessment:

> It is evident that John has had some experience with books and stories. He enjoys being read to and sustains interest in the reading for extended periods. He has internalized the usual pattern of stories well enough to be able to reconstruct major elements of the story in sequence. However, he does not elaborate or include many details, and he makes very little use of language from the story.

As you did with Kim, speculate about an appropriate instructional program for John. Then read on to compare your ideas with our suggestions.

John's Instructional Program

Virtually all the suggestions for Kim's instructional program would apply to John as well. He needs a print-rich environment in which reading and writing are integral parts of every school day. He needs many opportunities to hear stories read aloud, to discuss and retell stories, to explore books independently, and to experiment with writing. His approximations and efforts to read and write should be accepted and encouraged. In addition, John would profit from some activities that would probably not be as appropriate for Kim:

- Encourage John (through extensive prompting) to expand on his story retelling. For example, after reading aloud *Where the Wild Things Are* to a group, the teacher might ask Kim "plot" questions such as "Do you remember what happened next?" With John, she would ask for elaborations and examples: "What did the wild things do to show they were fierce?"
- Engage John in activities that involve matching and naming letters.
- Model invented spelling, using letter–sound correspondences. As he tries to spell a problematic word, help John develop the strategy of stretching the word out, separating it into its component sounds.
- Call John's attention, from time to time, to the structure of print. For example, pointing to the words *the* and *then* in a story, the teacher might ask John, "Are these two words alike? What's different?" or, "Can you find another word that begins like *John?*"

Although John will continue to refine his understanding of the nature and purpose of print, he is ready to focus on more parts of written language and how they "work."

▪ Theresa

From Theresa's first day of kindergarten, her teacher was struck by her language facility. She had an extensive vocabulary and used more complex sentence structures than most children her age. Her play was always accompanied by elaborate

commentary, explanations of what she was doing and thinking. She loved listening to stories and could retell them in detail from memory. She could read some predictable books independently and frequently brought favorite books from home to share at school. She enjoyed writing and often chose to spend time in the writing center, where she produced elaborate drawings and wrote about them independently, using her knowledge of letter–sound correspondences.

Because of her outstanding language facility and apparent experience with print, Theresa was one of the first kindergarten children chosen by her teacher to go through the early literacy assessment.

PART I: Familiarity with Books

Theresa's teacher had already observed her book-handling skills, so he began the assessment by reading *Where the Wild Things Are* to Theresa. He asked her to tell back everything she could remember about the story as though she were describing it to another child who hadn't heard it.

> ***Theresa:*** Well, one night Max put on his wolf costume, and he was running around and chasing the dog. His mother told him to stop but he said, "I'll eat you up!" So his mother sent him to his room. So, he went to his room and pretty soon a forest grew up right in his room until he thought he was in a forest. Then a boat came along over the ocean and he got in and sailed away over night and day, and he came to the land of the wild things. The wild things looked terrible! And they roared their terrible roars and rolled their terrible eyes. But Max wasn't afraid of them. He stared at their eyes without blinking once, and they made him the king.
>
> Then they had a wild rumpus; they jumped all around and acted wild. And they hanged off the trees and yelled. But they got so wild that Max sent them to bed without any supper.
>
> Then he was sitting in the tent, and he got lonely and wanted to go home. And far away he smelled good things to eat. So he got back in his boat and started to sail away. The monsters woke up and came after him and said, "Please don't go! Please don't go! We'll eat you up 'cause we love you so." But Max went anyway. And he sailed back to his room, and when he got there his mother left his supper there for him. And it was still hot.

> ***Teacher:*** You really remembered a lot of that story, didn't you? Theresa, what was your favorite part of the story?

> ***Theresa:*** I liked the wild rumpus. And I liked when the wild things roared their terrible roars and gnashed their terrible teeth.

> ***Teacher:*** They were really wild, weren't they? Would you like to have an adventure like Max?

> ***Theresa:*** Oh yes! It was exciting!

PART II: Phonological Awareness

When the teacher asked Theresa the same question she had asked John, to supply a rhyme for *thing* and *sing*, Theresa said, "Let's see. *Thing, sing, ring, sting* . . . and *string!* And if she really wanted to, his mother could call him a *wild child!*"

When asked to produce words beginning like *Peter packed* . . . , Theresa said, "Peter packed purple pants . . . and pink pants . . . and pills and pots and presents. He could pack lots of things for p!"

PART III: Print Concepts

When asked, Theresa pointed out letters, words, and a sentence, commenting, "There's a period at the end." She could identify and name all the letters. When asked if she could read any of the words, Theresa read several phrases from the book.

She drew a picture of Max in his boat and wrote for it the caption shown in Figure 1.3. Theresa was a true phonetic speller. When writing, she used letters to represent every sound element she heard in each word. She left spaces between the words. This told her teacher that she had developed phonemic awareness, or the ability to separate words into all component sounds, and that she was conscious of word boundaries.

Interpretation of Theresa's Assessment

Theresa demonstrated well-developed awareness of story language and structure. Her retelling was very complete, in proper sequence, and included many details and some story language. She used mature syntax and precise vocabulary.

Theresa showed that she had well-developed phonological awareness and print concepts as well as considerable understanding of the reading and writing processes. She had attained the goals of the emergent reading stage and passed beyond it.

FIGURE 1.3 *Theresa's Writing Sample*

Theresa presented a challenge to the kindergarten teacher. Speculate as to what the teacher did to accommodate Theresa's needs and help her build on her accomplishments. Then read our suggestions for purposes of comparison.

Theresa's Instructional Program

Although Theresa has advanced literacy skills for her age, she can still profit from participating in emergent reading activities. Socially and emotionally she fits in very well with her kindergarten peers. It is not necessary to accelerate her in order to promote her literacy development. Like the other kindergarten children, Theresa will make optimum progress in a print-rich environment that provides daily opportunities for her to read and write. As she participates in such activities as listening to stories, reading along with the teacher, retelling or dramatizing stories, and writing, she will not only extend her own literacy development, but she will also become a role model and a resource for other children. In addition, Theresa needs to engage in some activities that allow her to read and write independently.

- ■ Encourage Theresa to try reading stories herself (or to another child or adult) that she has heard read aloud by the teacher.
- ■ Give her opportunities, during free choice time for example, to read books of her own choosing.
- ■ Have Theresa draw or write about what she has read and share her work with the other children.

Since Theresa has already entered the initial reading stage, additional suggestions for her kindergarten program will be found in Chapter 3.

Summary

If reading and writing have been modeled extensively, children in the emergent literacy stage will experiment with print in many ways. With help, they gradually "puzzle out" the nature, purpose, and use of print. Their attempts at reading and writing approximate conventional forms more and more closely. Conditions of literacy learning reflect conditions of language learning, as described by Brian Cambourne. Moreover, literacy learning proceeds from general to more specific understandings, it is a problem-solving process, and it occurs in a print-rich environment. Emergent readers who are moving into the initial reading stage are familiar with story structures and story language. They have developed many understandings about printed language and can identify some words from very familiar stories or environmental contexts.

BIBLIOGRAPHY

Allington, R. (2001). *What really matters for struggling readers*. New York: Longman.
Allington, R., & Cunningham, P. (1996). *Schools that work*. New York: HarperCollins.
Anderson, R. C., Hiebert, E., Scott, J., & Wilkinson, I. (Eds.). (1985). *Becoming a nation of readers*. Washington, DC: National Institute of Education.

Bonne, R. (1985). *I know an old lady.* New York: Scholastic.

Brown, M. (1957). *The three billy goats gruff.* New York: Harcourt Brace Jovanovich.

Cambourne, B. (1987). Language, learning and literacy. In A. Butler & J. Turbill (Eds.), *Towards a reading-writing classroom* (pp. 5–10). Portsmouth, NH: Heinemann.

Cambourne, B. (1988). *The whole story: Natural learning and the acquisition of literacy in the classroom.* Auckland, New Zealand: Scholastic.

Cambourne, B. (2001). Conditions for literacy learning. *The Reading Teacher, 54,* 784–786.

Carle, E. (1995). *The very lonely firefly.* New York: Philomel Books.

Chomsky, N. (1965). *Aspects of a theory of syntax.* Cambridge, MA: MIT Press.

Clay, M. (1979). *The early detection of reading difficulties: A diagnostic survey with recovery procedures.* Auckland, New Zealand: Heinemann.

Cowley, J. (1980). *Mrs. Wishy-Washy.* Bothell, WA: Wright Group.

Cunningham, P. (1992). What kind of phonics instruction will we have? In C. K. Kinzer & D. J. Lau (Eds.), *Literacy research, theory and practice: Views from many perspectives* (pp. 17–31). Chicago: National Reading Conference.

Durkin, D. (1966). *Children who read early.* New York: Teachers College Press.

Dykstra, R. (1967). The use of reading readiness tests for prediction and diagnosis: A critique. In Thomas B. Barrett (Ed.), *The evaluation of children's reading achievement* (pp. 35–51). Newark, DE: International Reading Association.

Farstrup, A., & Myers, M. (1996). *Standards for the English language arts.* Urbana, IL: National Council of Teachers of English.

Foertsch, M. A. (1992). *Reading in and out of school: Achievement of American students in grades 4, 8, and 12 in 1989–90.* Washington, DC: National Center for Educational Statistics: U.S. Government Printing Office.

Gadsden, V. L. (1994). Designing and conducting family literacy programs that account for racial, ethnic, religious, and other cultural differences. In H. F. O'Neil Jr. & M. Drillings (Eds.), *Motivation: Theory and research* (pp. 31–38). Hillsdale, NJ: Erlbaum Associates.

Gambrell, L., Pfeiffer, W., & Wilson. R. (1985). The effect of retelling upon comprehension and recall of text information. *Journal of Educational Research, 78,* 216–220.

Gentry, J. R. (1987). *Spel is a four letter word.* Portsmouth, NH: Heinemann.

Gentry, J. R. (1997). *My kid can't spell.* Portsmouth, NH: Heinemann.

Gentry, J. R. and Gillet, J. W. (1993). *Teaching kids to spell.* Portsmouth, NH: Heinemann.

Golden, J. M. (1984). Children's concept of story in reading and writing. *The Reading Teacher, 37,* 578–584.

Graves, M., Juel, C., & Graves, B. (2001). *Teaching reading in the 21st century* (2nd ed.). Boston: Allyn and Bacon.

Heath, S. B. (1982). What no bedtime story means: Narrative skills at home and school. *Language in Society, 11*(1), 49–76.

Hickman, J. (1995). Not by chance: Creating classrooms that invite responses to literature. In N. Roser & M. Martinez (Eds.), *Book talk and beyond* (pp. 3–9). Newark, DE: International Reading Association.

Hoban, R. (1964). *Bread and jam for Frances.* New York: Harper & Row.

Holdaway, D. (1986). The structure of natural learning as a basis for literacy instruction. In M. Sampson (Ed.), *The pursuit of literacy: Early reading and writing.* Dubuque, IA: Kendall/Hunt.

IRA (International Reading Association). (1985). *Literacy development and pre-first grade.* Newark, DE: International Reading Association.

Lindfors, J. (1987). *Children's language and learning* (2nd ed.). Englewood Cliffs, NJ: Prentice-Hall.

Mandler, J., & Johnson, N. (1977). Remembrance of things parsed: Story structure and recall. *Cognitive Psychology, 9,* 111–151.

Martin, B. (1982). *Brown Bear, Brown Bear, what do you see?* Toronto: Holt, Rinehart & Winston.

Mayer, M. (1968). *There's a nightmare in my closet.* New York: Dial Books for Young Readers.

McCloskey, R. (1948). *Blueberries for Sal.* New York: Penguin.

Morrow, L. M. (1982). Relationships between literature programs, library corner designs, and children's use of literature. *Journal of Educational Research, 75,* 339–344.

Morrow, L. M. (2001). *Literacy development in the early years* (4th ed.). Boston: Allyn and Bacon.

Pinker, S. (1994). *The language instinct: How the mind creates language.* New York: William Morrow and Company, Inc.

Potter, Beatrix. (1902). *The Tale of Peter Rabbit*. London: Frederick Warne & Co.

Pressley, M., Wharton-MacDonald, R., Allington, R., Block, C. C., Morrow, L., Tracey, D., Baker, K., Brooks, G., Cronin, J., Nelson, E., & Woo, D. (2000). A study of effective first grade reading instruction. *Scientific Studies of Reading*.

Ruddell, R., & Ruddell, M. (1995). *Teaching them to read and write*. Boston: Allyn and Bacon.

Schmitt, M. C., & O'Brien, D. (1986). Story grammars: Some cautions about the translation of research into practice. *Reading Research and Instruction, 26*, 1–8.

Sendak, M. (1963). *Where the wild things are*. New York: Harper & Row.

Seuss, Dr. (1957). *The Cat in the Hat*. New York: Random House.

Seuss, Dr. (1960). *Green Eggs and Ham*. New York: Random House.

Smith, F. (1988). *Understanding reading* (4th ed.). Hillsdale, NJ: Erlbaum.

Snow, C., Burns, S., & Griffin, P. (Eds.). (1998). *Preventing reading difficulties in young children*. Washington, DC: National Academy Press.

Sulzby, E. (1992). Research directions: Transitions from emergent to conventional writing. *Language Arts, 69*, 290–297.

Sulzby, E., & Barnhart, J. (1992). The development of academic competence: All our children emerge as readers and writers. In J. W. Irwin & M. A. Doyle (Eds.), *Reading/writing connections: Learning from research* (pp. 120–144). Newark, DE: International Reading Association.

Sulzby, E., Barnhart, J., & Heishima, J. (1989). Forms of writing and rereading from writing: A preliminary report. In J. Mason (Ed.), *Reading/writing connections*. Boston: Allyn and Bacon.

Taylor, D., & Dorsey-Gaines, C. (1988). *Growing up literate*. Portsmouth, NH: Heinemann.

Teale, W. (1982). Toward a theory of how children learn to read and write naturally. *Language Arts, 59*, 555–570.

Teale, W., & Sulzby, E. (1989). Emergent literacy: new perspectives. In D. Strickland & L. Morrow (Eds.), *Emergent literacy: Young children learn to read and write*. Newark, DE: International Reading Association.

Trelease, J. (1985). *The read aloud handbook* (rev. ed.). New York: Viking.

Viorst, J. (1972). *Alexander and the terrible, horrible, no good, very bad day*. New York: Atheneum.

Weaver, C. (1994). *Reading process and practice* (2nd ed.). Portsmouth, NH: Heinemann.

Weaver, C. (1998). Considering the research on phonological awareness and phonics. In C. Weaver (Ed.), *Reconsidering a balanced approach to reading*. Urbana, IL: National Council of Teachers of English.

Wells, G. (1986). *The meaning makers*. Portsmouth, NH: Heinemann.

Whaley, J. F. (1981). Story grammars and reading instruction. *The Reading Teacher, 34*, 762–714.

Wood, M. (1999). *Essentials of classroom teaching: Elementary language arts* (2nd ed.). Boston: Allyn and Bacon.

Wood, M. (2001). Project Story Boost: Read-alouds for students at risk. *The Reading Teacher, 55*, 76–83.

2 Initial Reading Stage

The Process of Learning to Read

■ *Overview*

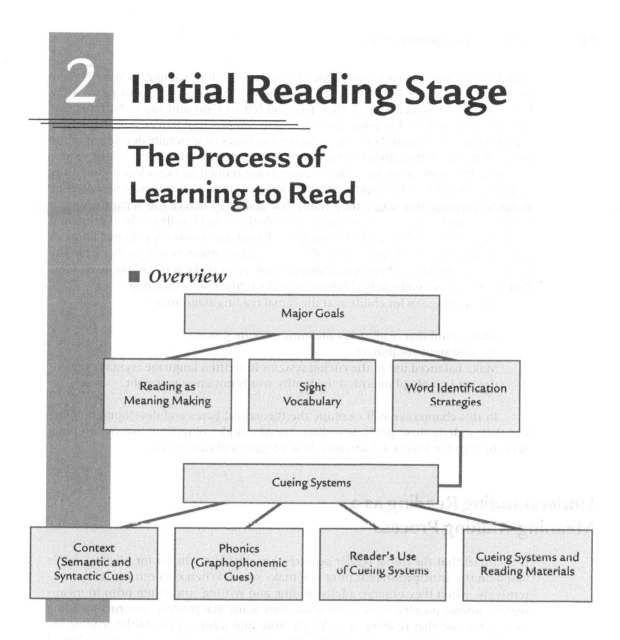

```
                        ┌─────────────┐
                        │ Major Goals │
                        └─────────────┘
        ┌───────────────────┼───────────────────┐
┌──────────────┐    ┌──────────────┐    ┌────────────────┐
│  Reading as  │    │    Sight     │    │Word Identification│
│Meaning Making│    │  Vocabulary  │    │   Strategies   │
└──────────────┘    └──────────────┘    └────────────────┘
                    ┌──────────────┐
                    │Cueing Systems│
                    └──────────────┘
┌──────────────┐ ┌──────────────┐ ┌──────────────┐ ┌──────────────┐
│   Context    │ │   Phonics    │ │ Reader's Use │ │Cueing Systems│
│ (Semantic and│ │(Graphophonemic│ │of Cueing Systems│ │    and       │
│Syntactic Cues)│ │   Cues)      │ │              │ │Reading Materials│
└──────────────┘ └──────────────┘ └──────────────┘ └──────────────┘
```

The literacy backgrounds of children entering the initial reading stage will vary considerably. Children who have been read to extensively and who have had opportunities to elaborate on these experiences either at home or at school are likely to make optimum progress in beginning reading. On the other hand, children who lack extensive literacy experiences will need to have many of these provided during this stage.

Literacy development is continuous. Although children's transitions from one stage to the next occur gradually, there are certain characteristics that distinguish the initial reader from the emergent reader. Initial readers, for example, recognize a few words consistently at sight. They have developed basic notions about print. They know that print is meaningful, that it is read left to right and top to bottom, that speech can be matched to print, that words are composed of letters, and that letters represent speech sounds. Their phonological awareness is generally developed to the point of manipulating rhymes and alliteration, and separating speech into words, syllables, and some phonemes. These concepts are refined and developed more fully as beginners gain reading and writing experience during the initial stage. As they progress through this stage, they refine the ability to detect the separate speech sounds in words, increase the number of words they can identify easily in print, and learn to use the cues in written language to figure out words they do not know at sight. If meaningful materials are used for instruction, students will predict what the print "says" and verify their predictions as they try to make sense of the text. Most first- and many second-grade children are at the initial stage of reading.

The major goals for children at the initial reading stage are to:

- Understand that reading is a meaning-making process
- Acquire sight vocabulary
- Make balanced use of the cueing systems in written language (syntax, semantics, and graphophonemics) to identify words not known at sight.

In this chapter we will examine the theoretical bases and developmental factors that underly these goals, as well as related samples of reading instruction practices. In Chapter 3 we will focus on whole programs of instruction.

Understanding Reading as a Meaning-Making Process

It is crucial that the initial reader acquire or maintain a schema for reading that is based on the anticipation that print will make sense. When children are read to extensively, when they observe adults reading and writing, and when print in meaningful contexts is called to their attention, they learn that readers construct meaning from print and that reading provides pleasure and information. Initial reading instruction must reinforce these insights. If instructional experiences are not balanced and appropriate, children may learn to view reading as sounding out words, guessing randomly, or memorizing isolated words. Care must be taken that reading does not become, for any child, a nonsensical, mechanical exercise.

Throughout subsequent sections of this chapter and Chapter 3, this goal will be addressed in discussions of theory and instruction. It pervades all other goals. Meaning is the essential function of language; similarly it is at the heart of literacy. When teachers lose sight of this in the interest of teaching children the mechanics of decoding, they risk creating a schema in which reading and writing are seen by the child as school-based chores that are irrelevant to his or her own life and interests. It is not only possible, it is also essential to teach children the skills of decoding and encoding print within contexts of meaning and personal relevance.

Acquiring Sight Vocabulary

An important goal at the initial stage of reading is the acquisition of a beginning sight vocabulary. The term *sight vocabulary* as used here refers to printed words that are recognized instantly (without analysis) in various contexts. Nearly all of the words encountered by a mature reader are recognized either at sight or (if they are longer or less common) by quickly recognizing familiar "chunks" or parts of words and effortlessly combining them into words that make sense in context. Both sight vocabulary and "chunk" recognition develop over a period of time as a consequence of multiple exposures to printed words in different language contexts. The first words children spontaneously learn to recognize at sight are not necessarily restricted to high-frequency words, nor have they been learned by isolated memory drills. Rather, a sight vocabulary develops naturally as children are repeatedly exposed to words that are personally meaningful to them in books that are read with them, in transcriptions of their own language recorded by parents or teachers, and in the environment. Many children, for example, learn that *STOP* says "stop" when stop signs catch their attention and adults explain what they are for. At first children identify the word *stop* only when it appears in the familiar context of a stop sign. When they begin to recognize the word in other contexts (advertisements, books), it has become, for them, a sight word. A child's own name is typically one of the first sight words if the adults in her environment write it on her drawings and label her possessions. In general, then, when children are immersed in print, they begin to notice or single out words that have some significance to them, and their sight vocabularies grow spontaneously.

When we examine recommended procedures for developing sight vocabulary in the context of reading instruction, we find two very different views represented. Many commercial materials that are used for beginning reading recommend the systematic teaching of sight words, particularly high-frequency (i.e., common) words (*of, to, the, my*) and "new" words (*friend, house*). Until recently, these words were introduced and taught before students attempted to read the story. Vocabulary used in the early reading selections was chosen from lists of high-frequency words. Introduction of these words was carefully controlled. Only a few words at a time were presented, and each new word was repeated several times, in an attempt to make it part of the child's sight vocabulary. The stories in the first books of the program were created from these explicitly taught words. Here is an example:

> We can go.
> Can you go?
> Help! Help!
> I can not go.
>
> I will help you.
> I will go.
> I will help you.
> You can not help.
>
> Can you go?
> I can.
> We can go.
> We can. (Goodman, Shannon, Freeman, & Murphy, 1988, p. 47)

The language of this story and others like it could not be called natural; it is unlike either the language of conversation or the language of literature. It is highly contrived, and therefore unpredictable to the beginning reader. The justification for creating contrived stories with highly controlled vocabulary was that the story is a vehicle for teaching words that will eventually be used in reading more realistic, meaningful texts (Goodman et al., 1988). The underlying assumption behind the creation and use of materials based on rigidly controlled vocabulary was that beginning readers must learn to identify a stock of individual words at sight before they are capable of constructing meaning from texts. You may remember reading this kind of material when you were a first-grader.

This view has largely been replaced by the belief that meaning making comes first and that acquisition of sight vocabulary follows (Weaver, 1994, 1998). Beginning readers who are helped to make meaning from texts will naturally develop sight vocabulary as a consequence. In this view, *learning to identify words at sight is a result of meaningful reading experiences rather than a prerequisite for them*. A teacher whose practice is derived from this theoretical base might read an enlarged-text version of a story with children several times, helping them to understand and enjoy it. After they have become very familiar with the text, she would focus their attention on selected individual words both in and out of context. This step is important; it enhances the speed and accuracy of sight vocabulary acquisition.

When children are immersed in print, their sight vocabularies grow spontaneously. The type of reading material that best facilitates this process is literature that is appealing to children, is predictable, contains patterns or repetitions, and has a limited amount of text. The specific vocabulary used need not be restricted. The story determines the vocabulary used, not vice versa. *Mrs. Wishy-Washy* is an excellent example of such a story. (The text, which is reprinted here, is enhanced by large, colorful illustrations in the original.)

"Oh, lovely mud," said the cow, and she jumped in it.
"Oh, lovely mud," said the pig, and he rolled in it.
"Oh, lovely mud," said the duck, and she paddled in it.
Along came Mrs. Wishy-Washy.
"Just look at you!" she screamed.
"In the tub you go."
In went the cow, wishy-washy, wishy-washy.
In went the pig, wishy-washy, wishy-washy.
In went the duck, wishy-washy, wishy-washy.
"That's better," said Mrs. Wishy-Washy, and she went into the house.
Away went the cow.
Away went the pig.
Away went the duck.
"Oh, lovely mud," they said. (Cowley & Melser, 1986)

One of the most important concerns in teaching initial readers is facilitating their acquisition of sight vocabulary. This is accomplished by providing many meaningful experiences with print in real communication contexts. The skillful teacher models reading using enlarged texts, invites children to read along and match their speech to the printed words, and helps them to make collections of meaningful words that they recognize easily. Each child's sight vocabulary will be a unique personal compilation of words. These techniques will be further elaborated in Chapter 3.

Developing Word Identification Strategies

At the beginning stage of reading, very few words are recognized at sight. Therefore, students must have strategies for figuring out words not recognized immediately in their printed form. In order to understand these strategies, it is necessary to examine how the child's experience with oral language contributes to the decoding of print.

Linguists define several components of language that are important for teachers of reading to understand. The *phonology* comprises all the speech sounds that are used in a given language. *Syntax* refers to the grammatical structures of the language, the ways in which we arrange words to form sentences. By the time children start school, they have acquired an implicit knowledge of the grammatical rules of their language through its meaningful use. They are unlikely to produce a sentence such as "John the ball threw," for example, because they have an implicit awareness that the direct object follows the verb in English. This sort of syntactic knowledge helps them to both create and understand an unlimited number of communications.

The *lexicon* of a language refers to all the individual words that comprise that language. There are hundreds of thousands of words in the English lexicon, including a small set of frequently used words and a much larger set of words that are used infrequently. One's individual lexicon consists of one's individual store of understood words in memory.

Semantics is sometimes referred to as the experiential component of language; it involves the derivation of meaning from language. The child's semantic knowledge consists of the meanings of words and the concepts they represent (lexicon) as well as their relationships, and is built through experiences of all kinds. The child who has been to a circus will understand the sentence "We saw clowns at the circus." The child who has not had this experience in real or vicarious form will not have "clowns" or "circus" in her lexicon, and will not understand the sentence.

Printed language differs from oral language primarily in the use of graphic symbols, which are unfamiliar to the beginning reader. The syntactic and semantic components are already familiar, due to the child's proficiency with oral language. For this reason, syntax and semantics provide powerful cues (hints, signals, or clues) that can help the beginning reader to identify words unknown only in their printed form. While the phonology of the language is also familiar to the speaker of a language, heightened awareness of the speech sounds in words must be developed if letter–sound relationships are to be used as cues successfully.

Linguists have described three cueing systems—graphophonemic, synt and semantic—that reside in print and that closely parallel the components language. While these kinds of cues operate simultaneously, it is neces teachers of reading to understand what each one contributes to the decoding process. They could be defined as follows:

letter sound relationship

structure

meaning

- *Graphophonemic cues:* Interrelationships between printed symbols (*graphemes*) and speech sounds (*phonemes*) and larger letter–sound patterns. The relationship between letters and sounds in written words is generally referred to as *phonics.*
- *Syntactic cues:* Grammatical cues such as word order, function words, and word endings. They involve grammar of the language implicitly known to speakers of the language.
- *Semantic cues:* The meaning relations among words and sentences in the text. The reader also draws heavily on personal knowledge and experience, providing additional semantic cues.

Graphophonemic cues reside in words; syntactic and semantic cues are found in larger units of language and are used heavily by beginning readers. For this reason, the syntactic and semantic systems will be discussed first.

what children bring: experience knowledge intuition

Syntactic and Semantic Cues: Using Context

The syntactic cueing system consists of patterns of language. Children come to reading with a vast background of experience with language. They use their knowledge of the ways in which sentences are formed to predict how speakers are likely to express their ideas. Similarly, when they encounter printed language, their knowledge of syntax enables them to predict the occurrence of words that fit the expected context or language patterns. For this reason, it is important that beginning reading materials contain sentence structures and language patterns that are familiar to children.

Semantic refers to meaning. Semantic cues enable beginning readers to use their knowledge of the meanings of known words to predict and work out the identification of unknown words in context. The semantic cueing system depends on the reader's world experience or background knowledge. The beginner draws on this knowledge to predict what words are likely to occur according to the meaning of the rest of the passage. In fact, the syntactic and semantic cueing systems are highly interdependent. Semantic cues carry syntactic information, and syntactic cues carry semantic information. The two cueing systems combined are commonly referred to as *context cues.*

To demonstrate how syntactic and semantic cues work, read the following sentence and predict what the omitted word might be:

Fish live in the _____.

Undoubtedly, the words you selected were in the noun or naming class (such as *ocean* or *brook*). On the basis of your experience with language, you expect the article *the* to be followed by a noun. The order of the words in the sentence, and the presence of *the* before the blank, in particular, were strong syntactic cues. You did not choose just any old noun, however. *Tree* or *sky* would have been unlikely choices. The words you came up with reflected your world knowledge about where fish live. This constitutes a strong semantic cue that limited your choices. When you used the combination of syntactic and semantic cues, you were using *context*.

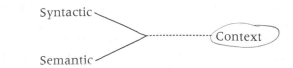

Research shows that reading words in context (as opposed to in isolation, in lists) improves the accuracy of initial readers' identification of words. This is true both of young, inexperienced readers and older, less proficient readers (Stanovich, 1991; Nicholson, 1991). Here we see a real difference between novice readers and proficient readers who can identify words equally accurately in context or in lists. For initial readers, words are also easier to identify if contexts are familiar and predictable (Weaver, 1994, 1998).

Promoting the Use of Context Cues

Context cues are used by all readers to construct meaning from print. However, there is a difference in the use of context by beginning readers and by more proficient readers. Fluent readers use context cues when reading sophisticated materials to figure out the meanings of words that are totally unfamiliar to them. Initial readers, on the other hand, use context cues primarily to help them identify words that are unknown in their printed form but that are already familiar in meaning. This process can be facilitated in several ways:

- Provide highly predictable materials that contain many syntactic and semantic cues. For example, *Mrs. Wishy-Washy,* cited earlier, contains many such cues because of the predictable, repetitive pattern of both the story and the language.
- When reading aloud from enlarged print, pause occasionally at the end of a phrase or sentence and allow children to supply the last word or two.
- When a child who is reading attempts an unknown word, ask, "Does that make sense?" Children will eventually internalize this criterion to monitor their own reading.
- Construct *cloze* exercises for occasional use. These are sentences with one or two key words deleted, such as *The train chugged down the _____.* Sentences may be taken from familiar stories or children's dictations. The children must use context cues to supply the deleted word. Of course, there will usually be several words that would make sense syntactically and semantically. Beginning readers who are over reliant on context cues may "guess" at unfamiliar words in context, based solely on syntactic and semantic cues. The use of graphophonemic cues (letter–sound correspondences) *with* context cues leads the beginner toward more accurate word identification.* (For more examples, see *Shared Reading* and descriptions of "masking" in Chapter 3.)

*The train chugged down the _____.

Graphophonemic Cues: Using Phonics

The term *graphophonemic* refers to the relationship between letters and the speech sounds they represent. Graphophonemic cues reside within words and are usually referred to by teachers as *phonics*. Phonics instruction consists of teaching spelling-to-sound correspondence rules that are supposedly designed to permit the beginning reader to translate written language into speech. This strategy, when used alone, has limited utility. The problem lies in the nature of correspondences between the letters of written language and the sounds of speech. If every letter consistently stood for one sound and each sound were represented by just one letter, then there would be a perfect one-to-one correspondence between phonemes and letters, and children could learn to decode words by mastering spelling-to-sound correspondence rules. The reason that use of graphophonemic cues alone is an ineffective strategy for beginning readers is that the links between letters and sounds cannot be specified exactly. This problem was highlighted in a study of 6,000 common words, all of which were one- and two-syllable words occurring in the spoken language of a group of 6- to 9-year-olds. No fewer than 211 different correspondences were found! Eighty-three of these involved consonants, which are thought to be relatively consistent. Seventy-nine involved the six vowels when they occurred alone in words. The remaining 49 correspondences involved combinations of vowels. This study gives some idea of the complexity of spelling-to-sound correspondences in English (Berdiansky, Cronnel, & Koehler, 1969).

Beginning readers use cues to identify words in print.

Phonics instruction is a topic of unending and largely unnecessary controversy among teachers of reading. This controversy was fueled by the publication in 1955 of a book by linguist Rudolf Flesch entitled *Why Johnny Can't Read.* Flesch proposed that the prevalent cause of reading problems was a lack of intensive teaching of phonics. The publication of his book was followed by a swing toward the emphasis of intensive phonics instruction in beginning reading programs. Another influential book, Jeanne Chall's *Learning to Read: The Great Debate,* appeared in 1967. Chall reviewed a large number of studies and came to the conclusion that a thorough knowledge of phonics was the basis of success in beginning reading. Subsequent researchers have criticized Chall's conclusion, claiming that studies on which it was based were flawed (Carbo, 1988; Turner, 1989). Her view still prevails among some reading educators and among many lay people and politicians. The debate has been further complicated by recent claims that lack of phonemic awareness by the reader is at the root of most reading problems.

Most reading researchers and educators have a different perspective on the role of phonics in reading today, due to the body of basic research that has accumulated since 1967 showing that reading is a complex language process rather than an aggregate of phonemic awareness and phonic skills that lead to word identification and, eventually, comprehension (Coles, 2000; Pearson, 1984; Stahl, 1992). There is widespread agreement that most students learn to use graphophonemic cues regardless of the type of instruction they receive. Learning about letter–sound correspondences is an integral and inevitable part of learning to read. This learning and its application do depend on the reader's phonemic awareness. The issue today is not whether phonemic awareness and knowledge of phonics should be fostered, but rather how these elements are most appropriately incorporated in the larger context of beginning reading instruction (Adams, 1990; Cunningham, 2000; Stahl, 1992). Teachers need to be familiar with the development of phonemic awareness, as well as with phonics content and terminology. They need to know how the use of graphophonemic cues develops in readers and what constitutes effective phonics instruction. Let us examine each of these areas.

Phonemic Awareness

During the emergent reading stage children begin to attend to the internal phonological (sound) structure of spoken words, as described in Chapter 1. They are typically able to recognize and supply rhyming words and words that begin with the same phoneme. Most often they are not able to separate words much further into their component sounds. *Phonemes* are what we perceive as the individual speech sounds that comprise words. The spoken word *rain,* for example, has three phonemes: /r/, /a/, and /n/. *Phonemic awareness,* or the awareness of the separate speech sounds in spoken words, goes beyond rhyming or alliteration. It is a more finely tuned manifestation of phonological awareness. The child who can detect that *blow* and *boat* begin with the same sound, that *cap* and *stop* end with the same sound, or (more difficult) that removing the *r* from *brat* leaves *bat,* has well-developed phonemic awareness. The most sophisticated levels of phonemic awareness involve *segmentation*—accurately separating and counting the phonemes in words, "stretching out" words (verbally—no print is involved) to identify the separate speech sounds, and *blending*—putting component phonemes in a "stretched" word together to identify the word. Since invented spelling involves these skills in a functional situation, it is perhaps the best way to develop them (see Chapter 3, p. 93). Print is involved in the product, but phonemic segmentation and blending are needed for the novice speller to decide what letters to write, and in what order.

The ability to segment words into phonemes is less natural and more difficult than cruder forms of phonological awareness and manipulation. There is evidence that relatively few children acquire phonemic awareness spontaneously (Adams et al., 1998) and that it constitutes a far more difficult task for some children than for others. There is also a large amount of research evidence that phonemic awareness and reading achievement are closely related (Snow, Burns, & Griffin, 1998). The dilemma comes in applying this information appropriately to educational practice, because it is also true that *the relationship between phonemic awareness and learning to read is reciprocal, or bidirectional.* In other words, increasing phonemic awareness may well contribute to increased decoding proficiency; however, it is also true that increased reading and writing practice results in improved phonemic awareness. (Snow, Burns, and Griffin, 1998; Weaver, 1998). While phonemic awareness must be at least partially developed in order for phonics instruction (formal or informal) to be effective, the reciprocal nature of the relationship has been well established. Hence it is of questionable value to devote instructional time in the primary grades to phonemic awareness drills and exercises that do not incorporate print on the theory that they are *prerequisites* to phonics and to beginning reading and writing. Phonemic awareness, phonics, and decoding ability can best be fostered simultaneously through a combination of language games, print activities, and attention to letters and words in the context of reading appropriate texts for beginners.

Phonics Content

In order to effectively integrate phonics into beginning reading instruction, the teacher of reading needs to be aware of basic phonics content. Common phonics terms that will be encountered in commercial materials include the following:

■ *Consonants* include all the letters of the alphabet except the vowels. Although certain consonants can represent more than one speech sound (*g*—*gun, giraffe,* and *c*—*car, circus,* for example), consonant sounds are generally much more consistent than vowel sounds. In addition, consonants frequently appear at the beginnings of words, and therefore provide strong cues for the beginner when coupled with context. For these reasons, the sounds of consonants are usually the first phonic elements learned.

■ *Consonant blends* consist of two or three consonants clustered together, each of which retains its individual sound, although pronounced in quick succession. Examples include *bl, st, str, br, fr,* and *spl.* Most beginning readers quickly develop an understanding of blends as they acquire familiarity with the individual consonants and build sight vocabulary.

■ *Consonant digraphs* consist of two consonants that, when they appear together, represent a single speech sound. (This sound is most often unlike the sound recorded by either letter.) Examples include *th, sh, ch, ng,* and *ph.* Beginning readers discover that in these special instances, two letters represent one speech sound.

■ *Vowels* are found in every syllable, and include the letters *a, e, i, o, u,* and sometimes *y.* (Some linguists also include *w* as a vowel when it has no distinct sound of its own, as in *cow* or *grow.*) Vowel sounds are extremely variable. Consider the sounds represented by *a* in these words: *cat, cane, car, care, again.* Dialect variations complicate the identification of distinct vowel sounds even further. Since consonants predominate in the majority of words, they provide more cues within words than do vowels. In fact, it is possible to read words in meaningful context when all vowels have been deleted. For example, read the following sentence:

M_x w_s s_nt t_ b_d w_th_t h_s s_pp_r.

Your implicit knowledge of English syntax coupled with the graphophonemic cues provided by the consonants enabled you to construct meaning in spite of the absence of vowels. Therefore, spending large amounts of instructional time focusing on mastery of vowel sounds is unlikely to be productive for the beginning reader.

■ *Short vowels* are difficult to define. They are described by some linguists as representing speech sounds not classified as consonants and not representing the letter name. Examples are *a—cat, e— bed, i—pick, o—hot, u—cup.*

■ *Long vowels* record the name of the letter: a—race, e—be, i—ice, o—old, u—mule.

■ *R-controlled vowels:* The letter *r* gives the preceding vowel a sound that is neither long nor short: *ar—car, er—her, ir—bird, or—corn, ur—fur.*

■ *Vowel digraphs* are pairs of vowels that represent the sound (long or short) of one of the vowels. For example, r*ain,* c*oat,* br*ead,* st*eak.*

■ *Vowel diphthongs* are also pairs of vowels that represent a single sound; however, in the case of diphthongs the sound recorded is unlike that of either vowel. For example, c*ouch,* t*oy,* f*ew.*

■ *Silent letters* result sometimes when consonants are combined. They may occur at the beginning, middle, or end of a word. Examples include: *wr* (*wrong*), *kn* (*know*), *lk* (*walk*), *gh* (*night*), *mb* (*climb*). In their early experiences, children are exposed to many words that contain silent letters. Beginning readers soon discover that some letters are silent.

While teachers need to be conversant with phonics terms in order to interpret commercial instructional materials, *it is not necessary for beginning readers to learn these terms and analyze words in this fashion.* Rather, the goal of phonics instruction should be to aid children in discovering patterns of letters and letter combinations that will help them identify words that are unknown (only) in their printed form.

Development of Phonics Use

Studies have indicated definite patterns or stages in the development of children's initial learning of words (Frith, 1985; McCormick & Mason, 1986; Stahl, 1992). Word identification and the use of graphophonemic cues take place during the emergent and initial reading stages and occur simultaneously with all the other early discoveries about reading, writing, and meaning making.

Frith (1985) described three stages children pass through as they learn to use letter–sound correspondences: *logographic*, *alphabetic*, and *orthographic*. In the logographic stage, words are recognized as wholes, usually embedded in a specific context or "log," such as a stop sign. As children learn letters and the speech sounds they represent, they enter the alphabetic stage, in which they labor through decoding and invented spelling letter by letter. With reading and writing experience, children move into the orthographic stage. They begin to detect patterns (letter groupings) and to use these to identify words without sounding out every letter. Most children pass through the first two stages and begin to see words orthographically by the end of first grade. Following this stage, sight vocabulary grows rapidly, and children no longer need to focus consciously on word structures and spelling (Frith, 1985; Stahl, 1992).

Promoting the Use of Graphophonemic Cues

Traditionally, phonics instruction has been classified along a continuum between two approaches: analytic and synthetic. A *synthetic* approach involves teaching letter–sound correspondences in isolation. When children have learned the sounds represented by various letters, they are asked to blend them into words. For example, children who have learned the sounds for *d, n, a,* and *p* would be asked to blend them to "read" the words *Dan, pan, nap,* and *Dad.* As more letter–sounds are taught, more "decodable" words are read. The first connected text children are given to read consists of words whose component sounds have been taught, along with a few high-frequency words (*the, is, on*) necessary in the construction of sentences. These are referred to as "decodable texts." Although "real" stories may be read aloud to children in such programs, their own reading consists of practice in decoding texts that are not necessarily meaningful. Their writing is likely to be limited to words that contain the letter–sounds they have been taught as well.

An *analytic* approach involves using known words containing a particular phonic element and helping children discover and describe that letter–sound relationship. For example, a teacher might list the words *big, bird,* and *bike* on the board. After reading them, she would ask, "What part of these words is the same?" Children would be encouraged to explain that all three words begin with the letter *b,* and with the same sound. When using an analytic approach, the teacher refers to sounds embedded in words, rather than in isolation. *B* does not merely represent *"buh"*; it represents the sound at the beginning of *big* and *bird.* Children analyze words, noting similarities and differences, and phonics content is taught gradually as they read and write all kinds of text. They are led to use context and sight words as well as phonics to help them figure out unknown words as they read, since their reading material is not restricted to the letter–sound patterns they have been taught.

A variation of this is *analogic* phonics instruction, which emphasizes the teaching of patterns in words, and using known "chunks" in words to figure out other words. This approach is based on research that has shown that it is easier for children to divide syllables into onsets and rimes than into separate phonemes. *Onsets* are defined as all the letters before the vowel(s), while *rimes* include the vowel and what follows. The word *jump*, for example, is more easily heard/divided as *j-ump* than as *j-u-m-p*. A teacher using an analogic approach would help children discover that if they can read and write the word *ran*, they can also read and write other words that rhyme with *ran: Dan, man, can*. Again, children's reading and writing are not restricted to the patterns they have been taught (Cunningham, 2000; Moustafa, 1998). Analogic instruction as well as other forms of analytic phonics instruction may be planned and taught in some sequence, or the instruction may be *embedded* in the context of authentic reading and writing activities, with teaching sequence determined by need, or by the words that arise in the texts children are reading and writing. Teachers who use a primarily analytic approach to teaching phonics will use isolated sound practice from time to time (when modeling invented spelling, for example). However, such practice is brief, and letter sounds are always related back to the context of whole words and meaningful messages.

Most beginning reading instruction does not rely exclusively on one of these approaches; however, programs usually emphasize one over the others. Although research supports some teaching of letter sounds in isolation (Adams, 1990), the analytic approach is favored by most literacy specialists for several reasons. First of all, a purely synthetic approach promotes the view that reading consists of making a sequence of discrete sounds and then blending them together. This can lead to the habit of sounding out every word, letter by letter, which can actually interfere with development of fluency and comprehension. A second concern is the variability of letter–sound relationships, discussed earlier in this chapter. Finally, instruction and practice in isolated letter sounds is unnatural for children, time consuming, and divorced from the meaning base of reading (Cunningham, 2000; Searfoss & Readance, 1994; Smith & Johnson, 1980).

The topic of how best to teach phonics probably receives more attention than it deserves. In a review of research on approaches to phonics instruction, Stahl, Duffy-Hester, and Stahl (1998) concluded that there is no research-proven, most-effective approach to phonics instruction. In their words:

> The notion that children construct knowledge about words may explain why the differences among programs are small. As long as one provides early and systematic information about the code, it may not matter very much how one does it. . . . If the information is made available to children, then it may not matter exactly how the instruction occurs. (pp. 350–351)

The following basic content for graphophonemics instruction is recommended for helping initial readers use this cueing system effectively in conjunction with the others. (This sequence assumes that the initial reader knows and can produce most letters of the alphabet, and has some phonological awareness.)

- Beginning consonants (onsets)
- Common phonograms (rimes)
- Beginning consonant blends and digraphs
- Ending consonants, blends, and digraphs
- Short vowels
- Long vowels
- Multisyllabic words

The proposed sequence for focusing on these elements may be useful for the teacher to follow; however, it should be noted that children do not necessarily learn to use these elements in any particular order. A beginning reader, for example, might be able to identify the *t* sound at the end of *cat* before he is able to identify the beginning letter sound of *house*.

Additional guidelines for the teaching of phonics that represented a consensus of experts in the field were summarized in *Becoming a Nation of Readers*, a nationally commissioned report published in 1985: "The right maxims for phonics are: Do it early. Keep it simple. Except in cases of diagnosed individual need, phonics instruction should have been completed by the end of the second grade" (Anderson, Hiebert, Scott, & Wilkinson, 1985, p. 43). Despite heated controversy about phonics instruction since that time, most educators would agree that these maxims hold true. Phonics instruction (as well as emphasis on other basic word identification strategies) is undertaken and largely completed during the initial reading stage. Instruction should emphasize the most helpful and consistent letter–sound relationships. For example, initial consonants provide helpful, reasonably reliable cues for word identification and should therefore be emphasized in instruction. On the other hand, vowel combinations are more variable in pronunciation and less used as cues in identifying words, except as parts of phonograms (rimes). Commercial reading programs have traditionally provided overly extensive and complex phonics instruction. The authors of *Becoming a Nation of Readers* commented:

> These programs seem to be making the dubious assumption that exposure to a vast set of phonics relationships will enable a child to produce perfect pronunciations of words. The more reasonable assumption is that phonics can help the child come up with approximate pronunciations—candidates that have to be checked to see whether they match words known from spoken language that fit in the context of the story being read. (Anderson et al., 1985, p. 38)

Considerable research has focused on the utility of teaching rules or generalizations to help students decode words (Clymer, 1963; Sorenson, 1983). Most commercial programs include phonics generalizations to be taught explicitly. The assumption is that students will apply these rules when they encounter unfamiliar words. Arguments against the teaching of generalizations are based on the answers to these questions:

- Are the rules true?
- If beginning readers learn them, do they apply them when reading?

In answer to the first question, there are very few generalizations that hold true 75 percent (or more) of the time. For example, a commonly taught rule is "When two vowels go walking, the first one does the talking." In other words, when two vowels appear together in a word, the long sound of the first one is pronounced. It turns out that this rule holds true slightly less than 50 percent of the time. Consider, for example, *bread, chief, does, wear, their, laugh, field*. In this instance, children might as well be advised to flip a coin; heads the rule works, tails it doesn't.

Even if rule application were extremely consistent, it is doubtful that the rules would be utilized by initial readers. Studies of the word identification strategies employed by beginning readers indicate that they use context and recognition of familiar letter patterns in words rather than conscious analysis of phonic elements. In view of these considerations, the extensive use of instructional time for teaching phonics generalizations is difficult to justify. Our recommended content for teaching phonics (specified earlier) acknowledges the assumption that the purpose of phonics instruction is to help readers discover and make use of the alphabetic principle. Once the most important, regular letter–sound correspondences are understood, children can best refine and extend their knowledge of graphophonemic relationships through repeated opportunities to read and write.

To summarize, while graphophonemic cues are useful to the novice reader, their use is limited because of the variability of spelling–sound correspondences, and because such cues are restricted to the word levels. The other cueing systems utilize larger units of language. Beginning readers who are over-reliant on phonics tend to lose meaning, or to mispronounce words without concern that the resulting sentences do not make sense. Although beginning readers benefit from instruction that focuses on letter–sound correspondences, in real reading situations they should be encouraged to use graphophonemic cues in conjunction with syntactic and semantic cues.

How Beginners Use the Cueing Systems

To demonstrate how a beginning reader might use the three cueing systems, consider how the reader might approach the unknown word *monkey* in the following sentence:

Mary saw a monkey at the zoo.

If the reader depends entirely on graphophonemic cues, confusion may result. The *o* represents neither the long nor the short sound of the letter. Does the *ey* represent the sound of *ey* in *they*, or *key* or *eye*? In this instance, graphophonemic cues alone provide too many possibilities. A more likely strategy would be to use the most obvious graphophonemic element, the initial letter (*m*) combined with the context. The reader's knowledge of syntax would help to reduce the number of possibilities. The unknown word follows the article *a*. The reader knows it is something that Mary saw. Using these cues, the reader might speculate that the word is *mountain* but would be unlikely to try *much*, or even *money*, because they do not fit the syntactic pattern. Continuing on with the sentence, the reader is likely to encounter an important semantic cue on recognition of the word *zoo*. Any reader who has had some experience with zoos (prior knowledge) will assume that the unknown word represents an animal. Therefore *mountain* becomes an unlikely alternative. *Monkey,* on the other hand, becomes a plausible alternative because it fits with the information from all three cueing systems. As the beginner is likely to say, "It makes sense."

Much of the research on initial reading conducted in the 1980s focused on successful beginning readers and how they approach word identification when reading connected text. A common finding was that efficient beginning readers (those who are able to identify a high proportion of words correctly in a meaningful text) make considerable use of contextual information and depend less completely on graphophonemic information than is often assumed. In a study conducted by one of the authors, first-graders were asked to try to identify unfamiliar words in context and then to verbalize the strategies they used. Although they had been taught to "sound out" unfamiliar words, successful decoders most often mentioned context first, using such statements as "I used all these other words" or "When I saw this word, I knew this one had to be _____." Analysis of the first-graders' interviews provided evidence that successful beginners rely heavily on their knowledge of language patterns as well as on their experiential background to narrow the possibilities for identifying an unknown word, after which they apply their phonic knowledge. For example, after successfully struggling through the sentence "The ball *bounced* across the road," one first-grader explained his choice of *bounced* as follows: "Well, I looked at all these words. 'The *ball* . . . across the *road.*' So I knew it had to be either bounced or crossed—or rolled. But I knew it couldn't be *crossed* or *rolled,* because it starts with *b.* So I figured out it was *bounced"* (Wood, 1986).

One key to success for beginning readers is the balanced application of the cueing systems. Teachers must be very sensitive to opportunities to model word identification strategies and make them explicit. For example, when children are reading orally and are stymied by an unknown word (or misread it), these interjections may be helpful:

- Let's read the rest of the sentence to see what would fit there.
- Does that make sense?
- Does that word (pronounced by reader) begin with (the first letter of the printed word)? Does it look right?

In addition to such modeling and guidance, the teacher must also design and select beginners' reading materials carefully, considering what cues are truly present in the text, and what text features will help the beginner to puzzle out unknown words.

Cueing Systems and Reading Materials

Materials that reflect the story structures and language patterns that are familiar to children facilitate the spontaneous use of the cueing systems that are already parts of their language repertoire (the syntactic and semantic systems), thereby making it easier for them to decode the words in print. In other words, beginning readers need materials that are highly predictable and meaningful to them. An examination of representative commercial material reveals striking contrasts in this regard.

Programs that use "decodable texts" teach short vowels and consonants one at a time through isolated words (*run, dad, add*). Students are then introduced to texts created from this limited collection of letter sounds. Here is an excerpt from one such text:

EXAMPLE 1

Add a ramp.
Run up, pup.
Add a pad. (Eaton, 1998)

This type of text is not predictable or meaningful to the beginning reader. The language patterns are totally unlike any the child has encountered either in conversations or in stories; the material lacks syntactic cues. Furthermore, the content of the "story" is nonsensical, so the reader is prevented from using experience (semantic cues) to predict what words will occur. The intent is to have the reader practice working with the letter–sound relationships that have been taught. Beginning readers must depend entirely on graphophonemic cues, which are the least familiar and reliable. The beginner must identify each word as if it had nothing to do with the other words in the line of print. In a meaningful text every word is largely predicted from the words preceding and following it. The type of text represented by Example 1 makes efficient, authentic reading virtually impossible because the reader is forced to labor along blindly, attempting to identify one word after another with no prior insight into what these words are likely to be. Decodable texts coupled with synthetic phonics instruction have become popular with those who subscribe to a heavily skills-oriented approach to reading instruction. They are also used widely in resource rooms with "special education" students and struggling initial readers. While it is necessary to make sure that such students understand how the alphabetic writing system works, these are also the readers who most need the support of the other cueing systems in order to decode print. Pattern, meaning, and sense are powerful supports for learning and applying the abstract matching of letters to speech sounds.

The second example represents a type of text that is widely used in beginning basal readers. Although it differs significantly from Example 1, it also restricts full use of the three cueing systems by the novice. Here is an excerpt from a basal reader:

EXAMPLE 2

Can you see me?
Here I am.
Time to get out.
This is hard.
Oops!
Can I make it? (Ford, 1996)

This story consists entirely of the words spoken by Little Elephant. No quotation marks are used. Since the language patterns used are similar to those used in conversation by young children, the reader may make considerable use of syntactic cues. Deriving meaning, however, is problematic. The text alone does not provide enough semantic information for the reader to construct a story line (what is going on?). In order to understand what the characters are doing and why, the reader must make extensive use of the accompanying illustrations. While the authors of the text may assume that conversations will be easy for young children to read, in fact this format is unlike the narrative format of the stories that have been read to children. Surely this will cause confusion in the young reader because it contradicts the notion that the text tells the story. In *Little Elephant,* as in many texts, the reader's attention is directed to photographs that depict the action (there is no story line). The text is actually superfluous.

Example 3 is an attempt to provide the beginner with a story that is very simple but that facilitates the use of all three cueing systems:

EXAMPLE 3

I like to ride my pony.
I ride to the lake.
My pony can walk in the lake.
I see a hill.
I ride up the hill.
I look down.
I see the woods.
I ride my pony down the hill.
I ride my pony in the woods.
I can't see the hill.
I can't see the lake.
I can't see my house.
My pony and I are lost.
We ride and ride in the woods.
Where are we?
We are lost.
I see my dog.
My dog runs.
I ride out of the woods.
I can see the hill.
I can see the lake.
I can see my house.
And I ride home. (*Lost and Found,* 1980, pp. 28–37)

This story differs from the other two in several respects. The reader can draw extensively on syntactic cues; not only are the language patterns familiar, but they are often <u>repeated</u>, which aids the novice in predicting what words will occur. In addition, the text is meaningful and contains (within a traditional story format) the semantic information necessary to construct meaning. This further enhances its predictability. For these reasons, Example 3 would prove much easier than Example 2 for the beginner to read. With a meaningful, predictable text, the reader can use experience with language to know which words go together to make sense and will therefore gain practice in successfully mapping speech to print. Once the reader has gained skill and experience at decoding and recognizes many words "at sight," heavily predictable texts become unnecessary, and readers appropriately move on to more challenging materials.

Summary

In this chapter we have examined in some depth the developmental milestones and instructional goals for initial readers. Even in this very early stage when reading competency is in its infancy, it is important that children associate reading with meaning making. The acquisition of a rudimentary sight vocabulary and use of all the interrelated cueing systems are taught and practiced with the goal of discovering the meaning of printed texts. It is therefore important that beginning reading materials be predictable, manageable by novices, and meaningful so that all the newly emerging skills of the reader can be used successfully. The discussion of instructional practices and materials has been general, up to this point. In Chapter 3 we will examine the ways in which all of these elements may fit together in specific reading approaches and programs that are designed to be comprehensive in leading initial readers to success in beginning reading.

BIBLIOGRAPHY

Adams, M. J. (1990). *Beginning to read: Thinking and learning about print.* Boston: MIT Press.

Adams, M. J., Treiman, R., & Pressley, M. (1998). Reading, writing, and literacy. In I. Sigel & K. Reninger (Eds.), *Handbook of child psychology* (5th ed.), Vol. 4: *Child psychology in practice.* New York: Wiley.

Anderson, R. C., Hiebert, E., Scott, J., & Wilkinson, I. (Eds.). (1985). *Becoming a nation of readers.* Washington, DC: National Institute of Education.

Berdiansky, B., Cronnel, B., & Koehler, A. (1969). *Spelling-sound relations and primary form: Class descriptions for speech comprehension vocabularies of 6–9 year olds.* Southwest Regional Laboratory for Educational Research and Development, Technical Report #1.

Carbo, M. (1988). Debunking the great phonics myth. *Phi Delta Kappan, 70,* 226–240.

Chall, J. (1967). *Learning to read: The great debate.* New York: McGraw-Hill.

Clymer, T. (1963). The utility of phonics generalization in the primary grades. *The Reading Teacher, 16,* 252–258.

Coles, G. (2000). *Misreading reading: The bad science that hurts children.* Portsmouth, NH: Heinemann.

Cowley, J., & Melser, J. (1986). *Mrs. Wishy-Washy.* Auckland, New Zealand: Shortland Publications.

Cunningham, P. (2000). *Phonics they use.* New York: Longman.

Eaton, D. (1998). The nap. In *Lippincott phonics,* Level A. New York: McGraw-Hill School Division.

Flesch, R. F. (1955). *Why Johnny can't read and what you can do about it* (1st ed.). New York: Harper.

Ford, M. (1996). Little elephant. In *Literature Works.* Collection 1/2. Needham Heights, MA: Silver Burdett Ginn.

Frith, U. (1985). Beneath the surface of developmental dyslexia. In K. E. Patterson, K. C. Marshall, & M. Coltheart (Eds.), *Surface dyslexia: Neuropsychological and cognitive studies of phonological reading.* Hillsdale, NJ: Erlbaum.

Goodman, K., Shannon, R., Freeman, Y., & Murphy, S. (1988). *Report card on the basal reader.* Katonah, NY: Richard C. Owen.

Lost and found. Preprimer. (1980). New York: McGraw-Hill Student Division.

McCormick, C. E., & Mason, J. M. (1986). Intervention procedures for increasing preschool children's interest in and knowledge about reading. In W. H. Teale & E. Sulzby (Eds.), *Emergent literacy: Writing and reading* (pp. 90–115). Norwood, NJ: Ablex.

Moustafa, M. (1998). Reconceptualizing phonics instruction. In C. Weaver (Ed.), *Reconsidering a balanced approach to reading* (pp. 135–157). Urbana, IL: National Council of Teachers of English.

Nicholson, T. (1991). Do children read words better in context or in lists? A classic study revisited. *Journal of Educational Psychology, 83,* 444–450.

Pearson, P. D. (Ed.). (1984). *Handbook of reading research.* New York: Longman.

Searfoss, L. W., & Readance, J. E. (1994). *Helping children learn to read* (3rd ed.). Englewood Cliffs, NJ: Prentice-Hall.

Smith, R. J., & Johnson, D. D. (1980). *Teaching children to read* (2nd ed.). Reading, MA: Addison-Wesley.

Snow, C., Burns, S., & Griffin (Eds.). (1998). *Preventing reading difficulties in young children.* Washington, DC: National Academy Press.

Sorenson, N. (1983). *A study of the reliability of phonic generalizations in five primary level basal reading programs.* Unpublished doctoral dissertation, Arizona State University, Tempe.

Stahl, S. (1992). Saying the "p" word: Nine generalizations for exemplary phonics instruction. *The Reading Teacher, 45*(8), 618–625.

Stahl, S., Duffy-Hester, A., & Stahl, K. (1998). Everything you wanted to know about phonics (but were afraid to ask). *Reading Research Quarterly, 33,* 338–355.

Stanovich, K. (1991). Word recognition: Changing perspectives. In R. Barr, M. L. Kamil, P. B. Mosenthal, & P. D. Pearson (Eds.), *Handbook of reading research: Vol. 2* (pp. 418–452). New York: Longman.

Turner, R. L. (1989). The "great" debate: Can both Carbo and Chall be right? *Phi Delta Kappan, 71,* 276–283.

Weaver, C. (1994). *Reading process and practice* (2nd ed.). Portsmouth, NH: Heinemann.

Weaver, C. (1998). Toward a balanced approach to reading. In C. Weaver (Ed.), *Reconsidering a balanced approach to reading* (pp. 11–74). Urbana, IL: National Council of Teachers of English.

Wood, M. (1986). The role of metacognition in the identification of words in context by beginning readers. Unpublished doctoral dissertation, Boston University.

3 Initial Reading Stage

Instructional Approaches and Programs

■ *Overview*

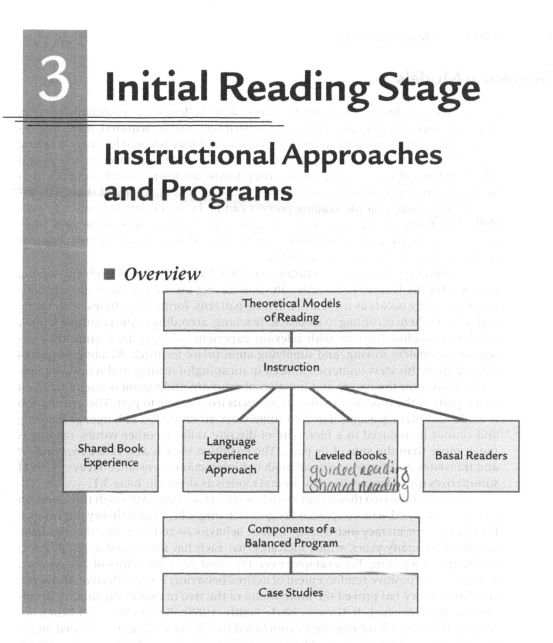

```
Theoretical Models
of Reading
        |
   Instruction
```

Shared Book Experience | Language Experience Approach | Leveled Books *guided reading Shared reading* | Basal Readers

```
Components of a
Balanced Program
        |
   Case Studies
```

*O*bservers of beginning reading programs are frequently struck by great differences from classroom to classroom in methods, materials, and teachers' expectations of children. One reason for these differences is that approaches to beginning reading have their origins in two opposing psychological theories about learning: behavioral and cognitive. These two schools of thought differ markedly in their views of the learner and the learning process, so it is not surprising that they give rise to very different instructional approaches.

Theoretical Models

Behaviorists view learning as habit formation and the learner as essentially passive. Teaching, then, involves identifying the desired habits to be acquired, providing related stimuli, and reinforcing correct responses until they become habitual. Reading programs that have their roots in the behaviorist tradition reflect these general views and are often labeled *atomistic.* They follow an instructional sequence that progresses from part to whole and involves mastery of a hierarchy of skills. The assumption is made that the reading process can be broken down into discrete subskills that, if mastered in sequence, will lead to proficient reading. This view is referred to in the educational literature as *reductionist* and the resulting instruction as representative of the *transmission* model.

Cognitive psychologists, in contrast, consider learning to be a problem-solving process and the learner to be active in constructing knowledge from the environment. Learning occurs as the learner detects patterns, forms hypotheses, tests them, and reviews them according to feedback. Teaching, according to the cognitive school, involves providing learners with relevant experiences (data), facilitating their attempts at problem solving, and supplying appropriate feedback. Reading programs derived from this view immerse children in meaningful reading and writing experiences. Only after the nature and function of print are understood is attention given to the parts of the process; instruction proceeds from whole to part. The assumption is made that literacy acquisition is in some ways an extension of language learning and cannot be reduced to a hierarchy of discrete skills. In other words, reading is much more than the sum of its parts. The cognitive view is also called *constructivist* and translates into the *transactional* model of instruction. Constance Weaver (1994) summarizes these contrasting educational models as shown in Table 3.1.

Which of the two theoretical models is the "true" one? Although this question is frequently asked, a more appropriate question might be, Which theory is most useful as a basis for literacy instruction? In fact, behaviorist and cognitive theories have coexisted for many years, which indicates that each has some valid applications to teaching and learning. For example, even the most adamant critics of behaviorism recognize that positive reinforcement of desired behaviors is very effective. However, cognitive theory has proved the more useful of the two in explaining literacy development (Graves, Juel, & Graves, 2001; Smith, 1988). Researchers and other observers of children have repeatedly concluded that literacy learning is indeed an active, problem-solving process (Altwerger, Edelsky, & Flores, 1987; Weaver, 1998). These findings have had instructional implications, but, more importantly, they have led to the recognition of optimum conditions for teaching reading. Regardless of the methods and materials used, beginning reading instruction will succeed only if children are immersed in print; provided with many opportunities to observe, imitate, and participate in meaningful reading and writing activities; and encouraged to experiment with language and print in a secure and supportive environment.

Basic instructional approaches for teaching beginning reading fall on a continuum from a heavy subskill orientation to a holistic or meaning-based orientation. On one end of this continuum it is presumed that mastery of subskills precedes reading. Programs built on this premise advocate the mastery of many subskills and extensive

TABLE 3.1 *Contrasting Educational Models*

Transmission	Transactional
Reductionist	Constructivist
Behavioral psychology	Cognitive psychology
Habit formation	Hypothesis formation
Avoiding mistakes prevents formation of bad habits	Errors necessary for encouraging more sophisticated hypotheses
Students passively practice skills, memorize facts	Students actively pursue learning and construct knowledge
Teacher dispenses prepackaged, predetermined curriculum	Teacher develops and negotiates curriculum with students
Direct teaching of curriculum	Responsive teaching, to meet students' needs and interests
Taskmaster, with emphasis on cycle of *teach, practice/apply/memorize, test*	Master craftsperson, mentor: emphasis on demonstrating, inviting, discussing, affirming, facilitating, collaborating, observing, supporting
Lessons taught, practiced and/or applied, then tested	Mini-lessons taught as demonstration, invitation; adding an idea to the class pot
Performance on decontextualized tests is taken as measure of learning of limited information	Assessment from a variety of contextualized learning experiences captures diverse aspects of learning
Learning is expected to be uniform, same for everyone; uniform means of assessment guarantee that many will fail, in significant ways	Learning is expected to be individual, different for everyone; flexible and multiple means of assessment guarantee all will succeed, in differing ways
Adds up to a failure-oriented model, ferreting out students' weaknesses and preparing them to take their place in a stratified society	Adds up to a success-oriented model, emphasizing students' strengths and preparing them to be the best they can be in a stratified society

(Weaver, [1994] p. 365.)

practice with phonemic segmentation activities, synthetic phonic exercises, and work with decodable texts before children engage with real texts. In the 1990s and early twenty-first century many claims were made about the "scientific" research base for such programs (Fletcher & Lyons, 1998; Langenberg et al., 2000). Reading instruction came to be seen as the province of legislators and policy-makers in a way that was unprecedented in the history of education in the United States. In reaction, many respected educators and scholars in the field of literacy education criticized the absence of educators' input into policies and the narrowness of the research base used to support skills emphasis and "phonics first" programs (Coles, 2000).

At the other end of the continuum is the holistic orientation, which presumes that authentic reading and writing experiences precede and then accompany attention to subskills. Meaning-based approaches, such as the shared reading and language experience methodologies, fall at this end of the continuum. They, in turn, have been criticized for leaving too much essential learning about print to children, for under-using direct instruction, and for lacking effective support for struggling readers.

Basal reading programs fall at various places along the continuum between these two extremes, although the majority are primarily subskills-oriented. Before examining specific methodologies for teaching initial readers, we will consider the general characteristics of basal-based programs because of their widespread use and long history; we will also examine whole-language philosophy because it has strongly influenced instruction since the 1980s. Following these general information discussions, we will examine four specific instructional methodologies in some detail: shared reading, language experience approach, guided reading of leveled texts, and basal programs. We will also consider elements of instruction that cross programs, such as word study and writing.

A traditional *basal reading program* consists of a series of books, graduated in length and difficulty, designed for the sole purpose of teaching reading. At the beginning levels, deliberate attempts are made to include words and word elements that have previously been introduced. In addition, stories are typically accompanied by workbooks and skill sheets that focus on a skills hierarchy created by the authors. Although there are significant differences in the story texts and organizations of different series, they are all based on the premise that reading is an aggregate of skills that must be gradually developed in a logical sequence. The publication and distribution of basal readers are multimillion-dollar businesses. The chief difference between older basal readers and those that have been published since 1993 is that the more recent editions seldom contain selections written specifically for teaching reading. Rather, they include anthologies of selections written by professional children's authors (Hoffman et al., 1994). In order to attract as many customers as possible in the educational community, each basal publisher typically claims that its series is "balanced," provides a "whole reading program," and uses real, meaningful literature. In reality the series typically include phonics, explicit teaching of word identification skills, rules, work with patterned words, and direct teaching of sight vocabulary. While many of today's teachers' manuals claim to focus on construction of meaning and to be "literature-based," close scrutiny reveals the limited accuracy of these claims. In fact the anthologies still include more excerpts from and adaptations of literature than complete, unabridged selections. They still implicitly define reading as mastery of specific skills, and explicitly prescribe how these skills should be taught and assessed (Weaver, 1994). Many elementary-level administrators and teachers subscribe to the apparent logic of this assumption and believe that basals represent a scientific approach to teaching reading (Shannon, 1990). While novice teachers may find the prescriptive nature of a basal series appealing, beginning reading instruction based solely on the use of a basal program may result in youngsters who lack reading proficiency and/or motivation. Reading, for them, can become an unsuccessful or unpleasant exercise prescribed and controlled by others (Anderson et al., 1985; Shannon & Goodman, 1994).

In the 1980s there was a strong impetus toward use of instructional approaches that were seen as more compatible with current knowledge about learning, literacy, and language development. These were often referred to as *whole-language* approaches because they reflected a whole-language philosophy, which includes the premise that literacy is most naturally learned from whole to part, in meaningful contexts. If children are exposed to a print-rich environment (i.e., they are read to, encouraged to explore books and to attempt to write, and given opportunities to observe adults reading and writing), they develop a general understanding of the existence, nature, and purpose of print. With continued, guided exposure to the world of print, their understandings become more refined and specific. Another characteristic of whole-language-based instruction philosophy is emphasis on meaning. For this reason, this approach is often referred to as meaning-based (in contrast to skills-based) instruction. While early reading materials may be predictable and brief, they have intrinsic literary value; stories, poems, and chants are chosen on the basis of their appeal and meaning to children, rather than their simplicity and brevity. Moreover, meaning-based instruction acknowledges the social aspects of literacy. Sharing of stories and compositions (both drawings and writing) capitalizes on the natural sociability of young children and plays a major role in meaning-based classrooms.

The atmosphere of a meaning-based classroom fosters problem solving and risk taking. Since the teacher understands that children engage in approximations en route to the eventual mastery of conventional reading and writing, experimentation is encouraged and positively reinforced. As children learn to speak, their parents never doubt that their approximations will eventually evolve into adult speech. Similarly, teachers who adopt a whole-language philosophy have confidence that children who have continuous, meaningful, and sensitively guided experiences with print will eventually become accomplished readers and writers. Such teachers incorporate the direct teaching of skills in a natural, functional way rather than according to a prescribed sequence.

In these classrooms, children help determine their own learning pace. The environment is designed to be secure and supportive of their efforts so that anxiety is not associated with reading and writing. Assistance is freely available to children on request. They receive much positive reinforcement; their reading and writing products are celebrated. More and more schools in recent years have moved toward a mix of directly taught skills and meaning-based instruction, devising what are often called "balanced" reading programs. The widespread acknowledgement of the importance of authentic reading and writing experiences and of children's literacy preferences and learning differences are lasting contributions of the whole-language movement. Having established this background, we now move to discussion of specific instructional approaches which are used in various combinations by effective teachers of initial stage readers

Perhaps the most significant characteristic of meaning-based programs is the use of highly predictable materials for beginning reading instruction. As previously noted, familiar, patterned texts enable beginners to use the full range of cueing systems to identify words that are unknown to them in printed form. Predictable materials appropriate for use with beginners fall into two categories: patterned literature (stories, poems, etc.) and transcriptions of children's own language. The shared book experience makes use of the former, while the language experience approach uses the latter type of material. Both are meaning-based approaches and are far less scripted than skills-based and basal approaches, and require more extensive literacy background and decision making on the part of the teacher. These approaches also tend to tie directly into children's interests, backgrounds, and feelings of success as beginning readers and writers. For these reasons we will focus our discussion first on these two approaches. They involve extensive modeling and "reading with" students and are, therefore, most often used with beginning readers.

Shared Book Experience

The *shared book experience* develops young children's awareness of the nature and purpose of print through the use of enlarged versions of favorite stories, poems, and songs. The approach was developed and tested in a ten-year project in the schools of New Zealand by Don Holdaway. He observed that many children learn to read by having stories read aloud to them. Typically, a parent reads favorite stories repeatedly, with the child sitting close enough to observe the print during this process. Teachers have always recognized the importance of reading aloud to groups of children. However, this activity was formerly considered to have limited instructional value since the print could not be seen, shared, and discussed by the children. Holdaway came up with the simple but ingenious idea of enlarging favorite children's books, so that whole groups of children can see and follow the print as the story is read aloud. Shared book experience is an extraordinarily effective vehicle for initiating children into reading and is therefore used primarily in kindergarten and early first grade. The teacher who wishes to use this approach must have access to a good selection of children's books, including several enlarged versions. These can be either commercially published or teacher-made and should represent choices that are popular with children, and that are short, predictable, and meaningful.

A typical shared book experience often begins with a warm-up session. The children gather comfortably (usually on a rug) around the teacher, who sits beside an easel used to display the enlarged reading material. The lesson begins with group reading of a familiar story or poem that the children have already encountered many times. The teacher uses a pointer to point to each word as it is read and encourages the children to chime in and read along at a fluid, natural pace. This is a thoroughly enjoyable activity for most children, who get the sense that they are participating in reading and that reading is pleasurable.

After the warm-up the teacher introduces a story that is new or at least less familiar. For example, suppose the teacher has selected the well-known verse "I Know an Old Lady Who Swallowed a Fly." This is a particularly appropriate selection for beginners because it is highly predictable. Phrases are repeated, it has a consistent refrain, and each verse builds on the previous ones. All these characteristics make it easy for children to predict and remember what words and phrases will appear in the text; they can participate even in the first reading by the teacher.

The teacher introduces the book, encouraging the children to discuss the cover illustration and the title and to predict what the story will be about. After building the children's anticipation, the teacher reads the book to them, following the print with a pointer and stopping occasionally to talk about the illustrations and to encourage further predictions about what will come next. "What do you think the old lady will swallow next? What do you think is going to happen to her? Let's read to find out." The primary purpose of the first reading is for the children to enjoy the story and become familiar with it.

During the second reading, the teacher helps the children focus on the print. The children are encouraged to read along. The teacher points to each word as it is spoken, which helps the children map speech to print. They are familiar with the rhyme; moreover, it is extremely predictable. Therefore, they will be highly successful at "reading" it back with the support of the group. Children who engage in shared reading immediately develop a sense of confidence in their ability to learn to read and in the willingness of others to help them. Because the environment is supportive and because the first texts they encounter are meaningful and delightful, they develop extremely positive attitudes toward reading. This is one of the most powerful arguments for using the shared book approach.

During the course of a lesson, which typically lasts 30 or 40 minutes, several pieces may be read or the same book may be read several times. During these readings the procedures of modeling, pointing, pausing, and masking are likely to be included.

Modeling of reading is provided by the teacher. The children observe her matching speech to print. In addition, the language of literature is modeled in spoken form. ("Fancy that! She swallowed a cat." ". . . perhaps she'll die.")

Pointing involves moving a pointer along each line of print to draw the children's attention to each word as the teacher says it. This helps the children follow along as the story is read, develop a left-to-right orientation to reading, and understand that each printed word represents a spoken word.

Pausing before key words enables the children to predict words on the basis of their own experiences and their familiarity with the story.

Masking is a technique used to focus children's attention on the details of print, such as a single word, letter, or letter combination. Teachers often make a masking device by cutting a window out of an index card or piece of oaktag and using the cutout portion as a sliding tab. For example, to help children use a graphophonemic element to predict a word, the teacher might frame the word *spider,* covering all letters except *sp.* She then leads the children to pronounce the blend of *s* and *p,* encouraging them to predict what the word might be. Finally, she uncovers the rest of the word, and compares it with the children's predictions. Through masking the teacher can help children develop and refine their word identification strategies.

Although the reading and rereading of enlarged texts is the heart of the shared book experience, the effectiveness of the approach is greatly enhanced by including appropriate follow-up activities. These fall into two broad categories: activities designed to extend children's experience with story language and structure and activities designed to develop beginning reading skills (sight vocabulary and word identification strategies).

Story extension activities include retelling of stories (often using simple props), art projects based on stories, and dramatizations of stories. A story retelling activity designed by teacher Judy Kennedy centers on the use of storyboards. The children construct a basic setting for a story by gluing construction paper scenery on a 10- by 18-inch piece of oaktag. (For example, the storyboards for *Peter Rabbit* include the rabbit hole, the fence, and Mr. McGregor's garden.) Next the children make stick puppets of the major characters in the story (mother rabbit, four little rabbits, and Mr. McGregor). The children delight in using the storyboards over and over as backdrops for the retelling of their favorite stories.

The teacher points to each word as it is being read.

Activities that focus on words and parts of words are designed to address the initial reading goals of acquiring sight vocabulary and learning to use word identification strategies. For example, first-grade teacher Kim Knapton prints key words from a big book on individual cards and has students match them to words in the text and read them in context. At other times she asks children to find words in the story that begin with a certain letter sound. Or they may be given a familiar sentence from the story with a word deleted and asked to supply the missing word. Many possible follow-up activities can be tailored to fit the children's capabilities. The teacher is limited only by her imagination.

For children who are in the emergent and early initial reading stages, the shared book experience is an extremely effective vehicle for promoting reading development. It can be used with a large group (the whole class) or small groups, and it is equally beneficial for children at slightly different developmental levels. Those who are in the emergent reading stage and have had relatively little experience with print develop basic print concepts. Initial readers build sight vocabulary and word identification strategies from the same lesson.

The Language Experience Approach

The *language experience approach (LEA)* is often used as a supplement to shared reading or basal instruction. Like shared book experience, it can be classified as a meaning-based approach. It involves teaching reading by using the students' own experiences and language. Following some discussion, the children dictate a message that is recorded by the teacher and then used for reading. The language experience approach begins with a focus on meaning. Students learn that their thoughts can be expressed in language, which can be recorded and read by themselves and others. Through this process, the teacher can facilitate understanding of the function of words and letter sounds and of the relationship between spoken and written units of language.

Using students' own language for their early reading experiences ensures that the reading material will be intrinsically interesting, understandable, and highly familiar or predictable since it consists of their own language recorded by the teacher. Properly implemented, the language experience approach also provides a natural and functional way to foster the development of print concepts and introduce the initial reading processes: building a sight vocabulary and learning to use word identification strategies to figure out unknown words. Since this approach provides students with models of pronunciation, spelling, syntax, and word meanings, it is particularly appropriate for struggling readers and children who are learning English as a second language.

The approach can be used either with individuals or groups of initial readers. The typical language experience lesson has three distinct parts: discussion, dictation, and follow-up. The effectiveness of the language experience approach depends largely on the teacher's ability to structure each of these components for maximum motivation and reinforcement.

Individual Instruction

The basic steps in generating and using language experience text are as follows:

1. *Discussion* The prelude to writing a language experience episode is conversation. The teacher talks with the student about a topic of interest: something the child has recently done, something that has happened to him, something he has drawn, or something that has been read to him, for example. The discussion provides an ideal opportunity for the teacher to help the student build concepts, enlarge vocabulary, and use expressive language.

2. *Dictation* After informal discussion, the teacher helps the student to summarize and relate ideas in sequence, choose the most relevant (to him), and dictate exactly what he wishes to have recorded. As he dictates, the teacher transcribes his language exactly. The student should watch the teacher write; student and teacher both say each word as it is recorded. When the student has completed the dictation (which should be limited to five or six sentences), student and teacher read it back together. The teacher moves her hand along under the sentence being read to focus the student's attention on the words and to ensure left-to-right progression. The student can then be asked to read the selection independently or with minimal help. As an alternative, the teacher can record the text with a word processor, with a copy printed out for the student to take home, illustrate, and practice reading.

3. *Follow-Up* The text can be reread the next day with help as needed. At this time the teacher can determine which words the student knows at sight. The teacher can frame various words in random order with hands or a window card. If the student seems to know the word out of context, he can add it to a collection of sight words. Or the student may be invited to point out words that are recognized without rereading whole sentences. Two or three of these words should be selected to add to the student's "word bank."

Selected words can be printed on cards and kept in a box, closable plastic bag, or envelope. It is helpful for the teacher to write the original sentence containing the sight word on the back of the card. If the word is not recognized subsequently, the student can turn the card over and read the word in context. As the child's collection grows, it can be used in many ways. Older beginning readers or students who have a large collection may prefer to keep their words in a notebook arranged alphabetically according to beginning letters.

The student should read the sight words to the teacher or an aide every few days. Words that are forgotten more than once should be discarded or kept separate; they are not sight words. The goal is to develop a collection of words that are easily and consistently recognized and that are personally meaningful to the student. A number of follow-up activities can be used to provide additional practice:

- Several dictations can be made into a reading book for children to read and take home.
- The teacher can prepare a copy of a dictated text cut into sentence strips, then present a packet of strips, out of order, to the child. Using the original story as a model, the student pastes the strips, in order, on construction paper to read and take home.

The following activities can be done independently:

- Illustrating the text
- Reading to a friend
- Looking for sight words in other printed materials and circling them
- Reviewing sight words with a friend

Such activities provide supplementary reading practice for the children; moreover, they require little teacher direction. Children can work independently or in small groups while the teacher devotes herself to working with other groups or individuals.

Group Instruction

The language experience approach can be used with a small group or a whole class as well as with individuals. Discussion is elicited, with participation by all the children. In a group situation, children take turns dictating sentences and recording is done on chart paper so that everyone can see it. The same steps used in generating, recording, and working with an individual should be followed. Children should "read back" as a group first. Then individuals can volunteer to read sentences.

A good immediate follow-up activity is "Hunt." Questions can be tailored to each child's capabilities. For example, using the same chart, the teacher may ask:

"Who can come up and find the word *dog*?" "John, can you point to a compound word?" "Melissa, find a word that begins with the same sound as *ship*." The teacher may wish to reproduce the text and make copies for the children to reread and use.

Whether working with individuals or with groups of children, the most important part of the language experience lesson is the dictation, reading, and rereading of meaningful material. Time spent calling attention to graphophonemic elements and sight words should not dominate the lesson. Initial readers can profit from use of the text for limited practice with word identification strategies; however, they will gain the most from dictation and reading of the whole text for both enjoyment and practice.

Dialect Variations

One aspect of the language experience approach that many teachers find problematic is the recommendation to record students' language exactly, even if it is grammatically incorrect. The reason for this recommendation is that the beginning reader's task is to match speech to print; the more closely the printed language corresponds to the child's oral language patterns, the easier it will be to accomplish this match. In many instances the differences between children's language patterns and standard American English are minimal and consist mostly of regional expressions ("We was going home") or immature speech ("Me and Tom played ball"). Calling attention to such minor differences can interfere with the primary goal of helping beginners understand the relationship between speech and print; hence the recommendation to transcribe speech exactly is a sound one.

In situations in which students' oral language patterns are markedly different from standard American English, the teacher may want to use other strategies. In the case of students who have pronounced dialect differences or for whom English is a second language, important social and cultural factors must be considered. The parents of minority children have expectations that school is the place where their children will acquire and practice the "language of power," which in this country is standard American English. This is a valid concern; however, it is equally important not to devalue in any way the language that children bring with them to school. Criticism of their language amounts to criticism of their family and culture.

Faced with this dilemma, innovative teachers have modified the language experience lesson in such a way that children are exposed to standard American English without compromising the integrity of their dialect. For example, in discussing an upcoming Easter party, a group of first-graders dictated four sentences, using the following language:

> We gon' make Easter egg.
> We done brang egg.
> We be waitin' on Friday.
> We wants to find de egg 'n candy.

The teacher used correct spelling in recording the dictation, but did not alter the children's language patterns.

We're going to make Easter eggs.
We done brang eggs.
We be waiting on Friday.
We want to find the eggs and candy.

The children read their story several times and engaged in the usual follow-up activities. The next day, after the children read the story again, the teacher put up a new chart next to their original dictation and explained, "This is how your story would look if it were in a book."

We're going to make Easter eggs.
We brought eggs.
We are waiting for Friday.
We want to find the eggs and candy.

The children read the new version and compared it to the original, noting which words were different. There was no implication that the first version was inferior to the second; the two drafts were simply presented as slightly different. The children had the opportunity to read their own recorded language as well as a "translation" in standard American English.

Combining LEA and Shared Book Experience

Language experience and shared book approaches naturally complement and enhance one another; for this reason it is strongly recommended that both be used in beginning reading instruction. While they have many features in common, each approach makes unique contributions to the child's early literacy learning. For example, both approaches involve the modeling of reading using enlarged print; however, the texts used in shared book experiences are already complete, having been created by someone else. The children do not observe this process, whereas during a language experience lesson composing is modeled as well as reading. The children see the generation of text, which provides insights into the relationship between speech and print and between writing and reading.

There are important differences in the text content of the two approaches. The shared book experience exposes children to traditional forms of literature that transcend their personal experience and provide strong emotional and aesthetic satisfaction. Language experience dictations, in contrast, are usually derived from children's real-world experiences and demonstrate how these can be recorded and read. The language experience approach integrates particularly well with science and social studies. Learning in these content areas involves observing, discussing, and summarizing information. Recording children's observations and summaries not only helps them to acquire and organize new information, it also provides another opportunity for literacy learning.

Many teachers use LEA as a follow-up to shared reading, inviting children to summarize stories in their own words, sequence key events from a story, create a new ending to a story, caption their drawings about a story, or give personal reactions to characters and plot. Teachers have found that participation in shared book experiences significantly increases the quality and richness of the vocabulary and language structures used by the children in their dictations. Conversely, the language experience approach adds to children's understanding of how texts are composed and recorded, thus expanding their awareness of the relationship between reading and writing (Holdaway, 1979). They know where books come from.

The next two approaches we will examine—guided reading with leveled books and basal reader instruction—involve less "reading with" students and more extensive teacher guidance before and during the child's independent reading. These approaches are likely to be most effective with children well into the initial reading stage, who have begun to acquire sight vocabulary and can apply their developing knowledge of letter–sound correspondences in reading and writing.

Use of Leveled Books

Reading Recovery, a first-grade intervention program that was developed by Marie Clay of New Zealand, has demonstrated high levels of success in accelerating the literacy progress of struggling initial readers. Many of the practices and materials used in Reading Recovery have made their way into regular primary-grade classrooms and have influenced the instruction of all initial readers. One of the most widespread of these influences has been the refocusing of teachers' attention on the match between beginning readers and the level of complexity of their reading materials. Reading Recovery teachers move their students through a sequence of short little books that gradually increase in complexity. Because the increase in difficulty of the books is so gradual (there are 24 levels), students typically experience a high rate of success. In assigning levels to the little books, Clay and her colleagues went far beyond mechanical readability formulas that depend on structure of sentences and numbers of multisyllable words. They took into account such additional features as the supportiveness of illustrations, predictability, repetition of language structures, and familiarity of subject matter. Moreover, they tried the books out on children to estimate the relative difficulty of individual texts for the majority of children (Allington, 2001).

The idea of "leveling" books to more accurately control the match of beginning reader with text has become more and more widely used. Fountas and Pinnell (1999) have extended this process through a typical fourth-grade level, and have attached difficulty levels to more than 7,500 books that are popular for use with children in grades K–4. Many publishers have followed the trend, providing levels for supplementary books as well as basal texts. Teachers are left with a problem, however, in that the leveling process, since it has become more inclusive in factors considered, is not uniform or even equivalent across published materials. If she is using books from various sources, a teacher is left to figure out level equivalencies on her own.

In his extensive work with schools and teachers, Richard Allington suggests a workable process for teachers to use in leveling their own texts for children in the primary grades and beyond. Adapting the recommendations of Chall et al. (1996), he recommends identifying "benchmark texts" that represent different grade levels, such as typical beginning first grade, late first grade, and so forth. Books from the leveled list in Fountas and Pinnell's book *Matching Books to Readers* (1999) or leveled books from a publisher may be used. Once benchmark books are identified, a teacher (or better yet groups of teachers from similar grade levels) may "level" some of the books to be used in their classrooms. The process works in this manner: first, you skim through the book whose level is in question, noting characteristics that determine difficulty such as amount of text, sentence length, page format, relation of illustrations to text, predictability of language and story, and vocabulary familiarity. Next, find the benchmark book that seems closest to the new text in level of difficulty. Label the book with the same level as the "closest" benchmark book. This is not the end of the process, however. As children read the books you have leveled, make comparisons. Do those who can successfully read the benchmark book find the new book harder? Easier? If there is consistency in what you are noticing, adjust the labeled level (Allington, 2001).

Leveled texts can provide a great aid to teachers, particularly with children who are struggling with learning to read and children who tend to consistently choose books that are much too difficult for them to read successfully. Most often teachers use these texts for guided reading, having small groups or pairs of students read a book individually, and then together with the teacher and/or each other. There are potential pitfalls in over-using leveled texts, however. School literacy specialist and former primary-grade teacher Tracy Warren cautions teachers she works with that over-use of leveled books can result in:

▪ *Over-restriction of reading choices.* If children have access only to books that match their identified level, their choices will be unnecessarily limited. Leveling of books does not take into account children's interests and reading preferences. Hence, restriction to leveled books may undermine motivation to read.

▪ *Neglect of comprehension.* Typically teachers assess the reader/book match in terms of word identification accuracy, documenting gains by means of running records and/or fluency of oral reading. Comprehension may not be addressed. Moreover, leveled books for initial readers often lack story elements or new information; hence meaning is not a focus when reading them.

▪ *Inappropriate matches of child to text.* Depending on who leveled the books and how, there may be major discrepancies in difficulty within a level.

▪ *Fixation on levels.* When too much of the students' reading is from leveled texts, both teachers and students can become overly conscious of the level, rather than the content, of the books. If achievement is seen as advancing upward in levels, children may push to move through levels at too rapid a rate, failing to consolidate their gains. If teachers see children's advancement through levels as the chief indicator of their own success as teachers, they may inadvertently contribute to this problem.

It is fair to say, then, that leveled books can be very useful in matching beginning readers to texts that stretch them just the right amount, but that misuse and overuse are to be avoided. Leveled books are perhaps most useful in guided reading lessons with small groups or pairs of children who are homogeneously grouped for these sessions. The total reading program, however, should also include many opportunities for children to choose from a variety of books including those that are below or slightly above their reading level. From the time children can recognize a small number of "sight words" and decode simple texts, comprehension and meaning making should play a role in both instruction and assessment.

Use of Basal Readers

Basal readers have changed dramatically in the past few years in response to research and teacher practice. Whereas older basals included contrived stories with limited vocabulary (remember "See Spot run"?), the newer basal series consist of anthologies of mostly unabridged literature selections by recognized authors. Literature is organized according to themes, and supplementary trade books are recommended or provided. Each basal selection is still accompanied by numerous skill lessons, workbooks (sometimes labeled "student resource books" or "journals"), and consumable worksheets. Although teachers are expected to select from resources presented in the teachers' guides, the notes for each selection are very extensive. Reading and deciphering them is extremely time consuming and can seem overwhelming. Typically the notes for the teacher are far longer than the actual student text.

Many school systems still require teachers to make use of a commercial basal series. There are several reasons for this. One is undoubtedly tradition. By the late 1920s, basal reading series had become widely accepted as the primary vehicle for reading instruction in American public schools. Three or more generations of Americans have undergone reading instruction that was driven by basal readers (Goodman et al., 1988). Because of their own school experiences, parents and educators alike tend to equate reading instruction (and improvement) with the use of basal readers and their accompanying workbooks.

Another appealing aspect of basal programs is what administrators refer to as "consistency." They are reassured by the fact that lessons are structured and sequenced for the teacher; all children will cover the same program at more or less the same rate. Teachers using a basal approach are required to make far fewer instructional decisions than teachers using approaches that are not pre-programmed, such as shared reading, language experience approach, and guided reading of leveled texts. The basal approach suggests what will be presented and when. This provides a certain kind of security, especially for the beginning teacher because she is relieved of the sole responsibility for making instructional decisions. Basal programs attempt to standardize the literacy learning process for all teachers and students. While this may help some teachers, literacy learning seems much too important to be constrained by inflexible external guidelines.

Teachers who have developed a thorough understanding of early literacy learning and of the conditions most conducive to children's reading growth can maintain control of reading instruction even when required to use basal readers. This is accomplished through thoughtful evaluation and modification of basal lessons. The teacher who is able to decide which parts of a lesson are essential and which parts can be eliminated or taught more effectively in another context is in a position to provide time for the more authentic reading and writing activities described elsewhere in the chapter. How does a teacher evaluate a basal lesson for these purposes? We have developed several criteria that education students and practicing teachers have found helpful in modifying basal lessons.

There are two aspects of each lesson that must be examined: the story itself and the accompanying skill activities. Knowing that materials for beginning readers should be meaningful and highly predictable, the teacher will note the kind of language used in the story. Does the story primarily (or completely) consist of conversation? Is the language contrived to include specific phonic elements? Is the story removed from the language and experiences of young children? If the answers to these questions is consistently "yes," the teacher would be well advised to create related but more appropriate text for additional reading practice, through language experience dictation or teacher-written text.

Next the teacher evaluates the accompanying skill activities. There are often simply far too many of them. Teachers frequently have difficulty determining which of these activities can be omitted. In making a decision, the teacher must consider three criteria. First, will the exercise contribute to the reader's ability to figure out unknown words? Second, will the students have an immediate opportunity to apply the skill in a real reading situation? And, third, is a disproportionate amount of time being spent on isolated skill activities?

In applying the first criterion, it is helpful to remember that the goal of phonics instruction is not for children to become proficient at analyzing and naming phonic elements of words in isolation; rather, it is to promote the use of letter–sound associations to aid in identifying words in context. This distinction should prove helpful in selecting appropriate activities. For example, consider the following workbook exercises:

1. *The Hard and Soft Sounds of C*

    Sometimes a *c* has a soft sound, as in the word *city*. Sometimes it has a hard sound, as in *call*. Write S after the words in which the *c* is soft and H after those in which the *c* is hard.

call _____	careful _____	crowd _____
Nancy _____	cake _____	cent _____
picnic _____	ice _____	cookie _____

2. *What Word Is Missing?*
    1. The children wanted to pl_____ ball.
    2. We can't watch TV. The TV set is br_____.
    3. The cow had white and bl_____ spots.
    4. Be careful when you cross the str_____.

The first exercise requires readers to analyze phonic elements in isolated words. Note that this task can only be successfully completed by students who can already identify the words. This is true of most exercises that focus on words in isolation. One must question the value of such analysis, since it does not help the reader identify unknown words. If the exercise were restructured so that the words appeared in context, students would use the sense of the sentence to identify the target words. Conscious analysis of the hard or soft sound of *c* would be very unlikely to enter into the process. This example is typical of exercises that require analysis for its own sake and contribute little to developing proficiency in reading.

function vs analysis

The second exercise, on the other hand, provides practice in functional application of phonics rather than analysis. The deleted words containing blends are embedded in sentences. Students are led to use the sense of the sentence in conjunction with their knowledge of letter–sound associations and familiar letter groupings (onsets and rimes) to supply the deleted words.

Basal reader lessons frequently provide phonics exercises to be led by the teacher just before the story is read. One would assume the phonic elements discussed before the story reading would appear in words in the story, thus giving children practice in functional application. In fact, this is often not the case. In examining lessons, teachers will find many instances of practice of skills that are not subsequently utilized in reading the story. For example, in a popular basal reader that we examined, an extensive exercise on words beginning with *d* was followed by a story that contained no words beginning with *d*. A good rule of thumb for teachers to follow is to select or generate skill activities that are derived from the reading material.

Another issue teachers should address is the number of isolated skill activities included in a lesson. One of the major conclusions of the national report of the Commission on Reading, *Becoming a Nation of Readers* (Anderson, Hiebert, Scott, & Wilkinson, 1985) was that our schools do not devote an adequate amount of time to extended reading and writing; instead, far too much time is spent on isolated skill activities that have little value in learning to read. Since the report was published in 1985, many teachers have increased the time their students spend reading; however, basal programs persist in offering far too many "activities."

Regardless of which skill activities are selected, children—even beginning readers—should spend most of the time allotted for reading instruction engaged in extended reading activities (Allington, 2001). Word study is an important part of the program for initial readers but should not be allowed to encroach on time for real reading and related meaning-making activities. Teachers can replace workbooks and non-reading drills with literature discussion groups, author studies, or reading of trade books related to the basal theme even at the first-grade level (Routman, 1996).

Several first-grade teachers in a school that was judged by local administrators, teachers, and parents to have an excellent reading program estimated their allotment of reading instructional time as follows:

Activity	Percentage of Time Allotted
Modeling reading	
Students "reading along"	
Independent reading	80%
Extension activities (e.g., story retelling)	
Writing	
Word study and isolated skill activities	20%

Note: These basic time-allotment guidelines do not depend on whether the teacher is using a basal reader.

The format given in figure 3.1 for assessing basal reading lessons at the initial levels can be used to provide a basis for modifications. The evaluation of a lesson according to the checklist guides the teacher's decisions about what to modify and

FIGURE 3.1   *Criteria for Analyzing a Basal Lesson*

Publisher: _____   Date of Edition: _____

Title: _____   "Level": _____

- Would the story make sense without the pictures?
- The story's language is: (a) that of literature (b) contrived to include certain phonic elements (c) primarily conversation.
- Which cueing system(s) could a beginning reader use a great deal in identifying the words: (a) semantic (b) syntactic (c) graphophonemic?
- Comment briefly on the quality (and interest) of the story and illustrations.
- How many skill activities (oral and written) are included in the lesson?
- Do the skill activities seem to relate directly to the reading material?
- Estimate the ratio between time devoted to reading and time devoted to skill activities.
- Would you omit any skill activities? If yes, which ones, and why?
- If you had to use this basal series, what might you do to supplement this lesson?

how. Changes that teachers frequently make in early reading lessons include the following.

Before Reading
- Eliminate skill activities that do not relate to instructional goals for initial reading and/or that appear to be confusing or unhelpful for readers at this level.
- Practice only those skills that are likely to be used in reading the selection.
- Rather than preteaching vocabulary, help children to anticipate the content of the story through prediction.

Reading
- Teacher and students read text together (choral reading) once or twice without interruption.
- Help children understand the story through discussion.
- Summarize the story in narrative form, using the language experience format. (Children retell story in their own words, teacher records on chart paper, they read it back.) This is a particularly appropriate activity if the basal story is primarily conversation.

Follow-Up
- In lieu of skill work and workbook exercises, read aloud a related children's literature book. (Most basal teachers' guides provide lists of recommended children's books to go with each theme.)
- If appropriate workbook exercises are available (according to criteria discussed earlier), select and assign one or two.
- Have children draw and write in response to the story.
- Read related trade books.

Many options are available for modifications, which will vary according to the particular group of students and the basal lesson being used. Skill at modifying lessons effectively develops as teachers gain experience working with beginning readers and with materials. Prospective teachers will find it helpful to examine several basal lessons using the checklist of criteria, and to speculate on appropriate modifications. The end result of this process is having more time to spend with beginning readers in the kinds of holistic reading and writing activities described in the discussions of shared book experiences and the language experience approach.

All initial reading approaches include the study of words and word parts. Teachers are challenged to balance word study with use of whole texts. Whether designing their own word analysis activities, or selecting appropriate exercises from a commercial program, guidelines are helpful.

Graves, Juel, and Graves (2001) recommend several general principles that may be used to guide word study instruction. We have modified these slightly:

■ *Start where the child is.* Effective word study instruction builds on what the child already knows about letters, sounds, and words, and the relationships among them. It also builds on the child's more holistic sense of how print functions. In fact, whether instruction moves from part to whole (beginning with teaching letter sounds and blending these into words) or from whole to part (beginning with words and analyzing component letter sounds), it will make no sense to a child who does not have a well-developed concept of the whole process and purpose of reading—what stories are like, how print relates to speech, and so on. Meaningful encounters with print provide the experience that makes phonics instruction useful. When children lack rich and varied experience with stories, this must be provided at school along with opportunities to build understanding of print itself.

■ *Make word study an active, decision-making process.* Effective word study instruction acknowledges that learning involves pattern detection and active classification. Children can be helped to analyze and classify words on the basis of component sounds and spelling features. Words can be grouped together if they contain the same onsets, rimes, letter patterns, or other common features. For example, *pig, wig,* and *rig* can be grouped together. Why? What part of these words is the same?

Effective word study instruction also makes extensive use of contrasts. Wth guidance, children learn how to contrast words having different onsets, rimes, and spelling patterns and learn to describe those differences. Contrasting the onsets in *pig, wig,* and *rig,* or the rimes in *hop* and *hat, pop* and *pat, mop* and *mat,* helps the child to discern which letters lead to which pronunciations. This in turn builds the child's ability to detect and use similar features in words when reading. Effective decoders tend to figure out words not by applying phonics rules, but by recognizing familiar patterns of letters, or "chunks," that they have encountered before (Stahl, 1992).

■ *Help children understand how the alphabetic writing system works.* Teachers of emergent and initial readers model how to segment spoken words into rimes and phonemes, and how to record these speech units with letters. Effective teachers then help children learn how to represent speech units in their own writing. "As children learn to write, they are learning the ways words are constructed. As they learn the ways to write, or encode, a word, they are learning what they will need to know to decode a printed word in reading" (Graves, Juel, & Graves, 2001, p. 163).

■ *Keep comprehension the primary goal.* This principle is especially important to keep in mind: the ultimate purpose of phonics instruction is for readers to learn to recognize words quickly, automatically, in order to fully focus their attention on comprehension of the text. Children who devote their attention, or mental energy, to sounding out words will not be able to attend sufficiently to making meaning from the text (Samuels, 1988). The purpose of phonics instruction should be verbalized to children, and they should be led to read and reread stories to solidify their decoding skills and develop fluency.

Graves, Juel, and Graves point out that these four principles apply to all word–study instruction for readers of all ages who are relative beginners. Teachers are urged to bear in mind, always, that word study is only one part of an effective reading instruction program, and as such, must be kept in perspective as a tool for developing literacy, rather than as an end in itself. If we return to Frith's (1985) stages of word recognition (see Chapter 2, p. 64) it is evident that good phonics instruction should help children pass through the logographic (whole words embedded in familiar contexts) and alphabetic (focus on letter sounds) stages and into the orthographic (visually recognizing familiar groups of letters) stage as quickly as possible. Emergent readers' experiences with story reading, book handling, shared reading, and other typical kindergarten activities support them at the logographic stage. Initial readers develop alphabetic knowledge particularly through direct instruction with letter-sound correspondences and practice in writing. Separating the sounds in words in order to record them in writing forces children to attend to the internal structure of words, as does onset/rime-based instruction. Such instruction moves children into the orthographic stage, which fosters their capacity to automatically recognize words. "Once a child begins to use orthographic patterns in recognizing words and recognizes words at an easy fluent pace, it is time to move away from phonics instruction and to spend even more time reading and writing text" (Stahl, 1992, p. 625).

Components of a Balanced Literacy Program

The approaches discussed thus far are teacher-guided and are core elements of initial reading programs. In addition, researchers and teachers agree on three other components that are a regular part of all effective beginning reading programs: listening to literature read aloud, independent and/or paired reading, and writing. Including the following strategies on a daily basis maximizes the potential for growth in literacy (Routman, 1996; Weaver, 1994):

1. *Read literature aloud to children every day.* By reading aloud, the teacher can introduce children to different types of literature and share wonderful stories and information that they are as yet unable to read themselves. Reading aloud creates a social bond and helps foster the perception that reading is a meaningful and enjoyable activity.

Listening to literature on an audiotape or interacting with text on a CD-ROM are valuable complements to reading aloud by the teacher, but should not replace it.

2. *Provide daily opportunities for independent reading.* Even before children can read independently in a conventional manner, they benefit from quiet time interacting with books they have chosen. This experience makes them feel like readers and assume many habits of a reader. They tend to select books that appeal to them because of the pictures or subject matter or books that are familiar because they have been read aloud. During silent reading time in a first-grade classroom, some children will be absorbed in perusing illustrations in their books, some will be quietly retelling a familiar text in their own words, and others will be attempting to puzzle out the print.

For most initial readers, *paired reading* is a natural alternative to independent reading. They enjoy looking at books with a friend or helping each other construct a story or negotiate text. Literacy is largely a social event for young children; for this reason, they often prefer paired reading to completely independent reading.

3. *Provide daily opportunities for writing.* "Writing" in kindergarten used to consist of instruction and practice in penmanship (the "correct" formation of letters). In first grade, copying of words or sentences was added to the curriculum. It was generally believed by most teachers that children were not capable of writing in the sense of composing their own messages until they had begun to read, acquired some sight vocabulary, and memorized the standard spellings of many words. Teachers now treat writing in the primary grades very differently. The research of Donald Graves and others has greatly expanded our understanding of early writing development and of the role of writing in literacy growth (Graves, 1983; Morrow, 2001). This new knowledge has had great impact on classroom practice. We now know, for example, that rudimentary attempts at writing actually precede reading; young children can and should be encouraged to compose. We also know a good deal about the process of writing. Writers of all ages generate ideas, draft their ideas on paper, revise or elaborate on their drafts, and edit them for correctness if they are to be shared with an audience. Very young children engage in all parts of this process except for the last step, editing, which requires considerable reading and writing experience. Since the major emphasis of the writing process is on meaning, children need not be constrained by their lack of knowledge of standard spelling and punctuation.

Kindergartners who are invited to write often begin by drawing. As a consequence of being immersed in a print-rich environment, they soon begin to include print with their drawings, often in the form of extended scribble, letter strings, or one-word labels spelled phonetically. The printed messages spelled in this way gradually expand to phrases, sentences, and eventually to longer texts. Spelling progresses (as described in Chapter 1) from random letters to phonetic spellings as children come to understand the alphabetic principle. As they continue to interact with print in meaningful ways and begin to develop sight vocabulary, their writing includes more and more standard spellings. Clearly, writing contributes significantly to children's literacy learning. Through independent attempts to spell the words they need, initial readers practice and refine their ability to match letters to the speech sounds they represent. Phonetic spelling requires a functional application of phonics. Moreover, writing ensures that children will see meaning as central to literacy. They write to communicate; an outgrowth of this is an expectation that all print will be meaningful.

Interactive Writing

Another teaching strategy that has gained in popularity since the mid-1990s is *interactive writing*, sometimes known as "sharing the pen." Interactive writing is a teacher-guided activity in which a group composition is recorded partly by the teacher and partly by students. Its purpose is to model the process of writing as well as to involve children in the process. Interactive writing sessions enable children to extend their understanding of how written language is constructed and to practice applying what they are learning about written language to the act of writing.

The teacher using this strategy may work with a whole class or a small group. (Of course, the smaller the group, the more each child can actively participate.) The students gather around an easel or other writing surface with chart paper attached. They must all be able to see the paper, and to reach it easily when asked to come forward and help with the writing. The teacher sits next to the easel and writes clearly with a dark marker. The purpose and format of the writing are generally set by the teacher and expanded by the group. Then teacher and children jointly compose a text. "Thinking aloud" about construction of the text, the teacher invites individual children to come forward to write word parts or whole words; the teacher then fills in the rest. Since the process is fairly slow, and is generally used with emergent or initial readers, the text is typically short (a list, a caption for a picture, a sentence or two about a class experience). Sometimes teachers use interactive writing for longer texts, such as story retellings, and spread the writing over several sessions on consecutive days (Pinnell and Fountas, 1998).

Many teachers find that interactive writing sessions can be valuable for enhancing children's early development as readers and writers, but the effectiveness of the session depends on how it is designed and used. The teacher's modeling and students' participation will only be effective if tailored to the developmental level of the children in the group. Moreover, the length and frequency of the sessions are an important consideration. Since only one student at a time can participate in the writing, much of the children's time is spent watching. Interactive writing sessions can easily become tedious if the teacher is not adept at pacing and at involving the children. Another potential pitfall identified by teachers who have used this strategy is that it can result in a focus on correctness. Since the text produced will be used for later reading, the teacher typically edits it as it is written. This can add to some children's concern about correctness in their own writing at a time in their development when they should gain independence and knowledge of letter–sound correspondences from experimenting with "invented" spelling. For these reasons, many reading specialists caution teachers to bear in mind that interactive writing is only one possible element in a balanced literacy program that should also include daily opportunities for other guided and independent writing activities. Teachers are urged to keep interactive writing sessions short, and to pay attention to appropriate pacing, content, and balance between student writing and teacher writing.

Sometimes novice teachers are confused by the overlapping characteristics of language experience dictations, interactive writing, and independent writing. Although reading and writing activities are inextricably linked in the early stages of literacy learning, these three instructional techniques have different emphases and purposes. It could be said that while writing is modeled in the LEA, its primary purpose is to generate *reading* (and word study) *material* that is short, familiar, and predictable. While the product of interactive writing is also useful for rereading, the chief purpose of the strategy is to model the process of writing and draw attention to the spelling features of words. The goal of independent writing activities is for children to compose and engage in the process of writing independently, practicing what they know about the way printed language is constructed.

In this chapter, you have learned about various approaches, methods of instruction, and materials for teaching beginning readers. No one combination of these will achieve equal success with all students at the initial reading stage; rather, each is useful in some form for some students some of the time. The constants in effective early literacy programs lie not in the details but in the larger components that make up a well-balanced program. What we can say with a high degree of confidence is that effective programs for beginners include reading to children, reading with children, guiding children's reading, and providing opportunities for children to read independently. Effective programs also include focused instruction and practice with the parts of written language: letters, words, spelling, and pronunciation patterns. Teachers in different contexts and conditions, working with different children, combine materials and approaches to balance these ingredients.

■ CASE STUDIES

Most children enter the initial stage of reading during the first grade. For this reason, we will examine our three case study children as first-graders. John's profile and instructional needs will be typical of the majority of first-graders, Kim will not yet have reached the initial stage, and Theresa will have gone beyond it; they represent the range of literacy development that a first-grade teacher must accommodate.

■ Kim

When Kim entered first grade, she was clearly still in the emergent reading stage. However, she had made a great deal of progress in her kindergarten program, which was rich in print experiences. At the end of her kindergarten year, Kim's sight and hearing were thoroughly tested. No significant problems were found.

As a first-grader, Kim enjoyed being read to. She remained attentive throughout read-aloud sessions and eagerly participated in discussion of stories. She particularly enjoyed story retelling with puppets. Her drawings were more elaborate than they had been in kindergarten and were often accompanied by letter strings or by copied lines of text from any readily available source. (Kim was not aware of the meaning of the print she copied.) Her oral language was more mature than it had been in kindergarten. She used more extensive vocabulary and generally spoke in complete sentences. In October of first grade, Kim's teacher administered an early literacy assessment similar to the one used in kindergarten. She found that:

■ Kim could retell a story including basic plot elements in the proper sequence. She did not include many details or story language. She used conversational language, for the most part, in her retelling.

- Kim was able to point out letters and words but could not identify a sentence. (When asked, "Can you show me a *sentence* in the book?" she pointed to a line of print.)
- She was able to name many letters but could not identify any words in the story.
- Her writing sample consisted of strings of letters (see Figure 3.2). She "read" her message, running her finger from left to right under the print. She wrote her name correctly.

The writing sample shows that Kim understands that print conveys a message and that it is composed of letters. She knows more than she did at the beginning of kindergarten about the way print looks and how it is constructed.

Interpretation of Kim's Assessment

Kim's story retelling reflects increasing familiarity with books and stories. She understands how stories are organized and is able to reconstruct major elements of the story in sequence. She does not yet include many details in her retellings, and she does not remember and repeat story language.

Her understanding of the nature and purpose of print is evolving. She has internalized the more global print concepts (print carries meaning, is read from left to right, and is comprised of words and letters). She has some phonological awareness; she can identify and create rhyming words. She has learned to identify most letters but is not yet aware of letter–sound correspondences.

Before reading on, speculate about an appropriate instructional program for Kim. Consider how her needs will be similar and how they will be different from those of the initial readers in her class and how, as her teacher, you could best accommodate those needs. Then compare your ideas with our suggestions, which follow.

FIGURE 3.2   *Kim's First-Grade Writing Sample*

"One day my cat had three kittens"

Kim's Instructional Program

Most of the recommendations that were made for Kim's kindergarten program would still be appropriate for her in first grade because she is still in the emergent reading stage. Expectations regarding the level of her responses, however, will be different since she is advancing through the stage. Like all primary-grade children, she needs a print-rich environment in which reading and writing are frequently modeled and practiced. Hearing stories read aloud will continue to build her familiarity with story language and structure. Discussing and retelling stories, exploring books independently, and experimenting with writing will continue to be important parts of Kim's program. These activities are appropriate for initial readers as well. A major difference between Kim and her classmates will be the level of her approximations of reading and writing; her teacher will need to understand, accept, and encourage her efforts. Suggested activities would include:

- During discussions of stories that have been read aloud, prompt Kim to elaborate, give examples, and recall language from the story. For example, after reading *The Magic Fish* (Littlehale, 1967), the teacher might ask, "What did the fisherman say every time he went back to ask the fish for something? Do you remember? 'Oh fish in the sea, . . .'"
- When reading aloud from either regular-size or enlarged texts, encourage Kim to make predictions about both content ("What do you think will happen next?") and language ("Blue horse, blue horse, what do you _____?") from familiar, repeated patterns.
- Give many opportunities to engage with print using enlarged texts. Both shared reading and the language experience approach will be appropriate for Kim, as well as for early initial readers.
- Build a repertoire of very predictable, short books read frequently enough so that Kim memorizes them. Encourage her to "read" these independently or with a friend. This will not only give her practice in matching speech to print but (more importantly) will give her a sense of accomplishment and confidence in herself as a reader.
- Using enlarged texts that are very familiar to Kim, draw her attention to features of print. For example, have her find words that begin with the same letter, match identical words, and discuss differences between words.
- Give practice in predicting words from context and beginning letter/sound. For example, "My wife begs a wish from the magic f_____."
- Encourage Kim to write independently, and accept whatever form of writing she uses (e.g., letter strings). In addition, model invented spelling daily, "stretching" words and focusing on letter–sound correspondences. Eventually she will incorporate this strategy in her independent writing.
- Support Kim's growth in phonemic awareness during reading and writing activities by regularly drawing her attention to component sounds and letters in words.

Appropriate reading and writing activities such as these will foster Kim's development as an emergent reader, while at the same time acknowledging her as a member of the first-grade community of readers and writers. It is important that children like Kim not be singled out and made to feel inadequate. Although Kim will undoubtedly profit from additional one-on-one attention if it is available, she does not need a "special" or different reading program. She can benefit from participation in most of the literacy activities that are used with initial-stage readers; her responses, however, will be at a different level. Under these conditions, Kim can be expected to progress slowly and steadily through the emergent reading stage and into initial reading.

■ John

When John entered first grade, he was at the beginning of the initial reading stage. He had acquired considerable understanding of the nature and purpose of print. He could match speech to print with a very familiar text (such as the rhyme "Humpty Dumpty"), moving his finger from left to right under the print. He had begun to acquire a sight vocabulary and could recognize several familiar words out of context, including his name, *Mom, stop,* and *spaceship.*

He enjoyed listening to a wide variety of stories and retold them with considerable elaboration and use of story language. He often chose books to look at independently in the library corner and seemed eager to be able to read them on his own.

A sample of John's writing (Figure 3.3), done in October of his first-grade year, shows that he is a semiphonetic speller, according to Gentry's stages, discussed on page 40. If we compare this writing sample with the one produced a year earlier, we see that John has acquired an understanding of the alphabetic principle and has begun to use his knowledge of letter–sound relationships in his writing. His phonemic awareness is increasing.

Before reading on, speculate about an appropriate instructional program for John. Then compare your ideas with our suggestions, which follow.

John's Instructional Program

John is a fairly typical initial reader; the instructional approaches described earlier in this chapter would be appropriate for him. He needs many opportunities to see reading and writing modeled, to read along with a model, and to practice reading

FIGURE 3.3   *John's First-Grade Writing Sample*

I GTAN BGWL

"I got a new big wheel"

and writing independently or with other children. Shared reading would be a particularly effective approach to use as the primary vehicle for reading instruction for the reasons cited earlier. This may be supplemented by the language experience approach, which John's teacher would be especially likely to use in conjunction with science and social studies. Writing process should be an integral part of his program. As he progresses, he may profit from guided reading of leveled texts. If a basal reader is used in John's first-grade classroom, the teacher will modify it to make certain that the majority of reading instructional time is devoted to reading and that the skills work undertaken is appropriate and supplementary.

Specific activities that could be incorporated with any mix of these approaches would include:

- Continue to read aloud frequently and to encourage discussion and retelling of stories.
- Use predictable, meaningful materials for modeling and practicing reading.
- Encourage awareness and use of word identification strategies. When John is reading aloud and encounters unfamiliar words, guide him with questions that focus on context ("Does that make sense?") and graphophonemic cues ("Look at that first letter. Could that word be _____?").
- Give John additional practice in the balanced use of word identification strategies through the use of cloze exercises such as the following: *The troll lived under the br_____.*
- Help John develop a word bank or collection of words he recognizes at sight. Use these word cards for independent activities.
- Provide many opportunities for John to read and reread familiar texts (read by himself, read with classmates, read to adults at school and at home, read to younger children).
- Provide daily opportunities for John to write independently on self-selected topics.

With the kind of program we have recommended, John is likely to progress through the initial reading stage during his first-grade year.

■ Theresa

Theresa entered first grade as a transitional stage reader. She could read many books independently, having already acquired quite an extensive sight vocabulary. It was evident that she was using word identification strategies efficiently and effectively. Her teacher administered an informal reading inventory (described in Chapter 11) to learn more about her general reading competence. He established that Theresa could read and understand materials that are typically read easily by third-graders or other children who are well into the transitional stage.

Her teacher noticed that Theresa's writing was more mature than that of most first-graders. She produced long texts and used a mixture of standard and phonetic spelling (Gentry's transitional stage, see page 40). Figure 3.4 shows a letter Theresa wrote early in her first-grade year to a friend who was ill with chicken pox. This

FIGURE 3.4   *Theresa's First-Grade Writing Sample*

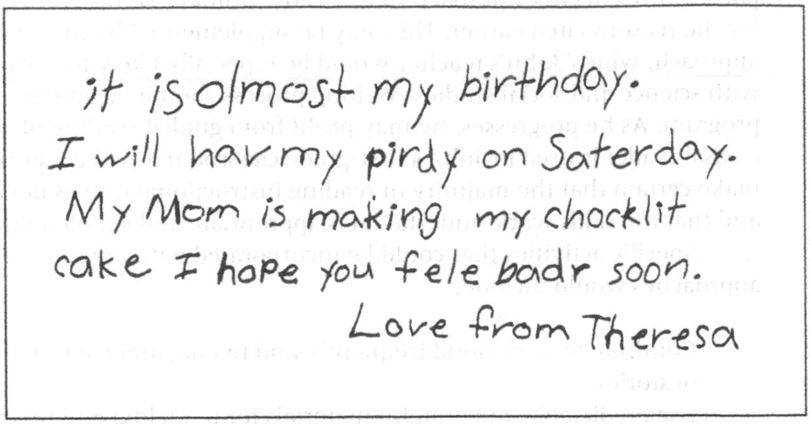

it is olmost my birthday.
I will har my pirdy on Saterday.
My Mom is making my chocklit
cake I hope you fele badr soon.
                    Love from Theresa

sample shows Theresa's confidence as a writer. She is willing to compose freely, unrestrained by undue concern with correctness.

As you did with Kim and John, speculate about what would constitute an appropriate, manageable program of instruction for Theresa. Then read on to compare your ideas with our suggestions.

Theresa's Instructional Program

Socially and emotionally Theresa is a typical first-grader; however, her reading and writing competencies are not typical. These two factors must both be considered in designing instruction for her. Shared book experience will play a prominent role in the first-grade reading program. Theresa should be included in whole-class shared reading activities; she will undoubtedly enjoy the stories as well as the feeling of belonging to the group. While the initial readers gain advanced print concepts, beginnings of sight vocabulary, and experience with word identification strategies, Theresa will be involved at a different level. She will add less common words to her sight vocabulary, gain fluency through reading with a model, and quickly add the stories read to the repertoire of books she can read without help. These same observations would apply to group language experience dictations. Theresa's instruction would diverge significantly from that of the initial readers during the follow-up phase of such lessons. While the beginning readers will need to read extensively with a model, practice using word identification strategies, and collect and work with sight words, Theresa should be engaged in extensive independent reading and follow-up activities that involve her reactions to and interpretations of stories.

If Theresa's teacher is using a basal reader as part of the reading program, certain issues will arise. The content of the basal lessons designed for first-graders will be inappropriate for Theresa because her reading development is so advanced. While she might enjoy participating in a reading group for social reasons, she would derive no benefits in terms of her literacy growth. Both the texts and the accompanying activities would be likely to bore her and might adversely affect her attitude toward reading. Sometimes teachers are inclined to place a student like Theresa in an advanced level of the basal series. This generally does not work well. First, the content and expectations of material designed for older children are often inappropriate for a younger child. Another potential problem is that if Theresa reads the "third-grade" basal texts in first grade, she will be "out of sync" in terms of the schoolwide program. The teachers she will have in subsequent years will inherit the same dilemma. For children like Theresa, then, a basal reading program is probably not a viable option. A better plan would be to expand the breadth of her reading through her self-selection of as many books as possible that appeal to her interests as a first-grader. It is noteworthy that in November of her first-grade year Theresa stated that her two favorites among the books she had read independently were *Little House in the Big Woods* (Laura Ingalls Wilder, 1932) and *Green Eggs and Ham* (Dr. Seuss, 1960).

Specific activities for Theresa might include:

■ Daily opportunities to read independently or to other children. Total time spent in this kind of reading should be at least 30 minutes a day.
■ Keeping a reading log or simple record of books completed.
■ Engaging in follow-up activities to books she has read, including writing, drawing, and conferring with the teacher or another adult.
■ Keeping a word book, a journal of new or interesting words encountered in reading. She can illustrate them or write sentences using them.
■ Daily writing on self-selected topics and in connection with special projects.

The next chapter in this text, "Transitional Stage," contains many more detailed descriptions of activities that would be appropriate for Theresa during her first-grade year. If Theresa is provided with the type of instruction suggested, her fluency will increase rapidly and she will in all likelihood pass through the transitional stage of reading during first grade. It is most important that Theresa be provided with authentic reading experiences appropriate to her level, so that she will continue to view reading as a pleasurable, desirable activity.

Summary

During the initial stage of reading, children need to have many, many encounters with meaningful print. They should see reading and writing modeled and should have daily opportunities to participate in reading and writing activities both with a model and independently. The materials they are exposed to should be enjoyable and highly predictable; good stories are the foundation of effective programs. If these conditions are present and are accompanied by a secure, supportive classroom environment, literacy learning will be inevitable for most children. They will see reading as a meaning-making process, acquire a beginning sight vocabulary, gain understanding of the structure of oral and printed language, and learn to use varied strategies to identify unknown printed words. By the end of the initial stage, students are approaching independence in reading.

BIBLIOGRAPHY

Allington, R. (2001). *What really matters for struggling readers: Designing research-based programs.* New York: Addison Wesley Longman.

Altwerger, B., Edelsky, C., & Flores, B. M. (1987). Whole language: What's new? *Reading Teacher, 41,* 144–154.

Anderson, R. C., Hiebert, E., Scott, J., & Wilkinson, I. (Eds.). (1985). *Becoming a nation of readers.* Washington, DC: National Institute of Education.

Chall, J. S., Bissex, G., Conard, S., & Harris-Sharples, S. (1996). *Qualitative assessment of text difficulty: A practical guide for teachers and writers.* Cambridge, MA: Brookline Books.

Coles, G. (2000). *Misreading reading: the bad science that hurts children.* Portsmouth, NH: Heinemann.

Fletcher, J. M., & Lyons, G. R. (1998). Reading: A research-based approach. In W. M. Evers (Ed.), *What's gone wrong in America's classrooms* (pp. 49–90). Stanford, CA: Hoover Institution Press.

Fountas, I., & Pinnell, G. S. (1999). *Matching books to readers: Using leveled books in guided reading, K–3.* Portsmouth, NH: Heinemann.

Goodman, K., Shannon, R., Freeman, Y., & Murphy, S. (1988). *Report card on the basal reader.* Katonah, NY: Richard C. Owen.

Graves, D. H. (1983). *Writing: Teachers and children at work.* Portsmouth, NH: Heinemann.

Graves, M., Juel, C., & Graves, B. (2001). *Teaching reading in the 21st century* (2nd ed.). Boston: Allyn and Bacon.

Hoffman, J. V., McCarthy, S. J., Abbott, J., Christian, C., Corman, L., Curry, C., Dressman, M., Elliot, B., Matherne, D., & Stahle, D. (1994). So what's new in the new basals? A focus on first grade. *Journal of Reading Behavior, 26,* 47–73.

Holdaway, D. (1979). *The foundations of literacy.* Sydney, Australia: Ashton-Scholastic.

Langenberg, D., et al. (2000) *Report of the National Reading Panel: Teaching children to read.* U.S. Department of Health and Human Services. NIH Publication No. 00-4769.

Littlehale, F. (1967). *The magic fish.* New York: Scholastic Book Services.

Morrow, L. M. (2001). *Literacy development in the early years* (4th ed.). Boston: Allyn and Bacon.

Pinnell, G. S., & Fountas, I. (1998). *Word matters.* Portsmouth, NH: Heinemann.

Routman, R. (1996). *Literacy at the crossroads.* Portsmouth, NH: Heinemann.

Samuels, S. J. (1988). Decoding and automaticity: Helping poor readers become automatic at word recognition. *The Reading Teacher, 11,* 756–760.

Seuss, Dr. (1960). *Green eggs and ham.* New York: Random House.

Shannon, P. (1990). *The struggle to continue.* Portsmouth, NH: Heinemann.

Shannon, P., & Goodman, K. (Eds.). (1994). *Basal readers: A second look.* Katonah, NY: Richard C. Owen.

Smith, F. (1988). *Understanding reading* (4th ed.). Hillsdale, NJ: Erlbaum.

Stahl, S. (1992). Saying the "p" word: Nine generalizations for exemplary phonics instruction. *The Reading Teacher, 45*(8), 618–625.

Weaver, C. (1994). *Reading process and practice* (2nd ed.). Portsmouth, NH: Heinemann.

Weaver, C. (1998). Toward a balanced approach to reading. In C. Weaver (Ed.), *Reconsidering a balanced approach to reading* (pp. 11–74). Urbana, IL: National Council of Teachers of English.

Wilder, L. I. (1932). *Little house in the big woods.* New York: Harper & Brothers.

Becoming Fluent

*F*luency, the ability to identify words quickly and accurately in context, is a prerequisite for skilled reading. The fluent reader is able to coordinate the word identification process with the process of constructing meaning from the text. The beginning reader also engages in these two processes, but not in the same fluid, coordinated manner. The beginner makes more conscious use of meaning (context) to predict and verify the occurrence of individual words since they are not yet recognized automatically. Reading is characterized by a sort of see-sawing between the two processes; word identification strategies are used to make meaning, and meaning is used to solve the puzzles of word identification. As the child gains reading experience and the identification of individual words becomes more automatic, the two processes operate in a more synchronized manner. During the transitional stage of reading growth, readers move from see-sawing between word recognition and meaning to a more simultaneous engagement in the two processes.

It is interesting to note that classic studies dating from the 1920s comparing the eye movements of initial readers with those of more accomplished readers show marked differences. Beginning readers not only make many more eye fixations on each line of print (i.e., they read far more slowly and haltingly); they also make more regressions, or backward eye movements (Buswell, 1922; Gilbert & Gilbert, 1942). This indicates that beginning readers focus on smaller units of text than fluent readers.

Historically, fluency has been measured in schools by documenting the rate of oral reading. As children advance through school, they generally demonstrate a steady increase in reading rate as measured by number of words they can read per minute (Rasinski, 2000). Of course, increase in reading rate or fluency is clearly related to amount of reading at an appropriate level, including silent reading. Herein lies the dilemma of the stage: the more fluent readers become, the more words, sentences, pages they read during a given time. Struggling readers, who are still processing text word by word and going back to reprocess when they lose meaning, will read far less volume in that same amount of time (Allington, 2001). When the child's struggle to read leads to loss of motivation to read, the problem is compounded.

It used to be assumed that fluent reading did not appear until a reader had passed through the initial stage, acquired considerable sight vocabulary, and become proficient at using word identification strategies (Chall, 1983). First-grade teachers who use extensive literature-based instruction now report that initial readers are capable of reading far more fluently than was previously believed possible (Avery, 1996; Routman, 1988). However, their fluency is limited to materials that they have heard or practiced repeatedly and that are extremely familiar to them. In contrast, the automaticity of word identification that develops during the transitional stage enables readers to read even unfamiliar materials with relative fluency.

The third stage of reading represents transition in many respects. As fluency develops, readers move from a necessary focus on identification of words to a focus on larger units of text. They also make a transition from relative dependence to independence in their reading. The initial reader requires much modeling of reading and reads with assistance, for the most part. During the transitional stage, independence grows to the point where the child can read and enjoy even unfamiliar materials (of appropriate difficulty) without help. At the same time, there is progress from approximation to accurate reconstruction of texts. Experience with print leads to increased sight vocabulary, which gives the reader more data to employ in recognizing familiar word parts and decoding by analogy.

The transitional stage is a unique period of literacy development between beginning attempts to read and fluent independent reading. Part II is devoted to an examination of the transitional stage, including characteristics of students at this stage, major goals, and appropriate means for facilitating passage through the stage. Chapter 4 concludes with continuations of the case studies of Kim, John, and Theresa.

BIBLIOGRAPHY

Allington, R. (2001). *What really matters for struggling readers: Designing research-based programs.* New York: Addison Wesley Longman.

Avery, C. (1996). *With a light touch.* Portsmouth, NH: Heinemann.

Buswell, G. T. (1922). *Fundamental reading habits: A study of their development* (Supplementary Educational Monograph No. 21). Chicago: University of Chicago, Department of Education.

Chall, J. S. (1983). *Stages of reading development.* New York: McGraw-Hill.

Gilbert, L. C., & Gilbert, D. W. (1942). Reading before the eye-movement camera vs. reading away from it. *Elementary School Journal, 42,* 443–447.

Rasinski, T. (2000). Speed does matter in reading. *Reading Teacher, 54,* 146–151.

Routman, R. (1988). *Transitions from literature to literacy.* Portsmouth, NH: Heinemann.

4 Transitional Stage

■ *Overview*

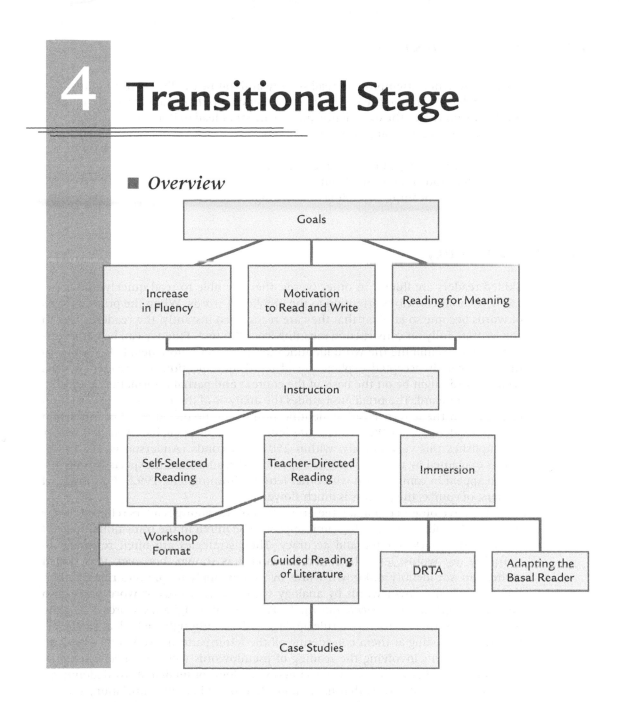

Students entering the transitional stage have acquired considerable sight vocabulary and are able to apply word identification strategies independently. As a consequence, they can begin to read easy texts that have not previously been read to them or with them. Although they are able to decode many words in context, their reading is often slow and laborious. They pause frequently to work out the pronunciations of words they have not encountered in print. Typical transitional stage readers subvocalize while attempting to read silently and follow the line of print with a finger. They have acquired the necessary competencies to make rapid progress in reading; they simply lack the experience and practice that lead to fluency.

The goals of the transitional stage are to:

- Increase fluency in reading and writing
- Foster motivation to read and write
- Focus on meaning in reading and writing

Increase in Fluency ≧ *constructing meaning*

Skilled readers are fluent; in other words, they are able to read quickly and accurately without conscious attention to the individual words. When the printed forms of words become so familiar that they are recognized instantly, the reader is free to concentrate fully on constructing meaning from the text. Fluency can be better understood by examining the word identification process in more detail. According to the most widely accepted explanation of word identification, the reader predicts what a word might be on the basis of the context and partial information about the letters in the word. The prediction guides the analysis of the remaining information contained in the letters. Positive identification of the predicted word occurs when enough evidence from the context and letters becomes available. A skilled reader accomplishes this very quickly, within 250 milliseconds (Anderson et al., 1985). This is explained by the fact that the experienced reader's brain expects certain letters to appear in combination with other letters (Cunningham, 1992). For unskilled readers, of course, the process is much slower.

We have observed that a large proportion of the young readers referred to our university's reading and writing clinic appear to be mired in the transitional stage of reading. They lack fluency and accuracy. Their strategies are often restricted to sounding out words, letter by letter. Research has shown, however, that skilled readers do not identify unknown words by rapidly applying phonics rules; rather, they identify unknown words by analogy with known words or word parts (also known as *mediated word identification*). In Patricia Cunningham's words, ". . . the brain is a pattern detector, not a rule applier, and . . . although we look at single letters, we are looking at them considering all the letter patterns we know" (1992, p. 28). Experiments involving the reading of pseudowords (*rab, zift, blipe*) have provided evidence that supports the decoding-by-analogy, or mediated word identification strategy. Pseudowords that have more than one likely pronunciation, such as *mive* (likely analogies would be *give* and *five*) are pronounced more slowly than other pseudowords and are sometimes pronounced with one vowel sound and sometimes with another. Readers do not need to know the difference between long and short *i* in order to pronounce the pseudoword *mive;* they need only an adequate stock of known words to be used as possible analogies. To support this process, sight vocabulary must grow. Extensive reading practice leads to increased sight vocabulary, as students encounter words repeatedly in different contexts. The more words they recognize at sight, the more resources they have available for the decoding-by-analogy strategy.

Fluency and comprehension are significantly related. Unskilled readers must devote most of their attention and effort to identifying the words in the text. When decoding skill has become automatic, readers are able to concentrate more fully on the meaning of the text. Many older students who are identified as having comprehension problems in fact lack fluency and therefore need extensive reading experience with easy materials.

It should also be noted that fluency exists in relation to the difficulty level of the material for the developing reader. For any given text, you may estimate the reader's fluency according to these general descriptors:

- Reading in phrases with varying intonation indicates *good* fluency.
- Reading mostly in phrases but often lacking appropriate intonation indicates *fair* fluency.
- Reading word by word, for the most part, indicates *poor* fluency (Allington, 2001).

The further along a student is on the continuum of literacy development, the higher the level of difficulty of material he or she will be able to read with good fluency. Initial stage readers will be unable to read any material fluently unless it is highly predictable (usually patterned) and has been read repeatedly. For transitional stage readers, fluency will vary widely according to the difficulty level of material. Readers who have reached the basic literacy stage will read most material fluently, but fluency will break down when the reader is confronted with texts containing complex sentence structures and a great deal of unfamiliar vocabulary.

Motivation to Read and Write

Children entering the transitional stage are struggling to read independently. Most children will take a year or more to attain enough fluency to read with ease and enjoyment. Their motivation must be sustained during this period; they must not lose the hope that eventually reading will become effortless. For many children who are skilled readers for their age, and even for some whose reading skill is average or below average, reading itself is enjoyable. They are "hooked on books." An obvious goal of reading instruction is increasing the number of children who are competent readers. An equally important goal, however, is increasing the number who read voluntarily, widely, and with evident satisfaction.

Unfortunately, traditional school reading programs can lead to negative attitudes toward reading. The purpose of many of the tasks assigned in the name of reading is not evident to the children. Many children who enjoy reading on their own dislike reading in school. In some cases, school reading instruction leads to such negative attitudes that children stop reading altogether except when it is required. Motivation to read is generally much higher when children are given frequent opportunities to choose, read, and discuss books that are of interest to them.

Research has identified common characteristics of classrooms where children like books and read extensively (Hickman, 1995). First, children mirror the teachers' enthusiasm about reading. Teachers in these classrooms are readers themselves. They convey to their students the pleasure and enjoyment that they derive from reading. They know the literature that is appropriate to the age level of their students, and they frequently share, promote, and recommend books to the whole class or to individual students. They read good literature aloud to their students every day. Their classrooms are well stocked with carefully selected books. Moreover, the books are attractively displayed and accessible to the students. Rather than being lined up in a bookcase with only the spines showing, the books are placed around the classroom in frequently changing displays. Children are given time to browse, choose, and read. Books are shared and discussed, and they provide the basis for more reading and writing activities (Hickman, 1995).

All of these recommendations are contingent on the availability of books. Richard Allington (1994) reports that one reason that many children read so little in school is that there isn't much time for them to read. Basal readers alone do not provide enough reading material for students to become skilled readers; however, in many schools the entire budget for reading is spent on basal anthologies and accompanying materials. One particularly disturbing finding is that availability of books is directly related to income levels of the families whose children attend the school. Studies have shown that schools that enroll large numbers of poor children have about 50 percent fewer books and magazines than schools with few children from poor families. This disparity may account for the limited use of literature in schools attended by large numbers of poor children (Guice et al., 1996). Even schools that serve more affluent students seldom have a wealth of trade books available (Guice & Allington, 1992). Moreover, classroom and school libraries tend to have a limited variety of current books and often provide many copies of a few titles rather than single copies of more titles. Easy, interesting materials needed by struggling readers are typically in short supply. Without access to a wide variety of interesting, appropriate materials, many children are busy throughout the school day, but have few experiences with real reading (Allington, 1994, 2001). It is not uncommon for teachers to spend their own money to build their classroom libraries so that their students will have access to appropriate literature.

Motivation to write arises from the same conditions as motivation to read. Classrooms in which children write willingly and with satisfaction provide them with time to write and encouragement to select topics they know and care about. Teachers model the writing process. Student writings are shared and valued. As with reading, fluency in writing evolves as a consequence of frequent, meaningful opportunities to write. When teachers overemphasize writing about teacher-assigned topics and formulaic writing, or are more attentive to correct mechanics than to message, children's motivation to write can diminish, resulting in reluctance to write and less writing.

Emphasis on Reading for Meaning

Although it has been noted that nonfluent readers devote a great deal of attention and effort to word identification, they will, if they have had appropriate experiences at the initial stage, continue to use context to construct meaningful interpretations of texts. Even at the beginning stages of reading, information from the text and the knowledge already possessed by the reader act together to produce meaning. During the transitional stage, as students attempt to read unfamiliar books independently, they must rely heavily on their prior knowledge to predict what words will occur and to make sense of the text as a whole. For example, the reader who selects a book about a circus and who has some background knowledge about circuses will expect certain words and concepts to appear in the text (*acrobats, clowns, trapeze, costumes*). These expectations help the reader to use the criterion "Does this make sense?" as an aid to word identification and comprehension. Understanding of text is maximized for transitional readers by providing them with well-written materials that are of personal interest to them and that relate to their background of experiences.

Students who are encouraged to read and who encounter a variety of books that they *can* read develop personal tastes and preferences. This spurs them on to further reading and helps them develop a sense of themselves as readers. Reading itself becomes meaningful. It is no longer directed toward developing skill with the process; readers begin to respond deeply and personally to books they can read themselves and to acquire unique identities as readers.

Instruction

Instruction at the transitional stage of reading must emphasize abundant real reading practice to build fluency. Two instructional approaches are commonly used for accomplishing this goal: self-selected reading and teacher-directed reading. *Self-selected reading* is an approach in which students choose their own reading materials, read them independently, and respond meaningfully, all of which is monitored individually by the teacher. Much of the responsibility for planning and implementing their reading rests with the students. An important strength of this approach is that it personalizes reading and reading instruction. *Directed reading activities*, in contrast, are planned and guided by the teacher. Groups of students read the same materials and often complete the same preparation and follow-up activities under the direction of the teacher. Directed reading activities include group and individual work focusing on literature as well as basal selections. We will examine each of these approaches, turning first to self-selected reading because we view it as the most important component in readers' development after they have reached the transitional stage.

Self-Selected Reading

One of the most important goals of education is to produce students who are not only competent readers but who also read frequently for information and for pleasure. The only way to accomplish this goal is to provide many opportunities for self-selected reading.

The benefits of voluntary reading are well documented. In terms of developing reading proficiency, extensive reading helps build the background knowledge that provides the foundation for comprehension. For example, a child who has read *Blueberries for Sal* (McCloskey, 1976) will have developed some concepts about blueberries and where they grow and will even be aware that bears like to eat them! In addition, there is a positive correlation between voluntary reading and general achievement in reading (Irving, 1980). Children who are voluntary readers not only score higher on standardized achievement tests than peers with low interest in books, but they are also rated higher by their teachers in general school achievement, work habits, and social–emotional maturity (Morrow, 1985). Strong evidence shows that voluntary reading as part of the school program increases children's inclination to read as well as their reading skill. When teachers systematically promote self-selected reading, their students tend to demonstrate enthusiasm and positive attitudes toward reading (Allington, 1994; Irving, 1980).

Over the years there has been increasing recognition of the importance of including voluntary reading as an integral part of reading instructional programs at all levels. Recently, critics have questioned the instructional value of independent reading, claiming lack of scientific evidence (experimental studies) to support the practice (Langenberg, 2000). As Allington (2001) points out, however, there is a great deal of evidence from contrastive studies (comparing the reading volume of low- and high-achieving students) that higher-achieving students engage in more reading than low-achieving students. Such studies do not prove a causal link between volume of reading and high achievement; nevertheless they give compelling evidence of a strong relationship. Large-scale correlational studies such as those based on the National Assessment of Educational Progress (NAEP) using a national sample add to this evidence. According to the *NAEP 1998 Reading Report Card for the Nation and States* (U.S. Department of Education, 1999; also available at http://nces.ed.gov/naep), at each grade level students who read more each day had higher reading scores. Given the rich research evidence documenting the relationship between reading achievement and amount of reading over time, we must conclude, once again, that voluntary reading is a crucial element in a successful literacy program. Nevertheless, the majority of our students are not getting adequate time for sustained silent reading in school.

Furthermore, it is not enough to simply provide time for reading. If children are to fully utilize individual reading time, they must feel motivated to read. How do teachers foster the desire to read in students whose independent reading is not yet fluent? The novice reader experiences feelings of success and achievement on completing an entire book. This positive response expands still further when children are led to share their reactions to books they have read. In classrooms where books are a major focus of discussion and where students' opinions and comments about books are solicited and respected, children see themselves as insiders, as members of a group of readers. This feeling of belonging contributes to their positive feelings about reading and adds greatly to their view of themselves as successful readers. These characteristics of children who are motivated, independent readers are best fostered in programs that include the following elements: choice, time, and sharing (Atwell, 1998) as well as record keeping. Each of these elements will be examined in relation to classroom practice.

Choice

First is the element of choice. Children must learn to choose books that are appropriate both in content and level of difficulty. This can only be accomplished in classrooms that contain a variety of reading materials. Even in schools that have well-stocked central libraries, a substantial collection of easily accessible books should be housed in each classroom. The classroom collection should include a variety of types of books and range of difficulty levels. Many professional publications and internet sites are available to help classroom teachers select appropriate, high-quality books for their classroom collections. Choosing appropriate books is a skill that evolves with experience. Teachers can facilitate this process by providing children with some guidelines. The teacher might begin by explaining to children that choosing a book is a tentative process. Readers (adults included) do not finish every book they start. If a book turns out to be too difficult or uninteresting to the reader, it may be discarded and a new choice may be made. One technique that children find useful in determining whether or not a book is too difficult for them to enjoy is the *five finger test*. Children are instructed to select a page in the book they are considering, read the amount of text that fits between their thumb and outstretched index finger, and raise a finger every time they come to a problematic word. If they use up all five fingers before they come to the end of the passage, the book is probably too difficult for them to enjoy. (This can be adapted as the *three finger test* for children who are reading books with limited amounts of text on a page.)

Teachers often worry that children will select texts that are too easy or too difficult for them. This concern is largely unwarranted. It has been demonstrated, for example, that reading (and rereading) of very "easy" materials increases both fluency and the feeling of success. It is typical for unaccomplished readers to select short, easy books that they can read quickly. If allowed to do this, they inevitably begin on their own to select longer, more challenging books. Many primary-grade teachers report that in May their students look back at their fall reading lists with amazement. As one second-grader remarked in May, "At the beginning of the year I read such simple books!"

At the other extreme are children who select books that appear to be far too difficult for them to read independently. This type of choice usually reflects strong motivation. The book may have been read by admired peers, or it may be on a topic of particular interest to the reader. In either case, the reader should be allowed to decide whether or not to stick with the book. When children keep working on difficult texts, we can assume that they are getting something of value out of the experience. To encourage real choice, it is generally not necessary or desirable for the teacher to classify all available books by readability level and restrict children's choices accordingly. According to second-grade teacher Peter Lancia, such restrictions in fact deter a child's motivation to read. One of our goals is for children to learn to select appropriate books independently.

Time

Another essential element of a successful self-selected reading program is the provision of time—time for browsing and choosing, time for reading, and time for sharing. Independent reading time must not be viewed as an optional enrichment activity; it should be treated as an integral part of the reading curriculum. Only through generous allotments of time for reading will students acquire the motivation, fluency, and breadth of experience necessary for becoming lifelong readers.

Sustained silent reading (SSR) is a commonly used term for the independent reading period and will be used in this text. Teachers have come up with other interesting acronyms such as DEAR time (Drop Everything and Read), DIRT (Daily Individualized Reading Time), and SQUIRT (Sustained Quiet Individual Reading Time). Regardless of the term used, sustained silent reading involves a regularly scheduled period of time during which children are expected to read their chosen books independently. In classrooms in which SSR is a popular and productive part of the school day, teachers have established workable routines and clear expectations.

Several rules are particularly helpful in ensuring the smooth operation of SSR:

- Students must have sufficient reading material to use during the reading period. Materials must be chosen ahead of time.
- SSR time is to be used only for reading. It is not a time for catching up on homework, socializing, drawing, or other activities.
- Readers are not to be interrupted during SSR.

In addition to these basic rules, teachers devise other guidelines that fit their management styles. Decisions must be made about various procedural details such as what records must be completed, how much movement will be permitted within the classroom, and what kinds of assistance will be provided for readers who are "stuck."

Sometimes teachers also read quietly during part of the SSR period, providing a valuable model for the students. Once the routines of SSR are firmly established, the teacher may choose to use some or all of this time for conferring with individuals or groups of students about their reading. Some teachers incorporate SSR in a larger reading workshop, and conduct guided reading quietly with a group in a corner of the room while the rest of the students are engaged in SSR. Any of these teacher activities are appropriate, since the teacher is engaged with her own reading or with students' reading. Activities that are not related to reading or reading instruction are inappropriate.

It is difficult to make specific recommendations regarding the amount of time that should be allotted for SSR. This will be influenced by such factors as the age and previous reading experience of the children and the extent of awareness of the value of independent reading on the part of the staff and administration. In general, however, it is recommended that beginning in the second grade, at least 2 hours a week (over 20 minutes a day) should be allotted to self-selected reading. It is important to include SSR daily, rather than once or twice a week. Beyond this, Allington (2001) and others recommend a total of 90 minutes of reading time per day. This includes all reading—guided, independent, oral, silent, in content areas, and so on. Regular, extended practice is the key to building students' fluency and motivation.

Record Keeping

A key element of successful independent reading programs is a simple, clearly defined record-keeping system. Maintaining reading records can be motivational for students, particularly for unaccomplished readers. Records enable students to see their progress and to feel a sense of accomplishment. Moreover, the teacher's insistence upon accurate, up-to-date records conveys that self-selected reading is an important and valued activity. It "counts."

The two most common types of records that can be maintained by students are the daily reading log and the list of books completed. Figure 4.1 shows a daily reading log that includes the date, title of book being read, and pages completed. Figure 4.2 shows a record of books completed. In this example, the teacher has included space for the student to comment on the book, as well as places to check whether the student conferred with the teacher about the book or responded to the reading in some other way.

Teachers also keep records of students' reading. One effective technique is the *status of the class check*. Immediately before reading time begins, the teacher asks each student what he or she plans to read during SSR and records it quickly on a chart (see Figure 4.3). The status of the class check takes only a few minutes but has many benefits. Students must have a book ready. Because they have stated their

FIGURE 4.1   *Reading Log*

Daily Reading Log	Mark Donnoly, grade 2			
Date	**Title**	**Pages:**	**Start**	**Stop**
Jan. 5	*Robert the Rose Horse*		1	15
Jan. 6	*Robert the Rose Horse*		16	25
Jan. 7	*Sam the Minute Man*		1	10

FIGURE 4.2   *Book Record*

Books Completed	Maria Cortez, grade 3	
	Conference	**Follow-up**
1. *Charlotte's Web,* by E. B. White	_____	_____
Comments: The saddest part was when Charlotte died. I used to hate spiders before I read this book.	_____ _____	_____ _____
2. *Little House on the Prairie,* by Laura I. Wilder	_____	_____
Comments: I loved this book. I read the first one too. I want to read all the books in the series.	_____ _____	_____ _____

FIGURE 4.3   *Status of the Class Chart*

	Monday	Tuesday	Wednesday	Thursday	Friday
Luanne	Little Bear	Little Bear	Frederick	abs.	Frederick conf.
Juan	Ghost-Eye Tree	Ghost-Eye Tree	Ghost-Eye Tree	G. E. Tree conf.	Worse than Willie
Pete	Stuart Little	S. Little	S. Little	S. Little	S. Little conf.
Mariann	Ramona Quimby	Ramona Quimby conf.	Little House in the Big Woods	L. House . . .	L. House . . .
Kelly	abs.	abs.	Rosie's Walk	R. Walk conf.	Tale of Peter Rabbit

intentions, they are more likely to feel accountable. Teachers have an ongoing record of student choices and progress.

Some teachers conduct their status checks after reading has begun, moving from student to student for a very brief check-in, and noting what each student is reading and whether he or she needs any particular guidance. Usually the records are anecdotal in nature, but each teacher designs record-keeping formats that meet his own needs. Reading records allow the students and the teacher to monitor reading; however, follow-ups to reading should include much more than this.

Sharing

Activities that allow students to share their impressions of books with peers, the teacher, and wider audiences add immeasurably to their appreciation and understanding of literature. Sharing can take various forms. Perhaps the least structured form of sharing is having students volunteer to comment on books or parts of books they have recently read. Such a sharing time is often held immediately after SSR, takes 5 to 10 minutes, and is invitational. A more structured form of sharing is the *book talk*, in which a reader prepares a book commentary designed to interest other readers in the book.

Children can extend their appreciation and understanding of books through other media. Groups or individual students may create retellings of stories or summaries of information learned from non-fiction books through illustrated writing or dramatizations, to be shared with their own classmates or with others. Janet Hickman (1995) studied classrooms in which children exhibited high motivation to read; she found that creative extension activities to reading were an integral part of their literacy programs. Such activities are valuable for two reasons. First, they are motivational. Second, they provide an opportunity for children to extend their understanding of the story through their own creations. Of course, time is an important consideration. Book extension projects should never encroach on reading time.

An extremely important follow-up activity is the student–teacher conference. Conferences are held periodically to give the teacher an opportunity to discuss completed books with students. The individual conference allows the teacher to discover the student's interpretation and personal opinion of the book and gives the student the message that her thoughts and opinions are valid and important to the teacher.

Conferences flow more smoothly if students and teachers prepare for them. Students should decide what aspects of the book they would like to talk about with the teacher. They may want to select and rehearse a short passage to read aloud. Many teachers ask their students to jot down new, interesting, or troublesome words they encountered in the text.

Teachers' preparation for conferences is ongoing. The more they know about their students and the books they are reading, the more productive the conferences are likely to be. (While it is desirable to have read most of the books their students read, it is possible for a teacher to lead a productive conference on a book that he has not read.) If the teacher is genuinely concerned about students' interests and personal preferences and uses this information to guide their choices and discussions of books, students almost always respond positively to reading. Perhaps the greatest motivator of all for a student is having the teacher personally recommend a special book for her to read.

A conference is not a comprehension test. Although the teacher will discover a great deal about the student's comprehension through the discussion, questions are designed to help the reader react to the book in terms of his own personal experiences. Examples of questions that many teachers use to stimulate this kind of interaction include:

What did you especially like/dislike about this book?
Was it hard/easy for you to read?
What part was most exciting (funny, sad, interesting)?
Did the story seem real or make-believe? Why?
Which character would you like to meet?
What did you learn that you didn't know before?
What would you have done about . . . if you had been there?

These questions are only a sampling. Although they are helpful for initiating discussion, the teacher should remember that the conference is a dialogue in which the student's responses guide the direction of the conversation. Many teachers keep anecdotal records of these exchanges.

In addition to end-of-book conferences, many teachers conduct frequent mini-conferences to support and monitor children's reading. Each mini-conference takes only a minute or two, as the teacher moves around the room, finding out how each child's reading is going. Through this process, the teacher shows interest in each student's reading and offers assistance, particularly to those who need frequent

Sharing adds to the understanding and appreciation of reading.

encouragement and guidance. She also collects useful assessment data about the child's book choice, use of time, and quantity and quality of reading.

An effective addition or alternative to oral conferences is a *reading response journal.* Students write about what they read—reactions, questions, comments— usually on a daily basis. The journal entries provide beginning points for oral conferences with the teacher or with other students. The teacher often collects the journals of students between conferences and writes back to students, responding to their comments, fostering further reflection and thought, and addressing issues raised by students. The teacher's oral and written responses are opportunities to nudge students' thinking processes and reading development (Atwell 1998; Avery, 1993; Hindley, 1996). Written exchanges between students and teacher allow for more frequent dialogue about reading than might otherwise be possible. Transitional stage readers are novices at reading, writing, and responding to literature. This is reflected in the way teachers guide children in their early attempts at written responses to literature. (Using response journals with more accomplished readers will be discussed in Chapter 9.)

Factors That Influence Independent Reading

Independent reading programs take many forms. Factors that influence the organization of programs include the teacher's confidence level and individual style of classroom management, the age and reading competency of the students, and availability of resources. Regardless of such variations, all effective reading programs incorporate student choice, time for sustained silent reading, and opportunities for sharing. Basal programs and guided reading of leveled texts do not emphasize these essential elements and therefore when used exclusively are generally not adequate vehicles for developing competent, motivated readers. In studies comparing the reading achievement, strategies, and attitudes of students in skills-based programs with students in literature-based programs, the use of children's literature as the primary instructional vehicle has been shown to develop more successful, enthusiastic readers (Bader, Veatch, & Eldredge, 1987; Eldredge & Butterfield, 1986; Freppon, 1991).

Teacher-Directed Reading

Children at the transitional stage need support and direction to gain skill and fluency. We use the term *teacher-directed* to imply involvement of the teacher in managing and orchestrating reading practice at this stage. Teacher-directed reading, in contrast to self-selected reading, involves the use of material selected by the teacher, who leads students through all phases of the reading. Although directed reading activities can be conducted with individuals (in tutoring situations), they are usually used with groups of students. There are several reasons for including directed or guided reading activities in an instructional program. Through such activities, the teacher can expose children to material that will broaden their reading experience and that they might not choose on their own. Another consideration is the need for direct instruction related both to content and to the reading process. Teacher-guided reading activities can help children cope with difficult materials and acquire strategies that will eventually lead to more independence in reading. An additional benefit of directed reading activities is that they provide common reading experiences and the opportunity for shared responses to the same text.

Guided Reading of Literature

Guided reading and group discussions are designed to stimulate the construction of new understandings and interpretations of literature rather than recall of information from stories. Literacy professor Lea McGee calls the group exchanges *response-centered talk*. When reading for enjoyment and understanding, readers experience fleeting thoughts, images, and reactions to the text, which become the basis for their unique personal responses to literature. In McGee's words:

> Response centered talk consists of a combination of children's responses and thinking and a teacher's responses and guidance. It moves from random and tentative sharing of salient events from a story to exploring a story's deeper meanings. The resulting literary interpretations arise from children's reasoning and problem solving. Through literature response conversations, children build shared, enriched interpretations of literary works and practice new strategies for thinking about literature. (McGee, 1996, p. 206)

There are various ways of organizing literature discussion groups. They may be teacher-led, student-led, or some combination of the two. The literature may be selected by the teacher, by the students, or by students and teacher together. Groups may be assigned by the teacher prior to book selection, or students who choose the same book may constitute a group (Galda, Cullinan, & Strickland, 1993). One of the most common organizations for novice readers (second- and third-graders) is exemplified in the third-grade classroom of Janet Rodriguez, who assigns her children to one of four heterogeneous groups that meet three times per week, on the average, to discuss the trade book that their group is reading. Each group gathers together in a circle. The discussion begins with an open-ended question provided by the teacher. They continue to share and discuss their impressions and interpretations for 10 or 15 minutes, referring to their books when necessary. This is followed by reading time, during which they read the next assigned section of the book. Finally, they write reactions, responses, or comments about their reading in a literature log to be shared with the teacher. The log entries and the teacher's responses provide a continuing personal conversation about literature between Ms. Rodriguez and each student in her class.

Because literature groups are new to the third-graders, Ms. Rodriguez spends time at the beginning of the year preparing the children for this type of literature study. Initially, she uses a book she is reading aloud to the whole class as a vehicle for discussion. *Charlotte's Web*, a third-grade favorite, is well suited for this. During her daily read-aloud sessions, Ms. R models how we think about and talk about literature—making predictions, creating mental images, analyzing characters, interpreting and appreciating the story. She involves the whole group in discussion before and after reading to them. Meanwhile, during other parts of the school day, she is gathering information about students' individual strengths and weaknesses as readers and about their social interactions. She provides many opportunities for them to develop their skills at working cooperatively in small groups, accepting all contributions, staying on topic, taking leadership roles, and ensuring that all members participate.

When she reaches the last few chapters of *Charlotte's Web*, she forms temporary groups and has the children engage in small-group discussion in response to a question she gives them following read-aloud time. The class then reconvenes to share observations about the process, formulate guidelines, and solve problems. When they have become comfortable with group procedures, Ms. Rodriguez assigns each group a short narrative to read and discuss. She observes these discussions closely to assess group dynamics and identify leaders, quiet introverts, personality conflicts, and able and struggling readers. Based on these observations, she assigns children to four heterogeneous literature discussion groups. The makeup of each group is carefully planned; the groups generally stay together for the remainder of the year. (Other teachers change the makeup of the groups from time to time.) Once the groups are organized, Ms. R introduces several novels of which she has multiple copies. The groups decide which books they would most like to read and indicate their preferences.

From this point on, as the groups begin work on their novels, teacher and students work out issues that arise. Ms. Rodriguez has to decide what kind of discussion questions to frame for each group. Some focus on specific books ("In Chapter 9, Harriet has a frightening dream. What horrible events might this dream foreshadow?"); some are more generic ("Authors have reasons for separating stories into chapters. Look over the last three chapters you have read and discuss why you think this author ended each chapter where he or she did.") (Keegan & Shrake, 1991). She develops categories of questions: those that focus on story content and interpretation, those that focus on the author's technique, and those that focus on personal responses. Students in each group must decide how to support group members who have difficulty reading the book independently (by using reading buddies, making audiotapes to follow, etc.); how to assign and perform roles within the group (leader, timekeeper, participation monitor); and how to deal with conflicts or distracting behavior. Ms. Rodriguez, of course, helps them come up with and implement solutions to such problems.

This teacher provides a great deal of structure and guidance as she initiates her students into effective management of and participation in literature discussion groups. Teachers of more experienced and more mature readers frequently release more of the responsibility for the groups to the students as they appear to be ready for it. (See Chapter 9.) Teachers who make use of guided reading through literature groups usually observe that their students broaden and deepen their responses to literature over the course of the year. The content of the response logs and of the discussions late in the year is likely to include unprompted comparisons of literature with people and events in their own lives and in other books, comments about authors' styles, and speculations about authors' intents (see Figures 4.4 and 4.5). The tenor of these conversations provides a marked contrast to the old teacher-directed question and answer sessions (Keegan & Shrake, 1991).

FIGURE 4.4 *Response Log Entry (October)*

title: More Spaghetti I Say
By Rita Golden Gelman

This Monkey loved Spaghetti, and evre. time His frid Said Come and I play he Said no I hate to finish my spaGetti. evre time he Said that His freind said if you Say that one more time I will throw out YouR spaGetti.

FIGURE 4.5   *Response Log Entry (May)*

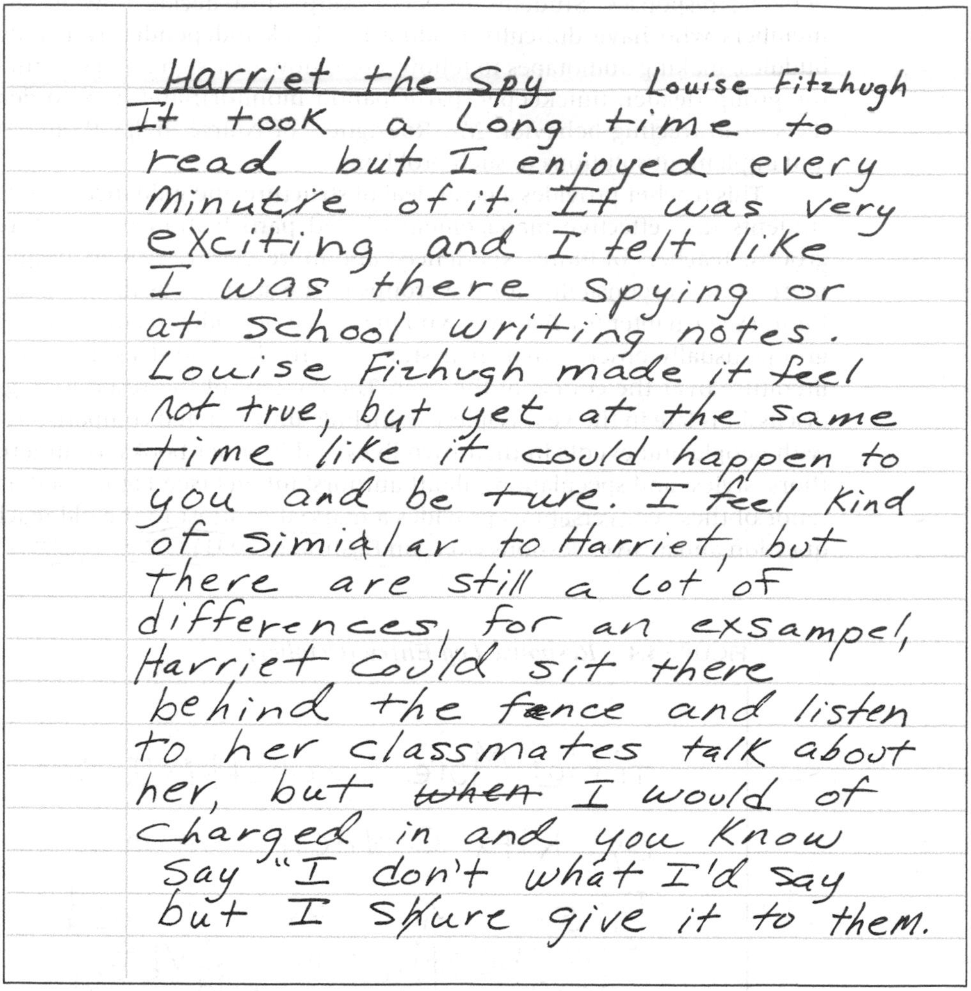

> <u>Harriet the Spy</u>   Louise Fitzhugh
> It took a long time to read but I enjoyed every minutre of it. It was very exciting and I felt like I was there spying or at school writing notes. Louise Fizhugh made it feel not true, but yet at the same time like it could happen to you and be ture. I feel kind of simialar to Harriet, but there are still a lot of differences, for an exsampel, Harriet could sit there behind the fence and listen to her classmates talk about her, but ~~when~~ I would of charged in and you know say "I don't what I'd say but I shure give it to them.

Combining Instructional Approaches: The Workshop Format

Second-grade teacher Peter Lancia combines guided and independent reading in his literature-based program. He manages instruction through a daily reading workshop with his students, using the following format:

Reading Workshop Format
Mini-Lesson (5–10 minutes)

Lesson topics are determined by the needs of the class. They are brief and often involve teacher and student modeling. Topics include: book selection strategies, book or genre previews, author traits (styles of writing and illustrations), independent reading strategies, discussions about characteristics of good readers, and procedures for the workshop such as conferences, book talks, and types of response.

Status of the Class (5 minutes)

After the children select or retrieve books, the teacher asks each student what he or she will be reading and records it on a chart. This provides an excellent opportunity for brief conversations with the children about their choices. Students are allowed to select books independently, although teacher guidance may be necessary.

Silent Reading (30–45 minutes)

Once the children have selected books, they are expected to read silently and independently (although many primary-age students still vocalize while reading and may need the support of oral reading with a partner). During the first few minutes, the teacher reads as well.

Conferences (during silent reading, 5–10 minutes each)

The teacher meets with each child once a week on a regularly scheduled day to talk about his or her reading in an informal conversation. The children are asked to prepare for this meeting by keeping their reading logs and response journals up-to-date and having a favorite book chapter to retell and share orally. The teacher prepares as well, by looking over the children's book lists, reading the response journals, and considering any special instructional needs. These preparations merely provide a beginning for conferences, as each conversation may take on its own direction and focus.

Response (10–15 minutes)

The children have opportunities for both written and oral responses to their reading. Written responses include journals whose entries are based on open-ended prompts supplied by the teacher, exciting word books (very simple vocabulary notebooks), and book reviews. More elaborate book projects are completed at home. Writing is always shared orally. Oral responses include book clubs, book talks, and commercials (mock advertisements for books).

Read Aloud (20–25 minutes)

The children interact with the story as the teacher reads it aloud. This provides an excellent opportunity for modeling of reading and response strategies.

Directed Reading–Thinking Activity

Teachers who are familiar with the components and characteristics of effective directed reading activities are able not only to design guided reading lessons for use with groups of students reading the same text, but also to modify and improve the commercially produced lessons found in the basal series they may be required to use. As students progress to reading more challenging informational materials in the upper primary grades, it becomes particularly important to scaffold and guide their reading.

A practical lesson format known as the *directed reading–thinking activity* (*DRTA*) is divided into three major parts: preparation for reading, silent reading, and follow-up activities (Graves, Juel, and Graves, 2001; Stauffer, 1976). The components of the DRTA can be modified to be used with most materials and at any grade level.

Preparation for Reading. Preparation is the most important phase of the DRTA, since it facilitates both word identification and comprehension. First, the teacher introduces the topic and helps students relate it to their previous experiences. This involves assessing what students already know about the topic and determining what relevant background they lack. Next, the teacher provides direct or vicarious experiences to build the concepts necessary for understanding the material. Let us suppose the children are going to read a story about sharks. An example of a direct experience would be a visit to a large aquarium where live sharks can be observed. Vicarious experiences are secondhand and would include showing pictures or videos, or visiting a web site about sharks. In all instances, the teacher would build concepts about sharks through discussion.

The issue of whether and how much to preteach new vocabulary is problematic. In order to make decisions about working with vocabulary before reading, the teacher must decide in what way the words are new to the reader. In some instances, new words are unknown to the reader only in their printed form and can be figured out independently through the use of the usual word identification strategies. It is generally not necessary or advisable to preteach these words. We want readers to practice decoding them independently. Attention to new vocabulary is beneficial, however, when the words represent concepts unfamiliar to the reader. Such words are often referred to as *wordstoppers*, since the students' comprehension will suffer if such words are not read with understanding. For example, some third-graders who were reading a story about a flood encountered the following sentence: "Bill and Laurie rushed to the river to help their neighbors make the *levee* stronger." Many children worked out the pronunciation of the new word *levee*; however, they did not understand the sentence since they did not know what a levee was. In this instance, their reading would have been facilitated by the teacher's introduction of the concept of "levee" prior to reading. Instructional strategies for helping children develop new concepts are discussed in Chapter 6 as part of the topic of vocabulary development. In general, however, it is recommended that only a limited number of new words (if any) be introduced before reading and that they be presented in context and thoroughly discussed and explained. Care should be taken to help students elaborate the meanings of wordstoppers so that they can apply their understanding of the new words in different situations. For example, when introducing *levee*, the teacher might help children compare levees to walls and fences and discuss what sorts of materials are used to build levees and why. This would be far more effective than simply defining the word or showing a picture.

In addition, when there are ESL (English as Second Language) students in the class the teacher must anticipate which vocabulary words might be problematic for them in particular. For example, idiomatic expressions and words that have multiple meanings may need attention and explanation by native English-speaking students or by the teacher.

Many basal lesson plans suggest that teachers work with isolated skills before having students read a selection. In most instances, this will not enhance the reader's ability to read the material, since <u>reading is an integrated process</u>. The reader is intent on constructing meaning, not on applying isolated skills. At the transitional stage, the goal is to help students develop fluency while <u>reading for meaning</u>. The skill to be developed, for them, is reading. Later on, after students have become fluent (i.e., have attained the <u>basic literacy</u> stage), they will profit from instruction in the use of <u>strategies</u> that will help them cope with more complex, abstract materials. For transitional readers, however, the focus of the DRTA should be on the reading itself.

The last component of the preparation phase, purpose setting, helps students <u>generate predictions and expectations about the content of the selection</u>. This is not a matter of raising specific questions and instructing students to read to find answers to these questions. Such focused purposes may actually lead readers to overlook much of the material, thus limiting the reader's comprehension. Rather, the process of purpose setting should help students develop a general set of expectations. How this is done will depend on whether the text is narrative or informational. For narrative materials, an effective strategy is to set up a situation that parallels the plot of the story and ask students to react in terms of their experience. If students are about to read a story about some children who get lost in the woods, for example, the teacher might ask them if they have ever been lost or if they know anyone this has happened to. How did they feel? What did they do? After this discussion, the teacher highlights the circumstances in the story the students are about to read. How might they react in those circumstances?

If the material to be read is informational, the teacher will lead students through the process of skimming the selection and drawing on their prior knowledge to generate predictions. Two questions that generally prove useful are: "What do you think the author is going to include?" and "Why do you think so?" As active readers, the students' goal will be to confirm or disprove their predictions.

Adequate preparation for reading helps ensure that students will read the material with understanding. The process of building conceptual background and helping students anticipate what they will read enables them to take an active role in reading. They will use their background knowledge and their expectations in combination with the author's text to construct meaning. Sound preparation for reading solves many "comprehension problems." For transitional stage readers, it also facilitates word identification through anticipation.

Silent Reading. Silent reading of the selection is the major event of a DRTA. During silent reading, readers are intent on getting meaning from the printed text, relating it to their predictions. Transitional stage readers, who are not yet fluent, are likely to move their lips and point to individual words as they read. Teachers often try to correct these habits. This is unnecessary; it is now recognized that these behaviors simply reflect that the reading is difficult and unfamiliar. Even very accomplished readers (college students, for example) manifest these behaviors when attempting to read very challenging, technical material. Calling attention to subvocalizing or pointing simply makes the reader self-conscious and detracts from focus on meaning. As readers gain experience and fluency, these behaviors spontaneously disappear.

Questions often arise about having transitional stage students read silently, rather than orally, during a DRTA. There are significant differences between oral and silent reading that must be understood. In general, there are two commonly cited purposes for students' oral reading: to provide the teacher with an opportunity to assess accuracy or speed, and to share in a real audience situation. Oral reading undertaken specifically for assessment is usually done privately and will be discussed at length in Chapter 11. However, teachers make ongoing observations about children's oral reading behaviors daily, as they listen to them read aloud to practice or share reading selections. This type of continuing evaluation in the context of everyday reading activities is an important part of effective reading instruction. Another purpose for oral reading is to share. Often young children choose to read together for social reasons. They delight in sharing their favorite books and stories. When students read aloud for the purpose of sharing more formally, or with a larger audience, they should be given the opportunity to rehearse by reading silently first.

There are important differences in purpose and function between oral and silent reading. The purpose of oral reading is to communicate the author's ideas to an audience. The reader concentrates on pronouncing words correctly and using the proper inflection and tone necessary to read expressively. As researcher Dolores Durkin points out:

> With oral reading, the customary function is similar to that of speaking: to communicate to one or more listeners. Although an effective oral presentation often indicates that the reader understands the text, comprehension is not an essential requirement. What is required are correct pronunciations and phrasing, suitable volume, and appropriate expression. These can all be present when the oral reader does not understand everything an author wrote. (Durkin, 1988, p. 38)

The purpose and focus of oral reading remain the same, regardless of what type of text is being read.

In contrast, during silent reading the reader is not concerned with pronunciation and therefore is free to concentrate on the construction of meaning. Beginning with the transitional stage, comprehension tends to be better during silent reading. Another major difference between oral and silent reading is that during silent reading, readers vary their rate of reading according to the purposes they have established, whereas oral reading rate usually does not vary.

Initial readers, who are primarily concerned with pronunciation and who have had limited exposure to words in print, tend to read everything orally. Once students are past this stage, however, silent reading begins to take precedence over oral reading. By the end of the transitional stage, as a consequence of silent reading practice, the silent reading rate has overtaken the rate of oral reading. Thus, an inordinate focus on oral reading at this stage may limit the amount of students' reading. Moreover, it is generally agreed that students should not be required to follow along silently while other students read orally, round-robin style. In this situation, the followers are forced to read silently at someone else's oral reading rate. Moreover, readers who are following along are tempted to correct the child who is reading orally. Too many interruptions by children or teacher promote word-by-word reading and prevent the reader from developing *eye–voice span.* (Good readers, when reading orally, actually read ahead silently before pronouncing the words. Their eyes are typically a few words ahead of their voices.) Transitional readers are in the process of increasing this eye–voice span (Cunningham & Allington, 1998). If a group of children are reading the same text from multiple copies, they can be instructed to place a finger on the page, close the book, and "follow along" with the meaning rather than the words, as their classmate reads.

Even though the problems associated with round-robin reading were identified long ago, the practice still persists in many American classrooms. Classroom observation research (Allington, 1994; Anderson et al., 1985) has documented that round-robin reading typically dominates reading instructional time in many primary grade classrooms. At later levels, it is used less frequently on the whole but is still often used with the poorest readers and in content areas.

When the group involved in a DRTA includes children of differing abilities and language backgrounds, teachers often read parts or all of the selection orally or in a shared reading format with those who need extra support to participate successfully. Alternatively, teachers provide taped readings of the text (read slowly but smoothly) and have struggling readers follow along with the tape.

In the context of directed reading activity, there is little rationale for extensive oral reading by students. In a DRTA, everyone reads the same material; there is no reason for student sharing through extensive oral reading. More appropriate opportunities for oral reading arise in the self-selected component of the reading program, when children rehearse and share favorite parts of their books with peers who have not already read them.

Follow-Up to Reading. The third main component of the DRTA provides an opportunity for students to discuss their reading in light of the purposes they established before reading and to engage in response activities. Checking students' comprehension need not involve asking numerous, specific questions about the content of the passage. Rather, the teacher helps the students compare what they expected the writer to say with what they actually found as they read the text. The discussion often involves summarizing the text, interpreting it, and relating it to prior knowledge, including parts of the text read previously. (Specific questioning strategies that help enhance students' comprehension are discussed in Chapter 7.)

Extension activities are usually optional and depend on the extent of students' interest, as well as the nature of the material. They can be used to elaborate concepts introduced in the reading or to introduce new, related concepts and texts. Examples of extension activities might include:

■ Locating and reading additional material related to text or topic or by the same author
■ Comparing different authors' treatment of the same topic
■ Summarizing information from the text

The basic components of the DRTA are summarized in Figure 4.6.

FIGURE 4.6 *Outline of DRTA*

I. Preparation

    A. Introduction and motivation

    B. Concept clarification
        1. Direct experiences
        2. Vicarious experiences (including discussion) related to students' personal experiences, if possible

    C. Introduction of difficult words in context

    D. Skill direction (optional): Introduce any strategies needed to read the selection.

    E. Setting purposes for reading
        1. Prereading questions
        2. Prediction of what the author will say

II. Silent Reading

III. Follow-Up

    A. Discuss prereading questions generated by students.

    B. Compare what students expected to find to what was actually found.

    C. Suggest appropriate related readings or activities.

Adapting the Basal Reader

The pros and cons of including basal readers in reading instructional programs continue to stir considerable debate. Authors and publishers of basals (as well as many administrators) suggest that reading instruction can be best managed and delivered by the use of materials that are structured and sequenced for the teacher. Although the value of exposure to literature is acknowledged, the basis for these programs is a subskills view of reading that leads to isolating and teaching various skills and strategies that are actually inseparable in real reading (Weaver, 1994). We subscribe to the view that meaning is central to all reading instruction and that teachers are in the best position to design that instruction. Our position is that *ideally* instruction should evolve from authentic literacy experiences; basal readers are not necessary. If they are used, they should be primarily used as anthologies, as sources of literature, and instruction should be based on the demonstrated needs and interests of the children rather than on prescriptive directions and "scripts" for teachers to follow.

Nevertheless, we recognize that the use of basals remains widespread. Many school systems require the use of a particular basal program. Novice teachers often prefer to use a basal reader, if only temporarily, because of the structure it provides. Given the reality that many teachers use basal readers, we will address the ways in which commercial programs can be modified and adapted to make lessons more effective and to allow sufficient time for authentic reading and writing.

Although the commonly used basal series vary considerably in format and sequence of teaching activities, nearly all incorporate the basic DRTA format to structure lessons. However, most of them tend to stress skill development. Most basal lessons contain an inordinate number of prereading and postreading activities, many of which are not related to the content of the reading selection (Shannon & Goodman, 1994). If basals are to be used, the effectiveness of the lessons can be greatly increased by restoring the balance between reading and other activities. The purpose of this section is to suggest the kinds of constructive changes teachers can make in basal lessons by deleting, modifying, and, in some cases, adding activities.

Preparation for Reading. The first step is to examine the recommendations for preparing students for reading. Recent editions of basal readers generally acknowlededge the importance of providing adequate background information prior to reading. Studies have shown, however, that this important step is often omitted by teachers in the interest of saving time (Durkin, 1984; Weaver, 1994). Concept building is one component of the DRTA that always deserves careful consideration. Decisions about the amount of time to be spent on this part of the preparation should be based on how much the students already know about the topic. If their background knowledge seems insufficient, the teacher may need to supplement the background preparation recommended in the manual.

As noted in the preceding discussion of the DRTA, wordstoppers crucial for understanding the selection should be introduced to students prior to reading. Most basal manuals recommend the preteaching of large numbers of words, many of which students could easily figure out independently while reading. It is not necessary to isolate these words and teach them, even in context. Not only is the preteaching of long lists of words boring for most students, it also deprives them of the opportunity to apply the word identification strategies they have already acquired.

Perhaps the most troublesome aspect of the DRTA as presented by basal reader publishers is skill direction. As previously mentioned, most basals devote an inordinate amount of time to instruction in isolated skills that have questionable value in contributing to reading progress. Teachers who are conversant with the stages of literacy development can recognize those skills that are not appropriate to their students' stages of reading and eliminate them. For example, third-grade-level basals usually contain numerous phonics exercises. However, it is widely recognized that readers in the transitional stage have already learned to use graphophonemic cues coupled with context. Reading skill and fluency develop primarily through reading practice. However, if teachers decide that a subskill from the basal lesson should be addressed with students, this may best be accomplished after reading, rather than before. Meaning should be the primary focus of any directed reading. With this emphasis in mind, the natural flow of the lesson is to move from activation of prior knowledge and concept building to prediction, reading, and discussion of the content of the text. It does not make sense to interrupt this process with analysis of the components of the reading process. Therefore, at the transitional stage, work with skills generally belongs after the comprehension activities. (At the next stage, the "skills" taught are more likely to be strategies for comprehending increasingly difficult or abstract material and are therefore introduced before reading to help students make meaning from the text.)

The last step in the preparation phase of the DRTA is setting purposes for reading. Basal manuals tend to approach this mechanically, by suggesting that the teacher give the children a directive, such as "Read this page to find out what happened to John next." It would be more appropriate to engage students actively in generating predictions about what the writer will say. "What do you think will happen to John next? Why do you think so?" (Is there a picture? Is the prediction based on what has already been read or on a student's experience?) Once students have established expectations about the content of the material, they are ready for silent reading.

Silent Reading. Most basal manuals instruct teachers to interrupt their students' silent reading periodically to check their comprehension. In some instances, readers are stopped at the end of every few pages and questioned. For example, consider the following list of questions for three pages of text in a third-grade basal:

1. Who was the young man? What was his recipe for?
2. What did Klaus say when the king asked what was in his recipe? Why do you think Klaus didn't tell the king?
3. Why did the king feel that he and Klaus would get along well? Why do you think Klaus didn't care?
4. Who really cooked dinner?
5. How did Klaus and the king feel about their arrangement? Why did they feel that way? (*Book 3*, 1989, p. 330)

Most readers find such interruptions annoying. Stopping to answer questions detracts from enjoyment of the story: it is not a natural reading behavior. Independent readers do not stop reading to take a quiz at the end of each page. However, there may be instances when the teacher feels that some monitoring and guidance during reading are necessary. If a story is long or contains potentially confusing elements, the teacher should identify an appropriate point in the story at which to stop the children and determine whether they are having difficulty. Such a break should be as natural and brief as possible. The purpose of the discussion is to make sure readers are on track and to have them predict what will occur next, not to test them with a list of literal recall questions such as those provided by many basals. If students are to read the entire text on their own, after preparation, teachers often supply them with post-it notes to mark parts that puzzled them or that they want to share in the discussion later.

Follow-Up to Reading. The comprehension check that follows completion of the reading should be scrutinized—and usually modified. Three problems commonly occur with the comprehension checks provided in basal manuals. First, there are often far too many questions. If teachers use them all, they may feel as though they are "milking a story to death" and boring their students. Second, this problem is exacerbated by the fact that many of the questions, particularly in older basal series, are trivial, framed at the literal level, and repetitive. A third concern is that the questions generally are unrelated to each other in any discernible way and therefore do not lead to a coherently developed discussion.

P. David Pearson has developed guidelines for generating comprehension checks or discussions that are more effective and interesting for both teacher and students (Pearson, 1985). A good way to begin, for example, is to have students reflect on their prereading predictions and compare what they expected to find with what they actually found. Next, the teacher can help the students generate a summary of the material, which provides the common basis for the rest of the discussion. In the case of narrative material, the teacher's questions will lead the children to recap the important elements and events of the story, creating a *story map* (Morrow, 2001). Students might be asked to describe the setting and the major characters, to explain the main character's problem or goal, and to describe the resolution of the problem or accomplishment of the goal. Although some of the questions used in this process will be requests for literal recall, they will not be random; they will follow the structure of the story, thus establishing a coherent framework for understanding and remembering the story. Following are examples of questions that would help students establish such a framework:

Beginning of Story

Setting: Where did the story take place? Who was the main character?

Problem: What was _____'s problem?

Goal: What did _____ decide to do?

Attempts: What did _____ do about _____?
What happened to _____?

End of Story

Resolution: Did _____ solve the problem? How would you have solved _____'s problem?

Reaction: How did _____ feel at the end?

Theme: What did you learn from this story? What's the major point of this story?
(Vacca & Vacca, 2002, p. 28)

The establishment of the story map is the first step in a logical line of questions. The next set of questions will be more interpretive and will enable readers to describe relationships among events, rather than just the sequence of events. In stories, as in real life, events often lead to other events; there are reasons for the order of their occurrence. Students should be asked to make comparisons (How was John's reaction different from Susan's?) and to detect cause/effect relationships (Why do you think John was so upset?). These kinds of questions often elicit more than one interpretation. It may therefore be appropriate to ask students to refer back to the text to explain their responses.

The final questions are designed to extend students' thinking well beyond the information in the text and require them to combine their own experiences with the information derived from the text to forge new insights. Questions about the writer's techniques (What did the author do that made you want to finish the story?) and questions that relate books to other books would be appropriate (Pearson, 1985).

If the content of the reading selection is informational rather than narrative, the teacher's questions will lead the students to summarize the information covered. The summary provides a basis for relating the new information to their prior knowledge of the topic and for exploring the implications of the content.

In summary, guidelines for effective questioning include relating predictions to what was read, following systematic lines of questioning, and emphasizing questions that promote reflection and personal reaction to the material and that do not have predetermined answers. Some of the most recent editions of basal readers reflect current thinking to the extent that they have revised follow-up activities to acknowledge these guidelines. Even though the individual activities are more defensible than those in earlier editions, most recommended activities are still extremely time consuming and unnecessarily extensive. On examining a lesson from a basal series that is marketed as "literature based," we found 15 workbook pages and 2 "activity cards" recommended for use after reading a children's literature selection involving a child who is interested in art. The teacher's guide contains 20 follow-up activities, including writing about drawing, categorizing characters, story mapping, summarizing the story, distinguishing reality from fantasy, reviewing the main character's problem and rewriting the ending of the story, recording realistic story events, working with vowel combinations, playing a vowel game, finding common syllables in words, working with commas, naming types of artists (vocabulary exercises), group discussion relating readers' imagined feelings if they were the character, writing a description of a gift for the character, making a pinwheel (following directions), making a web about artists, learning to spell words from the story, experimenting with old crayons, and researching careers in art. While some of these activities relate directly to the story and may well be worthwhile, the sheer number of activities is daunting. Even if the teacher selects from among these, an inordinate amount of time is likely to be spent on activities that do not provide additional reading practice or enjoyment. Some teachers report spending seven or eight days working with a single story! Surely this is not how literature is intended to be used.

Teachers often are aware of these drawbacks; however, they continue to use prescribed follow-up activities for purposes of classroom management. Children who have completed their reading time with the teacher are kept busy while the teacher works with other groups. While management of groups of children is a legitimate concern, there are many appropriate options for independent work, such as those used in Mr. Lancia's Reading Workshop, described earlier in this chapter.

As a general rule, productive follow-up activities are those that engage children in meaningful reading and writing.

Modifying the DRTA Format. The DRTA format, which is used as the basis for most basal reading lessons, can be modified by the knowledgeable teacher to make it more effective and interesting. The modified lesson emphasizes development of concepts, purposeful reading, and extension of understanding through thoughtful discussion and related activities. Focus on these elements ensures that children will spend a significant proportion of their reading time on reading rather than on unrelated activities. The teacher uses activities suggested in the teacher's guide very selectively, eliminating all those that seem superfluous, inappropriate, or simply too time consuming. The goal is to spend well over half the lesson time on *reading authentic material*.

Modifications of basal readers enable the conscientious teacher to improve on the lessons as they are presented in the series' manuals. However, even the most skillful alterations cannot compensate for absence of quality in the literature on which the lessons are based. The teacher must be responsible for identifying stories that are poorly structured, uninteresting to students, or inappropriate for some other reason. It is in the best interest of the students to eliminate such stories and to replace them with readings the teacher deems more appropriate.

Immersion Techniques

Many older students who have been labeled learning disabled or remedial readers are stuck in the transitional stage of reading. They have not developed sufficient reading fluency to pass on to the basic literacy stage. For such students, special techniques designed specifically for increasing fluency may prove beneficial. These "immersion" techniques help readers develop knowledge of particular texts and increase their ability to predict effectively while reading—in other words, to read more fluently. *Immersion methods* improve reading competency by immersing the student in meaningful reading material and leading him into fluency. He learns what balanced, fluent reading feels like and eventually approaches even unfamiliar material in a balanced way. Two of these techniques are known as *assisted reading* and *repeated reading*. Both of these methods lead students through the experience of fluent oral reading. Oral reading fluency is not the primary goal; silent reading fluency is ultimately far more important. Nevertheless, we know that both oral and silent reading practice increases fluency.

Immersion techniques should be explained to students as reading exercises. They can be likened to muscle building or calisthenics for the football player. They are preparations, not substitutions, for the game. Immersion techniques are appropriate for readers at the late initial and early transitional stages who are overly analytical or who lack fluency. The techniques can be profitably used with students of any age who fit this description.

Assisted Reading

Assisted reading consists of reading along with a more able reader. It is best accomplished with a text that is already familiar to the reader, usually through hearing it read aloud. If an unfamiliar text is used, the first step in the process is for the teacher to read the book to the student. The actual assisted reading is similar to shared reading (discussed in Chapter 3) except that a regular-sized text is used. The student is invited to read orally along with the teacher, who reads smoothly and evenly at a rate the student can follow. In most cases, it is recommended that the student follow the print with a finger, pointing to each word as it is pronounced to ensure a speech–print match. As the reader acquires more fluency with the selection, pointing becomes unnecessary.

Assisted reading can also involve having the student read along with an audiotape of a text. While there are excellent published tape recordings of children's literature with accompanying books, they are best suited for listening enjoyment. The pace of the reading is generally too rapid for a nonfluent reader to follow. Teacher-made tapes are more appropriate for assisted reading because the length and type of selection, the pace of reading, and the cues provided can be tailored to meet student needs.

Many teachers and tutors of struggling readers have found the following adaptation of assisted reading to be effective:

Make a tape recording of the chosen reading selection. (Length should be very brief to begin with, a few sentences or one paragraph. This can be adjusted later according to the reader's capabilities.) When recording, give the student the title, page number, and location of the selection on the page. Instruct the student, "Put your finger under the first word: _____. Point to each word as you hear it, and read along with the tape. Ready?" In recording, read the selection slightly faster than the student would read it independently, but keep the pace slow. At the end of the selection, instruct the student, "Rewind the tape and practice reading this selection with the tape as many times as you need to read it easily by yourself. Then read it to your teacher."

Repeated Reading

Repeated reading is closely related to assisted reading; the two approaches are often used in combination. The practice of repeated reading is not a new one. Parents have always read favorite stories to their children over and over, often to the point where the stories are memorized by the children. In school, repeated readings involve having a student listen to and read a selection or story many times with a tape or with the teacher. Generally a complete piece (chapter, short book) is used, and the tutor's reading proceeds at a more natural pace than in assisted reading. When the student has listened to and read with the model many times, she attempts to read the material independently.

Both assisted reading and repeated reading make maximum use of prediction on the part of the student, who knows exactly what words to expect by the time she reads the selection independently. This leads her to use word identification strategies in balance. Moreover, in following the model's reading, she is prevented from overanalyzing (there isn't time) or randomly guessing (the correct word is immediately pronounced and heard).

Components of Effective Programs

In this chapter we have examined various instructional approaches and types of material that are appropriate for use with students in the transitional stage of reading, including self-selected reading, guided reading, responses to literature, DRTA, adapted basal programs, and immersion techniques. As we pointed out in the earlier discussion of instruction of initial stage readers (Chapter 3), options for instruction can be combined in various ways to suit the individual and collective needs of students, the teachers' preferences, and the school context. Once again, the consistent components of effective instructional programs in grades two and three (and with readers in other grades who are transitional stage readers) are reading to children, reading with them, guided reading, independent reading, and relevant strategy instruction. Compared with initial stage instruction, programs for transitional readers incorporate less reading with the teacher and more guided and independent reading. Writing connected to literature also assumes a more prominent role. Effective teachers of transitional stage readers combine these ingredients in ways that help novices increase their reading skill and experience while maintaining their enthusiasm and confidence until they achieve fluency.

■ CASE STUDIES

The majority of children enter the transitional stage of reading during their second-grade year. For this reason, we will describe the literacy development of our three children as second-graders. John's profile and instructional needs will be typical of the majority of second-graders, Kim will have entered the initial stage of reading, and Theresa will have gone beyond the transitional stage. Together, these three students represent the range of literacy development that a second-grade teacher must typically accommodate.

■ Kim

When Kim came into second grade, she had entered the initial reading stage. As a consequence of her immersion in print and the appropriate instruction and support by her first-grade teacher, she had made excellent progress. By the end of first grade, she was retelling stories in considerable detail and using some story language. She demonstrated understanding of basic print concepts. When producing and "reading" written texts, she proceeded from left to right and attempted to match printed words with spoken words. She knew the names of all letters and many of the sounds they represent. Her writing reflected this new knowledge and was semiphonetic. She could read short, very familiar materials such as language experience stories and a few favorite books. She had begun to acquire sight vocabulary and consistently recognized a few words that were personally significant to her (*Kim, Mom, baby, monster*). At the beginning of second grade, she viewed herself as part of the community of readers and writers in her classroom. Although she was fully aware that other children in her class were more proficient readers and writers than she was, she did not see herself as unsuccessful. She freely solicited their help and advice and felt good about sharing her own accomplishments with other children. Kim was fortunate in having had teachers in kindergarten and first grade who accepted and celebrated all children's efforts. For this reason, her classmates also accepted each other's accomplishments and provided support for each other.

FIGURE 4.7 *Kim's Second-Grade Writing Sample*

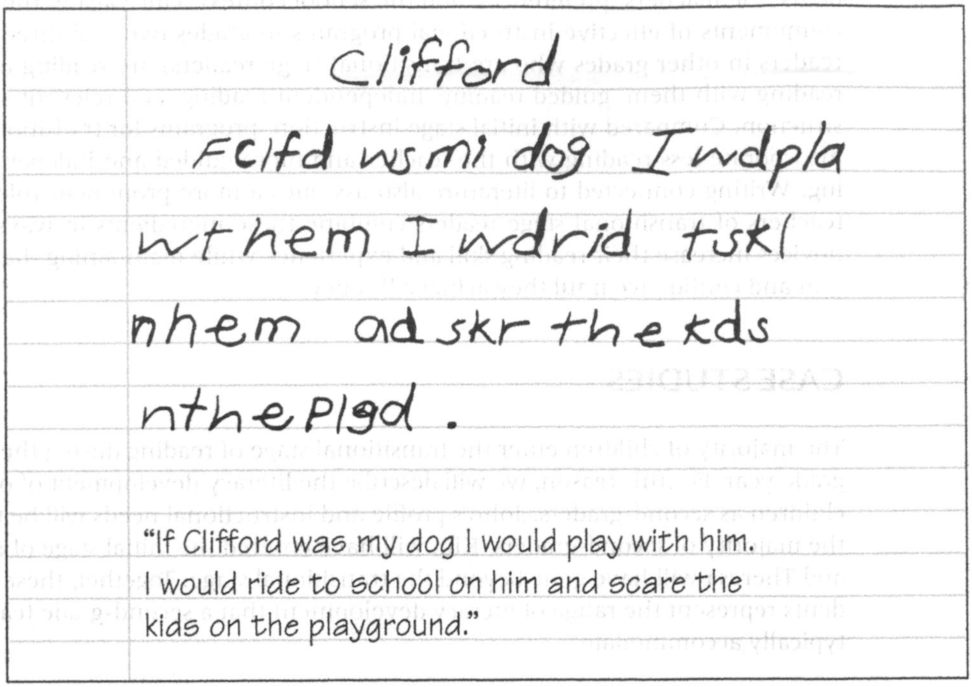

Clifford

FClfd ws mi dog I wdpla

wt hem I wdrid tskl

nhem ad skr the kds

nthe Plgd .

"If Clifford was my dog I would play with him.
I would ride to school on him and scare the
kids on the playground."

Kim produced the writing sample shown in Figure 4.7 in October of her
second-grade year after reading several "Clifford" books, including *Clifford's
Halloween* (Bridwell, 1985). The sample shows that she understands that letters
represent speech sounds. She attempts to hear the component sounds in words
(phonemic segmentation) and uses this information to construct her message. She
is beginning to use lowercase as well as uppercase letters. Her text is much longer
and more complete than earlier writings.

Before reading on, consider how you as a second-grade teacher might address
Kim's needs. Then compare your ideas with our suggestions, which follow.

Kim's Instructional Program

Kim is at the beginning of the initial stage, while most of her classmates are approaching or are into the transitional stage. However, there are many literacy
activities that can be responded to at various levels and which are therefore as
appropriate for Kim as for her more advanced classmates. Some activities that Kim
could successfully participate in along with her classmates include listening and
responding to literature read aloud by the teacher, shared reading, writing process,
and voluntary self-selected reading (SSR).

Reading good literature aloud should continue to be a daily occurrence.
Stories that are read aloud by the teacher at this level are often longer and more

complex than those read aloud in kindergarten and first grade. Like her classmates, Kim will benefit in several ways. Her understanding of more complex story structures will expand. Her vocabulary will grow as she is exposed to new or unusual words and phrases in texts. Her world knowledge will be enhanced through the vicarious experiences of stories heard and discussed.

If her teacher still makes use of enlarged texts for shared reading, Kim will respond by building her ability to predict, her sight vocabulary, and her use of word identification strategies. Her more advanced classmates will be likely to use the shared reading as a rehearsal for independent reading of the same book.

Writing process is particularly important for Kim's teacher to include during the school day because it accommodates the full range of literacy development in the class. Like her classmates, Kim can participate in all aspects of the writing process, with the exception of editing. She can plan, draft, share, revise, and publish her work just as the other children do. Her independent attempts at drafting will be far less advanced than those of the majority of her classmates, and she will still need to have a more literate person edit for her, whereas the more advanced second-grade writers will be starting to assume some responsibility for their own editing.

Sustained silent reading of self-selected books is an essential component of any second-grade reading program. During SSR, Kim can read over very familiar books, her own published stories, or dictations. She may also choose to browse and look at books that she cannot yet read independently, in the conventional sense.

"Special" Instruction. Although Kim can participate in many literacy activities along with her classmates, she will also need some instruction that is unlike that of her classmates because of her level of literacy development. Kim needs to engage in activities that specifically address the instructional goals for an initial reader, including the following:

- Continue to work with Kim on the repeated readings of short, predictable books that she enjoys. Read each story to and with Kim many times, encouraging her to follow the text with her finger. Teacher-made tapes can be used (see the discussion of assisted reading in this chapter). She can practice reading these books independently, both at school and at home.
- Continue to use the language experience approach. Kim can generate dictations in reaction to literature, personal experiences, drawings, or observations. She may be helped to build a collection of easily recognized words, kept in a word bank and used for various activities. These can be selected from language experience dictations, books, or other printed materials.
- Lead Kim through the process of using word identification strategies. When she encounters unfamiliar words in her reading, focus her attention on context ("What would make sense?" "Does that make sense?"). Use of graphophonemic cues can be encouraged by drawing her attention to the initial letter of the unknown word. ("Could that word be _____? Look at the first letter. What letter sound do you hear at the beginning of _____?")

[handwritten margin notes: "letters before vowel" / "vowel and what follows" / "onset" "rime" / "J-ump"]

- Continue work with onsets and rimes.
- Encourage Kim's attempts at invented spelling. Model the use of letter–sound correspondences in the context of writing. This will help Kim refine her ability to hear component sounds in words and to use phonics to produce increasingly complete spellings of words.
- If a commercial or formal spelling program of any kind is used in her second grade, do not make it part of Kim's instructional program. She will not be able to remember conventional spellings of words that are not part of her sight vocabulary. At her level, continuing refinement of her own approximations is far more appropriate.
- If a basal reader is used with Kim, modify its use as suggested in Chapter 3. The most appropriate application would probably be to have Kim use the easiest readings in the series for additional reading practice, while having guided reading instruction with predictable texts or leveled texts.

Again, a major consideration in designing Kim's instructional program must be to sustain her motivation to read and write and her view of herself as a competent learner whose efforts are worthy of recognition.

■ John

During the fall of his second-grade year, John became a transitional stage reader. He had acquired considerable sight vocabulary. His sight word collection had become so unwieldy that it was no longer appropriate for him to keep a word bank. He was able to apply word identification strategies independently and was beginning to read unfamiliar books independently. Like most transitional stage readers, he could read familiar texts fluently, but his reading of unrehearsed texts was slow and laborious. He followed each line of print with his finger as he read, which he said helped him keep his place.

John produced the writing sample shown in Figure 4.8 in October of second grade. His spelling was largely phonetic, but he had begun to spell some commonly encountered words conventionally. His writing was much more fluent than in the fall of first grade, and his texts were becoming longer.

Before you read on, formulate an instructional program that you think would be appropriate for him.

John's Instructional Program

[handwritten margin notes: "More reading + writing – journaling", "Positive", "Motivation"]

John needs the same type of instructional program as any typical transitional stage reader. Above all else, he needs many opportunities to practice reading in order to build fluency and independence. The teacher's role in helping a transitional reader such as John to realize his potential as a reader is crucial. She must provide a variety of interesting, meaningful, easy-to-read materials and guide John in learning to make appropriate choices. She must ensure that he has plenty of time to read, every day, and that he and his classmates share their reading experiences. His teacher will be on the alert for difficulties that John and his classmates show in

FIGURE 4.8 *John's Second-Grade Writing Sample*

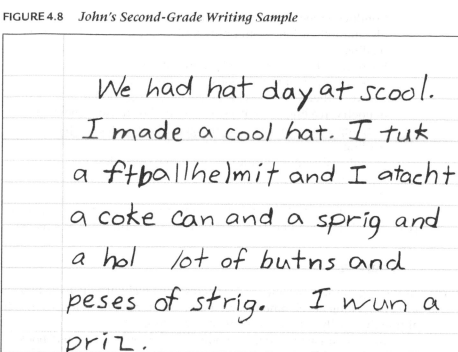

We had hat day at scool.
I made a cool hat. I tuk
a ftballhelmit and I atacht
a coke can and a sprig and
a hol lot of butns and
peses of strig. I wun a
priz.

applying the reading strategies they learned as initial readers. Skills at this stage should be taught on the basis of demonstrated needs of individuals or groups of children.

Teacher-directed or guided reading activities will give John the opportunity to read slightly more difficult materials and to engage in a common reading experience with a group of peers. The teacher may design guided reading activities based on trade books (multiple copies would be necessary) or DRTAs using informational materials or basal reader selections. If a basal is used, it should be modified to ensure that the majority of time is spent reading. Both teacher-directed reading and self-selected reading with responses should form the core of John's instructional program.

The teacher should continue to read aloud daily to John and his classmates. Writing process should also continue to be an integral part of the language arts program.

Specific activities appropriate for John would include:

■ Require John to keep simple records of his reading: for example, a daily reading log including book title and number of pages read and a list of books completed.
■ Invite John to share his reactions to reading through book talks, discussions, and writing activities.

■ Conduct periodic conferences with John to discuss his impressions, assess his comprehension, monitor his reading progress, and stimulate further reading.

■ Encourage John to extend his appreciation and understanding of favorite books through journal responses and book talks.

■ Create authentic reasons for practicing sharing oral reading. Choral readings of poetry, reading parts of a story to the class during a book talk, and re-hearsing a story to read to a younger child are all examples of authentic oral reading.

■ Provide daily opportunities for John to write independently on self-selected topics.

If John is given these and other similar opportunities during his second-grade year, he will gain in fluency, independence, and confidence as a reader.

■ Theresa

At the beginning of second grade, Theresa was well into the basic literacy stage; her level of reading development corresponded to that of most fourth- or fifth-graders, although socially she was very much a second-grader.

She was an avid reader, and now enjoyed longer "chapter" books. Her favorites, she told her teacher, were *Stuart Little* (White, 1973) and all the books in the *Little House* series (Wilder, 1986). Theresa loved to talk about the books she read. It was evident that she was reading for both pleasure and information. When questions arose in class, she usually volunteered to look up information and report back to the class.

Theresa had begun to encounter words and concepts in her reading that were new to her in meaning as well as form. She was curious about new words and often asked her teacher what they meant.

Theresa's writing reflected her generally advanced literacy development. The sample in Figure 4.9 shows Theresa's ability to compose a long, complete text, using a great deal of conventional spelling and punctuation.

Before reading on, consider how you would design and manage an instructional program for Theresa. Then read our recommendations and compare them to yours.

Theresa's Instructional Program

The second-grade instructional program for transitional stage readers should include two basic components: self-selected (individualized) reading and teacher-guided reading. Theresa's needs can be accommodated within this structure, even though she is beyond the transitional stage. She will be able to participate in the same kinds of activities as the other children; however, there will be differences in the materials she reads and in some of the follow-up activities she pursues. One of the best features of self-selected reading is that a wide range of literacy levels can be accommodated within the same structure.

FIGURE 4.9 *Theresa's Second-Grade Writing Sample*

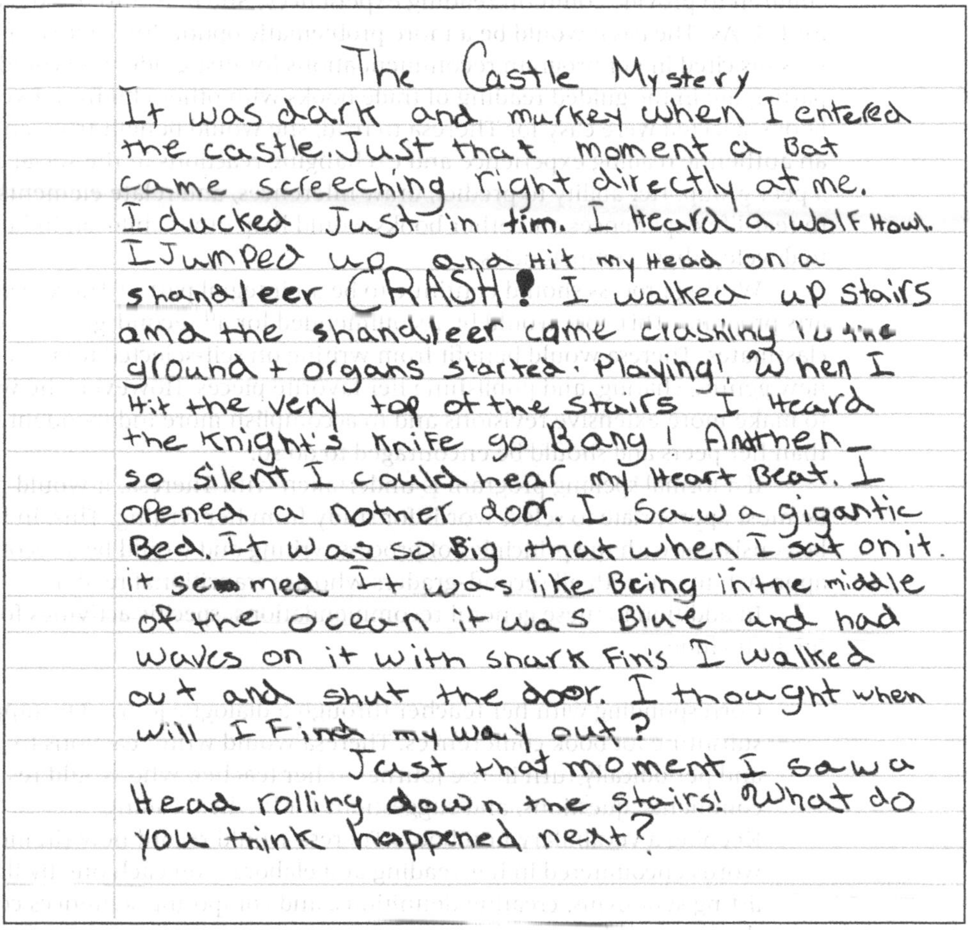

> The Castle Mystery
>
> It was dark and murkey when I entered the castle. Just that moment a Bat came screeching right directly at me. I ducked Just in tim. I Heard a Wolf Howl. I Jumped up and Hit my Head on a shandleer CRASH! I walked up stairs and the shandleer came crashing to the ground + organs started Playing! When I Hit the very top of the stairs I Heard the knight's knife go Bang! And then — so silent I could hear my Heart Beat. I opened a nother door. I saw a gigantic Bed. It was so Big that when I sat on it. it semmed It was like Being in the middle of the ocean it was Blue and had waves on it with shark Fin's I walked out and shut the door. I thought when will I Find my way out?
>
> Just that moment I saw a Head rolling down the stairs! What do you think happened next?

For her self-selected reading, Theresa is likely to choose longer, more challenging books than her classmates. Her teacher should not restrict her choices by prohibiting her from reading "easy" books; however, she can encourage Theresa to read more demanding books by making personal recommendations. Like everyone else in her class, Theresa will engage in sustained silent reading, keep records of her reading, and share her reading experience through book talks and projects. However, some of Theresa's follow-up activities will be different from those of her classmates and will be more characteristic of basic literacy stage readers.

For example, she can engage in more sophisticated reactions to her reading and make extensive use of writing in her sharing. Her vocabulary work will focus on learning the meanings of new words rather than on developing fluency through recognizing the printed forms of words already familiar in meaning.

The second-grade teacher may use guided reading activities with groups of children to provide common reading experiences. She may also use basal readers for DRTAs. The basal would be a more problematic option for Theresa, for the reasons cited in her program recommendations for first grade. She could, however, participate in the guided reading of trade books with other children. Even if the books selected were easy for Theresa to read, she would benefit from engaging in an authentic reading experience and exchanging reactions in the social context of a peer group. Her ability to predict, draw inferences, and relate elements of a story to real-life experiences and other books would help other children in her group to develop these competencies.

Writing process should continue to be an integral part of Theresa's language arts program. This, too, would be recommended for all second-graders. Like her classmates, Theresa would benefit from writing on self-selected topics, exploring new genres, sharing, and publishing her favorite pieces. However, she will be able to make more extensive revisions and to accomplish more independent editing than her peers and should be encouraged to do so.

If a formal spelling program is undertaken with Theresa, it would probably be most appropriate to select words for study from her writing. This, in fact, would be consistent with the principles of process writing and would be a recommended approach to use with all second-graders who are transitional readers.

In addition to these general recommendations, specific activities for Theresa might include:

- Corresponding with her teacher through a dialogue journal to supplement or substitute for book conferences. Theresa would write reactions to her reading and periodically turn in the journal to her teacher, who would respond with comments, questions, and suggestions for further reading.
- Keeping a vocabulary notebook. Theresa would record new (in meaning) words encountered in her reading and elaborate on each one by illustrating, listing synonyms, creating definitions, and composing sentences containing the new words.
- Serving as a resource for less accomplished readers and writers in the class. This will work best if all children are encouraged to help each other, and all children's particular strengths and interests are valued.

If Theresa is provided with the type of instruction that has been suggested, she will progress through the basic literacy stage, adding breadth and depth to her reading experiences, increasing her skill as a reader, and maintaining her motivation to read and write.

Summary

During the transitional stage of reading, students need extended independent reading practice in order to gain fluency. This is best accomplished in classroom settings in which children can choose their reading from an abundance of appropriate literature, in which adequate time for independent reading is an integral part of the school day, and in which sharing of responses to reading is actively promoted. Directed and guided reading activities should be structured so that the emphasis is on reading, not on practice of isolated skills. If these conditions are met, most children will pass rapidly through the transitional stage, emerging as fluent, motivated readers.

SOURCES OF APPROPRIATE LITERATURE FOR TRANSITIONAL STAGE READERS OF DIFFERENT AGES

Cummings, J., & Blair, H. (Eds.). (1990). *A core collection for young reluctant readers* (Vol. 2). Evanston, IL: Burke.

Keane, N. (2001). *Booktalks and beyond: Thematic learning activities for grades.* Atkinson, WI: Upstart Books.

Peterson, B., & Huck, C. (2001). *Literary pathways: Selecting books to support new readers.* Portsmouth, NH: Heinemann.

Routman, R. (1991). *Invitations: Changing as teachers and learners K–12.* Portsmouth, NH: Heinemann.

Worthy, J. (1996). A matter of interest: Literature that hooks reluctant readers and keeps them reading. *The Reading Teacher, 50*(3), 204–214.

Note: The National Council of Teachers of English and the International Reading Association periodically publish recommended booklists for readers of all ages.

Web Sites:
Children's Book Council: www. cbcbooks.org
Scholastic Books: www.scholastic.com

Popular Series Books:

Arthur	*Cam Jansen*
Frog and Toad	*Henry and Mudge*
Clifford	*Magic Treehouse*

BIBLIOGRAPHY

Allington, R. (1994). The schools we have. The schools we need. *The Reading Teacher, 48*(1), 14–29.

Allington, R. (2001). *What really matters for struggling readers: Designing research-based programs.* New York: Addison Wesley Longman.

Allington, R., & Cunningham, P. (2002). *Schools that work: Where all children read and write* (2nd ed.). Boston: Allyn and Bacon.

Anderson, R. C., Hiebert, E., Scott, J., & Wilkinson, I. (Eds.). (1985). *Becoming a nation of readers.* Washington, DC: National Institute of Education.

Atwell, N. (1998). In the middle: *New understandings about writing, reading, and learning.* Portsmouth, NH: Boynton/Cook.

Avery, C. (1993). *With a light touch.* Portsmouth, NH: Heinemann.

Bader, L. A., Veatch, J., & Eldredge, J. (1987). Trade books or basal readers? *Reading Improvement, 248,* 62–67.

Book 3. (1989). Literacy Readers. Boston: Houghton Mifflin.

Bridwell, N. (1985). *Clifford's Halloween.* New York: Scholastic Books.

Cunningham, P. (1992). What kind of phonics instruction will we have? In C. K. Kinzer & D. J. Leu, eds. *Literacy research, theory, and practice: Views from many perspectives* (p. 28). Chicago: National Reading Conference.

Cunningham, P., & Allington, R. (1998). *Classrooms that work: They can all read and write* (2nd ed.). NY: Addison-Wesley .

Durkin, D. (1988). *Teaching them to read* (5th ed.). Boston: Allyn and Bacon.

Eldredge, J. L., & Butterfield, D. (1986). Alternatives to traditional reading instruction. *The Reading Teacher, 40,* 32–37.

Freppon, P. A. (1991). Children's concepts about the nature and purpose of reading in different settings. *Journal of Reading Behavior, 23,* 139–163.

Galda, L., Cullinan, B., & Strickland, D. (1993). *Language, literacy and the child.* Fort Worth, TX: Harcourt Brace Jovanovich.

Graves, M., Juel C., & Graves, B. (2001). *Teaching reading in the 21st century* (2nd ed.). Boston: Allyn and Bacon.

Guice, S., & Allington, R. (1992, December). *Access to literacy variations in schools serving low income children.* Paper presented at the meeting of the National Reading Conference, San Antonio, TX.

Guice, S., Allington, R., Johnson, P., Baker, K., & Michelson, N. (1996). Access?: Books, children and literature-based curriculum in schools. *The New Advocate, 9,* 197–207.

Hickman, J. (1995). Not by chance: Creating classrooms that invite responses to literature. In N. Roser & M. Martinez (Eds.), *Book talk and beyond* (pp. 3–9). Newark, DE: International Reading Association.

Hindley, J. (1996). *In the company of children.* York, ME: Stenhouse.

Irving, A. (1980). *Promoting voluntary reading for children and young people.* Paris: UNESCO.

Keegan, S., & Shrake, K. (1991). Literature study groups: An alternative ability grouping. *The Reading Teacher, 44*(8), 542–547.

Langenberg, D., et. al. (2000). *Report of the National Reading Panel: Teaching children to read.* U.S. Department of Health and Human Services. NIH Publication No. 00-4769.

McCloskey, R. (1976). *Blueberries for Sal.* New York: Penguin.

McGee, L. (1996). Response centered talk: Windows on children's thinking. In L. Gambrell & J. Almasi (Eds.), *Lively discussions! Fostering engaged reading* (pp. 194–207). Newark, DE: International Reading Association.

Morrow, L. M. (1985). Voluntary reading: Forgotten goal. *The Educational Forum, 50*(2), 161–168.

Morrow, L. M. (2001). *Literacy development in the early years* (4th ed.). Boston: Allyn and Bacon.

NAEP 1998 *Reading report card for the nation and states.* U.S. Department of Education.

Pearson, R. D. (1985). Changing the face of reading comprehension instruction. *The Reading Teacher, 38*(8), 714–737.

Shannon, P., & Goodman, K. (Eds.). (1994). *Basal readers: A second look.* Katonah, NY: Richard Owen.

Stauffer, R. (1976). *Teaching reading as a thinking process.* New York: Harper & Row.

Vacca, J. L., & Vacca, R. T. (2002). *Content area reading* (7th ed.). Boston: Allyn & Bacon.

Weaver, C. (1994). *Reading process and practice* (2nd ed.). Portsmouth, NH: Heinemann.

White, E. B. (1952) *Charlotte's Web.* New York: HarperCollins.

White, E. B. (1973). *Stuart Little.* New York: Harper & Row.

Wilder, L. I. (1986). *Little house on the prairie* series. New York: Harper & Row.

Fluent Readers

*R*eaders who have achieved fluency are well on their way to functional, permanent literacy. With continued reading experiences, students will reach a competency level that will enable them to cope with the everyday reading tasks they will encounter outside of school throughout their adult lives. Moreover, they will acquire the basic foundation for continued academic literacy development. School literacy tasks (from approximately fourth grade on) demand an array of strategies and competencies to cope with increasingly long, complex texts.

An analogy may help to illustrate the difference between the first three stages of reading (prefluency) and the last two (postfluency). In some respects, learning to read can be compared to learning to drive a car. The novice driver must pay attention to myriad specific actions that must be coordinated to make the car go. Similarly, beginning readers focus their energy on decoding the printed message, coordinating the use of word identification strategies. Even though beginners learn to read in the context of real, meaningful reading experiences, they are constrained by their lack of reading proficiency. The novice driver can learn to drive while trying to reach a real destination for a real purpose; nevertheless, he pays strict attention to the mechanics of driving. For the more experienced driver, these mechanics have become automatic; less consciousness is devoted to them, and, therefore, more consciousness can be devoted to the journey. It will become increasingly easy to try new routes, drive securely under different conditions, and travel to new destinations. The reader who is in the basic literacy or refinement stage is in a similar position. Attention can be fully devoted to the interpretation of reading rather than the act of reading, which has become automatic.

New instructional concerns come to the fore with the basic literacy stage, since the ability to comprehend a range of materials requires guidance. As students proceed into the refinement stage, a great deal of independent learning through reading is required for success in school. The eventual ability of students to function as independent, strategic readers is based on earlier guidance and modeling. Assisting students to make the transition from dependence (on teacher modeling and guidance) to independence is the overall focus of Part III.

Another aspect of reading development of particular concern to teachers of basic literacy and refinement stage students is helping them retain (or build) their motivation to read for their own purposes. All too often, voluntary reading diminishes as students reach the upper elementary grades, partly, at least, because of the demands of the curriculum. Both students and teachers often report that they simply "don't have time" to read for pleasure. It is imperative that regularly scheduled time for self-selected reading be incorporated into the language arts curriculum and that it be treated as a valid, essential component of the literacy program (Allington, 2002; Morrow, 1986). Throughout the discussion of the last two stages of reading development, we have attempted to convey the importance of voluntary reading and to suggest ways in which it can be promoted.

BIBLIOGRAPHY

Allington, R., & Cunningham, P. (2002). *Schools that work. Where all children read and write.* Boston: Allyn and Bacon.
Morrow, L. (1986). Voluntary reading: The forgotten goal. *Educational Forum, 50,* 159–168.

5 Basic Literacy Stage

■ *Overview*

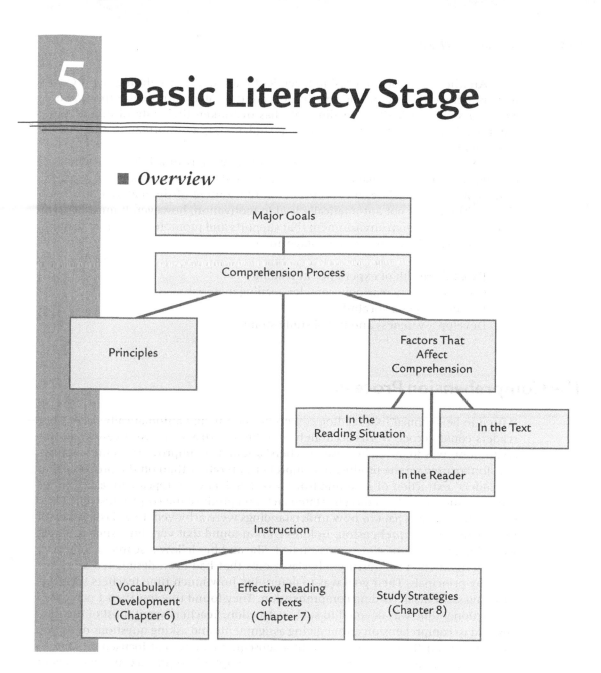

By the time students enter the basic literacy stage, they have had extensive independent reading experience and are, therefore, able to read longer and more varied texts. However, most of the materials they have read independently have related closely to their personal experiences. As they enter this stage, they encounter more and more materials that transcend their background knowledge. This has major implications for instruction.

Another result of students' independent reading practice during the previous stage is a great increase in fluency. Readers are now able to recognize thousands of words at sight. Their silent reading rate has overtaken their rate of oral reading; silent reading is used almost exclusively as students gather information and read for enjoyment.

For many children the attainment of fluency leads to a fuller enjoyment of reading. They no longer have to labor over word identification; reading is more effortless, and they are free to concentrate on the content of the material they read. Fluency alone does not automatically lead to motivation, however. It must be combined with a classroom environment that supports and promotes voluntary reading.

The goals of the basic literacy stage are to:

- Expand breadth of experience in reading
- Comprehend increasingly complex reading material
- Extend meaning vocabulary
- Develop awareness and use of study strategies
- Foster Motivation

The Comprehension Process

It used to be assumed that reading comprehension would automatically occur once readers could decode words accurately and fluently (Irwin, 1998). Even when this assumption was found to be false, teachers' attempts to improve students' comprehension focused on the product of comprehension rather than on the process—that is, readers' extraction of meaning from text. Readers were repeatedly asked to respond to questions about directly stated facts and produce the correct answers. Little or no attention was paid to how understandings were achieved. In a classic study of the teaching of comprehension, Dolores Durkin found that very little such teaching was taking place in the classrooms studied. She and her fellow researchers observed reading instruction in fourth-grade classrooms that had been designated as exemplary by principals. Their goal was to determine how much time teachers spent instructing students in reading comprehension. They found that less than 1 percent of instructional time was devoted to such instruction. Teachers spent most of the time devoted to comprehension either giving assignments and asking questions or testing comprehension (Durkin, 1978–79). In a subsequent study that focused on materials, Durkin found that basal teachers' manuals emphasized practice and assessment activities and gave few suggestions for instructional procedures (Durkin, 1984).

One might think that these conditions would have changed since 1979. However, a study conducted a decade later had equally disappointing results (Wendler, Samuels, & Moore, 1989). The researchers compared the teaching of comprehension by three groups of teachers: those who had won awards for exemplary teaching, those who had master's degrees in reading, and others. There were no significant differences among the three groups. In general, the teachers with extensive literacy training and experience were found to allocate comprehension instructional time in much the same way as the teachers did in Durkin's 1979 study, despite the considerable amount of research on comprehension that was published during the intervening decade.

A 1996 statewide survey of third- and fifth-grade teachers in Maine's elementary schools revisited the earlier studies on the teaching of comprehension (O'Donnell, 1996). The results were similarly disappointing. While most teachers embraced a view of comprehension as the construction of meaning, many still had an old paradigmatic approach to teaching comprehension as a process involving discrete linear skills. More than 60 percent of the teachers used traditional workbook exercises for fostering comprehension. Less than 5 percent designed activities for fostering meaning vocabulary as a conceptual process.

The current view of comprehension, derived from learning theory and research, is that it is an active, constructive process. Comprehension occurs when readers combine information from the text and knowledge they already possess to produce meaning. Readers do not passively take in authors' messages; rather, they assume an active role, constructing meanings from the text (Alvermann & Phelps, 2002; Vacca & Vacca, 2002).

Comprehension Principles

Three principles guide our understanding and teaching of the comprehension process:

- Prior knowledge strongly influences comprehension.
- Relating the new to the known determines what meanings will be derived.
- Organizing and classifying new information determine how well it will be understood and remembered.

While these principles are closely related and often overlap, it is important for teachers to understand the contribution of each principle to the overall comprehension process.

Prior knowledge refers to all the knowledge of the world that we have catalogued, so to speak, in our memories. It is sometimes referred to as *world knowledge* or *background knowledge* (Tierney, 1990). Frank Smith describes prior knowledge as our personal "theory of the world in our heads" (Smith, 1985). Comprehension involves constructing a relationship between what we already know about a topic and what is included in a text. What the reader brings to the text strongly influences how much will be understood. Prior knowledge provides a framework of expectations. In the words of Henry David Thoreau, "We hear and apprehend only what we already half know" (quoted in Richardson, 1993). Comprehension cannot take place when nothing is known about a topic, because there is nothing to which the reader can link the new information.

Relating the new to the known is often described by researchers as building bridges to the known (Brown & Stephens, 1995; Pearson & Johnson, 1978). To demonstrate this analogy, consider how we explain a new experience to a friend.

Our description is filled with such phrases as "Well, it was a lot like . . . , except that . . . ," "it was sort of like . . . , but it's different from that, because . . .". We try to help our friend relate the new experience we are describing to anchor points in her own store of experiences. Effective teachers always help their students make connections between what they are about to read and what they already know (Brozo & Simpson, 2003). For example, a teacher who is preparing her sixth-graders to read a chapter from their social studies text that discusses the caste system in India might help them use their knowledge of less rigid social structures in the United States as an anchor point. In doing so, she is helping them relate the new (caste system in India) to the known (social class structure in the United States). As a consequence, they can establish expectations for reading, and, as they are reading, they will be able to fill in gaps in their world knowledge with new information taken from the text.

The third principle relates to how our world knowledge is organized, classified, and stored. This aspect of comprehension can be explained by schema theory (Ruddell, Ruddell, & Singer, 1995). A *schema* is a network of related concepts; *schema theory* explains how knowledge is classified and stored in memory. Each schema represents knowledge of a concept along with associations that link it to things, events, or ideas that are related to the same category. For example, your schema for the concept of restaurant includes everything you know about or associate with all types of restaurants within your experience as well as personal memories of incidents that took place in restaurants. Schemata constantly change and grow to accommodate new information. As learning occurs, the categories within a schema are modified and new categories are established (Irwin, 1998).

Knowledge is best understood and remembered when one has a schema, or framework, within which new information can be quickly related and classified. It is virtually impossible for us to remember bits and pieces of unrelated information; only information that we can fit into a schema can be consigned to long-term memory and later retrieved.

The three comprehension principles provide the basis for our discussion of comprehension. They serve as criteria for selecting and designing effective instructional activities. Before undertaking an activity, the teacher can ask, "Will this activity draw upon students' prior knowledge? Will it help them link the new information to what they already know? Will it help them classify or organize the new information?" We will return to these questions again and again as we examine comprehension instruction in subsequent chapters.

Teachers often ask whether our discussion of the comprehension principles can be applied to English-as-a-second-language learners as well. On the whole, research supports the notion that the cognitive processes used by ESL students are substantively the same as those used by native English speakers (Fitzgerald, 1995). ESL students draw on their prior knowledge to make sense of text, use personal experience to make connections to new information, and attempt to use problem-solving strategies to "fix up" comprehension problems. They acknowledge the same metacognitive strategies as native English speakers; of course, differences in their experiences and expectations affect their comprehension of English texts. Findings from studies of ESL learners lend strong support to literacy programs for ESL students that are grounded in cognitive, interactive models of reading such as the ones described in Chapter 3.

Factors That Affect Comprehension

When comprehension is obviously taking place (in ourselves or our students), we have evidence that the three principles are working. When comprehension breaks down, however, we need to be able to determine why the principles are not operating. Several factors are simultaneously involved. These factors can be divided into three categories: those that reside in the reading situation, those that reside in the reader, and those that reside in text (Roe, Stoodt, & Burns, 1998).

Factors in the Reading Situation

Comprehension is affected by the nature of different reading situations, some of which are easy, while others are very challenging. The reading situation is influenced by the authenticity of the material, attitudes, interests, purposes, predictions, prior knowledge, and the reader's use of reading strategies (Roe, Stoodt, & Burns, 1998, p. 89). When the text makes sense and the material can be processed comfortably, readers approach the task with a purposeful stance; they have a sense of ownership and they are willing to expend the energy necessary for processing and applying the information. They are aware of their own and the teacher's expectations. The value and relevance of their reading are apparent to them, and they are actively engaged. Responding successfully to sophisticated and complex reading situations is the result of much reading experience and modeling of strategies.

Factors in the Reader

Experience. Readers filter the meanings of the texts they read through their own personal backgrounds of experience. *Experience,* as the term is used here, has a broad definition and includes not only world knowledge but also language experience, cultural experience, and literacy experience. Experience, or prior knowledge, is often considered to be the most important factor in determining the reader's comprehension (Irwin, 1998). Consider the necessity of adequate prior knowledge in understanding this message:

> There's a bear in a plain wrapper doing flip-flops around 77 and passing out green stamps.

The vocabulary in the passage is simple; readers have no problem understanding the individual words. The sentence as a whole is meaningless, however, unless the reader is familiar with CB language. To a truck driver who has a CB radio the message is "There's a policeman in an unmarked car going back and forth around mile marker 77 and giving out speeding tickets." Whether or not you understand the message in its original form depends on your experience.

Interest/Motivation. Interest in the material provides motivation to read; motivation drives comprehension, probably because the motivated reader concentrates more. We have all experienced unmotivated reading. When reading something uninteresting, we find it difficult to concentrate; our minds may wander, and we find we have "eyeballed" the text without understanding. Existing knowledge and reading strategies go unused if readers do not have the motivation to prime their activation. Strong interest in the material, on the other hand, has the opposite effect. In fact, motivated readers sometimes astonish their teachers by reading and comprehending texts that were considered too difficult for them. For example, the authors of this book have often observed adolescent students in our university reading clinic who scored at a third- or fourth-grade level on reading tests yet read highly technical motorcycle manuals with good comprehension. In such cases, motivation interacts with background experience to enhance comprehension. Comprehension is seldom a problem when students are allowed and helped to choose their own reading fare. Even when reading is required, students' motivation and comprehension will be enhanced if the teacher provides adequate background and helps students develop purposes for reading.

Fluency. The importance of helping students become fluent readers has been discussed in the previous chapter. Lack of fluency detracts from comprehension, since readers are using their cognitive energy to identify words rather than to construct meanings from larger units of text. Older students who are still transitional stage readers are often diagnosed as "having a comprehension problem." In fact, their problem is likely to be lack of fluency, which is a prerequisite for comprehension (Weaver, 1994).

Metacognition. *Metacognition* can be defined as awareness of one's own thinking and problem-solving processes. When applied to reading, the term refers to the reader's awareness and use of reading strategies. Strategic readers, for example, monitor their comprehension while reading. If they are not comprehending a passage, they become aware of this and draw on strategies to correct the situation. They may reread the text more slowly, or they may decide to continue reading looking for further clarification, or they may abandon the reading and find a more appropriate text (Baker & Brown, 1984). Metacognitive awareness contributes to comprehension and will be examined in depth later in this chapter, in connection with study strategies.

Factors in the Text

Concept Density. Different texts vary in the number and type of concepts presented. Reading material is said to be *concept-dense* when it contains many concepts in a short amount of text, especially if these concepts transcend the reader's personal experience. Expository materials are generally more concept dense than are narrative materials. Science textbooks tend to be most concept dense of all, since they contain many new and abstract concepts. This text factor interacts closely with

Students in the basic literacy stage learn to use content texts.

one of the factors in the reader: background experience. When a reader who lacks relevant prior knowledge encounters a concept-dense text, a comprehension problem is virtually inevitable.

Organization. Most texts fall into one of two basic categories: narrative or expository. Each has a consistent structure that, if known to the reader, makes the text more predictable. These two structures are quite different, however. Narrative texts are organized according to a sequence of events and follow a "story grammar," as described in Chapter 1. Expository texts are organized according to the relationships of the information or ideas to be presented. The story grammar of well-written narratives is very consistent. There are many variations within the elements of the story, but the overall pattern remains constant. This is not true of expository texts, which vary considerably in both format and structure of content. For this reason, organization is a more significant factor in influencing comprehension of expository materials than of narrative materials.

Content area texts are particularly variable in terms of organization. Some texts are "reader friendly." They are organized in ways that help the reader see the relationship among the ideas presented. The chapters provide a logical flow of ideas. Texts that are not reader friendly follow an obscure organizational pattern, making it difficult for the reader to see relationships between ideas discussed (Armbruster, 1984). In fact, some texts appear to be random collections of information, organized loosely by topics, but with no attention given to relationships. Compare these two chapter formats from different social studies textbooks:

EXAMPLE 1: *Problems of the New Government*

A. Basic Problems
B. Economic Problems
   1. Lack of Money
   2. Economic Depression
C. Political Problems
   1. Disagreements among the States
   2. Threats from Foreign Governments
D. Assembling the Constitutional Convention

EXAMPLE 2: *Growing Cities and Industrialization*

■ First Cities
■ More Cities
■ Industrial Growth and Immigration
   New Americans
   Labor Unions
   Eugene Debs
   Prosperity Grows
■ Modern Cities
■ Industrial and Technological Growth
   New Inventions
   New Technology

Example 1 suggests a logical sequence of examples that have an obvious relationship to the title of the chapter. This enhances the reader's ability to connect the ideas and to recognize that the last section is a culmination, or logical conclusion, of the points discussed earlier in the chapter. Example 2, in contrast, does not lead the reader through a logical sequence. Relationships among the title and the subtopics are not apparent.

Other organizational factors contribute to the "friendliness" of the text, as well. Its physical layout can be more or less helpful to the reader. Introductions, relevant visual aids (maps, graphs, illustrations), boldfaced topic headers, and summary statements are examples of features that contribute to the reader's understanding. The visual presentation can also affect the reader. Generous margins, clear print, and highlighting of major points give the reader the impression that this is a manageable text.

While overall organization, sometimes referred to as *global* or *macro organization*, affects the reader's comprehension, organization at the paragraph level is also important (Armbruster & Anderson, 1981). There are five structures for paragraph organization that are commonly used by writers of expository texts: simple listing, temporal sequence, cause/effect, comparison/contrast, or problem/solution. Helping students achieve awareness of such patterns contributes to their comprehension and is discussed in Chapter 7.

Style. In the context of text, *style* refers to the sentence patterns and word choices used by the writer. The author's style interacts with the reader's previous literacy experiences to affect comprehension. For example, ninth-graders are frequently required to read *David Copperfield*. The majority of them find this reading difficult to the point of being painful, mostly because Dickens's writing style is so unfamiliar to them. A student who has had experience with the syntax and vocabulary of the Dickensian period will understand and enjoy far more of the novel.

Similarly, expository texts are often written in a style that is unfamiliar and therefore confusing to students. Common contributors to comprehension difficulties are use of unexplained technical terms, insufficient elaboration and explanation, and complicated syntax. Authors who are aware of readers' needs assist them by providing numerous context clues and definitions of terms, by elaborating on key concepts and ideas, and by using as clear and direct a style as possible.

Readability. The traditional use of the term *readability* refers to the difficulty of a piece of material, based on two variables: length of sentences and difficulty of vocabulary, usually measured by the number of syllables in words. This definition of readability provides the basis for the design and use of readability formulas, which are widely used by publishers and school personnel to assess the difficulty of student texts. While this notion of readability has been widely criticized because it captures only some of the syntactic variables necessary for comprehension, it does provide a useful starting point for estimating the difficulty of reading materials. Several formulas are currently available to teachers. The *Fry Readability Formula* is one of the most popular and easy to use. This formula determines readability by randomly selecting three 100-word passages from a text, counting the number of sentences and syllables in each passage, and averaging these counts. The next step is to locate the average number of sentences on the vertical axis and the average number of syllables on the horizontal axis. The point on the graph where these two lines intersect indicates the approximate readability, expressed as a grade-level equivalency. The graph, accompanied by directions for its use, is reproduced in Figure 5.1.

The limits of the accuracy and usefulness of readability formulas are readily apparent. True readability is a composite of all the elements within a given text that affect the success readers have in constructing meaning from it. Current literature has largely replaced the term *readability* with *processability,* to reflect this broader view. All the comprehension factors discussed so far influence how well readers process texts. The most glaring weakness of mechanical readability formulas, perhaps, is their failure to take into account the concept density of the material and the experiential background of the reader. These essential factors cannot be reduced to numbers in a formula; they can only be determined by a teacher who is familiar with the text and with the backgrounds of the students who are expected to read it.

Another way to apply readability formulas is as a guide for writing or rewriting materials to ensure that they will be easy for students to read. (Most word processing programs include a feature for estimating technical readability.) Great caution must be exercised when formulas are used for this purpose. Simply shortening sentences and replacing multisyllabic words with more common, "easier" words do not necessarily make a passage easier to comprehend. In fact, it may make it more

FIGURE 5.1   *Graph and Directions for Estimating Readability—Extended*

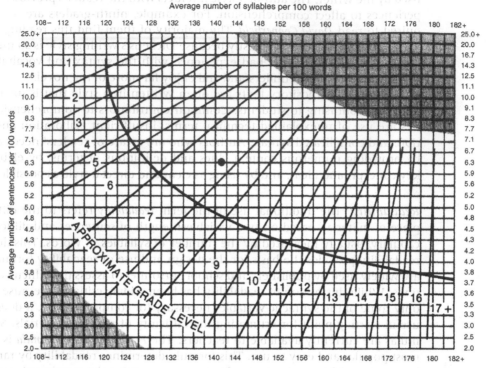

Average number of syllables per 100 words

Expanded Directions for Working Readability Graph

1. Randomly select three (3) sample passages and count out exactly 100 words each, beginning with the beginning of a sentence. Do count proper nouns, initializations, and numerals.
2. For each passage, count the number of sentences in the 100 words, estimating length of the fraction of the last sentence to the nearest one-tenth.
3. Count the total number of syllables in the 100-word passage. If you don't have a hand counter available, an easy way is to simply put a mark above every syllable over one in each word, then when you get to the end of the passage, count the number of marks and add 100. Small calculators can also be used as counters by pushing numeral 1, then pushing the + sign for each word or syllable.
4. On the graph enter the *average* sentence length and *average* number of syllables; plot dot where the two lines intersect. Area where dot is plotted will give you the approximate grade level.
5. If a great deal of variability is found in the syllable count or sentence count, putting more samples into the average is desirable.
6. A word is defined as a group of symbols with a space on either side; thus, *1945* is one word.
7. A syllable is defined as a phonetic syllable. Generally, there are as many syllables as vowel sounds. For example, *stopped* is one syllable and *wanted* is two syllables. When counting syllables for numerals and initializations, count one syllable for each symbol. For example, *1945* is four syllables.

Source: Edward Fry, Rutgers University Reading Center, New Brunswick, NJ 08904.

Note: This "extended graph" does not outmode or render the earlier (1968) version inoperative or inaccurate; it is an extension. (Reproduction permitted—no copyright.)

difficult. Short, simple sentences do not usually convey relationships between ideas or events as well as longer sentences do. Short, commonly used words often do not have the preciseness of meaning that longer or less common words convey. Simplification may result in loss of meaning. For example, compare the following original passage with its rewritten counterpart:

> Whenever the moon was full and the meteors streaked across the night sky, the witches gathered on the mountain side to work their magic.
> The moon was full. Shooting stars fell through the sky. The witches got together on the hill. They made magic.

The rewritten version may be technically easier to read, but it lacks the full meaning and imagery of the original. Awareness of these potential pitfalls enables writers to create simplified texts without sacrificing meaning.

Although it is useful for the teacher to examine each of the comprehension factors in the reader and in the text, they overlap and interact in real reading situations. If a student is having difficulty understanding a text, there is usually more than one factor involved. For example, a sixth-grader who is reading a technical description in a science text of how a steam engine works may be hampered initially by lack of prior knowledge. If, furthermore, the text is poorly organized and full of highly technical diagrams, the student's interest and motivation to read the material diminish in the face of these obstacles.

Summary

Awareness of comprehension factors enables the teacher to anticipate difficulties students are likely to have in understanding a given text and to plan instruction accordingly. This knowledge is also helpful in identifying the sources of difficulties readers encounter that were not anticipated by the teacher.

The three comprehension principles and the factors in the reading situation, reader, and text that influence comprehension must be constantly considered while planning and implementing instructional programs. The teacher must often provide direct instruction in comprehension strategies and processes. Sound comprehension instruction should encompass three major areas: concept building/vocabulary development, effective reading of texts, and study strategies. The next three chapters will deal with each of these topics in turn.

BIBLIOGRAPHY

Allington, R., & Cunningham, P. (2002). *Schools that work. Where all children read and write.* Boston: Allyn and Bacon.

Alvermann, D. E., & Phelps, S. F. (2002). *Content reading and literacy.* Boston: Allyn and Bacon.

Anderson, R. C., Heibert, E., Scott, J., Wilkinson, I. (Eds.). (1985). *Becoming a nation of readers.* Washington, DC: National Institute of Education.

Armbruster, B. B. (1984). The problem of inconsiderate text. In G. Duffy, L. Roehler, & J. Mason (Eds.), *Comprehensive instruction perspectives and suggestions.* New York: Longman.

Armbruster, B. B., & Anderson, T. (1981). *Content area textbooks.* (Reading Education Rep. No. 23). Urbana, IL: University of Illinois Center for the Study of Reading.

Baker, L. and Brown, A. (1984). *Cognitive monitoring in reading.* In J. Flood (Ed.), *Understanding Reading* (pp. 21–44). Newark, DE: International Reading Asociation.

Brown, A. L., & Stephens, E. (1995). *Teaching young adolescent literature.* Belmont, CA: Wadworth.

Brozo, W. G., & Simpson, M. L. (2003). *Readers, teachers, learners: Expanding literacy across the content areas.* Upper Saddle River, NJ: Merrill Prentice Hall.

Durkin, D. (1978–79). What classroom observations reveal about reading comprehension instruction. *Reading Research Quarterly, 14*(2), 123–126.

Durkin, D. (1984). Do basal manuals teach reading comprehension? In R. C. Anderson, N. Osborne, and R. Tierney (Eds.). *Learning to read in American schools: Basal readers and content texts.* Hillsdale, NJ: Erlbaum.

Fitzgerald, J. (1995). English-as-a-second-language learners' cognitive reading processes: A review of research. *Review of Education Research, 65,* 145–190.

Irwin, J. (1998). *Reading and the middle school student* (2nd edition). Boston: Allyn and Bacon.

O'Donnell, M. P. (1996). *A survey of reading instruction in Maine's elementary schools.* Gorham: University of Southern Maine, College of Education Research Report.

Pearson, P. D., & Johnson, D. D. (1978). *Teaching reading comprehension.* New York: Holt, Rinehart & Winston.

Roe, B. D., Stoodt, B. D., & Burns, P. C. (1998). *Secondary school literacy instruction: The content areas* (6th ed.). Boston: Houghton Mifflin Company.

Ruddell, R., Ruddell, M., & Singer, H. (1995). *Theoretical models and processes of reading* (4th ed.). Newark, DE: International Reading Association.

Searfoss, L. and Readance, J. (1994). *Helping children learn to read.* Boston: Allyn and Bacon.

Smith, F. (1985). *Reading without nonsense.* New York: Teachers College Press.

Tierney, R. (1990). Redefining reading comprehension. *Educational Leadership 47,* 37–42.

Vacca, R. T., & Vacca, J. A. (2002). *Content area reading* (7th ed.). Boston: Allyn and Bacon.

Weaver, C. (1994). *Reading process and practice* (2nd ed.). Portsmouth, NH: Heinemann.

Wendler, D., Samuels, S. J., and Moore, V. K. (1989). Comprehension instruction of award-winning teachers, teachers with masters' degrees, and other teachers. *Reading Research Quarterly, 24*(4), 382–401.

6 Basic Literacy Stage

Vocabulary Development

■ *Overview*

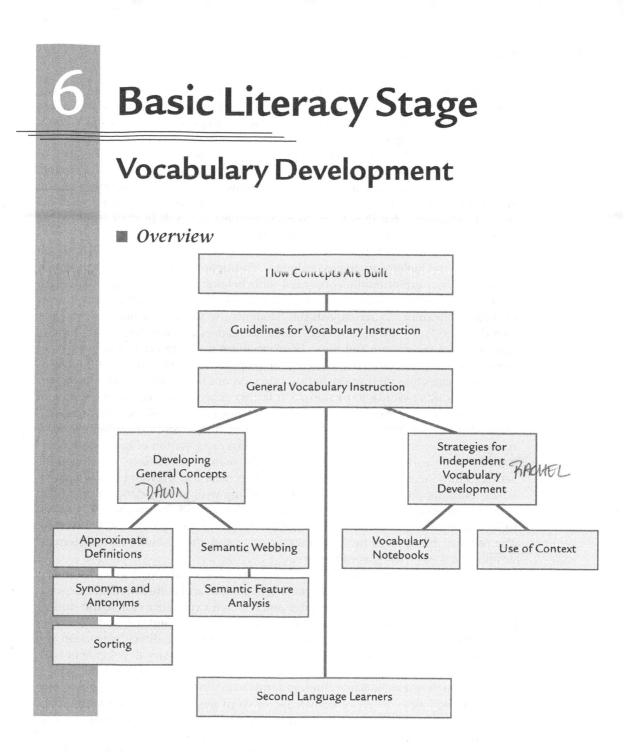

The relationship between knowledge of word meanings and comprehension has been well established (Nagy & Scott, 2000). Words are used to represent concepts. Increasing awareness of the influence of prior knowledge, or conceptual background, on comprehension has underscored the importance of vocabulary development, since building vocabulary is synonymous with building concepts. Acquiring a vocabulary involves much more than looking words up in the dictionary and memorizing meanings. Words are labels for concepts that can be acquired only through repeated exposure in a variety of meaningful contexts.

A fourth-grader who was referred to the university reading clinic because of poor comprehension described his problem as follows: "I don't have any trouble with the sentences. It's the *words* that get in my way." This is actually rather typical of students who are entering the basic literacy stage, for it is at this point in their literacy development that they begin to encounter many words in their reading that are not in their listening/speaking vocabularies.

It is important for teachers to understand the difference between building *sight* vocabulary and building *meaning* vocabulary. Throughout the initial and transitional stages, teachers are primarily concerned with helping students enlarge their sight vocabularies, that is, to recognize the printed forms of words that are already known to them in meaning. To accomplish this, students use word identification strategies (see Chapter 3). At the basic literacy stage, as readers progress into more difficult material they meet more and more words that are not only unknown to them in printed form but are also not in their listening/speaking vocabularies. Word identification strategies lose their utility because they do not help readers deal with meanings of unfamiliar words. For example, a fourth-grader who encounters the word *ecology* in the science text may use graphophonemic cues to work out the pronunciation of the word. This will not suffice, however, if the word's meaning is not already known or revealed through the context. An examination of basal readers designed for fourth- and fifth-graders reveals many "vocabulary development" activities that focus on pronunciation rather than meaning. Breaking words into syllables, marking prefixes and suffixes, and working with pronunciation keys in dictionaries are examples of such activities. An awareness of the distinction between sight and meaning vocabulary is important for planning appropriate instruction. The primary emphasis at the basic literacy stage and after should be on systematic development of meaning vocabulary.

What does it mean to "know" a word? There are varying degrees of understanding of word meanings. Word learning is gradual and cumulative and depends heavily on experience. Prior knowledge and relevant experience enable the student to learn some new words from context; when words go beyond the student's experience, they will be difficult to learn from context, and more direct instruction will be needed (Nagy & Herman, 1987). For this reason, vocabulary development is an area that needs special emphasis for students whose first language is not English.

Although researchers use different terms to describe word learning, they commonly identify three levels of knowledge of word meanings. The most superficial level is *associative,* a general sense of a word's meaning based on association with related words. Memorizing definitions of words often results in this superficial level of word knowledge. At the second level, *comprehension,* the reader understands the meaning of the word when it is read in context; however, she may not be able to use the word appropriately in speaking or writing. The most sophisticated level of understanding is *generative.* The student can produce and use the new word in novel contexts, in other words, in speaking and writing (Stahl, 1986).

A slightly different way of describing degrees of word ownership refers to *definitional knowledge* and *conceptual knowledge*. Definitions alone provide only superficial (associative) and limited understanding. Faced with many new words to teach, teachers often resort to assigning their students familiar definition-based activities: looking up words in glossaries and dictionaries, defining and memorizing the words, and attempting to use them in sentences. These activities will not improve reading comprehension or result in word ownership because they do not develop conceptual knowledge (Nagy, 1988; Vacca & Vacca, 2002).

How Conceptual Knowledge Is Acquired

Concepts are acquired naturally and without much conscious thought as we act on and interact with our environment. Concepts are best learned through direct, purposeful experience. A *concept* is a mental image that represents anything that can be grouped together by common features. One way to think of a concept is as an abstraction; it pulls together many facts. It organizes them and even makes sense of them. We would be overwhelmed by the complexity of our world if we responded to each object or event as a separate and distinct thing (Vacca & Vacca, 2002).

An understanding of how concepts are acquired is essential for the effective teaching of vocabulary. *Concept attainment* can be loosely defined as the ability to categorize, and thereby order, experiences. *Concept acquisition* involves comparing, contrasting, perceiving relationships of increasing complexity, sorting, and classifying. A construct for describing this process was developed by O'Donnell (2002) to help teachers recognize how learners come to understand new concepts. This knowledge enables teachers to better match instruction to students' levels of understanding. As you study the construct, do not be overly concerned with the labels and definitions of the various levels; rather, try to gain an appreciation of the developmental progression described.

The acquisition of a concept involves passage through four levels of understanding. The first of these is the *perceptual* level, which involves general awareness or literal knowledge. At this level, basic characteristics of things and ideas are recognized on the basis of very limited experience. Recognition without understanding is characteristic of this level. For example, a student might first encounter the term *mammal* in a sentence in a science book: "The rabbit, like other mammals, takes care of its young." On the basis of this sentence, the reader would probably assume that a mammal is an animal but would not be aware of the attributes that distinguish mammals from nonmammals.

The next level is called the *contextual* level because the learner encounters the new concept in different contexts or situations and, as a result, greatly expands awareness of its attributes. This leads to comparisons, or noting similarities and differences between the new concept and concepts that are already known. To continue with the example of *mammal*, the teacher might show the children pictures of many familiar mammals as well as pictures of animals that are not mammals (reptiles, for example) and discuss the similarities and differences. Through this and other experiences, children would develop awareness of the attributes of mammals.

The third, or *conceptual* level, is marked by the ability to accurately and consistently identify examples of the concept. The learner is able to recognize the essential attributes that define the concept. Consequently, the learner cannot be confused. He distinguishes examples of the concept from nonexamples and explains his rationale. This is referred to as *sorting,* or "downward" classification. The concept is fully formed. At this level, children could describe the essential features of mammals and could select from a mixed assortment all the animals that belong to the category *mammal.*

At the *classification* level, the learner is able to assign the new concept to a larger category, which includes other concepts as well. The process involves recognizing similarities among concepts and, on this basis, creating broader classes. This is sometimes referred to as "upward" classification. Children who have reached this level of understanding of the concept *mammal* would recognize that although mammals form a unique class, they have certain commonalities with nonmammals and are part of larger classes, such as animals and living things. Although the children may have started out at the perceptual level with a general awareness of *animal,* their understanding of this term is greatly refined as a result of their numerous experiences with classes of animals. No longer is *animal* simply a general label. It now reflects an understanding of the similarities and differences among the many kinds of animals. With further experience, learners will come to recognize even more sophisticated relationships, such as the similarity between animals and plants, both of which are living organisms.

Concepts vary a great deal in abstractness. Regardless of the complexity of the concept, learners of all ages pass through the same levels of understanding as a new concept develops. This is not a strictly linear process, however. The learner may explore more than one level at a time as new relationships are detected. For example, children's concepts of *animal* are being refined as they learn the attributes that distinguish mammals from reptiles.

Another example of the recursive (nonlinear) nature of concept attainment can be taken from literacy education. Consider a preservice teacher's understanding of the term *whole-language.* Initially, this is often vaguely (and often incorrectly) conceived of as a method of teaching reading through the use of "big books," whole-class instruction, and lack of instruction. A possible breakdown of the development of an accurate concept of whole language includes the following:

■ *Perceptual:* A method of teaching reading
■ *Contextual:* Various approaches (shared reading, language experience approach, writing process, and literature-based instruction) may be included in a whole-language program.
■ *Conceptual:* All whole-language instruction embraces certain principles—use of authentic purposes for reading and writing, instruction based on characteristics of language learning (whole to part, problem solving, immersion), teaching of skills in context, and use of predictable, meaningful materials.
■ *Classification:* A manifestation of constructivist theory that has its origin in cognitive psychology. Whole-language, meaning-based instruction, experiential learning discovery approaches to math, and social studies as inquiry process all come from this common theoretical, philosophical base.

A well-developed concept of whole-language will eventually include all of these component understandings; however, teachers will not necessarily experience them in the same sequence. One teacher, for example, may begin by learning about the differences between behavioral and cognitive psychology and where whole-language fits in this larger picture. This might be followed by understandings at either the contextual or the conceptual level until all the component parts are understood and related. Others may learn these various components in a different sequence. Regardless of the order in which the information is acquired, a full understanding of the concept will result in operational knowledge on which appropriate instructional decisions can be based. Teachers will easily be able, for example, to incorporate phonics appropriately or to select the best possible reading instruction that contributes to children's literacy development.

Let us examine the application of this process to a concept that basic literacy stage students would be likely to encounter: *senator*. At the perceptual level, students might know only that a senator has something to do with the government. At the contextual level, students would become aware of the qualifications and functions of senators, the differences between senators and other elected officials (representatives, governors), and their relationships with political parties, among other things. Although their awareness of the concept would be expanding, students at this level might still harbor many misconceptions and confuse many of the attributes of senators with those of other elected officials. Students have reached the conceptual level when they no longer have difficulty distinguishing between senators and nonsenators. At the classification level, the senators' place in the larger context of representative government would be understood. Senators would be seen as members of broader classes, such as politicians, elected officials, and people with power.

So far, we have focused on the levels one progresses through in acquiring a new concept. The teacher's task is to help students advance from one level to the next. This can best be accomplished if the teacher is aware of the cognitive processes that characterize each level. For example, the cognitive processes associated with the perceptual level, which involves first encounters with concepts, are perception and observation; therefore, experiences that are as direct as possible would be the most appropriate. Examples of activities include observing or conducting an experiment, examining a model, or viewing a videotape. The cognitive processes that characterize the contextual level are making associations and comparing. Activities that lead students to engage in these processes include brainstorming and noting similarities and differences. At the conceptual level, students must distinguish essential attributes and classify according to given categories. Sorting activities, excluding nonexamples, and constructing definitions for concepts are appropriate conceptual-level activities. The classification level requires the most creative, abstract modes of thinking. The cognitive processes and activities for this level involve the recognition of similarities among concepts and the grouping together of such concepts, forming broader categories. Students need opportunities to create new categories according to their own unique perceptions of similarities among concepts. Table 6.1 summarizes essential characteristics and types of instructional activity at each level of concept attainment.

Descriptions of the levels of concept attainment often strike teachers as difficult and obscure. They ask, "How is this information going to be useful to me?"

TABLE 6.1   *Concept Attainment Activities*

I. Perceptual Stage

- Memorizing facts
- Definitions
- Literal awareness
- Copying/tracing

II. Contextual/Attribute Stage

- Brainstorming attributes
- Comparing and contrasting
- Vocabulary notebooks
- Cloze activities
- Word maps
- Venn diagrams

III. Concept Attainment Stage

- Classifies according to differences
- Semantic mapping
- Inclusion and exclusion activities
- Semantic feature analysis
- Constructs new and different applications

IV. Categorization Stage

- Classifies according to similarities among concepts
- Creates networks of related concepts
- Venerates analogies

Virtually all learning involves attainment of new concepts and integration of these concepts with an existing body of knowledge. Although in this text concept attainment has been treated in the context of teaching vocabulary, in reality it pervades the entire curriculum. The teacher who understands this process is better able to orchestrate it. Awareness of the levels of concept attainment and the accompanying cognitive processes enables the teacher to design appropriate, effective instructional activities in all content areas.

In response to the question of usefulness, we are not suggesting that teachers get bogged down in terminology or in time-consuming analyses of activities. Rather, teachers need to develop a sense of the overall process of concept attainment and an awareness of the quality and relevance of activities they have their students engage in. Research shows that in many classrooms too much time is devoted to perceptual-level activities. Sensitivity to the process of concept attainment can help teachers change this situation and make thinkers out of their students.

Understanding the process of concept attainment, or how we acquire knowledge of new words, helps us realize why traditional approaches to vocabulary development are relatively ineffective. Most of us remember how we were expected to learn new words in school. We were assigned a list of unrelated words each week. We were expected to look up and memorize their definitions, use them in sentences, and prove mastery by regurgitating the definitions on a test. Unfortunately, we often did not understand the words well enough to use them, and we forgot them quickly. This is not surprising, in view of the principles of comprehension. The words in the lists were not related to our prior knowledge, and they were not grouped or classified in any way. We were unable to make connections, to relate the words to any existing schema. Newer approaches to teaching vocabulary avoid these pitfalls.

Guidelines for Vocabulary Instruction

A substantial amount of research has indicated several guidelines that are useful for effective vocabulary instruction.

■ *The teacher demonstrates and stimulates interest in word meanings and enthusiasm for vocabulary study.* Most of us can remember our disinterest and boredom in the face of dictionary drills in the upper elementary grades. The purpose of many of these was to learn how to use the dictionary, not to learn meanings of words we were curious about. Although it is certainly important to know how to use the dictionary, children must have a reason for using it. The teacher's attitude toward words and their meanings is extremely important. In fact, many researchers claim that the curiosity and excitement about words generated by the teacher are the most influential factors in improving students' vocabulary (Anderson & Nagy, 1993; Blachowicz & Fisher, 2000). Effective teachers share interesting new words with students, draw students' attention to their special features, and encourage experimentation with new words.

■ *In order for students to learn new words, they must have experiences from which concepts can be derived.* In general, the less background and experience students have in relation to a concept, the more they will need direct experiences in building the concept. Abstract, verbal experiences alone are unlikely to be sufficient for elaborated knowledge of complex concepts.

■ *Only key words from target passages should be taught.* Words are not selected simply because they are unusual or obscure. They are words that students need to know because they are essential for understanding the passage (Roe, Stoodt, & Burns, 1998). Words likely to be encountered repeatedly in different reading materials are also good choices for direct instruction.

■ *Words must be taught thoroughly and used by students in many different ways.* Looking up a definition and placing the word in a sentence are not sufficient. Students need frequent and varied encounters with selected words to learn them well. It is very important for students to experience the rich meanings underlying words by

examples

offering their own explanations of how words can be used in different situations or in combination with other ideas (Nagy & Scott, 2000). Active engagement promotes interest and strengthens associations for new concepts. A number of activities and strategies for accomplishing this will be discussed later in the chapter.

▪ *Words should be taught in semantically and topically related groups.* Related concepts should be taught together so that students' vocabulary and background knowledge will improve simultaneously (Kibby, 1995). Moreover, new words should be associated with known words that are topically related. This guideline reflects the importance of using prior knowledge and linking the new to the known—basic principles of comprehension.

▪ *The number of words taught should be limited.* Only a limited number of concepts can be thoroughly examined and assimilated in a short time. Basic literacy stage students will encounter many new words each week in the various subject areas they study. Many of these words will be understood only superficially or generally, used to comprehend the material at hand but not understood in depth or "worked on" to the extent that students can use them in new contexts. The teacher should select a few words for students to learn in much greater depth. These core words will be the focus of concept-building activities planned by the teacher.

▪ *Students should be given instruction that will help them become more effective independent word learners.* They can learn, for example, to make effective use of context, identify familiar parts in new words and relate them to parts of known words, and use reference sources such as glossaries and dictionaries. Teaching students individual word meanings only helps them learn and use these particular words. However, if they learn independent strategies for dealing with new words, they will be able to expand their vocabularies far more rapidly (Nagy, Herman, & Anderson, 1987).

▪ *Students should have daily opportunities for wide, independent reading.* Research has shown that a great deal of incidental learning of vocabulary takes place in the context of extensive independent reading (Anderson, 1996). If we consider that students learn to read an estimated 3,000 to 4,000 words each year, it becomes apparent that many of the words students learn cannot be directly taught (Graves et al., 2001). In fact, vocabulary instruction orchestrated solely by the teacher has significant limitations. Teaching the meanings of new words one at a time cannot possibly result in the vocabulary growth necessary for continued literacy development. In light of the limitations of teacher-directed vocabulary instruction, a primary goal for any vocabulary development program must be to foster independent word learning through a large volume of reading (Allington, 2001; Anderson, 1996; Nagy & Herman, 1987).

General Vocabulary Instruction

Our discussion of vocabulary development so far has included theories about vocabulary acquisition, the nature and the process of concept attainment, and guidelines for promoting vocabulary growth. The examples we have used (*mammal, senator, whole-language*) to illustrate how concepts are acquired might be called *specialized vocabulary*. They represent the kinds of new words/concepts that are encountered and taught in specialized areas of the curriculum. We now turn our attention to the kind of vocabulary instruction that occurs on a day-to-day basis within the context of language arts. The kinds of new words generally encountered in reading novels, newspapers, and magazines are words for which the learner already has an experiential base. Synonyms are known. For example, when a fifth-grader comes across an unfamiliar word and asks his teacher, "What does 'ecstatic' mean?" the teacher can explain easily, since the student knows what "very happy" means. (Contrast this with trying to explain *senator*.) The process of concept attainment is reflected in the development of *general* as well as technical vocabulary; the difference is that students have more related prior knowledge to draw on when learning general vocabulary. Therefore, the acquisition of general vocabulary can occur at a faster pace.

General vocabulary instruction has two main components. First, teachers must know how to direct and facilitate students' learning of new words and concepts, both in group situations and individually. Second, the teacher must help students acquire strategies for independent vocabulary learning. We will treat each of these in turn.

Developing General Concepts and Word Meanings

The activities used to help students develop their general vocabulary parallel the levels of concept attainment. Students' initial encounters with a new word constitute the perceptual level, or the beginning point for learning the word's meaning. Activities for word study usually begin at the contextual level and involve building many associations for the word. The teacher might help students generate definitions, brainstorm associations, and work with synonyms and antonyms.

Students learn new concepts best through a variety of experiences.

Approximate Definitions

The teacher can help students create an approximate definition in many ways. Suppose the new word is *irate*. The teacher might use the word in a sentence ("I was *irate* the third time you forgot your homework."), giving clues as to its meaning, and ask students to speculate on what it means. The students can easily conclude, from the context, that *irate* probably means angry or upset. The teacher might provide other sentences to help them confirm their hypothesis.

Another way teachers sometimes introduce new words is to dramatize them. After introducing the word *irate* by writing it on the board and pronouncing it, the teacher might say, "Now I am going to act *irate*," whereupon she slams a book on the desk, stamps her foot, and shouts. "I have *never* been more angry in my whole life!" Students are invited to describe their interpretation of the word. This type of vocabulary introduction has a real impact on students, making it likely that they will remember both the word and the performance!

Another activity that would help students relate the new word to their own personal experiences is brainstorming. For example, the teacher might ask students to describe many situations that would make them irate. These could be recorded and discussed. The discussion would be likely to lead naturally into work with synonyms.

Synonyms and Antonyms

Synonyms are words that have very similar meanings; however, no two words have exactly the same connotations. Nuances in meaning are what make word study interesting. *Irate* does not mean exactly the same thing as *angry*. *Mad, annoyed, upset,* and *furious* are related in meaning to *angry* and *irate*, but each has its special connotation. Once students have a grasp of the meanings of various related words, they can be asked to try to arrange them in order of intensity (see Figure 6.1). This activity requires that students compare word meanings and become aware of differences among them. The dictionary may appropriately be used to resolve students' disagreements about such differences.

Antonyms are words that have opposite meanings. Most words that are high in meaning (nouns, verbs, adjectives, adverbs) have synonyms; not all these words have antonyms, however. An antonym does not merely represent a difference; it represents an exact opposite meaning. However, designing activities using antonyms is complicated by the fact that there are various kinds of opposition. For example, *alive* and *dead, fast* and *slow, build* and *raze,* and *top* and *bottom* are not opposite in exactly the same way; however, they are all pairs of antonyms (Pearson & Johnson, 1978). In a typical activity on antonyms, the teacher gives students sentences with a key word underlined and asks them to replace that word with its antonym to change the meaning of the sentence. If students have worked with the words *lenient, hinder,* and *raze,* the teacher might be give them the following sentences:

His parents are very *strict*.

The people tried to *help* each other.

This machine can be used to *build* large houses.

FIGURE 6.1 *Words Ranked by Intensity*

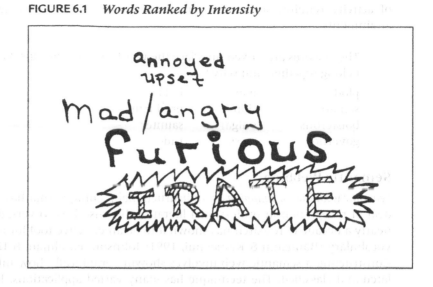

The purpose of the activities described so far is to help students develop many associations for new words so that they acquire a sense of their appropriate use. We will now turn to conceptual- and classification-level activities that involve categorizing new words and concepts in various ways. Being able to group or classify new words requires considerable understanding of the new concepts involved and the relationships among them.

Sorting Activities

Sorting activities require students to assign items to given categories based on their similarities and differences. For example:

Write these headings: Ways of Moving, Ways of Eating, Ways of Communicating. Then write the following words under the appropriate heading:

amble	preach	soar
mutter	devour	nibble
gnaw	leap	gesticulate

In doing this activity, students must decide which words to include in each category. An alternative activity requires *exclusion* of items that do not belong in a category.

Cross out the word that does not belong with the others:

lake	ocean	pond	desert
island	peninsula	ocean	continent

Note that inclusion and exclusion activities require students to have already developed approximate definitions of the words used. A still more sophisticated type of activity requires students to create categories (classification level of concept attainment).

> These words are mixed up. Place the words in three groups. Which ones belong together, and why?
>
> | plod | mayor | hobble |
> |------|-------|--------|
> | senator | skip | president |
> | boisterous | vulgar | saunter |
> | governor | crass | rude |

Semantic Webbing

Semantic webbing, or *mapping*, is an instructional technique that has received a great deal of recognition in professional literature because it is so versatile and because nearly a decade of research has shown it to be an effective tool for introducing new vocabulary (Baumann & Kameenui, 1991; Johnson, Pittelman, & Heimlich, 1986). Constructing a semantic web involves showing graphically how information is related and classified. The technique has many varied applications. It is used before reading to build background knowledge and before writing to organize the piece; it is also used after reading to organize new information, and it is used in connection with vocabulary development. Regardless of the application, semantic webbing is effective because it acknowledges the three basic principles of comprehension (using prior knowledge, linking the new to the known, and classifying information) and also incorporates the process of concept attainment.

The first step in constructing a semantic web is to brainstorm on the designated topic. Students are encouraged to volunteer anything they can think of that relates to the topic. The teacher records all contributions on the board. Figure 6.2 shows the result of a brainstorming session by a group of fourth-graders who began with the word *tree*. The first step in semantic webbing parallels the contextual level of concept attainment. As they brainstorm, students are generating a collection of attributes and examples of the concept. Because this is done in a group, children add to each other's pool of information about the topic. For example, many fourth-

FIGURE 6.2   *Brainstorming Results for* **Tree**

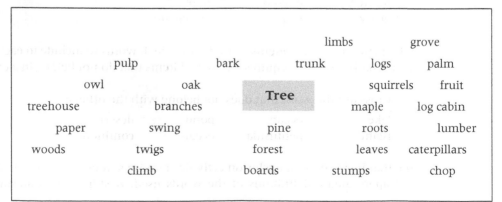

graders had never heard of the word *grove*. The student who suggested that word explained to the others what it meant.

The next step involves grouping the associations into categories. This can be accomplished in two ways. The teacher may supply the categories and ask students to sort items accordingly by asking "Which of these are kinds of trees? Which are parts of trees?" This process would be characteristic of the conceptual level of concept attainment since it involves downward classification. An alternative would be to have students generate the categories. The teacher might ask, "Which of these shall we group together? Why?" In this instance, students are creating categories, an action that reflects level four (the classification level) of concept attainment. They are engaging in upward classification.

The teacher whose class was working with *tree* decided to specify the categories and have students classify the items accordingly. The result was the semantic web shown in Figure 6.3. Even though the teacher supplied the categories, there was lively debate over some of the items. Some children thought *fruit* names a type of tree, while others maintained that *fruit* is a product. Since both were correct, *fruit* was listed in both categories. Some students questioned the placement of *stumps*. Stumps are parts of trees, but not living parts. They are also in a sense products, but not products useful to people. One student suggested creating an additional category containing *stumps, chop, logs,* and *log cabin*. Others came up with other alternative groupings. The discussions that accompany the creation of the semantic web tend to be lively and enlightening, as students sharpen their awareness of the relationships between items and become aware of new alternatives.

FIGURE 6.3   *Semantic Web for* **Tree**

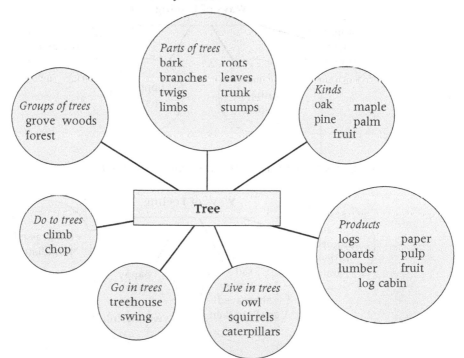

The example of semantic webbing for *tree* was not designed to introduce new vocabulary. Rather, it was used to elaborate students' knowledge of a familiar concept and give them experience with the classification process. After children have made several webs of known concepts, the teacher can use the technique as an effective vehicle for vocabulary development. This works best if the teacher selects several vocabulary words that are clearly related. For example, a sixth-grade teacher decided to introduce four words that reflect emotion: *irate, bereaved, ecstatic,* and *humiliated.* He began by giving the group a topic, Ways of Feeling, and asking them to supply examples. They grouped the examples as shown in Figure 6.4. He then put the new words on the board and asked the students whether they knew the meanings of any of them. One student was familiar with *humiliated.* After she described the word, the group decided it belonged in the same category as *embarrassed.* The other three words were unknown to all the students in the group. The teacher made up sentences using the words—for example, "I was *irate* when I got my car back from the garage and it still wouldn't start." Students easily figured out from the contexts which group each word belonged in (see Figure 6.5).

The teacher continued the discussion by helping the students compare the new words with the more familiar words in each group, thus sharpening their understanding of the precise meanings of the words. Additional exercises helped to accomplish this. For example, the students were asked to examine the words in the happiness category and to arrange them in order, from the least happy to the most happy.

FIGURE 6.4   *Grouping of Topic Examples*

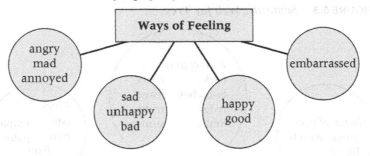

FIGURE 6.5   *Groups with New Words Included*

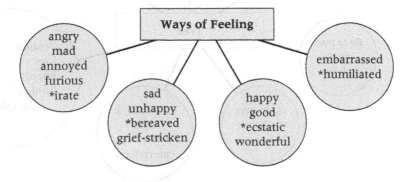

This is an exceptionally productive activity, since students must think about and agree on the fine differences between words that may be nearly synonymous. In the process, they may need to justify their opinions by citing examples of their experiences with the words or by looking them up in the dictionary. On completion of this activity, they will not only have a precise understanding of the new word's meaning, but they will have a sense of its relationship to words they already know.

Teachers agree that semantic mapping is a very effective approach for presenting new vocabulary; however, they often complain that they cannot use the procedure because they are expected to teach unrelated words that are included in a given lesson. While it is true that a unifying topic, or larger category, is needed to create a full semantic web, parts of the process can be used even with unrelated vocabulary. A separate category can be created for each new word, using words that are already familiar to the students. Even though the groups are not connected, students are still engaged in relating the new words to words they already know and in grouping them meaningfully.

In the following example, the teacher wanted students to understand fully and remember four unrelated words from a story they had read. She identified two known words or phrases for each new word (see Figure 6.6). The students were asked to place each new word in the appropriate group (see Figure 6.7).

Semantic Feature Analysis

Semantic feature analysis is another popular and effective instructional practice that helps students elaborate meanings for related words by noting their similarities and differences. Like semantic mapping, it capitalizes on prior knowledge and demonstrates the relationships among concepts within categories (Baumann & Kameenui, 1991; Johnson & Pearson, 1984). A grid is constructed in the following manner. First, the teacher selects several known words that belong to the same category and lists them vertically on the left side of the grid. For example, the teacher might begin with animals and list *cow, dog, cat, horse, rabbit,* and *porcupine.* Next, the students suggest features that at least one of the animals possesses. These are listed horizontally

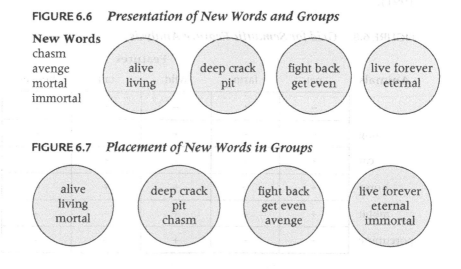

FIGURE 6.6 *Presentation of New Words and Groups*

New Words
chasm
avenge
mortal
immortal

alive / living

deep crack / pit

fight back / get even

live forever / eternal

FIGURE 6.7 *Placement of New Words in Groups*

alive / living / mortal

deep crack / pit / chasm

fight back / get even / avenge

live forever / eternal / immortal

across the top of the grid. The grid is filled in by discussing which features belong to each animal and marking these with pluses (has the feature) or minuses (does not have the feature) as shown in Figure 6.8.

Following the completion of the grid, the children can extend it by supplying more examples of the category and more features. They complete the enlarged grid by adding pluses and minuses, as before. Discussion of the words and their features is an essential part of this process. Children may learn new words within a category and semantic features they had not previously associated with the category (Baumann & Kameenui, 1991; Johnson & Pearson, 1984). For example, for some students the realization that horses and dogs can be wild or that rabbits have tails may be new. Another important outcome of the discussions is that students discover that no two words have identical patterns of pluses and minuses. No two words are really synonymous. Teachers must help children recognize that synonym means "something like" rather than "the same as" (Johnson & Pearson, 1984). Both semantic mapping and semantic feature analysis can be used to develop this understanding when children are asked to discriminate between similar words. Semantic precision is a hallmark of good readers and writers. Calling attention to the fine differences between words helps students use words in more varied and precise ways.

As children begin to see that some concepts share certain features but vary in the extent to which they possess those features, the plus or minus system used for filling in the grid may prove inadequate. Some teachers switch to a numerical scale that reflects greater precision in describing degrees of relationship (0 = none, 1 = few or some, 2 = most or usually, 3 = all). For example, in the Animals grid, *dog* was assigned a plus for *pet* and also for *wild*. However, there are many more pet dogs than wild dogs. Using a numerical system, children could show this difference by assigning a 2 to *pet* and a 1 to *wild*.

Semantic feature grids can be designed using any category of words. It is recommended that teachers begin with concepts that are already familiar to their students and then progress to more difficult or less familiar categories and concepts. The procedure can eventually be used effectively with content area materials as well as for general vocabulary instruction (Alvermann & Phelps, 2002; Pittelman et al., 1991).

FIGURE 6.8   *Grid for Semantic Feature Analysis*

			Features			
Animals	pet	farm	wild	tail	hooves	barks
cow	–	+	–	+	+	–
dog	+	–	+	+	–	+
cat	+	–	+	+	–	–
horse	+	+	+	+	+	–
rabbit	+	–	+	+	–	–
porcupine	–	–	+	+	–	–

The group instructional activities of brainstorming, semantic mapping, and semantic feature analysis all reflect the three principles of comprehension: They involve use of prior knowledge, help students relate the new to the known, and demonstrate the relationships among concepts through classification.

Strategies for Independent Vocabulary Development

Effective vocabulary development programs generally include both teacher-directed group activities and student-generated individual activities, all of which acknowledge the principles of comprehension. One outcome of effective vocabulary instruction is that students develop an interest in word meanings and begin to take responsibility for their own vocabulary growth.

Vocabulary Notebooks

A *vocabulary notebook,* maintained by each student, promotes independent vocabulary study. The notebook consists of a personal compilation of new words encountered by the student. Although the recommended format of notebooks varies according to different teachers' preferences, several guidelines are usually adhered to. Each student has a notebook in which he or she is encouraged (or in some cases required) to record three or four new words each week that the child has encountered in books, newspapers, magazines, or conversations. A single page is devoted to each word. Once students have established what a word means, they are encouraged to work with the new word in many different ways. The following is a starter list of suggestions for completing a vocabulary page; children will think of other unique ways of presenting their words, as well:

- At the top of each page, write the new word in the sentence in which it is used. You may copy the appropriate dictionary definition (optional).
- Draw or paste in magazine pictures to illustrate the vocabulary word and its meaning.
- Draw a box labeled *Associations.* In it write words that relate in some way to the new word.
- Write an original, interesting, humorous, or serious sentence using the new word.
- List several synonyms and antonyms for the word.
- Pretend you are introducing the word to a friend. Write a description of it including its part of speech, components (prefixes or suffixes), derivation, and how it can be used. Figure 6.9 shows a page from a vocabulary notebook.

The purpose of vocabulary notebooks is to promote many associations with the new word. Manipulating it in different contexts enables students to "own" a word, or incorporate it into their working vocabulary. Although students are expected to develop each vocabulary page independently, the process should be closely monitored by the teacher to ensure that students' interpretations and uses of the new word are appropriate. Simply having students look up new words in the dictionary is not sufficient. Common problems that arise when students use the dictionary include selecting the wrong definition, copying the definition of a related word that has nearly the same spelling (i.e., *brilliant* instead of *brilliance*), and mis-

FIGURE 6.9   *Vocabulary Notebook Page*

Sample Page - Vocabulary Notebook
(Kate)

| Expand | The balloon began to expand. p. 18 |

To make or grow bigger or wider as by unfolding.

BiG   WIDE   WIDER   W I D E R

<u>same</u>
grow
get bigger
enlarge

<u>opposite</u>
get smaller
shrinking

Science: Mr. Davis said the air expanded when it got heated.

The frog's throat expands when he sings.

understanding the definition. These difficulties might provide the content for focused mini-lessons on the effective use of the dictionary. On a day-to-day basis, however, many of these pitfalls could be avoided simply by encouraging students to verify word meanings with the teacher or other students before completing pages in the vocabulary notebook.

Context Clues

?How to build these?

Another facet of vocabulary instruction is the teaching of strategies that students can use independently to derive meanings for new words they encounter. It is generally agreed that *use of context clues* is the most useful strategy for figuring out the meanings of unknown words. Efficient use of context requires the reader to make inferences. The skilled, strategic reader uses context intuitively. Less accomplished readers at the basic literacy stage have not acquired this skill. When they encounter an unknown word, they focus on the word itself and do not make use of relevant contextual information. Such students can be taught to make more informed guesses about the new word's meaning and to verify their hypothesis for semantic and syntactic appropriateness. To begin the process, the teacher can demonstrate the identification and use of context clues in the following manner: Include a nonsense word in a sentence with very limited contextual information.

I bought a *blipe.*

Students speculate on the meaning of *blipe* and note that there are no clues except that a blipe is something you buy. By adding to the sentence, the teacher provides an additional clue.

I bought a *blipe* at the grocery store.

Students are now able to conclude that a blipe is probably some form of food. However, there are still many options. Continuing, the teacher adds more and more context.

I bought a *blipe* at the meat counter at the grocery store.

I bought a *blipe* at the meat counter at the grocery store and asked the clerk to cut off the tail and fins before wrapping it.

Each time the students guess what *blipe* means, they are also encouraged to justify their hypotheses based on the context. Examples of this nature graphically illustrate what context is and how it is used to derive word meanings. Once the power of context has been demonstrated with obvious examples, the teacher can move from contrived examples to more realistic situations, using real words embedded in meaningful contexts. Students should always be encouraged not only to guess what the words mean, but also to justify their hypotheses on the basis of the context.

The focus now shifts to independent application of these strategies in reading situations. Students can practice making a hypothesis about what a word means, substituting their hypothesis (synonym) into the sentence in place of the new word, and deciding whether the resulting sentence makes sense semantically and syntactically. For example, a group of students found the following passage containing an unknown word:

The coffee hit the spot. The bacon was just crisp enough. The butter melted on the pancakes, which dripped with real maple syrup. The men declared that they had never had better *victuals.*

Focusing on the unknown word, one student guessed that it meant "vicious." When asked why he thought so, he said, "It looks kind of the same." When he substituted *vicious* into the sentence, however, it became immediately apparent to him that *vicious* didn't make sense. Another student suggested that *victuals* must have something to do with food, because of the preceding description of coffee, bacon, and pancakes. This hypothesis was confirmed when the students substituted *food* in place of *victuals.* The teacher helped the students conclude that substitution of a possible synonym in place of an unknown word is a good way to verify their initial hypothesis. The teacher could continue to provide practice with this strategy for those students who tend to ignore context and formulate guesses based on features of the word that are not meaning-related.

The purpose of instruction in the use of context is not mastery of exact word meanings; rather, it helps the reader come up with approximate meanings, thus allowing general comprehension (which is the goal of independent reading) to continue. Students should also be aware of the situations in which context cannot be relied on. For example, in some situations the contextual information is insufficient to lead to even an approximate meaning of a word. In such situations, the reader's options are either to skip the word or turn to another source for a definition (the dictionary or another person). A second situation in which context clues should not be relied on occurs when a precise definition of the new word is required (in the content areas, for example).

Another strategy that should be mentioned is the analysis of unknown words to identify meaningful parts, commonly referred to as *structural analysis*. This involves drawing attention to root words and teaching the meanings of frequently encountered prefixes and suffixes. The assumption is that students will then recognize these units in unfamiliar words, which will help them determine the meaning. There is little research evidence to support the value of teaching structural analysis thinking without connecting it to other vocabulary activities that allow for more elaboration of meanings (Johnson & Baumann, 1985). Common sense suggests that drawing students' attention to frequently occurring prefixes and suffixes will expand the bases for hypothesizing new word meanings. This information will be of little help to them, however, unless they can combine it with knowledge of how to use context effectively.

Second-Language Learners

Students who are learning English as a second language (ESL) often find mastering new vocabulary a difficult challenge (Alvermann & Phelps, 2002). Even when they have acquired basic English fluency, they continue to struggle with the new concepts they encounter in mainstream content areas because of their limited prior knowledge. Unfortunately, these students are often expected to function with little or no accommodation for their evolving language status (Garcia & Pearson, 1994). It is not uncommon for second-language learners to require five or more years to develop the academic proficiency necessary to become independent learners (Cummins, 1994).

Second-language learners have considerable difficulty deriving meanings from words embedded in context. Unlike native speakers, they do not have a sizeable core vocabulary to connect with new words in context (Blachowicz & Fisher, 2000). Many programs for ESL students provide them with bilingual dictionaries; however, they often find these reference tools frustrating because they cannot recognize inflected forms or select the dictionary definition that makes sense in context (Gonzales, 1999). Moreover, figurative or idiomatic usages and unknown connotations for words are often problematic for second language learners. For example, "plane" in a geometry class may be confused with the plane that transports people. All these vocabulary problems interfere with comprehension.

Blake and Majors (1995) found that second-language learners with intermediate English proficiency can benefit from holistic instruction that reinforces new vocabulary through reading, writing, listening, and speaking. They suggest a five-stage instructional process for these students:

1. *Prereading activities* The teacher presents selected vocabulary, leads students to practice pronunciation, and supplies definitions. Other activities, such as brainstorming, semantic mapping, or semantic feature analysis, could be used as well.

2. *Oral reading and responses* Students and teacher take turns reading aloud with periodic stops for comprehension. Targeted vocabulary is given special attention. Students may write about new concepts in their learning logs.

3. *Focused word study* Students work with individual study cards that include target words, a meaningful sentence, a definition, and perhaps the word written in the students' first language. Students play word games. They could also use any of the various vocabulary-reinforcing activities that are described in the last section.

4. *Evaluating word knowledge* Students are quizzed on their understanding of new words through crossword puzzles, and cloze passages (using very familiar texts) with definitions provided.

5. *Writing workshop* The teacher models a written summary or short composition that includes as many of the target terms as possible. The final step of the process is for students to brainstorm, draft, and revise their own written pieces featuring the new vocabulary.

Summary

In this chapter we have demonstrated the importance of the role of vocabulary development in comprehension. Vocabulary development is a natural outgrowth of many direct and vicarious experiences. It increases concurrently with word knowledge; experiences lead to the acquisition of new concepts, which are represented with words. This process accelerates and becomes a prominent part of literacy development during the basic literacy stage, as students encounter more reading materials that transcend their experiences.

The teacher's role is primarily to provide experiences and facilitate students' interpretation and elaboration of new concepts. Direct teaching of definitions of individual words is not sufficient. Rather, the teacher's goal is to enable students to build understandings of words and to acquire strategies for independent use. Vocabulary development is a lifelong process; it continues far beyond the school years as a consequence of efforts to interpret and incorporate new language experiences.

BIBLIOGRAPHY

Allington, R. (2001). *What really matters for struggling readers.* New York: Longman.

Alvermann, D. E., & Phelps, S. F. (2002). *Content reading and literacy.* Boston: Allyn and Bacon.

Anderson, R. C. (1996). Research foundations to support wide reading. In V. Greaney (Ed.), *Promoting reading in developing countries* (pp. 55–77). New York: International Reading Association.

Anderson, R. C., & Nagy, B. (1993). *The vocabulary conundrum.* Champaign: University of Illinois, Center for the Study of Reading.

Baumann, J., & Kameenui, E. (1991). Research on vocabulary instruction: Ode to Voltaire. In J. Flood, J. M. Jensen, D. Lapp, & J. R. Squire (Eds.), *Handbook on the teaching of language arts* (pp. 604–632). New York: Macmillan.

Beck, J., Perfetti, C. A., & McKeown, M. (1982). Effects of long-term vocabulary instruction on lexical access and reading comprehension. *Journal of Educational Psychology, 74,* 506–521.

Blachowicz, C., & Fisher, P. (2000). Vocabulary instruction. In M. Kamil, P. Mossenthal, P. D. Pearson, & R. Barr (Eds.), *Handbook of reading research,* Vol. 3 (pp. 269–284). Mahwah, NJ: Erlbaum.

Blake, M., & Majors, R. (1995). Recycled words: Holistic instruction for LEP students. *Journal of Adolescent and Adult Literacy, 39,* 132–137.

Cummins, J. (1994) The acquisition of English as a second language. In K. Spangeenburg-Urbschat & R. Pritchard (Eds.), *Kids come in all languages: Reading instruction for ESL students.* Newark, DE: International Reading Association.

Garcia, G. E., & Pearson, P. D. (1994). Assessment and diversity. *Review of Research in Education, 20,* 337–391.

Gonzales, O. (1999). Building vocabulary: Dictionary consultation and the ESL student. *Journal of Adolescent and Adult Literacy, 43,* 264–270.

Graves, M. F., Juel, C., & Graves, B. (2001). *Teaching reading in the 21st century.* Boston: Allyn & Bacon.

Heimlich, J., & Pittelman, S. (1986). *Semantic mapping: Classroom applications.* Newark, DE: International Reading Association.

Herman, P., & Dole, J. (1988). Theory and practice in vocabulary learning and instruction. *The Elementary School Journal, 89,* 43–54.

Johnson, D., & Baumann, J. E. (1984). Word identification. In P. D. Pearson (Ed.), *Handbook of reading research* (Vol. 19, pp. 583–608). New York: Longman.

Johnson, D., & Pearson, P. D. (1984). *Teaching reading vocabulary* (2nd ed.). New York: Holt, Rinehart & Winston.

Johnson, D., Pittleman, S., & Heimlich, J. (1986). Semantic mapping. *The Reading Teacher, 39*(8), 778–783.

Kibby, M. W. (1995). The organization and teaching of things and the words that signify them. *Journal of Adolescent and Adult Literacy, 39,* 208–223.

Nagy, W. (1988). *Teaching vocabulary to improve reading comprehension.* Newark, DE: International Reading Association.

Nagy, W., & Herman, P. (1987). Breadth and depth of vocabulary knowledge: Implications for acquisition and instruction. In M. McKeown & M. Curtis (Eds.), *The nature of vocabulary acquisition* (pp. 19–35). Hillsdale. NJ: Erlbaum.

Nagy, W., Herman, P., & Anderson, R. (1987). Learning word meanings from context and during normal reading. *American Educational Research Journal, 24,* 237–270.

Nagy, W., & Scott, J. (2000) Vocabulary processes. In M. Kamil, P. Mossenthal, P. D. Pearson, & R. Barr (Eds.), *Handbook of reading research,* Vol. 3 (pp. 269–284). Mahwah, NJ: Erlbaum.

O'Donnell, M. P. (2002). Teaching and learning through literacy. Unpublished manuscript. Gorham: University of Southern Maine.

Pearson, P. D., & Johnson, D. D. (1978). *Teaching reading comprehension.* New York: Holt, Rinehart & Winston.

Pittelman, S., Heimlich, J., Berglund, R., & French, M. (1991). *Semantic feature analysis and classroom applications.* Newark, DE: International Reading Association.

Roe, B. D., Stoodt, B .D., & Burns, P. C. (1998). *Secondary school literacy instruction: The content areas.* Boston: Houghlin Mifflin Company.

Stahl, S. (1986). Three principles of effective vocabulary instruction. *Journal of Reading, 29,* 662–668.

Vacca, R. T., & Vacca, J. L. (2002). *Content area reading* (7th ed.). Boston: Allyn and Bacon.

7 Basic Literacy Stage

Effective Reading of Texts

■ *Overview*

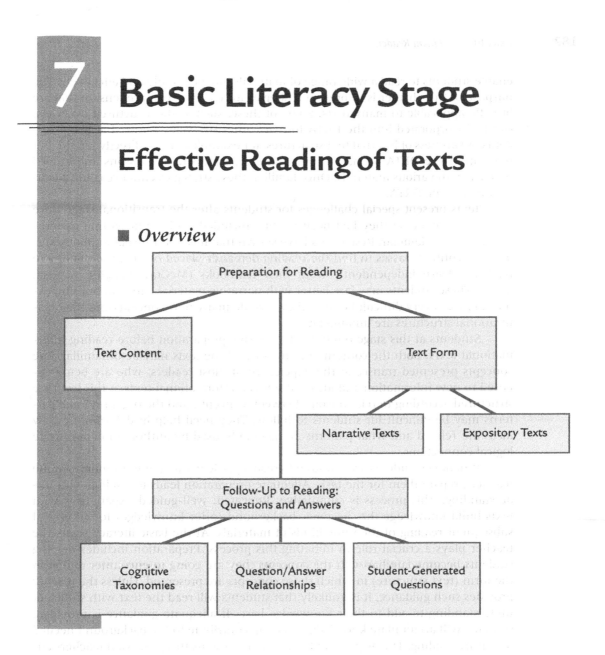

*A*lthough students at the basic literacy stage have achieved fluency and are therefore considered independent readers, their proficiency as readers can still be enhanced by direct instruction. In Chapter 4, we discussed how teachers can improve students' comprehension of specific reading selections through well-designed directed reading activities. While the DRTA remains an effective procedure to use at the basic literacy stage, students are encountering increasingly demanding and abstract reading materials. For this reason, it is now necessary for the teacher to provide additional direct instruction in comprehension processes that will eventually enable students to read a wide range of materials independently and effectively. The purpose of this chapter is to present strategies for teaching comprehension that are broadly applicable to many texts. Some of these, such as the structured overview, can be incorporated into the DRTA format. Other strategies (those that foster students' awareness of internal text structures, for example) can be directly taught, but not within the DRTA format. They require separate strategy lessons and guided practice with various materials. Once familiar, these strategies enhance comprehension within the DRTA.

Texts present special challenges for students after the transitional stage since most of the material they had been reading included stories and writing patterns that were very familiar. Reseachers have shown that it is not unusual for many students in content classes to find the reading demands placed on them too taxing to read and learn independently from their textbooks (McCray, Vaughn, & Neal, 2001). These students may fare better with narrative material (stories), but find expository texts very difficult because they include many new concepts and the organizational structures are unfamiliar.

Students at this stage often need extensive preparation before reading informational texts. Both the content and the form of the texts may be unfamiliar. The concepts presented transcend the experience of most readers, who are being exposed to new information and ideas. Moreover, informational texts at this level are structured according to relationships between concepts, and the organizational patterns may be difficult for students to follow. They need help in determining how ideas are related and what patterns are generally used by authors to demonstrate logical connections.

Whenever students are required to read a particular text, it is essential that the teacher prepare them for the task. Adequate preparation leads to reading with understanding. This process is cumulative. Repeated, well-guided experiences with texts build knowledge that becomes background (prior knowledge) for successful subsequent reading of the same kinds of materials. At the basic literacy stage, the teacher plays a crucial role in initiating this process. Preparation includes helping students become familiar with the concepts they are going to encounter and with the form (text structure) in which those concepts are presented. Unless the teacher provides such guidance, it is unlikely that students will read the text with sufficient understanding to add to their knowledge base. If adequate guidance is provided, students will accumulate knowledge that will contribute to the background needed for future reading. The diagram in Figure 7.1 represents this process. If teachers engage their students in this cycle frequently, by the time they reach the end of the basic literacy stage they will be well on their way to independence in dealing with new texts.

Preparation for Reading: Content

The DRTA format discussed in Chapter 4 can be used to prepare students for the reading of both narrative and informational materials that are to be read by a group. However, informational materials are likely to require far more attention than nar-

FIGURE 7.1 *Preparation-Reading-Knowledge Cycle*

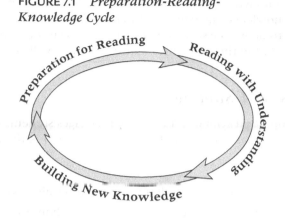

Preparation for Reading

Reading with Understanding

Building New Knowledge

rative materials to concept building. You may find it helpful to refer back to the discussion of the DRTA on pages 123–128 as we briefly review the steps teachers must take in preparing students for reading. Before meeting with the students, the teacher identifies the concepts that are crucial for understanding the reading selection and plans how best to build these concepts. (Many specific suggestions for elaboration of concepts are described in Chapter 6.) In introducing the text, the teacher

The teacher must determine what students already know about a topic.

determines what students already know about the topic, helping them activate their prior knowledge and generate interest. This discussion enables the teacher to make decisions about the scope and extent of concept-building activities that will be necessary. Within these activities, new vocabulary will be introduced.

The K–W–L Strategy

One popular teaching technique that engages students in assessing their own prior knowledge (and later, what they have learned) is the *K–W–L* (Carr & Ogle, 1987; Ogle, 1986):

> *K* stands for what students already know about the topic.
>
> *W* represents what they want to know about the topic, and
>
> *L* stands for what they learned from the reading.

The teacher prepares a K–W–L chart. Students fill in the K and W categories as the first step of the DRTA. This can be done individually, with partners or small groups, or as a whole class. The teacher uses the information gained about students' prior knowledge to plan pre-reading discussion and concept-building activities. After reading the selection, students note in the L column what they have learned. They may categorize the information, if appropriate.

The K–W–L procedure can be summarized as follows:

1. Have children brainstorm on what they know about the lesson topic (you may want to use partnerships or teams).
2. Direct them to organize what they know about the topic and make a list of their knowledge. Help them create semantic maps from their lists (Chapter 6) and add them to the K column of the K–W–L worksheet.
3. Have children then list what they want to know about the topic in question under the W column; they should anticipate what they're going to read as much as they can.
4. Direct children to read the assignment; they may add questions to their list as they read, if they wish.
5. Have children list what they learned under the L column and then categorize learned information and label the categories.
6. Ask children to develop their own maps using the categories and information learned.
7. Lead a discussion as children display and explain their maps.
8. Develop appropriate follow-up activities. (Ruddell & Ruddell, 1995, pp. 449–450)

Figure 7.2 is an example of a completed K–W–L chart. Figure 7.3 shows a map generated from the L column.

FIGURE 7.2 *K–W–L Chart on Killer Whales*

K (Know)	W (Want to Know)	L (Learned)
They live in oceans.	Why do they attack people?	D—They are the biggest member of the dolphin family.
They are vicious.	How fast can they swim?	
They eat each other.	What kind of fish do they eat?	
They are mammals.	What is their description?	D—They weigh 10,000 pounds and get 30 feet long.
	How long do they live?	
	How do they breathe?	F—They eat squids, seals, and other dolphins.
		A—They have good vision underwater.
		F—They are carnivorous (meat eaters).
		A—They are the second-smartest animal on earth.
		D—They breathe through blow holes.
		A—They do not attack unless they are hungry.
		D—They are warm-blooded.
		A—They have echo-location (sonar).
Description		L—They are found in the oceans.
Food		
Location		

Final category designations developed for column L, information learned about killer whales: A = abilities, D = description, F = food, L = location.

Whether or not students are using the K–W–L strategy, the teacher helps them set purposes for reading by speculating about what the author will discuss. With informational texts, she may lead the students in a survey of the material, calling attention to headings and visual aids. (A thorough discussion with examples of the application of the DRTA to content area texts may be found in Chapter 10.)

FIGURE 7.3   *Map Generated from a K–W–L Worksheet*

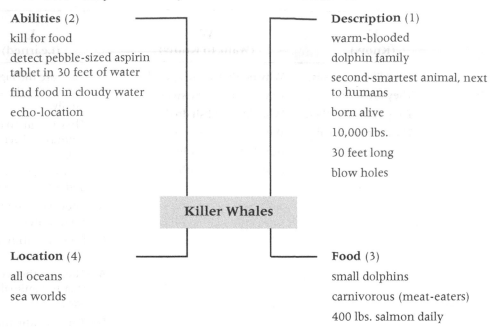

Abilities (2)

kill for food

detect pebble-sized aspirin tablet in 30 feet of water

find food in cloudy water

echo-location

Description (1)

warm-blooded

dolphin family

second-smartest animal, next to humans

born alive

10,000 lbs.

30 feet long

blow holes

Killer Whales

Location (4)

all oceans

sea worlds

Food (3)

small dolphins

carnivorous (meat-eaters)

400 lbs. salmon daily

(1) through (4) indicate the order of categories the student chose later for writing a summary.

Reproduced with permission from "KWL plus: A strategy for comprehension and summarization," by E. Carr and C. Ogle, 1987, *Journal of Reading, 30*, p. 631. Copyright by the International Association of Reading. All rights reserved.

Preparation for Reading: Form

In the basic literacy stage, awareness of the way texts are organized and the thought patterns of writers greatly enhances readers' comprehension (McKenna & Robinson, 2002). This outcome is most likely to occur when readers can use their prior knowledge to make connections between the new and the known. As educators have come to recognize the value of direct instruction in comprehension, they have identified effective strategies for promoting such awareness. Most of these strategies require sustained time for instruction and practice and are taught outside the context of the DRTA. The strategies used depend on the type of material to be read: narrative or expository.

Narrative Texts

Improving students' ability to handle narratives more effectively involves increasing their explicit awareness of the elements of story structure. In the previous stages of literacy development, an implicit understanding of story patterns sufficed, since stories were simple and closely related to students' experiences, for the most part. The major goal was to help students achieve fluency through extensive reading practice. As they progress through the basic literacy stage, readers encounter increasingly complex and unfamiliar types of narrative. Therefore, more attention to story structure is often recommended. Schmitt and O'Brien (1986), however, have expressed some concerns about the translation of story grammar research into instructional practices. They point out that although general features of story grammars can be identified, there are wide variations among stories; not all stories fit neatly into the same story grammar format. Nevertheless, the ability to see the common organizational pattern of narratives and to apply this awareness of underlying structure to a wide range of stories will enhance comprehension. How can teachers help students develop this sense of structure? One appropriate sequence of instruction is to begin with a presentation of a simple story map (see Figure 7.4). Next, retell a story that is well known to everyone and show how its elements fit into the story map (see Figure 7.5).

After this demonstration, the teacher might read a new story aloud, or select one that several students have read independently, and help them generate a similar story map as a group. Story mapping should always be done in groups, with opportunity for discussion and feedback. It is not a standard exercise to be required after every reading of a narrative; its occasional use alerts students to the organization of a narrative.

The completed story map can be used in several ways. The teacher can use it as a guide for framing questions in a way that will help students understand relationships among events in the story. For students it creates a coherent framework for

FIGURE 7.4 *Blank Story Map*

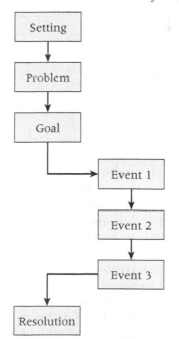

FIGURE 7.5   *Story Map Filled In*

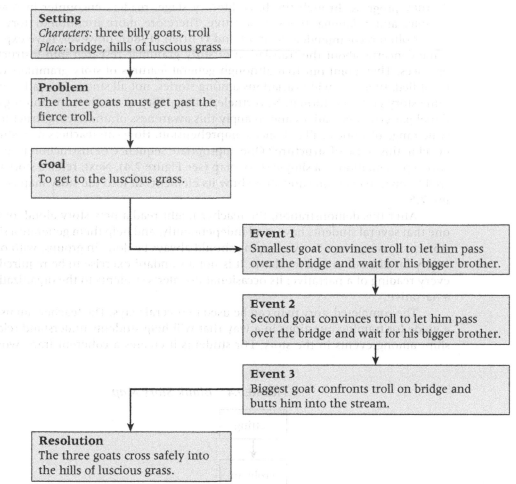

Setting
Characters: three billy goats, troll
Place: bridge, hills of luscious grass

Problem
The three goats must get past the
fierce troll.

Goal
To get to the luscious grass.

Event 1
Smallest goat convinces troll to let him pass
over the bridge and wait for his bigger brother.

Event 2
Second goat convinces troll to let him pass
over the bridge and wait for his bigger brother.

Event 3
Biggest goat confronts troll on bridge and
butts him into the stream.

Resolution
The three goats cross safely into
the hills of luscious grass.

understanding and remembering the story. It may provide a starting point for focusing on the writer's techniques in presenting one or more story elements. For example, one fruitful topic for discussion is character development—the way the author reveals a character's traits and the degree to which the character is made to seem believable. Students can be encouraged to comment on the way the author achieves certain effects, such as capturing the reader's interest with the introduction, building suspense, and creating a satisfying resolution.

Awareness of story grammar and of authors' skill in using this structure effectively and creatively increases students' sophistication, both as readers and as writers. Knowledge of narrative structure and technique enlarges their repertoire of responses to literature. Sixth-grade teacher Susan O'Roak's program includes extensive self-selected reading and group mini-lessons on story elements. The elements she introduces and discusses with her students include:

■ *Setting:* The time and place of the story. In some stories the setting serves only as a backdrop, while in others it is far more integral to the plot.

■ *Character:* The person (or animal or object) involved in the story's action—whoever the story is about. Characters often develop or change over the course of the story.

■ *Plot:* The order of events, or story line. There is usually a problem or conflict from which much of the action stems. Children can learn to identify the characters' goals, the sequence of events, and the story's resolution. The writer may present events in chronological sequence or through flashbacks.

■ *Theme:* The primary idea or message conveyed by the story as a whole. This is often a lesson or truth about the human condition (i.e., *people can overcome adversity if they work together,* or *loss and grief can lead to new insights*). Sometimes the theme is stated or obvious, sometimes it must be inferred, and some stories that are written simply to entertain do not have a theme.

Susan found that her students' responses to books became more insightful and mature as a result of these mini-lessons and discussions. Students began to comment routinely on character traits and development, themes or central conflicts of books, and authors' techniques.

Another outcome of this sort of instruction can be seen in students' writing. As they increase their awareness of story structure and various authors' writing techniques, their own writing begins to reflect this knowledge. Their stories become gradually more complete and better crafted (Goldman & Rakestraw, 2000; Miller & George, 1992). The strong relationship between reading and writing development is once again underscored.

Expository Texts

Strategies that help students cope with expository text also focus on awareness of structure; however, since expository texts are not organized the same as narrative texts, the activities for teaching text structure are different. Students benefit from learning about overall organization of expository texts (what information will be presented, in what order) and also about structure within texts (how ideas are interrelated and explained). Before students begin reading any large piece of expository text (book, chapter, or article), the teacher should lead them to preview the material to determine what information will be covered. This is valuable for two reasons. First, it provides an opportunity to activate their prior knowledge about the subject and make predictions about what the writer will cover. In addition, it makes students aware of the organization of the information that will be presented. (Suggestions for accomplishing this are given in Chapter 4 as well as earlier in this chapter, as part of the preparation phase of the DRTA.) The teacher might also use some variation of semantic mapping to help students consolidate their prior knowledge and deal with difficult new concepts. If the material to be read is especially difficult, containing many new concepts for which the students lack prior knowledge, the teacher must use other techniques to help students deal with the organization of the new information. The structured overview is an extremely effective vehicle for accomplishing this.

Structured Overviews

A *structured overview* or *graphic organizer* is a visual representation of the organization of a text (Barron, 1979). There is considerable research to support the use of structured overviews to help students build a frame of reference as they approach new material (Robinson, 1998). The teacher creates one to show how the major ideas and topics in the text are related and the order in which they are presented. You have been using the structured overviews at the beginning of each chapter of this text to preview the information you will encounter in the chapter and to see how it is organized. As a teacher, you would prepare, present, and discuss a structured overview of a chapter of informational material you assign your students before the chapter is read. Thus, the ideas presented in the text are given to students in advance, arranged in a form that highlights the relationships and order underlying the presentation. This preview provides an opportunity to assess students' prior knowledge of the various topics included in the overview and, for those who have had experience with a topic, to relate what they know to the new information. Since the key ideas are visually represented in order, the structured overview also serves as a map, enabling students to see where they have been (i.e., what has already been read and discussed in class), where they are, and where they will be going.

The structured overview can be used in yet another way during and after reading—to provide a format for summary and review of information. Students can use the overview to structure their note taking and summarizing. An effective way to accomplish this is for the teacher to make an enlarged version of the overview with space under each topic heading. Students can use this as a shell, inserting brief notes on what they have learned through reading and class discussion. As noted previously, one of the major principles of comprehension is that organizing and classifying new information facilitates understanding and remembering.

Teachers of content area subjects must carefully evaluate their textbooks to determine the extent to which they are reader friendly and logically organized. If a text meets these standards, preparing a structured overview is straightforward; the teacher simply makes a visual representation of the key ideas and their relationships as presented in the text. If the text is poorly organized or relationships between key ideas are not apparent, designing an overview is more challenging, since it must be based on the teacher's knowledge of the topic rather than on the text. In this situation, the overview would be used differently. Rather than a preview of the text, the overview represents the teacher's schema of a topic, which would include but not be limited to the material in the text. The teacher would present information from other sources and show how this relates to the content of the text.

For example, a chapter in a sixth-grade text had the title "Pollution of Our Environment." The chapter subtopics included packaging, landfills, sewage disposal, agricultural wastes, acid rain, and automobile exhausts. The teacher found the chapter inadequate in the following ways: First, there was no mention made of the particular problems of disposing of nuclear wastes; second, the organization of the chapter did not show relationships among ideas. The teacher constructed a structured overview of the topic of pollution that not only organized the content of the chapter, but also included additional information to be explored through other

FIGURE 7.6   *Structured Overview for Pollution Chapter*

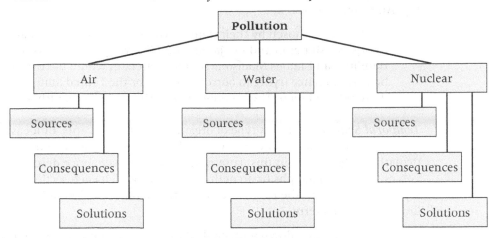

sources (see Figure 7.6). The teacher used the overview to help the students organize the information they collected from the text and other sources.

Recent educational textbooks and reading journals are replete with variations on the construction and use of structured overviews, many of which teachers will find useful and effective. Teachers may also create variations tailored to suit the needs of their particular students and their particular texts. Regardless of the format, this effective strategy for helping students perceive and use text structure incorporates the basic principles of comprehension.

Awareness of Internal Text Structures

In addition to learning to detect and use the overall structure of a text, students will also benefit from attention to the *internal structure*, or the way in which specific ideas are juxtaposed and explained by the author. The purpose of expository writing is to inform—in other words, to demonstrate, tell, describe, or explain. The more logically connected one idea is to another, the more coherent the message. Writers use different patterns of organization to show the nature of the connections among ideas. When readers recognize the structure of thought relationships in a text, their comprehension is enhanced (Vacca & Vacca, 2002). Through direct instruction, students can learn to look for major thought relationships that tie together the ideas presented in a text.

Richardson and Morgan (2000) have identified seven organizational patterns that appear to predominate in expository writing. We have targeted five and have chosen to call them *listing, temporal sequence, comparison/contrast, cause/effect,* and *problem/solution.*

Listing.   Listing of information about a topic is the most common internal organizational pattern found in textbooks (Bartlett, 1978). It is also probably the most difficult for the reader to understand and remember, since relationships between items are not apparent. This pattern is sometimes referred to as enumeration or fact packing. An example follows:

> Leaders were chosen by their states to come to the constitutional convention. George Washington and Benjamin Franklin were there. So were Alexander Hamilton and James Madison. Thomas Jefferson would have been there, but he was in France trying to borrow money for the United States. Altogether there were 55 men. They represented all the states except Rhode Island.

Temporal Sequence. In this type of organization, facts, events, or ideas are put into a sequence based on the order in which they occurred. Social studies texts are particularly likely to contain this pattern. However, the sequence described usually involves several paragraphs or an entire chapter in which each section is devoted to a separate event, with the events treated in temporal order. The following paragraph illustrates this pattern:

> Columbus knelt down and thanked God for the safe voyage. Some of his men cried and kissed the ground. Then they raised the Spanish flag. Columbus raised his sword and said, "I claim all this land in the name of King Ferdinand and Queen Isabella of Spain. I name this island San Salvador. "

Comparison/Contrast. Writers use this type of organization to point out likenesses (through comparison) and differences (through contrasts) among things, people, events, or ideas. For example:

> Senators and representatives to Congress are both elected by the people of their state. However, they do not serve for the same length of time. Senators are elected for six years, while congressmen are elected for two.

Cause/Effect. This organizational pattern is used to show causal relationships or how events lead to certain consequences:

> The gravitational pull of the moon causes ocean tides. Twice each day the pull of the moon, as it circles the earth, makes the ocean water rise and fall.

Problem/Solution. This organizational scheme describes the development of a problem and its solution or solutions. The problem/solution pattern is closely related to the cause/effect pattern. The problem may be viewed as a special kind of cause that leads to an attempted solution that may produce an effect. The following paragraph is an example of a problem/solution scheme:

> Acid rain is killing large numbers of fresh-water fish and gradually destroying vast forest regions. Conservationists are fighting for laws that will address this problem. Ways to burn fuel more efficiently must be developed even though they are expensive. Antipollution devices should be required in all coal-burning plants. Countries should work together to solve the acid rain problem.

Most texts are not written in clearly identifiable organizational patterns (McKenna & Robinson, 2002). Rather, they usually consist of complex combinations of patterns. Within individual sections or paragraphs, different kinds of thought rela-tionships may exist. An author may begin a passage by stating a problem. In explain-ing the development of the problem, listing, comparison/contrast, or cause/effect may be used. We believe that extensive time spent analyzing texts is not productive for teachers or students, since organizational patterns are so often intermixed. It is often recommended that students learn key words that will alert them to the organi-zational patterns being used by an author. (For example, *because, as a result of, there-fore*, and *consequently* alert the reader to a cause/effect or problem/solution relation-ship.) Learning to use signal words when writing helps students demonstrate relationships between ideas. However, analysis of text structures based on the identi-fication of a memorized list of key words tends to be a mechanical exercise that does not necessarily enhance comprehension. The goal of instruction, then, should not be to analyze complicated text structures, but to help students become aware of the way authors use organizational patterns as tools to present information. The suggested instructional activities that follow reflect this premise. These activities, which should precede any discussion of internal structure of texts within a DRTA, focus on writing, and on learning about patterns by creating them rather than simply analyzing them.

Middle school teachers have used an instructional sequence that begins by demonstrating and discussing how writers present information. The teacher pre-sents clear examples of the five basic paragraph patterns and leads a discussion of each model, asking, "What kind of relationship is the author trying to show? How can you tell?" Students are led to conclude that writers use different organizational patterns to show different relationships. In addition, they get a sense of the charac-teristics of each common pattern.

Next, the teacher shows several more paragraphs to the students to establish whether they are able to identify the patterns represented. Care should be taken at this level to use only short, simple paragraphs that represent an obvious pattern. (Teachers often find it easier to create clear examples than to search for them in texts.) Once students have become familiar with the five basic patterns, writing ac-tivities can be profitably used. The structured overview, described earlier in this chapter, can be used as a guide for writing different types of paragraphs. The teacher prepares a structured overview, like the one in Figure 7.6 that reflects an organiza-tional pattern. Students discuss the organization of the information in the overview and write paragraphs that follow the appropriate pattern. A student paragraph based on the overview shown in Figure 7.7. might be:

> Florida and Maine are both popular vacation states. However, they are very different. Florida has a very warm climate, whereas Maine's climate is cold. The land in Florida is flat, and there are many swamps. Maine, on the other hand, has mountains and hills. Palm trees grow in Florida, but not in Maine. People who like to swim can go to Florida and swim year round, but this is not possible in Maine because it is too cold in winter.

Students could compare their paragraphs and note the different ways in which they conveyed contrasts. This activity provides a good opportunity for students to become aware of signal words and phrases (such as *however, on the other hand*) and practice using them appropriately.

If the teacher uses a paragraph or section of a textbook as the source of the structured overview, students can compare their paragraphs with the original in the text. This is an effective technique for helping students become aware of organizational patterns; moreover, it often results in students beginning to evaluate the effectiveness of authors' presentations.

Another effective technique that can be used in conjunction with science and social studies involves giving students a topic they have studied and asking them to write about it using the various types of paragraphs. Unlike the previous exercise, which provides students with the content and structure for generating paragraphs, this activity requires them to create their own responses. For example, if the class had just completed a social studies unit on Canada, information about Canada would provide the content of their paragraphs. The teacher might begin by asking, "Suppose you are going to give information about the provinces of Alberta and New Brunswick. Which organizational pattern would you use?" Most students would suggest a comparison/contrast structure. The teacher might then encourage them to suggest other information about Canada that could best be presented in this format. A similar procedure could be followed for each of the other organizational patterns. For instance, events leading up to Canadian independence would probably suggest a temporal sequence, while territorial disputes with the United States could be described through cause/effect or problem/solution patterns.

As students participate in activities that require them to identify thought relationships and construct patterns that reflect these, they build schemas for internal structures of texts (Jones, Pierce, & Hunter 1988–89). In other words, they acquire background knowledge about the structure of expository prose, which helps them process information as they read.

FIGURE 7.7   *Structured Overview for Writing Paragraph*

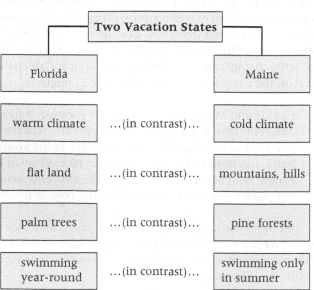

Follow-Up to Reading: Questions and Answers

Up to this point, our discussion of effective reading of texts has focused on facilitating comprehension through preparation for reading. This has involved helping students develop the necessary background knowledge for dealing with the content (ideas that will be described) and structure (ways ideas are organized) of the text. It is also important to enhance students' comprehension *after* the text has been read, through questioning and discussion.

Questions have been called the tools of the teacher's trade; yet teachers are often criticized for the kinds of questions they ask and the reasons they ask them. For example, consider these common situations: The teacher uses questions to "spot-check," to determine who is paying attention. The spot-check question is often asked in a menacing tone and is addressed to a student who has not volunteered. Closely related to the spot check is the "guess-what-I'm-thinking" question. The teacher asks a question, and students volunteer answers. However, the teacher has a specific response in mind, which is unknown to the students. The question/answer exchange becomes a game of trying to guess what the teacher wants to hear. Questioning can also become an interrogation session. In this situation, the teacher uses a barrage of literal questions to check whether or not students have read the material (Dole et al., 1991; Pearson & Johnson, 1978). None of these scenarios contributes to students' comprehension. In every instance, the teacher is trying to elicit a specific response but fails to acknowledge or build on the thinking that is reflected in students' answers. The issue, according to Pearson and Johnson, is not whether to use questions, but how, when, and where they ought to be used (Pearson & Johnson, 1978).

Cognitive Taxonomies

Good questions can trigger inquiry and help students elaborate their knowledge of the text. Until recently, teachers were advised to use taxonomies as a basis for analyzing the questions they asked and for generating questions representative of specified levels of cognitive functioning. Probably the most commonly used taxonomy was developed by Benjamin Bloom, who identified six levels of cognitive performance:

Cognitive Processes	*Student Behaviors*
1. Knowledge	The student recalls or recognizes information.
2. Comprehension	The student changes information into a different symbolic form of language and discovers relationships among facts, generalizations, definitions, values, and skills.
3. Application	The student solves a lifelike problem that requires the identification of the issue and the selection and use of appropriate generalizations and skills.
4. Analysis	The student solves a problem through conscious knowledge of the parts and forms of thinking.

5. Synthesis   The student solves a problem that requires original, creative thinking.

6. Evaluation   The student makes a judgment of good or bad, or right and wrong, according to designated standards (Bloom, 1956).

Another cognitive taxonomy that is simpler, yet compatible with Bloom's taxonomy, is Herber's Levels of Comprehension construct. He describes the three levels as follows:

Literal level   What the author said

Interpretive level   What the author meant

Applied level   What was learned from the text, applied to new situations

Herber relates the reading process to these three levels of comprehension, stating that the reader begins by identifying the words in the text to determine what the author is saying. Next, the reader looks for relationships among ideas (interpretive). Finally, the reader applies this knowledge to previous experiences, thus increasing understanding (applied) (Herber, 1978). Many content teachers use Herber's taxonomy to construct three-level reading guides (McKenna & Robinson, 2002).

Cognitive taxonomies represent attempts to classify learning experiences in a hierarchical fashion, progressing from concrete to abstract. While study of taxonomies may help teachers identify the degree of abstractness of instructional objectives and questions, their usefulness is limited in view of what is currently known about the comprehension process. There are two major problems with traditionally used taxonomies. First, their design implies that learning progresses in a linear way—that is, that students must become proficient with lower-level tasks before they are capable of handling tasks that require more abstract thinking. While it may be true that concrete thought precedes abstraction, comprehension actually occurs on many levels simultaneously (Vacca & Vacca, 2002). For example, kindergarten children who have just heard the story *Where the Wild Things Are*, by Maurice Sendak, could discuss whether the story was real or make-believe (a higher-level question) as well as describe what the monsters did (a lower-level, literal recall task). The second problem with using the older taxonomies to frame questions is that this process does not acknowledge the active/constructive nature of comprehension. Good questions must take into account the reader's prior knowledge and the role this plays in constructing meaning from text (Busching & Slesinger, 1995). The relative difficulty of a question does not depend on what type it is according to a taxonomy. Rather, the difficulty is determined by the extent to which the reader is able to draw on appropriate prior knowledge and make connections between this information and information in the text. Recent studies have shown that questions must be considered within a context including both the reader and the text, rather than in isolation. Newer taxonomies have been proposed (and used successfully) that are based on the relationship between question and text. One such taxonomy is the Question/Answer Relationships (QAR) model used by Raphael (1986) to train students to identify information sources necessary to answer questions. Researchers have shown that QAR remains an effective strategy for helping students succeed in answering comprehension questions (Benito et al., 1993; Roscshine, Meister, & Chapman, 1996).

Question/Answer Relationships (QAR)

According to QAR, there are three types of questions: *textually explicit, textually implicit,* and *schema-based.* Questions are categorized according to the source of information the reader will use to answer the question. The answers to some questions are directly stated in the text; such questions are *textually explicit.* In the preceding chapter, as part of the discussion of directed reading activities, it was noted that students should be encouraged to make predictions before reading. Following reading, when they are asked to compare their predictions with information presented in the text, they are using textually explicit information. Similarly, when students construct a story map after reading narrative material, they are using this same type of information. If a question requires students to consider various parts of the text and make inferences, it is a *textually implicit* question. The answer is implied rather than explicitly stated in the text. The third type of question, *schema-based,* cannot be answered on the basis of the text alone. It requires the readers to draw on previous knowledge (their schema) and to juxtapose this background information with ideas presented in the text.

A brief reading selection and examples of the different types of questions follow:

> An echo is a sound that bounces back. If you shout near a steep cliff, you can hear the sound bouncing back from the rocks. The walls that send the sound back must be clear and hard. The sound will not return unless you are at least 30 feet away from the cliff. The louder the yell, the more bouncing. An echo is like a rubber ball made of sound. Echoes are used in different ways. Many animals find their way by listening for echoes. Bats and fish use echoes to catch their prey. Radar sends out echoes to locate things in the air and underwater. Pilots use radar to locate storms. Echoes guide planes to safe landings in bad weather. Some day cars may use echoes to prevent crashes.

Textually explicit:
- What is an echo?
- How far away from a cliff must you be to get an echo?

Textually implicit:
- Compare the ways echoes are used by animals and people.
- What would be a good title for this selection?

Schema-based:
- What are some other things radar is used for that were not discussed in the selection?
- Why would it be impossible to make an echo in a room that has rugs and curtains?

Answers to the first two questions are stated in the text; therefore, they are textually explicit. The next two questions require the reader to examine and relate information from different parts of the selection. Facts from the text are assembled, and the reader uses them to make comparisons, draw inferences, and summarize. In order to answer the last two questions, the reader must draw on prior knowledge about radar and about sound.

A comparison of the taxonomies discussed shows that all of them describe three kinds of cognitive activity: recall of literal concrete information that can be retrieved from the text, interpretation of information that is in the text, and use of text information in conjunction with prior knowledge. It should be noted, however, that the parallels among the three taxonomies are only approximate. QAR categories are not simply new names for literal, interpretive, and applied comprehension. Rather, QAR represents a different perspective on analyzing questions. The basic premise behind QAR is that questions cannot be independently classified; they can only be categorized in conjunction with the process used by the student to formulate an answer. Because of this, QAR is an important contribution to our understanding of effective questioning.

Teachers familiar with these constructs can influence what their students will think about, learn, and remember. Students' interactions with questions have a direct impact on their learning. According to Wixson (1983), children apparently learn and remember best the information they are questioned about, regardless of whether it is important or trivial. Thus, text questions are powerful teaching aids. By asking a greater proportion of textually implicit and schema-based questions, teachers stimulate interpretation and higher-order thinking in their students.

Another factor that influences the effectiveness of questioning is time. Teachers should be aware that students need "think time" when responding to textually implicit and schema-based questions. Researchers have found that if teachers allow 5 seconds or more of think time, the length and quality of student responses increase significantly (Conley, 1987).

Unlike the older taxonomies, QAR has been successfully used with students to help them become aware of the different information sources necessary for answering different types of questions. Such awareness increases their ability to answer questions. In training students to analyze question/answer relationships, Raphael (1982) simplified the terminology and labeled the three types of questions "Right There," "Think and Search," and "On My Own" (see Figure 7.8). Raphael later expanded the definition of schema-based questions to include two subcategories: "Author and You" and "On My Own." The difference, according to Raphael, is that "Author and You" questions involve using both information provided by the author and the reader's background knowledge, whereas "On My Own" questions can be answered solely on the basis of background knowledge, without reference to the text (Raphael, 1986). In actual practice, we have found a range of relationships between the text and the schema-based questions generated by teachers. Some questions are closely tied to text information: "Why would it be impossible to make an echo in a room that has rugs and curtains?" To answer this, the reader would need some text information (echoes bounce off hard surfaces, from a distance of at least 30 feet) and some prior knowledge (sound is absorbed by rugs and curtains). Some questions are

FIGURE 7.8 *Introducing QARs*

Where Are Answers to Questions Found?

In the text:

Right There

The answer is in the text. The words used in the question and the words used for the answer can usually be found in the same sentence.

OR

Think and Search

The answer is in the text, but the words used in the question and those used for the answer would not be in the same sentence. You need to think a lot before you can answer the question.

OR

On My Own

The text got you thinking, but the answer is inside your head. So think and use what you already know to answer the question.

only minimally tied to text information: "There is an old wives' tale that bats are to be feared because they get tangled in your hair. Do you think this is true? Why or why not?" The only relevant text information is that bats use echoes, a type of radar. Beyond this fact, readers would have to depend on their own knowledge and reasoning. Still other questions relate to the topic, but are entirely independent of the text information: "Can you describe any ways that echoes are used by doctors?" Given this wide range of relations between text and schema-based response, we prefer to use Raphael's original designation, "On My Own," for all of these questions. We also note that the most thought-provoking questions and productive post-reading discussions tend to come from "on my own" questions that are connected in some degree to the text. Following is an instructional sequence based on Raphael's suggestions:

■ Introduce the concept of QARs by showing a teacher-made chart or overhead transparency that illustrates or describes the three question/answer relationships.

■ Give additional practice using short selections. Students may be provided with questions, answers, and identified QARs and asked to justify the labels. This is followed by giving questions and answers for which students must identify the QAR.

■ Longer passages can be used; eventually students can be asked to generate questions of the various types. Finally, they should be given opportunities to analyze questions from their text.

Student-Generated Questions

Teaching students to use QAR strategies reflects a recent trend in literacy instruction: to teach processes rather than to simply assess products. Such a focus enables students to become more independent and efficient consumers of texts as they become aware of how questions are framed and answers are generated. It is particularly worthwhile to involve students in generating their own questions as well as answering them. There are many ways in which teachers can engage students in generating questions. *Reciprocal questioning,* or *ReQuest,* in which teacher and students take turns generating and answering questions, is one way to accomplish this. Manzo (1969) devised this procedure to aid students in learning how to generate questions. His strategy, which was originally used on a one-to-one basis with remedial students, has been modified for use with groups by classroom and content area teachers.

Students and teacher start at the beginning of a text and read a short portion (one or two paragraphs). The students generate questions about the passage, and the teacher tries to answer these without referring to the text. Then roles are reversed; the teacher questions the students. This procedure is repeated with several additional paragraphs. Eventually the teacher asks the students to make predictions about the rest of the chapter. Predictions are discussed, and the students are asked to read the remaining part of the text silently. After the reading, the teacher leads a discussion in which students compare their predictions with the text information. Both teacher and students should make a deliberate attempt to diversify the kinds of questions asked, according to QAR.

A problem that often arises when the ReQuest procedure is initially used is that some students do not know how to generate questions. Others will ask only literal, "Right There" questions. The influence of the teacher's modeling is significant; however, explicit discussion of question types and how they are generated is also necessary. Activities that lead to understanding and analysis of question/answer relationships provide excellent background for work with ReQuest. The teacher can further help students by "thinking aloud" while generating a question.

"I want to ask a 'think and search' question. The selection described ways that animals use echoes, and also how people use them. I could ask students to compare these; they would have to use information from the text, but the answer isn't right there. I think I'll ask, 'Can you compare the ways animals and people use echoes?' No, that's too general. I want them to think about the *differences*. I think I'll ask, 'What are some differences between the way animals use echoes and the way people use them?'"

The teacher shares his thought processes, so that students gain a sense of the thinking involved in framing a question. He could invite students to think aloud their processes for further illustration. Practice in generating questions results in increased ability to frame good questions at different levels.

Once the majority of students are able to ask appropriate questions, the ReQuest procedure can be used by groups of students independently (without the teacher present). This gives each individual more opportunities to serve as questioner and responder. Students discover that asking, as well as answering, good questions helps them to better understand what they have read.

From the teacher's perspective, effective questioning leads to discussions that can increase students' insight about what they have read. By understanding and using questioning strategies that acknowledge the relationships among reader, text, and questions, teachers can enhance students' comprehension.

Summary

This chapter has focused on ways that teachers can help their basic literacy stage students deal more effectively with texts. Teacher guidance, particularly with the reading of informational texts, is vitally important at this stage. Independence in the effective processing of texts at the refinement stage depends largely on the effectiveness of direct instruction by the teacher during the basic literacy stage. In addition to an abundance of self-selected reading, students at this stage need teacher-directed guidance in preparing for reading texts that transcend their experience, developing awareness of text structures, and elaborating understanding through questioning strategies that enhance reader-text interaction at different levels.

BIBLIOGRAPHY

Barron, R. F. (1979). Research for classroom teachers: Recent developments on the use of the structured overview as an advance organizer. In H. L. Herber & J. D. Riley (Eds.), *Research in reading in the content areas* (4th rep., pp. 171–176). Syracuse, NY: Reading and Language Arts Center, Syracuse University.

Bartlett, B. (1978). Top level structure as an organizational strategy for recall of classroom texts. Unpublished doctoral dissertation, Arizona State University, Tempe.

Benito, Y. M., Foley, C., Lewis, C. D., & Prescott, P. (1993). The effect of question-answer instruction relationships and metacognition on social studies comprehension. *Journal of Research in Reading.* 16, 20–29.

Bloom, B. (1956). *Taxonomy of educational objectives: Cognitive domain.* New York: David McKay.

Busching, B., & Slesinger, R. (1995). Authentic questions: What do they look like? Where do they lead? *Language arts, 9,* 341–351.

Carr, E., & Ogle, D. (1987). KWL plus: A strategy for comprehension and summarization. *Journal of Reading, 30,* 626–631.

Conley, M. (1987). Teacher decision making. In D. Alvermann & D. Moore (Eds.), *Research within reach: Secondary school reading* (pp. 142–152). Newark, DE: International Reading Association.

Dole, J. A., Duffy, G. G., Roehler, L. R., & Pearson, P. D. (1991). Moving from the old to the new: Research on reading comprehension instruction. *Review of Educational Research, 61,* 239–264.

Goldman, S., & Rakestraw, J. (2000). Structural aspects of constructing meaning from text. In M. Kamil, P. Mosenthal, P. D. Pearson, & R. Barr (Eds.) *Handbook of reading research*, Vol. 3 (pp. 311–335). Mahwah, NJ: Erlbaum.

Herber, H. (1978). *Teaching reading in the content areas* (2nd ed.). Englewood Cliffs, NJ: Prentice-Hall.

Jenkins, J., Matlock, B., & Slocum, T. (1989). Two approaches to vocabulary instruction: The teaching of individual word meanings and practice in deriving word meaning from context. *Reading Research Quarterly* (24), 215–235.

Manzo, A. V. (1969). The ReQuest procedure. *Journal of Reading, 11*(2), 123–126.

McCray, A., Vaughn, S., & Neal, L. (2001). Not all students learn to read by third grade: Middle school students speak out about their reading disabilities. *The Journal of Special Education, 35,* 17–30.

McKenna, M. C., & Robinson, R. D. (2002). *Teaching through text: Reading and writing in the content areas* (3rd ed.). Boston: Allyn & Bacon.

Meyer, B. J. F., & Freedle, R. O. (1984). Effects of discourse type on recall. *American Educational Research Journal, 21,* 121–143.

Miller, K., & George, J. (1992). Expository passage organizers: Models for reading and writing. *Journal of Reading, 35,* 372–377.

Ogle, D. (1986). A teaching model that develops active reading of expository texts. *The Reading Teacher, 39,* 568–570.

Raphael, T. E. (1982). Question-answering strategies for children. *The Reading Teacher, 36,* 186–191.

Raphael, T. E. (1986). Teaching question answer relationships, revisited. *The Reading Teacher, 39,* 516–555.

Richardson, J. S., & Morgan, R. F. (2000). *Reading to learn in the content areas.* Belmont, CA: Wadsworth/Thomson Learning.

Robinson, D. H. (1998). Graphic organizers as aids to text learning. *Reading Research and Instruction, 37,* 85–105.

Roseshine, B., Meister, C., & Chapman, S. (1996). Teaching students to generate questions: A review of intervention studies. *A Review of Educational Research, 66,* 181–221.

Ruddell, R., & Ruddell, M. (1995). *Teaching children to read and write: Becoming an influential teacher.* Boston: Allyn and Bacon.

Schmitt, M. C., & O'Brien, D. G. (1986). Story grammar: Some cautions about the research of theory into practice. *Reading Research and Instruction, 26,* 1–7.

Sendak, M. (1963). *Where the wild things are.* New York: Harper & Row.

Vacca, R. T., & Vacca, J. L. (2002). *Content area reading* (7th ed.). Boston: Allyn and Bacon.

Wixson, K. K. (1983). Questions about a text: What you ask about is what children learn. *The Reading Teacher, 37*(3), 287–293.

8 Study Strategies

■ *Overview*

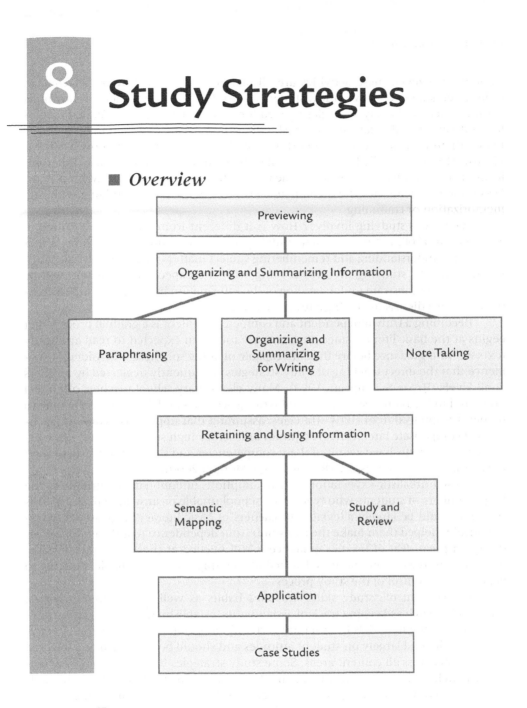

Brozo & Simpson (2003) describe study as "deliberate, planned, and conscious activities that students select to achieve a particular goal. Students typically employ study strategies when they need to retain material for the purpose of taking a test, writing a paper, participating in classroom discussions or any other demonstration of their learning" (p. 361). The use of study strategies is dependent on students' motivation to learn and on their awareness of reading processes. All the activities described earlier in Chapter 7 are designed to develop these kinds of awarenesses in students. However, these activities are all planned and guided by the teacher. In order to engage in effective study, students must develop independence; they must learn to select and apply strategies needed for specific reading tasks. Skilled readers take into account the nature of the task (what they will be expected to do with the material) and the nature of the text (how familiar the content is and how it is organized). Moreover, skilled readers are able to identify and summarize important ideas. They even have strategies for dealing with difficult or poorly written texts. Less skilled students lack these competencies; they often equate studying with rote memorization or cramming.

What does studying involve? How is it different from reading? According to Moore et al. (2002), "the way that studying differs from 'ordinary reading' is that studying is understanding and remembering subject matter independently" (p. 217). In other words, studying involves reading with the expectation that one will be required to demonstrate understanding of the information in some way such as participating in a discussion, taking a test, or writing a paper.

Becoming a truly independent and competent student is a gradual process that begins at the basic literacy stage. Students are too often expected to read and study texts without guidance before they are capable of doing so. There is considerable evidence that the direct teaching of study strategies is frequently neglected by teachers at all levels (Brozo & Simpson, 1999). Many elementary school teachers often feel pressured to focus on basic reading and writing activities and do not take the time to model the application of study strategies, assuming that upper-level content teachers will compensate later. However, junior and senior high school teachers often assume that students have acquired these competencies and that direct instruction on how to study is not necessary (Richardson & Morgan 2000).

These unrealistic expectations and assumptions undoubtedly contribute to the large numbers of students who reach high school unable or unwilling to study. This situation could be largely alleviated if teachers of basic literacy stage students systematically helped them make the transition from dependence to independence. Although a great deal of teacher guidance is still needed at the basic literacy stage, there are strategies appropriately learned at this stage that will enable students to begin to take control of the study process.

The content of "study skills" includes habits as well as learning strategies. Study habits such as keeping track of assignments, establishing a schedule for studying, and keeping materials in order are certainly important to school success; however, they depend largely on student attitudes and should be addressed and fostered by teachers across all content areas. Some study strategies focus on specific competencies such as locating information in the library and interpreting graphic aids (maps, charts). Other strategies require a greater degree of problem solving and decision making and lead to more general competencies. Organization and retention of information are examples of general competencies that students can fruitfully apply to each reading task.

McKenna and Robinson (2002) comment that skilled readers are versatile and flexible but that many students fail to become "strategic readers." Before examining specific strategies, it is necessary to review what is meant by *strategic*. Skilled readers not only use strategies; they also are aware of how and why they use them. This is referred to as *metacognitive awareness*. As we stated in Chapter 5, *metacognition* means awareness of one's own thought processes; when applied to reading, the term means awareness of one's own reading processes as well as the ability to monitor and control them. Studies show that immature readers do not assess the demands of the reading task or monitor their comprehension while reading. Moreover, they are at a loss as to what to do if comprehension fails. In contrast, readers with metacognitive awareness are flexible. How they read depends on how difficult the text is, how much they already know about the topic, and what purposes the reading serves. They know when their comprehension breaks down, and they take appropriate action. The goal of study-skills instruction is to enable students to become more strategic, or metacognitive. Metacognitive knowledge and the ability to devise and use study strategies are closely related and can be developed with systematic guidance by teachers. Effective study strategies help students organize information in such a way that it is understood, retained, and available for recall.

In this chapter, we will delineate specific strategies that can be undertaken with basic literacy stage students. We have included activities that help students preview material before reading, organize and summarize what they read, and retain and use information.

Previewing

A major problem that typically arises in the basic literacy stage is the difficulty students experience in reading and learning independently from content area texts. We will consider several specific techniques that help students approach textbook reading strategically. First and probably most important is adequate preparation for reading. Teachers begin by demonstrating previewing or surveying techniques that students can eventually learn to use independently. (Once again we would like to emphasize that extensive modeling and guided practice must be provided before basic literacy stage students can be expected to apply such strategies independently.) The following strategy can be used with the whole class to preview content area text chapters that include some or all of the following features: title, introduction, bold print headings and subheadings, graphic aids, and summary. The steps involved in previewing are adapted from Vacca and Vacca (2002) and Alvermann and Phelps (2002):

■ *Title:* The title can be used not only to predict what the chapter will be about, but also to activate prior knowledge. Students should be encouraged to speculate about what they already know about the topic and how the topic relates to preceding chapters they have read.

■ *Introduction and Summary:* The teacher can point out that chapter introductions and particularly summaries provide readers with the gist of the chapter and the most important points. Read these sections with students and have them identify the main ideas of the chapter.

■ *Bold Print Headings:* Examine headings and subheadings with students. Use them to formulate questions going beyond merely turning subtitles into literal questions. For example, in a science text chapter about weather, students might encounter the subtitle Tornadoes within a section on Major Weather Disturbances.

Questions that might be generated would include not only "What is a tornado?" but also "How are tornadoes different from the other types of storms described?" or "Where do tornadoes usually occur?" Good questions stem from speculation about what information the text may include. When students are being introduced to previewing, these questions should be recorded by the teacher on the board or on an overhead transparency and used to remind students what they will be looking for as they read. The questions can be used after reading to verify predictions and guide discussion of what was learned.

▪ *Graphic Aids:* Students frequently ignore graphic aids such as charts, tables, maps, and graphs, which are valuable sources of information, summarizing or illustrating key ideas from the text. During the preview, the teacher can call attention to the graphic aids and pose questions that lead students to examine them. "Why do you think the writer included this map?" "What information can we get from this chart?" If students are having difficulty understanding certain types of visual aids, the teacher may conduct mini-lessons (at another time) in which she models, through thinking aloud, how to glean information from charts or graphs, and students can analyze and practice using or creating them. Before students read, the teacher helps them review and summarize their predictions about the reading they are about to undertake.

At this point, you may be wondering how the previewing technique relates to the directed reading–thinking activity described in Chapters 4 and 7. Actually, the previewing sequence just described is an elaborated form of *purpose setting*, a regular part of the DRTA. However, previewing would generally not be emphasized with students prior to the basic literacy stage. It is at first teacher-directed, like other components of the DRTA. The goal of teaching students to preview, however, is to promote eventual independent application of the technique. This is not true of other preparation components of the DRTA, such as creating motivation or building students' conceptual background, which must be led by the teacher regardless of the students' stage of reading. Strategies that can be used by students primarily to organize information involve recording, sorting, and manipulating the information. Instruction in such strategies cannot be successfully undertaken, however, unless students comprehend the material. In other words, they should have adequate background for the information, be able to relate the content to their prior knowledge, and perceive the basic structure of the text. (Development of these basic components of comprehension is described in Chapters 5, 6, and 7.) Provided these basic conditions have been met, students can profit from learning to use strategies such as summarizing and note taking.

Organizing and Summarizing Information

Condensing important information into a summary requires that students identify key ideas and restate them in their own words. Novice readers of texts tend to *retell* rather than condense. They include information indiscriminately or choose what is of most interest to them rather than what is essential for understanding the passage. More sophisticated readers write in their own words summaries that correspond closely to the important ideas in the text. Good summary writers infer main ideas when they are not explicitly stated and create their own topic sentences. Basic literacy stage students can begin to move toward competency in this area, which will continue to be refined during the next stage of reading progress.

Paraphrasing

An appropriate preliminary strategy for students who have entered the basic literacy stage is *paraphrasing.* The teacher requests students to tell in their own words what they think the author conveyed in a passage or chapter. Initially very short segments of text (perhaps only a sentence or two) are used for teacher modeling and student practice or paraphrasing. As students become adept at this, longer pieces of text can be used. Eventually students can be asked to paraphrase a whole section of text, which requires them to identify key ideas.

Paraphrasing can also be of great value in monitoring comprehension. Students should be encouraged to ask themselves as they read, "What does this mean?" and to restate in their own language what they think the author is saying. Whether it is undertaken as a self-monitoring strategy or in response to a teacher's direction, paraphrasing aids comprehension and strengthens memory for the material because it forces students to reconstruct the ideas in the text.

Summarizing textbook material is an important and useful study strategy. Since readers obviously cannot remember everything they read, they must be able

A middle-grade student practices summarizing text.

to identify the most important ideas. According to Coffman (1994), the ability to do this is characteristic of skilled readers. Middle-grade students typically have great difficulty summarizing text material. Perhaps they see textbook selections as collections of unconnected statements or pay most attention to details that interest them or have high imagery value, whether or not they are important. The most likely reason for inability to summarize, however, is that students have not been taught how to identify and remember important information. Instructional strategies that teach students to summarize must address *how* one reads for important information.

Organizing and Summarizing for Writing

Effective activities for helping students organize and summarize information often involve developing several related competencies simultaneously. The following activity, designed by fourth-grade teacher Marcia Blake, exemplifies this.

The teacher helps the students identify key ideas from a selection that is read aloud to them. As a group, they condense the information and decide which supporting details are important to include. The mechanics of note taking are demonstrated as the teacher records their paraphrasing on the blackboard in abbreviated form. The students make decisions about the order in which the information can logically be arranged, and then (still working as a group) compose a brief report from the notes. Specific directions follow:

1. The teacher locates a short informational piece on a topic of interest to the students. Readability level is not important, since the piece will be read aloud; however, it must be well within the students' ability to comprehend. New vocabulary or concepts should be discussed prior to reading.
2. The teacher reads the entire selection aloud to the students. She reads it aloud a second time, instructing the students to stop her every time they hear something that sounds important.
3. Each time the teacher stops, she encourages the students to try to state the specified idea in condensed form. Help is given as needed, and notes are recorded on the board.
4. Teacher and students read over the list of notes together. Students identify those items that seem to belong together and come up with a heading or label for each grouping.
5. The students arrange the topics in preferred order.
6. Together, the group writes a summary of the article using the "outline." This is recorded by the teacher on the board or on an overhead transparency.

Note Taking

Note taking is another aid students use to organize and summarize information. It can be introduced at the basic literacy stage through teacher modeling and guided practice. Summarizing gives students practice in identifying key ideas and supporting details and summarizing them—important prerequisites for effective note taking. Students at this stage will use note taking primarily as a prewriting activity, a way of efficiently recording information they wish to include later in a written report. Instruction and practice in note taking should emphasize helping students condense information, put it in their own words, and record it in abbreviated form. At the basic literacy stage, note taking is usually taught in the context of summarizing and manipulating information. It is not until seventh or eighth grade, when most students are in or approaching the refinement stage, that note taking will be consistently required for other purposes such as recording important information from lectures and discussions or from the independent reading of content area texts.

Retaining and Using Information

The strategies discussed so far have focused on organizing material in order to understand it better. Another important purpose of study is to transfer information into long-term memory, so that it can be retrieved as needed or required. Understanding what is read is only the first step in studying; in addition to understanding, students must develop strategies for remembering and retrieving the content of what has been read.

Semantic (Cognitive) Mapping

The *semantic mapping* technique can be used after students have read a piece of informational material. The completed map, or web, is a visual representation of the important ideas and shows how they are related. The technique might be particularly helpful to use with material that does not include headings and subheadings. Creating a semantic map involves the following steps:

1. Before students read the selection, help them prepare for reading by previewing, as described earlier.
2. Have students read the text to confirm their predictions.
3. Have students work together in small groups to brainstorm information they can remember from the reading. Vacca and Vacca (2002) suggest that each group be given index cards and instructed to write each piece of information on a card. This enables students to physically group and sort information easily.
4. Write the central focus of the selection (i.e., the title) on the board. Select one key concept and ask students what information from their cards relates to this concept. As they volunteer information, record it on the board under the key concept. Discuss their choices and, when appropriate, the relationships among them. This process will result in a visual representation of these relationships (see Figure 8.1).
5. Invite the students to continue their work in their groups, grouping their cards into categories that represent key concepts and creating a semantic map of the whole selection. The maps can be copied onto chart paper or overhead transparencies for sharing.

FIGURE 8.1   *Example of Semantic Webbing*

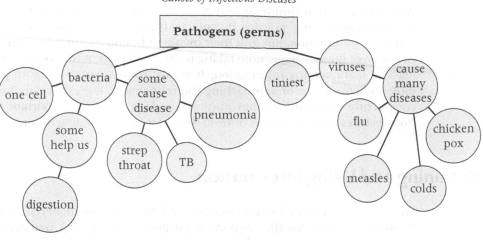

Causes of Infectious Diseases

6. Each group shows and explains its semantic map and the groups compare their results.
7. The teacher may then guide the whole class in developing a composite semantic map, such as the one shown in Figure 8.2, reflecting the work of all groups and demonstrating the relationships among key ideas and information.

Instruction, as always, should begin with modeling and explanation and proceed to increasingly independent use by students. Semantic mapping helps students learn to identify key ideas and illustrate how they relate to each other. Moreover, the completed maps become a valuable tool for review and recall of content read.

Study and Review

Several of the activities described in this chapter result in written representations of important information gained from reading. Teachers can use any or all of these graphic products to help children develop strategies for study, review, and retention of information. On completion of a chapter or unit of study, students can be taught to review whatever graphic representations they have made. For example, if summaries have been developed, students may be asked to study them in the following manner:

■ Read over your summary several times, repeating the information to yourself until you can remember most of it.
■ Work with a partner. Take turns telling each other what was included in your summary. The "listener" can ask questions and point out important information she thinks was omitted.

FIGURE 8.2 *Composite Semantic Web*

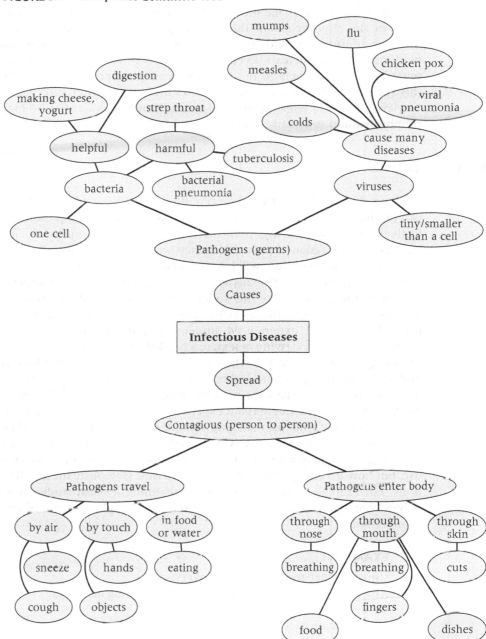

This process of rehearsal, recitation, and feedback constitutes practice studying. The teacher directs and monitors the process. With periodic repetition, students discover the effectiveness of these techniques for helping them organize and remember information. Studying in this way becomes a routine, manageable part of working with content texts. Eventually students will be able to make graphic representations and use them to rehearse and review material independently. Contrast this approach with the untrained student's inclination, when directed to "study" or "review," to reread whole sections of text. It is small wonder that so many students simply abandon systematic attempts to review.

Application

We have described here several specific study strategies and teaching activities that can profitably be used with basic literacy stage students to help them deal more effectively with their reading, particularly of informational materials. To the novice teacher, this collection of possibilities may seem overwhelming. Questions that are likely to arise include "How will I decide which activities to use?" and "Which activities can be combined?" The answers to these questions depend largely on the degree of maturity and skill of the students, the nature and difficulty of the material, and the teacher's instructional goals. Activities that would probably be most appropriate for the least experienced students include the teacher-made structured overview, guided previewing of text, teacher-led organizing/rewriting, and semantic mapping conducted with the whole class. These activities are the least complicated and time-consuming and are orchestrated almost entirely by the teacher. Nevertheless, they do provide students with the means to organize and assimilate difficult reading material. As students gain experience and maturity as readers, they are better able to profit from summarizing activities, writing about what they read, and more independent use of previewing, semantic mapping, and review strategies.

When planning a lesson, the teacher must decide not only which activities to use, but how to combine them in an effective way. Obviously there will be many options. For example, a fifth-grade teacher planning a social studies lesson that involves reading a chapter from the children's text might use one of these possible combinations:

EXAMPLE 1

Use of teacher-made structured overview
Assessment of prior knowledge, concept-building activities
Guided preview of text
Silent reading of text
Teacher-directed creation of semantic map (whole group)

EXAMPLE 2

Guided preview of text
Silent reading of text
Summarizing
Study/review using summaries

EXAMPLE 3

Use of teacher-made, partially completed structured overview of text
Guided preview of text
Silent reading of text
Completion and elaboration of structured overview
Study/review using overviews

Other effective combinations could be devised. The main concern is choosing a balance of activities to be used before, during, and after reading.

CASE STUDIES

We have chosen to describe our three case-study children as fifth-graders. The structure of fifth-grade classrooms varies from school to school. Our three students are in self-contained classrooms and have one teacher for all subject areas. Most children are well into the basic literacy stage by the time they reach fifth grade. John's literacy level and instructional needs are typical of many fifth-graders. Kim, whose literacy development is slower than average, is still at the transitional stage of reading. Theresa has passed through the basic literacy stage and is now in the refinement stage of reading. The three children represent the wide range of literacy development that fifth-grade teachers encounter.

Kim

When we looked at Kim in third grade, she was progressing through the initial stage of reading. Appropriate instruction was continued, and she entered the transitional stage during her fourth-grade year. By the time she entered fifth grade, Kim was able to read many easy books independently; however, her reading was not yet fluent except when she read books that were very familiar. She especially liked humorous books and mysteries. She had discovered Beverly Cleary's books about Henry Huggins and Ramona Quimby, and she loved Edward Packard's series of Choose Your Own Adventure books. She participated successfully in sustained silent reading and frequently took books home to read. Although she could not read as well as most of her classmates, Kim enjoyed reading. Her motivation was sustained by awareness of her progress in reading skill and by her increasing independence as a reader.

Kim was also showing more independence in her writing. She chose from a greater range of topics than she had in third grade and wrote informational pieces as well as personal and fictional narratives. Her drafts were often two or three pages long. She was beginning to revise her pieces by adding material suggested by questions raised during writing conferences with her peers or teacher. Her spelling was transitional; she remembered and used conventional spellings for some words and spelled others phonetically. She was developing sentence sense and used periods and capital letters more and more appropriately. Figure 8.3 shows a first draft of a piece Kim wrote in October of her fifth-grade year.

FIGURE 8.3   *Kim's Fifth-Grade Writing Sample*

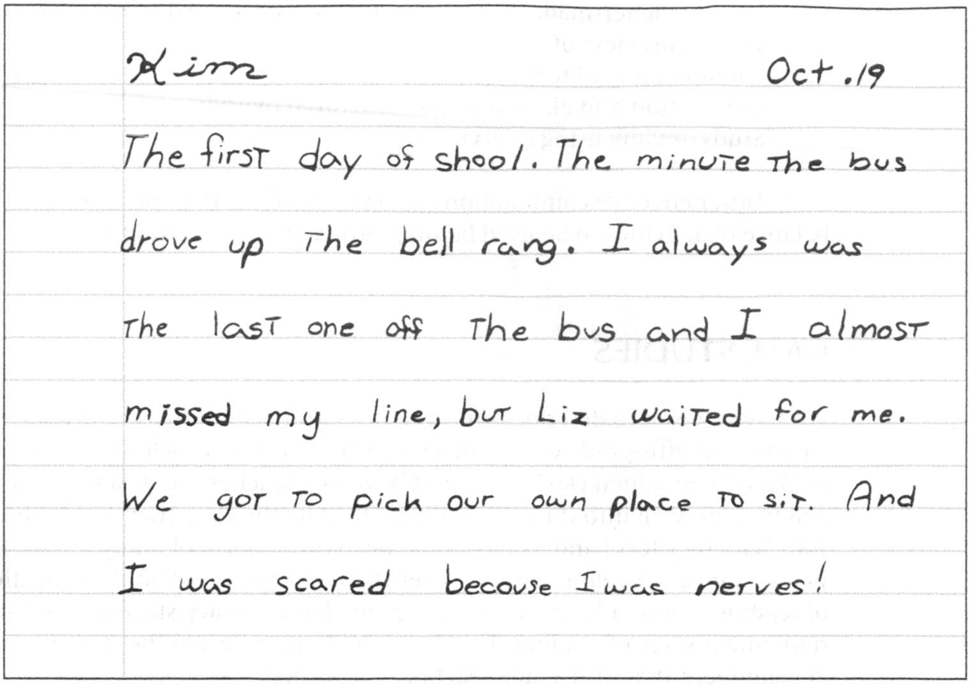

> Kim   Oct. 19
>
> The first day of shool. The minute the bus
> drove up the bell rang. I always was
> the last one off the bus and I almost
> missed my line, but Liz waited for me.
> We got to pick our own place to sit. And
> I was scared becouse I was nerves!

Before reading on, speculate about an appropriate instructional program for Kim. Consider which of her needs will be consistent with those of her classmates and which needs will be different from those of the basic literacy stage students in her class. How, as her teacher, would you accommodate Kim's needs? Compare your ideas with our suggestions, which follow.

Kim's Instructional Program

Since Kim is at the transitional stage of reading, major instructional goals for her will be to develop fluency, to continue to motivate her to read and write, and to promote reading for meaning. To some extent these goals can be addressed through activities that are common to everyone in her class. However, special instruction will also be needed. For example, Kim can participate in the whole-class voluntary reading and writing programs. She can select appropriate books, read independently during SSR, and share her reading through conferences and follow-up activities. (Description of these activities can be found in Chapter 4.) She can select writing topics and develop them during the whole class "writing workshop." If the classroom literacy program emphasizes process, reading and writing activities can be responded to at any level. Kim can progress successfully within this structure, as can all her classmates.

For additional practice in developing fluency, Kim would profit from immersion techniques such as repeated reading or reading along (see Chapter 4). This assistance, which her classmates do not need, might be provided by a teacher's aide or volunteer who could read with Kim for 15 or 20 minutes several times a week.

If a basal reader is used as a part of the classroom reading program, two important concerns will shape Kim's instruction. First, the material chosen for her teacher-directed reading must be at an appropriate level for her to read with guidance. (A fifth-grade basal reader would be far too frustrating for Kim, even with teacher assistance. The use of material that is very difficult for her would, in all likelihood, prevent her from increasing fluency, maintaining motivation, and comprehending what she reads.) The second concern has to do with the way time is allocated within the reading lesson. As a transitional stage reader, Kim needs practice reading above all else. Her teacher must emphasize preparation for reading, the reading itself, and elaboration of content through discussion; isolated skill activities should be kept to a minimum and used only when their application is apparent.

The most difficult part of Kim's program to structure will be teacher-directed activities in which the whole class is expected to read the same text. This situation is most likely to occur in the content areas, as the teacher guides students in reading and studying content area texts. Not only will the material be extremely difficult or impossible for Kim to read, but many of the reading/study strategies that are appropriate for basic literacy stage students will be too advanced for her. How to meet the needs of students like Kim in content area instruction is a common dilemma for upper-grade teachers. Decisions are affected by classroom management considerations and by the social needs of the students, as well as by the need to provide for individual differences. Classroom management concerns would include the teacher's responsibility to present content information and study strategies appropriate for the majority of students, the availability of help (assistants, aides, volunteers), and the size and makeup of the group. Social needs must also be considered. Inclusion in the group, a feeling of belonging, is important to all children. For this reason, Kim's teacher might decide to include her in content area instruction (with as much support as possible) even though she knows Kim will not gain as much academically as the other students from many of the activities. Kim should be included with the rest of the class in any activities that involve concept building or demonstration and modeling of strategies. Whenever the independent reading of text is required of the class, the teacher or her aide (when available) could take Kim (and sometimes other students) aside and read the text aloud with her. Occasionally the teacher can tape a section of text ahead of time and have Kim listen to the tape while others are reading silently.

Another alternative that Kim's teacher could use from time to time is to provide several different readings that vary in difficulty but relate to the same topic. Students would be allowed to choose one of the readings, work with it alone or in small groups, and report their findings to the rest of the class. In such instances Kim should be guided to select reading material that she can manage. These sorts of management techniques will enable Kim to participate to the greatest extent possible, to increase her knowledge base in the content areas, and to be exposed to approaches to text reading that she will be able to use later, when her reading skill has increased.

The management of Kim's instruction will be a challenge to her teacher. Nevertheless, through careful planning and coordination with others who provide

Kim with special help, she will be able to give Kim what she needs most—many opportunities to practice reading and writing in functional settings, and a feeling of belonging. If these recommendations are followed, Kim is likely to make steady progress and see herself as a successful member of her fifth-grade class.

■ John

When John entered fifth grade, he was well into the basic literacy stage. A fluent reader, he read a variety of materials independently. His comprehension of books he chose and read on his own was excellent. Like other children in his class, he needed teacher guidance in dealing with content area textbooks, however. At the beginning of the year, his teacher administered a reading interest inventory. John identified Roald Dahl as his favorite author and listed *The BFG* (1982) and *James and the Giant Peach* (1961) as his favorite books. He reported that he did not read extensively outside of school; he spent a great deal of time riding bikes and playing sports with his friends, and he enjoyed watching T.V. and playing computer games.

By the time he reached fifth grade John had had several years of process-oriented writing instruction. He selected topics that reflected a variety of genres. Early in fifth grade, he was particularly interested in writing fictional adventure narratives. Whereas in third grade he had produced many pieces, tending to lose interest in them once a draft was completed, by fifth grade John was showing more sustained interest in most of his compositions. He often made extensive content revisions and frequently rewrote a story several times before considering it "done." He took responsibility for editing, correcting much of the spelling and punctuation on his own or with peers before having a final editing conference with his teacher. Figure 8.4 shows a revised draft of a story John wrote in October of his fifth-grade year.

Before reading on, speculate as to what would be appropriate components of an instructional program for John. Then compare your ideas with our suggestions, which follow.

John's Instructional Program

Voluntary reading remains the most important part of John's instructional program. Through self-selected reading, John and his classmates will maintain motivation and further their skill and experience in reading. Time for independent reading in school is particularly important for students like John who engage in many out-of-school activities that compete with reading as a leisure time pursuit. John should be accountable for keeping records of his independent reading, and he should have many opportunities to share his responses to reading with his peers and his teacher through conferences, book talks, and written reactions. The principles of a sound independent reading program—provision for time, choice, and sharing—are as applicable in fifth grade as they were earlier.

Basic literacy stage students such as John also profit from teacher-directed reading. At this level, teachers often assign a group of students to read the same trade book, provided multiple copies are available. The teacher guides the reading and discussion. Because the students have had a common reading experience, they are able to explore the book in depth and profit from the exchange of reactions and

FIGURE 8.4 *John's Fifth-Grade Writing Sample*

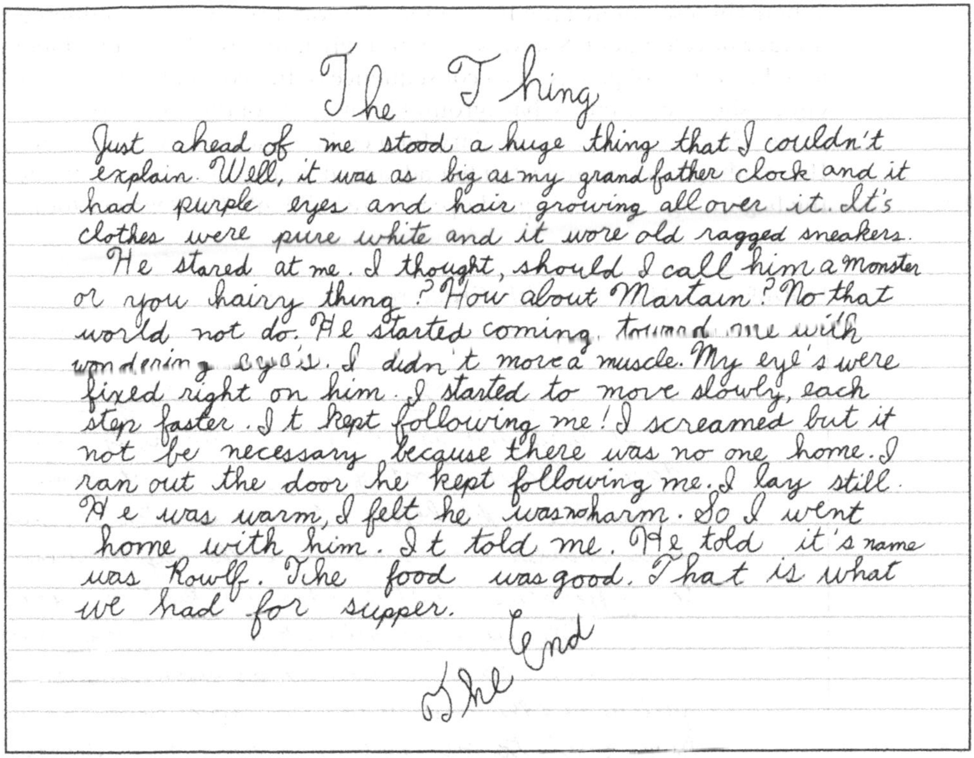

The Thing

Just ahead of me stood a huge thing that I couldn't explain. Well, it was as big as my grandfather clock and it had purple eyes and hair growing all over it. It's clothes were pure white and it wore old ragged sneakers.

He stared at me. I thought, should I call him a monster or you hairy thing? How about Martain? No that world not do. He started coming toward me with wondering eye's. I didn't move a muscle. My eye's were fixed right on him. I started to move slowly, each step faster. It kept following me! I screamed but it not be necessary because there was no one home. I ran out the door he kept following me. I lay still. He was warm, I felt he was warm. So I went home with him. It told me. He told it's name was Rowlf. The food was good. That is what we had for supper.

End

The End

ideas. The DRTA structure is best used "loosely" by the teacher in such contexts. In other words, only appropriate components are used.

If a basal reader is used as a part of John's instructional program, care should be taken to emphasize the reading and activities that enhance comprehension, such as developing background for reading and follow-up discussions. Isolated skills such as structural analysis of words and use of the dictionary, which are often incorporated in basal lessons at this level, should be used selectively and should not be allowed to consume valuable reading time.

Another recommended feature of John's instruction would be a structured program of vocabulary development. He can add to his meaning vocabulary through such whole-class activities as semantic mapping, semantic feature analysis, strategies for using context clues, and other activities described in Chapter 6. John, like other fifth-graders, would also profit from keeping a vocabulary notebook in which he enters new words found in his reading and develops and uses them in various ways. In the content areas, John will profit from teacher guidance in preparation for reading, reading strategies, and follow-up activities described in this chapter and in Chapter 7. He needs to acquire background concepts and relate them to new material. He also needs to become aware of text structure and begin to develop study strategies. At this stage, John's reading instruction should extend across the curriculum.

■ Theresa

When Theresa entered the fifth grade, she was already in the refinement stage of literacy development. She was an extremely fluent reader, read widely, and enjoyed a variety of genres. As a consequence of her considerable literacy experiences, she had extensive background knowledge of the world, of books, and of language. She had a large vocabulary for a child her age and was extremely articulate. Her reading interests reflected her advanced literacy development; her favorites at the beginning of the fifth-grade year were Tolkien's *The Hobbit* (1966) and L'Engle's

FIGURE 8.5   *Theresa's Fifth-Grade Writing Sample*

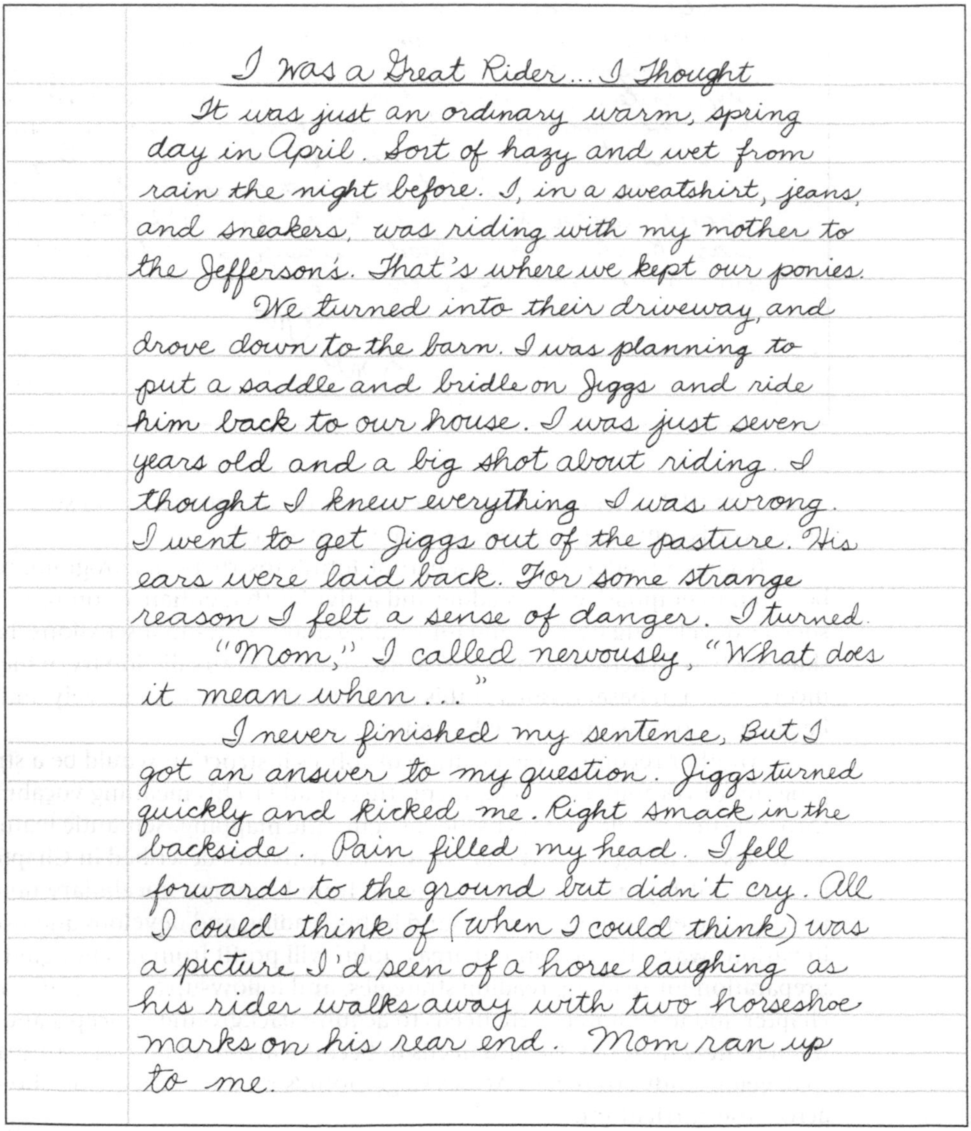

> ### I Was a Great Rider... I Thought
>
> It was just an ordinary warm, spring day in April. Sort of hazy and wet from rain the night before. I, in a sweatshirt, jeans, and sneakers, was riding with my mother to the Jefferson's. That's where we kept our ponies.
>
> We turned into their driveway, and drove down to the barn. I was planning to put a saddle and bridle on Jiggs and ride him back to our house. I was just seven years old and a big shot about riding. I thought I knew everything. I was wrong. I went to get Jiggs out of the pasture. His ears were laid back. For some strange reason I felt a sense of danger. I turned.
>
> "Mom," I called nervously, "What does it mean when..."
>
> I never finished my sentence. But I got an answer to my question. Jiggs turned quickly and kicked me. Right smack in the backside. Pain filled my head. I fell forwards to the ground but didn't cry. All I could think of (when I could think) was a picture I'd seen of a horse laughing as his rider walks away with two horseshoe marks on his rear end. Mom ran up to me.

A Wrinkle in Time (1962). Unlike many of her classmates, Theresa continued to read a great deal outside of school.

Theresa's writing was quite sophisticated by the time she reached fifth grade. She wrote in many genres but had developed a particular interest in poetry writing. She had internalized the components of the writing process, often revised her pieces extensively, and edited her own work with very little help from the teacher. During her fourth-grade year, two of her pieces were selected for publication in children's magazines. She enjoyed keeping a diary and wrote in it daily at home. Figure 8.5 shows a finished composition written by Theresa in October of her fifth-grade year.

"Are you all right?" she asked.

"Yeah," I replied, "but I won't be able to sit down for a month.

"Why don't we take Thumper," she said thoughtfully.

"O. K." I agreed, "if it doesn't hurt too much."

Thumper was a big, fat, lazy pony, who wouldn't move. Somehow we got a saddle and bridle on him and got him up on the road. Mom led us along for aways then said, "I'll go get the car. You wait here for me."

"Alright," I answered hesitantly, "But hurry."

She'd left us in a field about half way home. Suddenly Thumper wheeled and ran towards the Jeffersons.

"Help! Mom!" I shrieked.

We were headed for a bunch of bushes. I couldn't think.; I just held on. Thumper turned sharply, but I didn't. I flew head on into the rose bushes. After I landed I sat up. I looked at the scratches all over me. I thought about what had happened that day, and I cracked up laughing.

Beginning in fourth grade, Theresa participated in a gifted and talented program for fourth-, fifth-, and sixth-graders that met several times each week. In this program she had opportunities to engage in special projects and to pursue some of her own interests in depth. For Theresa, this usually involved extra reading and writing. Before reading further, consider what you would include in an instructional program for Theresa. What needs does she have in common with her less advanced classmates? How would you meet her special needs? After you have formulated some recommendations, read on to compare them with our suggestions.

Theresa's Instructional Program

Since Theresa is already a skilled and highly motivated reader, her teacher's major role will be to support her reading and writing and to stimulate her to extend her literacy experiences. Theresa will be able to participate in whole-class self-selected reading and related activities. Providing her with appropriate choices will be a particular concern for Theresa's teacher. On the one hand, it is important for Theresa to have access to books that challenge and interest her but are not necessarily typical fifth-grade reading fare. On the other hand, she should not be prohibited from reading books that appear to be easy for her but that she has a genuine desire to read. In other words, Theresa needs a wider range of choices than many of her classmates, but she should be allowed to make choices in the same way as the other children. Theresa, like her classmates, should be given time to read books of her choice and opportunities to share her reactions to her reading.

Theresa could participate with other children in the more teacher-directed reading of common trade books. While this might not be a challenging situation for her, she would be included in a group experience and would undoubtedly contribute a great deal to the quality of group discussions. Inclusion in a basal reading group, on the other hand, would not be advised, for the same reasons that have been set forth earlier in her case study.

A very appropriate teacher-led experience for Theresa would be participation in a Junior Great Books program (Feiertag & Chernoff, 1987). In this program, sponsored by the Great Books Foundation, children who are accomplished readers are assigned readings that lend themselves to discussion and interpretation. Discussions follow the shared inquiry model; questions are used by the teacher only to elicit interpretations. The teacher only asks questions that do not have a preconceived answer. Readers are encouraged to refer back to the text to support their interpretations.

Theresa would benefit from the same group and individual vocabulary-building activities that are recommended for John. In group activities she will be an asset in extending other students' understanding of new words. Her own vocabulary growth will probably occur primarily through individual work, such as keeping a vocabulary notebook in which she enters new words encountered in her reading. Since Theresa has a high interest in words, her teacher may introduce her to more sophisticated word development activities to include in her notebook, such as the origins of words or the analysis of their parts.

In the content areas, Theresa will profit from the same kind of teacher guidance described in John's recommendations. Because of her extensive reading experience, she is likely to "catch on" quickly to the use of strategies described in this chapter and Chapter 7. Theresa can be encouraged to supplement text reading with other sources and to share what she learns with the class. The teacher of her gifted and talented program should keep in close contact with her classroom teacher, so that special research or projects can be related, if this seems appropriate and practical.

Theresa can engage in many of the same instructional activities as her classmates; however, she will respond at her own (advanced) level. Her special needs may be addressed through participation in a gifted and talented program; however, if such a program were not available, Theresa's classroom teacher would be able to accommodate her special needs by providing challenging activities and materials, while taking care not to single her out to the extent that she suffers socially.

Summary

The goal of study-skills instruction at the basic literacy stage is to expose students to strategies that will eventually enable them to become independent and efficient learners. The competencies that should be addressed through instruction include previewing texts to be read, organizing and summarizing material, and retaining and using information. We have described several specific activities for fostering these competencies. In all cases, the teacher's role is of the utmost importance. Strategic approaches to reading and studying must be demonstrated, modeled, and practiced with guidance and feedback. At the basic literacy stage, most of the learning from content area texts will be accomplished under the direction of the teacher. By the time students reach the end of the basic literacy stage, they have had extensive reading experience and have explored a wide variety of materials through self-selected reading. They have encountered information and ideas that transcend their personal experience, and as a consequence, they have expanded their background of world knowledge. New words and the concepts they represent have been incorporated into students' meaning vocabularies. Their reading vocabularies have now grown larger than their speaking vocabularies. Students who have passed through the basic literacy stage have increased their awareness of text structure and approach narrative and expository texts with different expectations. They have developed some skill in organizing and summarizing the information they get from texts to enhance their comprehension. They have been exposed to basic study strategies that enable them to cope with different kinds of materials and to retain and recall information. By the end of the stage, students are functionally literate by most definitions; their literacy skills are permanent. They are at the threshold of becoming truly independent students.

BIBLIOGRAPHY

Alvermann, D. E., & Phelps, S. F. (2002). *Content reading and literacy* (3rd ed.). Boston: Allyn and Bacon.

Anderson, T. H., & Armbruster, B. B. (1984). Studying. In R. D. Pearson (Ed.), *Handbook of reading research*. New York: Longman.

Brozo, W. G., & Simpson, M. L. (2003). *Readers, teachers and learners* (4th ed.). Upper Saddle River, NJ: Merrill.

Cleary, B. (1979). *Henry Huggins*. New York: Dell.

Cleary, B. (1982). *Ramona Quimby, age eight*. New York: Dell.

Coffman, G. A. (1994). The influence of question and story variations on sixth graders' summarization behaviors. *Reading Research and Instruction, 34,* 19–38.

Dahl, R. (1961). *James and the giant peach*. New York: Knopf.

Dahl, R. (1982). *The BFG*. New York: Farrar, Strauss, and Giroux.

Feiertag, J., & Chernoff, L. (1987). Inferential thinking and self esteem through Junior Great Books Program. *Childhood Education, 6,* 252–254.

Hayes, D. A. (1989). Helping students grasp the knack of writing summaries. *Journal of Reading, 33,* 96–101.

L'Engle, M. (1962). *A wrinkle in time*. New York: Farrar, Strauss, and Giroux.

McKenna, M. C., & Robinson, R. D. (2002). *Teaching through text* (3rd ed.). Boston: Allyn and Bacon.

Moore, D. W., Moore, S. A., Cunningham, P. A., & Cunningham, J. W. (2002). *Developing readers and writers in the content areas K–12*. Boston: Allyn and Bacon.

Richardson, J. S., & Morgan, R. (2000). *Reading to learn in the content areas* (2nd ed.). Belmont, CA: Wadsworth.

Tolkien, J. R. R. (1966). *The Hobbit*. Boston: Houghton Mifflin.

Vacca, J. L., & Vacca, R. T. (2002). *Content area reading* (7th ed.). Boston: Allyn and Bacon.

9 Refinement Stage

■ *Overview*

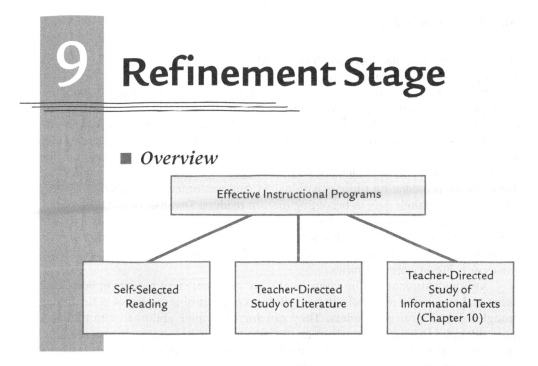

```
Effective Instructional Programs
```

Self-Selected Reading

Teacher-Directed Study of Literature

Teacher-Directed Study of Informational Texts (Chapter 10)

*S*tudents entering the refinement stage have acquired functional literacy. They can competently read and use a variety of everyday materials, including newspapers, magazines, novels appropriate to their age and interests, directions, and reference materials. Literacy has become a major tool for them to use in solving problems and coping with various life situations. Their reading and writing skills have become permanent. Even if formal schooling is discontinued, there will be little if any erosion of these competencies. These children have achieved permanent membership in the "literacy club," the community of readers and writers.

In addition, at this stage readers' interests are expanding. Whereas in previous stages, students often limited their voluntary reading to a particular author or genre, by the time they reach the refinement stage those who have been exposed to a wide variety of reading fare through sharing with other readers are generally interested in sampling a broader range of authors and genres. However, when they discover a new author, refinement stage readers still tend to focus on that writer's works for a while. At this stage, readers have greater awareness of why a particular author's works appeal to them. For example, Nancy Hutton, principal and middle school language arts teacher, reports that her students often choose to read Cynthia Voigt because they can count on meeting realistic situations and characters. They may choose Lois Duncan's books if they like suspense or "happy" endings. From Robert Cormier, they learn to expect complex plots and characters and endings that leave the reader thinking. Readers can identify and explain the authors' approaches and techniques on which their preferences are based.

Provided they have been exposed to discussion and modeling of reading strategies, students who have reached the refinement stage will have begun to approach reading strategically. They differentiate between the requirements for reading narrative and informational texts and know the difference between recreational reading and study reading. They usually monitor their comprehension and are aware of breakdowns in understanding, although they may not yet have effective strategies for remediating these situations. As students enter the refinement stage, they are well on their way to becoming mature readers. The goal of the refinement stage is to extend goals undertaken at the basic literacy stage, using increasingly advanced and abstract materials. From this point on, further reading development is contingent on appropriate instruction and on the extent to which the reader embraces new literacy opportunities.

Although students in the refinement stage are competent readers of both narrative and expository materials, they profit from opportunities to develop further as thoughtful and strategic readers. They can increase their ability to comprehend more difficult, abstract materials, they can add to their repertoire of concepts and the words that represent them (meaning vocabulary), and they can gain access to a greater variety of metacognitive strategies.

The majority of students who are at the beginning of the refinement stage are in middle schools or junior high schools. Virtually all the instructional suggestions for basic literacy stage students remain appropriate for them. Literacy instruction tends to be organized differently at this level, however, because most middle and junior high schools are departmentalized. Since students move from teacher to teacher for different subjects, the responsibility for literacy instruction must be shared. For many students, however, reading instruction across the curriculum is not available. Two related problems persist in the upper grades. First, there is still a perception on the part of some teachers that reading instruction is the province of the elementary grades and that it is not a primary concern of subject area specialists. The other (related) problem is that although teachers recognize that certain students do not read adequately, they often consider this to be a problem for a reading specialist to address; they do not see themselves as part of the solution. Fortunately, these perceptions are beginning to change as teachers become more aware of the process of literacy learning through the reading of professional literature and participation in conferences and in-service courses. In an increasing number of schools, upper-grade teachers are working together to ensure that students' literacy continues to develop beyond the functional level.

Effective Instructional Programs

An effective program for fostering literacy development at the refinement stage includes three major components: provision of opportunities for self-selected reading and sharing; teacher-directed reading of high-quality, age-appropriate literature;

and systematic guidance in reading and study of informational texts in the content areas. Who assumes responsibility for addressing each of these instructional components depends primarily on the organization of the school. In a small rural school where each grade is self-contained, one classroom teacher may be responsible for implementing all reading instruction. The majority of refinement stage students, however, are in departmentalized middle, junior high, or high schools, where different teachers have responsibility for different aspects of the reading curriculum.

In most middle schools and high schools, self-selected reading and teacher-directed study of literature are the province of the English or language arts teacher. These two components of the literacy program will be discussed in this chapter. The remaining component, teacher-directed study of informational texts, will be treated separately in Chapter 10. Throughout our discussion of instruction at the refinement stage, it will be evident that the teaching strategies represent extensions of work undertaken at the basic literacy stage, adapted to meet the more sophisticated needs of refinement stage students.

Self-Selected Reading

At the earlier stages of reading progress, self-selected reading is a primary component of effective reading programs. Extensive independent reading, as we have seen, is crucial to developing fluency, motivation, and experiential background. Provided they have had these experiences, students in the refinement stage are more

Students at the refinement stage need extended reading time.

able to profit from teacher-directed reading of literary works and of content area texts. While self-selected reading no longer dominates the program, it remains an essential component for maintaining motivation and continuing to extend literacy experiences. The three conditions for a successful self-selected reading program—choice, time, and sharing—must continue to be acknowledged.

In order to facilitate appropriate choices by middle school students, teachers must be conversant with the range of materials that appeal to this age group. The genre of "young adult" literature has come into its own over the last few decades. There is now a tremendous variety of high-quality literature available that addresses the concerns and interests of adolescents (Moore et al., 2003). Since the maturity levels of students at this stage vary significantly, it is important that classroom libraries also include books that characteristically appeal to less mature readers (adventure stories, for example) as well as those that appeal to more sophisticated tastes (period novels, classics). Another important concern is the inclusion of multicultural literature that reflects diversity; although not different in form from other literature, the content acknowledges a pluralist view of society, providing students with a realistic picture of the world at large. Reading material that reflects diversity such as ethnicity, race, region, age, gender, and exceptionality allow students whose cultural backgrounds may be different to understand how their culture fits into the mainstream (Roe, Stoodt, & Burns, 1998).

As in the lower grades, it is important to have collections of books readily available to readers. Teachers have consistently reported that well-stocked classroom libraries significantly increase students' interest in reading as well as the amount of time they spend reading (Hickman, 1995). Time for self-selected reading should still be an integral part of the school day. This ensures that all students do at least a minimal amount of voluntary reading, in spite of the increasing demands of out-of-school activities such as homework, sports, babysitting, and socializing. Providing time for reading in school is more problematic in the upper grades than it was in the lower grades since the middle school curriculum is generally departmentalized. English teachers take responsibility for conducting directed study of literature, and other content area teachers are concerned with students' reading of informational texts. Who is responsible for "teaching" self-selected reading—and when? In schools that recognize the value of voluntary reading, answers to these questions have been worked out in various ways. Some English teachers who only see students for one period each day devote certain days or portions of class on certain days to self-selected reading. Other teachers have scheduled a double period for language arts and use part of this period every day for such reading. In still other schools, homeroom periods have been extended to include independent reading and conference time, managed by every homeroom teacher.

Refinement stage students usually choose novels, biographies, and informational books that require extended reading time. As a result, sharing will take different forms. Rather than always conferring about completed books, teachers often conduct mini-conferences about reading in progress. More use can be made of structured peer conferences. The teacher models conferring procedures, and students are invited to confer with each other. Some teachers and their students devise simple conference forms to guide peer conferences. An example follows:

Name of Reader _____

Name of Conference Partner _____

Title/Author of Book _____

Check the questions or items you discussed. Limit your conference to 8 to 10 minutes.

1. What did you especially like or dislike about this book?
2. Were there any characters in this story that impressed you?
3. Were there any parts of this story that were especially interesting or exciting?
4. Were there any parts that were boring to read?
5. If authors of stories received awards for the following categories, for which awards would you nominate the author of this story?
   a. creating characters that are realistic
   b. developing exciting plots
   c. giving readers vivid mental images
   d. writing humor
   e. other

The use of dialogue response journals is another form of sharing that is particularly effective for refinement stage readers. This technique was discussed in Chapter 4. Dialogue journals exemplify the strong link between reading and writing, as students formulate reactions to their reading and verbalize these in writing. The teacher must write back frequently, validating the student's reactions, raising further questions, and suggesting other books that may interest the student. Figure 9.1 shows an excerpt from an eighth-grader's journal. The dialogue journal gives students the

FIGURE 9.1 *Sample Dialogue Journal*

Jan. 23—I am on my third book by Cynthia Voigt, and I still like them a lot. One reason is that her dialogue seem very realistic. I often have the feeling that I probably would have said the same things! Mrs. Voigt seemed to know what the reader would think. The dialogue in *The Callendar Papers* is harder to understand than the others. (I'm reading *The C. P.* now.)

Carol A.

Jan. 24—Why do you suppose the dialogue in *C. P.* is more difficult for you? Have you noticed any other differences between this book and the others you've read by Voigt? Which is your favorite?

Mrs. P.

Jan. 25—The *C. P.* took place long ago. Maybe this is why the dialogue was harder for me. The characters seemed much more proper and well learned than others I've read about, and they talked that way too.

opportunity to have frequent personal exchanges with the teacher. Not only do students benefit from the content of the teacher's feedback, they also enjoy the focused attention extended to them as individuals. This is a powerful source of motivation for reading. Students know that their teacher is very interested in what they read and values their reactions and opinions.

Dialogue journals can be especially useful for helping second-language learners develop a grammatical and lexical base for language acquisition (Fitzgerald, 1993). Although many ESL students may have limited use of English, they can make notes and/or drawings in their journals to express their thoughts. The teacher scaffolds and supports students' early writing efforts and creates a model for writing through her responses. Some second language learners may prefer to read their journals orally to their peers until they feel more secure with the mechanics (Roe, Stoodt, & Burns, 1998).

A word of caution may be in order here. Since personal reactions are encouraged, some students may want to bare their souls or make intimate revelations through their journals. This puts the teacher in the uncomfortable position of having to decide how to respond and whether to report the confidential information to others. This type of situation can be avoided if the teacher explains to all students that although the journal exchanges are private, revelations of serious personal problems, particularly those that involve potential injury, will have to be reported and the student referred for help. In less drastic situations in which students digress excessively, the teacher should guide them back to responses to the literature through questions that encourage them to interpret and seek evidence for their conclusions (Parsons, 2001).

The more frequent the dialogue, the more students will derive from the process. Responding to journals, however, is time-consuming; therefore teachers must devise manageable systems for dialoguing with students. Most teachers who instruct many students in the course of each day rotate the collection of journals in such a way that each student receives a response at least once a week. There is considerable variation in the specifics of teachers' use of dialogue journals; however, the following guidelines should be acknowledged:

- Respond on a regular basis.
- Avoid general, trite responses ("Good work," "Keep up the good reading").
- Responses should convey real interest in the students' reactions. Include statements or questions that promote further inquiry.
- Help students make connections and recognize patterns among books, ideas, and characters.
- Make recommendations for further reading, based on students' reactions.

There are many possible alternatives for sharing reading in upper-grade classrooms. The particular techniques used are not important, as long as certain outcomes are realized. First, students reflect about what they have read, organize their thoughts, and articulate their impressions to others. Second, students learn that their interpretations and reactions are valued. Third, they receive feedback that extends their thinking. Last, their interest in reading is stimulated, and their options for reading are expanded through others' recommendations.

Teacher-Directed Study of Literature

In most upper-grade schools, teacher-directed study of literature receives a great deal of emphasis. While voluntary reading is primarily recreational and very individualized, directed reading ensures exposure to chosen pieces of high-quality literature and the benefits of group study. It adds breadth and depth to the readers' literacy experiences. The study of literature exposes students to legends, myths, experiences, beliefs, values, and aspirations that are part of our cultural heritage. Good literature explores human relationships with nature, deity, self, and society and is characterized by expert use of language and narrative structure. Certainly literature that fulfills these criteria will sometimes be selected by students in the course of their voluntary reading, but the inclusion of directed reading in the program ensures that all students will have at least a minimal exposure to this body of writing.

Reading selections that are carefully chosen by the teacher can lead students to appreciate, rather than simply endure, high-quality literature. Assigned books are usually books that students are unlikely to choose to read on their own. However, they often find that they enjoy these books tremendously. For example, Nancy Hutton reported that Hemingway's *The Old Man and the Sea* became a favorite of most of her eighth-grade students after she assigned it and led a class study of it, although no one had previously chosen it for self-selected reading.

When students and teacher have all read the same piece of literature, they are able to pool their impressions, thus extending their interpretations of the reading. Such group discussions are characterized by lively comparisons of ideas, reactions based upon life experiences, and exploration of alternatives. These kinds of exchanges are most likely to occur when a group of readers shares a common reading experience.

Another outcome of effective teacher-directed reading is heightened awareness of the writer's craft, or the ability to "read like a writer." The teacher draws students' attention to literary elements and how they are used by a given author. Some elements commonly explored with middle school students are character development, manipulation of time sequence (such as flashbacks), use of imagery and figurative language, and creation of mood or tone. On a more abstract level, awareness of the universal themes of literature and their relevance to readers' own life experiences begins to emerge. This level of appreciation is evolutionary and will continue to develop throughout the refinement stage as students are exposed to more and more high-quality literature.

Teacher-directed study of literature can be organized in two ways: whole-group study of a piece of literature that is read by all students, and small-group examination of different texts. The former is orchestrated entirely by the teacher, while the latter typically involves limited student choice of texts and more student-directed discussion. Following are examples of whole- and small-group literature study.

Whole-Class Literature Study

Structure of individual literature lessons will vary according to the selection to be read and the characteristics of the students in the class. Presenting a piece of literature may take one class period or several. When dealing with long selections such as novels or plays, the time spent will be even longer and may consist of a number of related lessons as each section is read. The teacher's presentation follows the general format of the DRTA outlined in Chapter 4. Preparation for reading includes assessing prior knowledge, building new concepts, and establishing purposes for reading. Silent reading is followed by discussion and interpretation, (possibly) rereading of portions of the piece, and extension activities.

The following literature lesson, used with refinement stage students by middle school teacher Martha Corkery, illustrates the use of a modified DRTA format in presenting a short story:

> The DRTA helps my students relate what they already know to their readings, thus facilitating their comprehension of the literature they study as a group. To accomplish this purpose, I have developed the following DRTA for Frank R. Stockton's short story "The Lady or the Tiger":

I. Prereading

I design prereading activities based upon student needs and interests. Following are three that have proved effective with most classes.

- First I pose one or two general questions to students. I ask, "When people commit crimes in our country, how are they punished?" and "How were people punished in semibarbaric kingdoms?" Broad questions such as these allow everyone to contribute. Sometimes I ask students to jot down their responses prior to the class discussion. As the discussion progresses, I attempt to relate general questions to the content of the selection.

- I provide students with a real-life situation that parallels the major issues in the story.

    > "Your boyfriend or girlfriend has broken up with you and you still have strong feelings for that person. If you had to choose one of two alternatives for him/her, which would you select: a beautiful or handsome person to replace you or death? Explain."

    With this age group, this particular dilemma provokes a lively discussion. I generally ask students to write about their choices based on their personal feelings and experiences. This enables them to identify with the perspective of the writer as they read the selection. I feel the writing activity promotes greater student involvement than simply participating in a discussion.

- Since this story has a unique ending, I focus on this particular element of story grammar (resolution). I ask students to think of other stories they have read that had, in their opinion, "good" endings. We discuss how stories usually end and generate a list of characteristics of effective story endings.

II. Reading

After students have developed some anticipation of the content of the story through the prereading activities, I have them read the selection silently, either in class or as a homework assignment. Occasionally I read a portion of the story aloud to further pique student interest.

III. Follow-Up Activities

Follow-up tasks are designed to serve a dual purpose: to assess comprehension and to provide opportunities for students to elaborate their understanding. These activities provide the basis for discussions. Again, I prefer to have students write responses individually or in small groups prior to discussion. I often offer students a choice of activities.

- Referring back to the prereading discussion concerning crime and punishment, I ask the following question: "In this story, one person entirely controlled the fate of the prisoner. Could this happen today?" This question provokes a lively discussion that usually covers a wide range of situations, from the handling of school infractions by the principal to the difference between trial by judge and trial by jury.

- Another activity requires students to relate their prereading discussion to the ending of the story. "What decision do you believe the princess made for her lover? Did she tell him to open the door to the lady or to the tiger? Use details from the story to support your view."

- Referring back to the prereading discussion of story endings, I ask, "Why did the ending of Stockton's story seem so unusual? If you decided to write a resolution to the story, how would you end it? Write your ending to the story." Students would be encouraged to compare their endings.

Ms. Corkery also finds the DRTA can be used very effectively for the study of poetry. Here is a description of her work with a poem by Robert Frost:

My ninth-grade English course is a survey of literary genres, including poetry. Ninth-graders generally enjoy writing poetry, but dislike reading it. The use of the DRTA format helps increase motivation. The perception that poetry is a mystery to everyone but the teacher is dispelled. Activities are designed that enable students to explore the meanings of poems with increasing confidence. In presenting poems, I consider situations, narration, and sometimes symbolism. I begin by addressing the literal meaning of a poem, and, depending on the group, I may also explore poetic structure. Following is the DRTA I use to guide our reading of *Stopping by the Woods on a Snowy Evening* by Robert Frost:

I. Prereading

I use the following prereading activities selectively:

- In an effort to elicit genuine reactions to poetry and to gain a sense of how students view poems, I begin working with this first poem of the year by asking very general questions. This gives students a chance to express their feelings about poetry prior to reading. I ask: "What is poetry? What are some of its characteristics? How do you feel about poetry? Why?"

- Next, I focus on the poem's setting: "How would you describe winter in New England? How do you think a poet might describe it?" To prepare students for the poem's images, I ask: "What are the woods like when it snows? List words you would use to describe snow falling in the woods."

- I lead students to compare traveling through the woods in winter today (snowmobiles, jeeps) with traveling through the woods in winter 100 years ago (horse-drawn carts and sleighs).

- In an effort to activate prior knowledge concerning two literary terms—narration and imagery—I ask students to brainstorm definitions and associations for the two terms. I record their responses on the blackboard and relate them to poetry.

II. Reading

I read the poem aloud to students, and then have them read it silently.

III. Follow-Up Activities

- I begin with a general discussion of the poem's effect on the readers, using some or all of the following questions: "How did the poem make you feel? What do you think Frost was trying to convey, why do you think he wrote the poem? What did the poem make you think about?" I record their responses to point out the variety of interpretations and the validity of all of them.

- Referring back to the prereading discussion, I help students define the term *narrator*. I ask them what they can tell about the narrator, based on the content of the poem. "Can you think of words that would describe the narrator and point out the parts of the poem that lead to your conclusions?"

- Referring once again to our prereading discussion, I help students define the term *imagery*. I ask, "In your opinion, what was the best description in the poem? In other words, which image could you best picture? Write the phrase and explain what you think makes it so descriptive. I provide time for students to share their reactions.

- I have students write a poem about a favorite place, incident, or time of year. I encourage them to use as many images as they can. We discuss the differences between rhymed poetry and free verse. Students are free to use either one.

I find the DRTA to be an extremely valuable tool in the teaching of literature. It provides a structure for group interaction and sharing of background experiences and responses. This process of structured sharing makes the study of literature more relevant and interesting for all of my students.

Small-Group Literature Study

There are many variations of organizational plans for literature study in small groups by refinement stage students. The one we have chosen as an example is used by eighth-grade teacher Noah Brown and emphasizes the following goals:

- To deepen students' understanding and appreciation of literature by talking and writing about their reading
- To promote student sharing of insights about and interpretations of literature
- To promote student responsibility and cooperation in managing their group reading and discussions

Following is a summary of the major components of Mr. Brown's format for small-group literature study:

Book Selection and Formation of Groups

- Mr. Brown obtains multiple copies of paperback books to be used for literature study groups. He tries to get five or six copies of at least twelve different titles. His criteria for choosing books include students' interests, level of reading difficulty, quality, genre, and multicultural interests. Knowledge of the literature is essential; Mr. Brown believes that it is crucial that the teacher read all of the books that are finally selected.
- Before forming literature groups, Mr. Brown gives a brief book talk on four or five books. (When he is conducting a genre study, the books will all be of the same genre; at other times they are unrelated.) He tells the students only enough about the book to "hook" them. Sometimes he shares a particularly interesting passage from the book.
- Next, he provides 15 or 20 minutes for students to look at the books and rank their choices. They fill out a book selection form indicating their first, second, and third choices.
- Next, he groups students, giving them their first choice whenever possible. Student selection is an important element. When first choices are not possible (because groups would be too large or too small), students are assigned to their second choice group. (He makes sure these students get their first choice next time.)

Daily Routine

- At their first group meeting, the students in each group decide how far they will be responsible for reading before they hold a discussion. Because Mr. Brown uses the books for all class periods, books do not leave the room; all reading is done in class. Each group plans how they will keep all group members up with their group reading schedule. Mr. Brown stresses to the students that they are responsible for setting the schedule and for monitoring their own progress. If someone is unable to keep up, the group must plan a way to get and keep that person current. Groups often use the following strategies: pairing a fluent reader with a less proficient reader; taping portions of the text for students who have been absent or who read slowly; and locating additional copies of the book that can be taken home.
- Each day there is time for reading. Mr. Brown has his students spend the last 10 minutes of the period writing their thoughts and reactions to the literature in response journals.

■ When the agreed-upon reading is done, the group members meet, decide what aspect of the book or chapter they want to discuss, and hold a discussion. (At the beginning of the year, Mr. Brown has modeled appropriate kinds of questions, responses, and group behaviors that facilitate maximum participation, interest, and learning. Sometimes he suggests questions or topics for a group to discuss, but often the students generate discussion topics themselves.)

■ Mr. Brown sits in on as many discussions as possible. He sometimes participates in the discussion as a group member. In addition, he monitors and evaluates the work of the group and the participation of individuals within the group. Figure 9.2 shows the simple form he uses to document student contributions and behaviors. He also makes brief notes about what each group is doing well or struggling with. On the basis of this information, he decides what type of teacher-directed strategy lesson, explanation, or group-process intervention is necessary. When a group is having difficulty, he helps them make a web of possible topics to discuss, including characters, favorite parts, theme or message, connections between the book and others the students have read, and connections between the book and their own lives.

FIGURE 9.2 *Teacher's Notes*

Conferencing—Literature Study Groups

Book Title: The Outsiders (group 2)

Week of: 2/5

Andy	2/5 Led discussion Monitored well -	2/8 Interesting questions re kids living on their own.
Lucille	2/5 Very quiet -	2/8 Related story to cliques in school - Personal experiences
Cindy	2/5 Has already judged characters! (Can she go deeper?)	2/8 Dialogue w Lucille about school - Brought back to book focus by Andy
Sarah	2/5 Seems to understand motives	2/8 Sees good side of all characters - (complexity)
Carl	2/5 abs.	2/8 Behind others in reading - Check in SSR -
Seth	2/5 Foresees consequences of actions! e.g. fights etc.	2/8 Brings group discus. to higher level - Comparison to Choc. War & Lord of the Flies.

■ When each group finishes their book, they jointly construct a brief book review and plan an extension activity to present to the rest of the class. Popular choices include dramatizations or readings of a part of the story, character descriptions, and comparisons with other books. Because Mr. Brown usually plans for a week or two of individualized self-selected reading between these culminating activities and the beginning of the next unit of literature study, the fact that the groups need different amounts of time to finish their reading and activities is not a problem.

Novice teachers are often concerned about classroom management, since this format releases a great deal of responsibility to the students. Mr. Brown stresses several prerequisites for successful literature study. He does not begin using the above format until he has become familiar with the class and the class has become familiar with his expectations and management style. Moreover, they have learned the process for supportive work in groups and have seen the components of the program (journaling, conducting and participating in meaningful discussions, and sharing responsibility for learning) modeled. Mr. Brown recommends that teachers who are concerned about classroom management experiment with one class first and then revise practices before implementing discussion groups in other classes.

Effectiveness of Literature Study

Although lesson format is important, the effectiveness of the directed study of literature depends largely on the teacher. The pieces of literature to be studied should not be determined solely by what is available in an anthology or by a rigid specification of curriculum; rather, the teacher should select the literature to be studied based on her judgment of what would be appropriate for her students, considering their maturity, background, and previous literacy experiences. In order to do this, a teacher must know her students and know the literature available. Most important of all, she must feel and project real enthusiasm for the literature she is teaching and convey to students that such study has real relevance and merit. The teachers who do this best are those who begin by helping students make connections between their own experiences (both "real life" and literary) and the piece of literature being studied. As students become involved in the reading, such teachers lead them to expand their interests beyond the limited perspective of the here and now. As we look back on our own experiences in school, most of us can remember teachers who made the study of literature seem boring and dull and others who brought literature alive for us, sparking an interest in authors and works that we would not have appreciated otherwise. The difference was the teachers' knowledge and enthusiasm about the literature and their ability to relate it to our interests and concerns.

Summary

Refinement stage students are functionally literate. As they extend and refine the competencies of the previous stage, they gain in independence and sophistication as readers and writers. Effective instruction for refinement stage readers generally includes three components: self-selected reading, teacher-directed reading of literature, and reading of informational texts and other content area materials.

Self-selected reading is the part of the literacy program over which students feel ownership. They are trusted to choose their own reading fare, maintain adequate records, and share their responses, which are genuinely sought and valued. This is particularly important for adolescents, who are seeking to establish their own identity and to be respected by their peers and by adults. Teacher Nancy Hutton has stated that the voluntary reading program in her classes provides a "doorway of respect" between teacher and students.

In the more teacher-directed components of the refinement stage literacy program, student motivation is less intrinsic. Choices about what is to be read, and how, will be made largely by the teacher; therefore he must have a great deal of knowledge and enthusiasm in order to motivate students to undertake the recommended reading and study. We will devote the next chapter to teacher-directed study of content area texts.

BIBLIOGRAPHY

Fitzgerald, J. (1993). Literacy and students who are learning English as second language. *The Reading Teacher, 46* (May 1993): 638–647.

Hickman, J. (1995). Not by chance: Creating classrooms that invite responses to literature. In N. Roser & M. Martinez (Eds.), *Book talk and beyond* (pp. 3–9). Newark, DE: International Reading Association.

Parsons, L. (2001). *Response journals: Maximizing learning through reading, writing, viewing, discussing and thinking.* Portland, ME: Steinhouse.

Roe, D. R., Stoodt, B. D., & Burns, P. C. (1998). *Secondary school literacy instruction: The content areas.* Boston: Houghton Mifflin Company.

10 Refinement Stage

Content Area Reading Grade 6 → 7

■ *Overview*

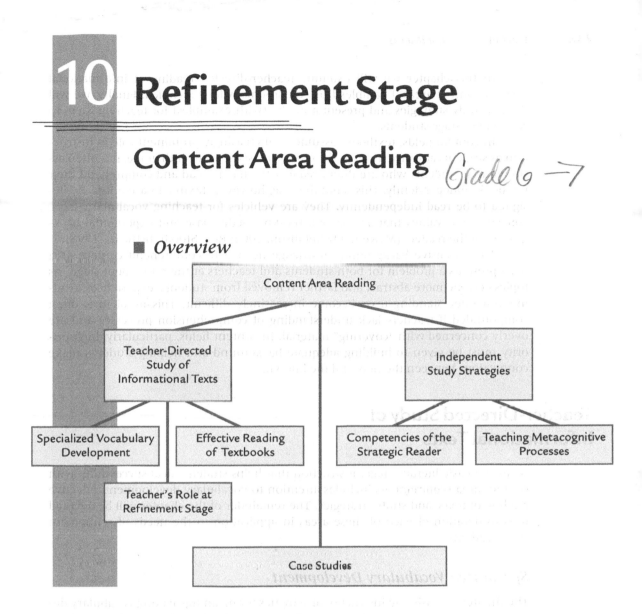

An important component of the literacy program in the refinement stage is teacher-directed study of content area materials. Building on their basic literacy competencies, students learn new reading/study strategies for successful processing of the various types of texts encountered in different curricular areas. In the guided study of literature, which typically takes place in language arts classes, students analyze, interpret, and appreciate narrative and poetic works and make connections between the perspectives of author and reader. In other content area classes, students read informational material for the purposes of understanding and remembering, adding to their store of world knowledge.

In this chapter we will examine teacher-directed reading of informational texts in content areas. Examples from classrooms will be included. Finally, we will discuss study strategies and present a model (with examples) for teaching them to refinement stage students.

In content fields, textbooks assume an increasingly prominent role in instruction as students advance through the grades. By sixth or seventh grade, it is often assumed that students who are fluent readers are able to read and comprehend their textbooks independently. This is not the case, however. Textbooks are not really designed to be read independently. They are vehicles for teaching vocabulary, facts, concepts, and values that are beyond the knowledge base and experiential background of the readers (McKenna & Robinson, 2002; Roe, Stoodt, & Burns, 1998).

The extensive background knowledge needed to comprehend content area texts presents a problem for both students and teachers at the refinement stage. As topics become more abstract and farther removed from students' experiences, reading and understanding texts become increasingly difficult. This problem is often compounded if teachers lack understanding of comprehension processes and are overly concerned with "covering" material. In content fields, particularly, high priority must be given to building adequate background and helping students make connections between the new and the known.

Teacher-Directed Study of Informational Texts

As in the basic literacy stage, instruction that helps students deal successfully with content area requirements includes attention to vocabulary development, effective reading of texts, and study strategies. The remainder of the chapter will be devoted to consideration of each of these areas in application to the needs of refinement stage students.

Specialized Vocabulary Development

The theoretical basis and instructional activities for meaning-making vocabulary development that were presented in the discussion of the basic literacy stage apply to the refinement stage as well. At this level, however, because of the increasing use of content area texts, students encounter far more new concepts and technical terms than they did at the preceding stage. This inundation of new vocabulary affects students' comprehension. The relationship between vocabulary knowledge and reading comprehension has been extensively investigated and has been summarized by Vacca and Vacca as follows:

> There is a strong connection between vocabulary knowledge and reading comprehension. If students are not familiar with most words they meet in print, they will undoubtedly have trouble understanding what they read. Long words bothered Pooh, probably as much as technical vocabulary—words unique to a content

Importance of vocab + comprehension (handwritten margin note)

area—bother students who are not familiar with the content they are studying. The more experience students have with unfamiliar words and the more exposure they have to them, the more meaningful (and less bothersome) the words will become. (Vacca & Vacca, 2002, p. 160)

It should be noted that Vacca and Vacca are not suggesting superficial introductions of word definitions in preparation for reading. In order to affect comprehension, vocabulary instruction must be embedded in the development of a larger schema for the topic and must go well beyond simply defining words. Yet so many new words occur in students' texts that teachers are faced with a dilemma.

Another complicating factor is that the greatest proportion of new vocabulary introduced at this stage is technical. Recognition of the difference between specialized (technical) vocabulary and general vocabulary (described in Chapter 6) is essential for teachers of refinement stage students. Technical vocabulary is rarely if ever used outside of the subject area in which it is taught. This is not the case with general vocabulary, which students have opportunities to hear, see, and use in a variety of settings, extending and reinforcing their understandings.

Another problematic characteristic of technical vocabulary is that each new word must be learned in relation to a cluster of equally unfamiliar words. For example, to truly understand the meaning of *atom*, one must also be familiar with the terms *electron, proton, nucleus, molecule,* and *element*. Teachers must ensure that students have adequate opportunities in class to develop meanings for such clusters of new technical words and to have the relationships among concepts demonstrated (Rupley, Logan, & Nichols, 1999).

The following "words to be learned," assigned to a group of sixth-graders in their science class, illustrate the problems of dealing with technical vocabulary:

annelida	endoskeleton	nymph
antennae	exoskeleton	ovary
arachnid	insect	placenta
arthropoda	invertebrate	platyhelminthes
coelenterata	larva	porifera
crustacean	mammal	pupa
echinodermata	metamorphosis	uterus
embryo	mollusca	vertebrate

Left to their own devices, students are likely to look up the definitions of the words in the text, write them down, and try to memorize them. This is likely to be a futile exercise. First of all, there are far too many words in the list to be memorized out of context. Moreover, they are listed in alphabetical order rather than by logical groupings based on their meanings. The list contains many terms in their Latin forms, adding to their unfamiliarity.

Teachers who are using texts with such lists must help students cope with vocabulary learning. The teacher's first concern should be to help students build familiarity with essential concepts and terminology *before* reading the chapter. The goal of

1. Vocab before read (handwritten margin note)

such background building is not to have students memorize every new term in the chapter; rather, the teacher attempts to demonstrate the relationships among the new terms and show how the new concepts relate to what students already know. As teachers work with content area material, they must keep in mind that new information, to be understood and used, must be related to a larger schema. Therefore, teachers must identify superordinate concepts ("umbrella" concepts that describe major categories) and begin instruction with them. Learners must know what, in general, they are going to learn about.

For example, the preceding vocabulary list was at the end of a chapter that discussed the animal kingdom. The teacher could begin by pointing out to students that the chapter, which is entitled "Animals: The Many Kinds," will explain how scientists classify or group animals. This may seem obvious; however, many students will not discern this unifying topic unless it is brought to their attention. This first, very general explanation should be nontechnical, using vocabulary and examples that are familiar to the students. Once this framework has been established, the teacher can elaborate, showing how *superordinate* and *subordinate* ideas are related and introducing new terms and examples. To illustrate this, we have designed a sample lesson for "Animals: The Many Kinds."

Sample Lesson

The chapter covers a large amount of information, as reflected in the vocabulary list, and its organization is difficult to discern—it is not reader-friendly. In the absence of extensive teacher assistance and preparation, students would have extreme difficulty comprehending the material. The teacher approaches the lesson by selecting the key concepts and related terms that he believes are most essential for understanding the chapter, and by grouping these terms in "clusters" for teaching. The teacher then proceeds as follows:

- First, he prepares a structured overview to introduce the vocabulary, show superordinate and subordinate relationships, and provide an advance organizer for reading the chapter (see Figure 10.1).
- After giving students the general orientation to what the chapter is about, the teacher explains that most of the new, unfamiliar vocabulary consists of scientific terms for groups of animals, most of whose common names are familiar. He then goes through the overview, pronouncing each new term and explaining how the terms are related. He alerts students to the fact that the text will contain descriptions of the characteristics of each class of animals. There will be information about their structures, ways of moving and eating, and reproductive functions.

  Several words on the vocabulary list relate to body structures or to reproduction. The teacher decided not to include these in the structured overview, but rather to elaborate on them following the reading if students were unclear about their meanings. The reasoning behind this decision was that *the number of new words introduced prior to reading should be limited, clearly related, and essential for making sense of the text.*

FIGURE 10.1 *Structured Overview*

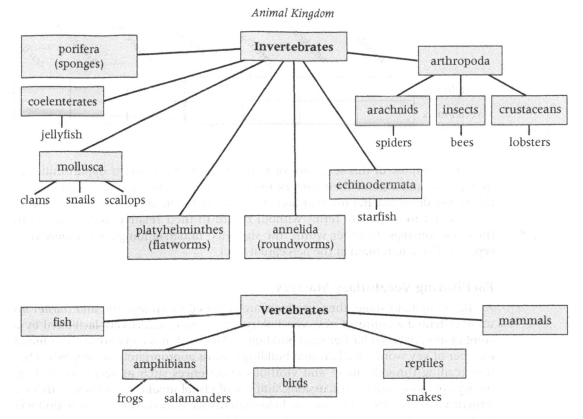

Collaboration
Sort/Classify
Brainstorm
Share
Read
Conference
Share
Extension
Activities

■ Before having students read, the teacher breaks the class into several groups and asks each group to take two or three classes of animals, generate examples of animals that belong in that group, and <u>brainstorm</u> the characteristics that are common to animals in that group. Students then share their responses. The teacher might record their observations on a large copy of the structured overview and remind them to verify and add to this information through reading.

■ Following the reading of the chapter (in class), students return to their groups to elaborate their examples of animals and their important characteristics. Again, they share their information with the class.

■ Additional follow-up activities would further reinforce students' understanding and application of the two major classifications, vertebrates and invertebrates. (These are terms the teacher has decided are most important for students to remember.) Students could be engaged in concept-building activities that involve <u>sorting</u>, or <u>downward classification</u> (see Chapter 6). One activity would require students to classify animals as vertebrates or invertebrates. Another would involve a simple <u>semantic feature analysis</u>, whose grid is shown in Figure 10.2

FIGURE 10.2   *Grid for Semantic Feature Analysis for Sample Lesson*

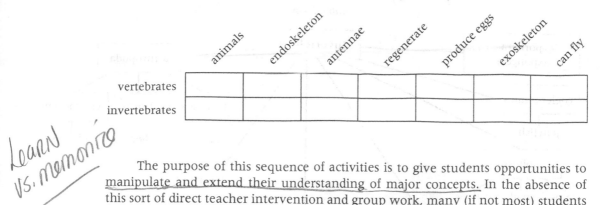

[handwritten: Learn vs. memorize]

The purpose of this sequence of activities is to give students opportunities to manipulate and extend their understanding of major concepts. In the absence of this sort of direct teacher intervention and group work, many (if not most) students will attempt to memorize terms without regard to their relative importance or to their relationships. In other words, the students' understandings of the new concepts are likely to remain at the perceptual level.

Facilitating Vocabulary Mastery

At the refinement stage, then, students are required to understand and master an unprecedented amount of new vocabulary. This is most effectively facilitated by a combination of broad background building and focused, intensive study of a limited number of key words. Background building is most appropriately accomplished before reading through direct and vicarious experiences such as seeing or making models, demonstrations, discussions, and use of visual media. After these activities, structured overviews can be used to help students see how the new information will be presented. With this knowledge base established, students will comprehend the text better and will further expand their understanding of the topic. If these conditions are met, focused study of the key vocabulary following the reading will lead to real ownership of the words. Focused study might include semantic mapping, semantic feature analysis, discovering relationships between words, creating definitions, and using the words in discussing or writing about the topic studied. Vocabulary learning requires the availability of good models as well as attention and effort on the part of the students; perhaps most important of all is the realization that vocabulary development is inextricably intertwined with concept attainment.

[handwritten: Scaffolding]

Effective Reading of Textbooks

It has long been recognized that students tend to have difficulty understanding textbooks; nevertheless, textbooks continue to predominate in content area classrooms at the middle school level and beyond. Many teachers deal with the problem by essentially ignoring the text (although readings are typically assigned) and presenting the material they think is important through lectures, activities, and guided discussions.

Another solution is to use simple, "watered down" texts that students find easier to read. While this may seem like a logical solution, it creates new problems. As we demonstrated in Chapter 5, rewriting textbooks according to a readability formula tends to rob them of content and make them more difficult to comprehend. Lack of precision, explanation, and elaboration results from restricting writers to the use of short, common words and simple sentence structures. Moreover, much content that is important to teach cannot be adequately described without the use of technical vocabulary. Can you imagine trying to teach how plants manufacture their own food without using the terms *photosynthesis, carbon dioxide, chlorophyll,* and *glucose?*

Neither of these solutions is in the best interests of students. There is no need to abandon texts simply because they appear difficult. Teachers need to become aware of the potential difficulties of texts in order to help students learn from them. Many obstacles to comprehension and learning can be eliminated by anticipating problems and compensating for them (Fielding & Pearson, 1994).

One of the most common sources of students' difficulty in comprehending textbooks is their lack of adequate background knowledge about the topic. This problem has already been extensively reviewed. Most other sources of difficulty relate to the organization and presentation of ideas in the text. Many texts, for example, do not include introductions that alert the reader to the content and plan of each chapter or section. Summary statements may also be absent. These aids highlight key ideas and often help the reader relate the new information to a broader framework. If the book does not include other aids, such as topical headings, italicized points, or other visual clues that signal main points of information, the reader may not identify key ideas. Writing style may also hinder the reader. If the writing is unnecessarily complex or if ideas and terms are not sufficiently explained, understanding will be difficult. Overuse of "fact packing" is common in many texts and makes reading tedious and difficult. The effective content area teacher must design strategies that will diminish the interference of all these problems as students read their texts.

Content Area DRTA

Many strategies to maximize the effectiveness of textbooks are described in professional content area material (Alvermann & Phelps, 2002; McKenna & Robinson, 2002; Richardson & Morgan, 2000). Since this is an introductory reading text, we will limit our discussion to one generally useful reading strategy, the Directed Reading–Thinking Activity (DRTA), which has already been described in several contexts but has special applications for refinement stage students dealing with content area textbooks. We will provide a detailed description of the content area DRTA.

Writers of content area textbooks have suggested various modifications of the DRTA and have used different labels to describe these formats—REAP technique: Read, Encode, Annotate, Ponder; GRP: Guided Reading Procedure; and IF: Instructional Framework (Richardson & Morgan, 2000; Stauffer, 1969). However, these techniques are all designed to help students deal more successfully with text content and all include preparation, reading, and follow-up. The DRTA can be appropriately used with content area texts provided it is modified to accommodate the special character of those materials. Table 10.1 shows the components of a content area DRTA. Let us examine each of these components in more detail, noting what is unique to the context of content area reading.

TABLE 10.1 *Components of a Content Area DRTA*

Instructional Plan	Rationale
Before reading	To build and sustain motivation, access prior knowledge, build conceptual background, and establish purposes, through previewing and predicting.
During reading	To promote reader–text interaction, prompt active response to reading, and promote comprehension monitoring.
After reading	To reinforce and extend ideas from text; organize and utilize information.

Preparation for Reading/Prereading. The components of this phase of the traditional DRTA—motivation, concept building, new vocabulary, and setting purposes for reading—must be extended when using content area texts because of their concept density and complexity of structure. *Motivation*, for example, requires more attention. Most students, under most circumstances, would not choose to read content area texts. When they engage in self-selected, recreational reading, the rewards are intrinsic; such reading is pleasurable. This certainly is not often the case with content area reading; more extrinsic rewards are required to sustain students' motivation. An important element in motivation seems to be the relationship between the effort required to perform a task and the reward. In upper-grade content area classes, the rewards usually consist of the personal satisfaction of succeeding, positive encouragement from the teacher, and a satisfactory grade. Students who initially spend considerable effort attempting to read and understand a difficult text only to meet with failure and poor grades soon give up the effort. How, then, can the teacher foster motivation? First, the teacher must demonstrate enthusiasm for the subject matter and make its relevance known to students. Second, the teacher must have realistic expectations of students and must make sure that success is within their reach and that their efforts will be rewarded. Last, the teacher must provide and model the strategies and skills that will enable students to complete the assignment successfully.

As students move into the refinement stage, their reading for content area subjects becomes further removed from their personal experience and more concept-dense. For this reason, more time has to be devoted to *background building* than was the case in earlier stages. This phase of the DRTA is crucial for students who are learning English as a second language since new concepts and vocabulary will present special challenges for them in content subjects (Alvermann & Phelps, 2002). Students need guidance both in understanding the ideas presented and in perceiving the organization of those ideas. Preparing students to deal with text content involves establishing what they already know and reviewing what they have learned about the topic from preceding readings and discussions. New concepts may be built through direct and vicarious experiences. New vocabulary will be introduced during this process. Many of the techniques described earlier, such as brainstorming or discussing responses to a semantic feature analysis, would be appropriate for this purpose. To help students discern the organization of the material, structured overviews are particularly effective.

The preparation for reading, up to this point, has helped to heighten students' anticipation of what they will encounter in the reading. The final step, _establishing purposes for reading,_ is simply a matter of previewing the text itself to predict in more detail what the author will cover. The teacher leads the students in surveying the chapter; noting organizational aids; considering the title, headings, and subheadings; examining illustrations, diagrams, and other visual aids; and finally reading the chapter summary, if there is one. This process develops in students an _anticipatory set_, a predisposition for reading with a sense of inquiry.

Look up

Silent Reading/Reader–Text Interaction. At the end of a well-executed preparation, students are ready to engage in reading the text with adequate background and reasonable anticipation of what they will encounter. They should be allowed and encouraged to read (silently) whole sections or chapters of text independently, without interruption. Unfortunately, there is a trend among publishers of content area texts toward production of teachers' guides that more and more closely resemble the teachers' manuals for basal readers. In many cases, the reading of text is overdirected; the teacher is advised to interrupt students at the end of each paragraph and prepare them for the next one. This practice turns reading of texts into drudgery

Students survey a chapter in preparation for actually reading it.

and certainly does not foster independence in reading. If preparation for reading has been adequate, most students will be able to process large chunks of text independently, stopping for further guidance at logical stopping points such as the end of a section or chapter.

Follow-Up to Reading/Postreading. Information acquired during reading is more likely to be assimilated if follow-up is undertaken. The teacher may begin by encouraging students to explain what they learned from the reading. The structured overview is often used as a point of reference or may be expanded. Paraphrasing, or expressing ideas from the text in their own words, requires students to organize and to demonstrate understanding. Until readers are able to express ideas in their own words, they do not really understand the material.

Once the teacher has established that students have grasped the basic content, they can be led to explore the relationship of this new information to broader contexts. "How does this information relate to what we learned in the last chapter?" "How did this new information change your notion about _____?" "Did this historical event remind you of anything that has happened recently?" Many teachers have students work in small groups to collaborate on such follow-up activities as completion of a semantic map or feature analysis chart, generation of "test" questions for other groups to answer, or brainstorming associations for new vocabulary encountered during the reading. Such follow-up activities, like all the elements of the content area DRTA, are designed to help students deal successfully with content area texts.

Sample Lesson

Following is a middle school science lesson that illustrates how the teacher incorporates the DRTA format. The text chapter, entitled "The Earth's Changing Crust," is about continental drift and plate tectonics theory. The chapter begins with a description of Wegener's theory that the continents of the earth were originally joined together and gradually drifted apart. Evidence for this theory, including the shapes of the continents, fossil remains, and geographical features along the coasts, is discussed. Next, the chapter goes on to describe the discovery of mid-ocean ridges and the evidence of sea floor spreading that led to plate tectonics theory, which describes the continents as parts of much larger "plates" that float on the earth's mantle, or liquid interior.

   I. **Prereading**
  - The teacher begins by drawing students' attention to the chapter title and asking:

    What do you think the chapter will be about?
    What is the earth's "crust?"
    In what way is it changing?
  - A globe is brought out, and names of the major continents are reviewed. The teacher asks, "Does land ever move? Could a whole continent move?"

■ The teacher has made several sets of cardboard cutouts of the continents. She divides the class into groups, gives each group a set of cutouts, and asks them to try to fit all of the continents together. (She explains that they will not fit exactly, like pieces of a jigsaw puzzle, but might fit more crudely.)

■ She shows an enlarged map of Pangaea, the original supercontinent hypothesized by Wegener, and students compare their solutions to the map. The teacher introduces the term *continental drift theory*, which assumes that the continents were once one land mass, which split into pieces that drifted apart. She invites students who have prior knowledge of this concept to contribute to the discussion and tells students, "When you read about this theory, see what other evidence there is to support the idea that the continents were once together."

■ The teacher asks students to share their impressions of what the ocean floor looks like. When they have done this, she shows a topographical map and points out the mountains and trenches in the ocean floor. She introduces the term *plates*, and explains that today scientists think the plates are moving, not just the continents. Next, the teacher asks, "What is below that, deeper in the earth?" She draws a cross section of the earth on the board, and with students' help, labels the liquid core, mantle, and crust (see Figure 10.3).

■ The teacher brings in several pieces of Styrofoam and a pan filled with a mixture of flour and water (the consistency of mud). First, she places the Styrofoam chunks close together on a hard surface, the top of a desk. "Will they drift apart?" she asks. Next, she places the pieces of Styrofoam together on top of the flour–water mixture and says, "Suppose the Styrofoam represents the earth's crust, and the flour–water mixture represents the earth's mantle, which is more liquid." (She refers to the diagram on the board, so students can see the relationship between the earth's crust, mantle, and core.) She asks students to predict what would happen to the styrofoam chunks if the mixture beneath them began to move. To test their hypotheses, she stirs the mixture gently, taking care not to touch the styrofoam with her spoon. The Styrofoam chunks shift position, showing how plates might "drift" on the mantle.

FIGURE 10.3   *The Earth*

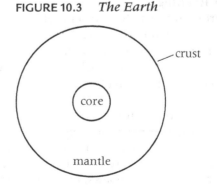

crust

core

mantle

FIGURE 10.4   *Structured Overview*

The Earth's Changing Crust

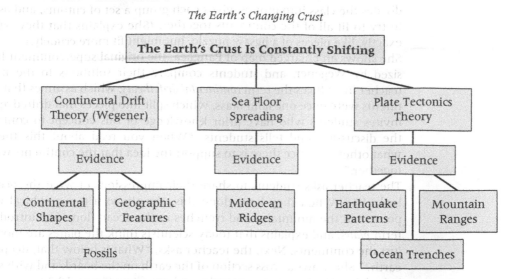

- The teacher hands out the following structured overview (Figure 10.4), and discusses the organization of the chapter. She points out that students will find information about the evidence for each theory and will be able to add to the overview after reading.

The preparation for reading this chapter takes two class periods. This is not unusual at this stage, since a great deal of background is necessary for understanding the reading. Immediately before the students read the chapter (during the third class period), the teacher leads them through a brief survey of the chapter, pointing out topics and visual aids and reminding students to pay particular attention to bold print terms.

II. Silent Reading

For various reasons, the teacher prefers to have the students read the text during class time rather than as a homework assignment. Anticipating that some students will complete the reading before others, she suggests that when they finish reading, they refer back to the structured overview and jot down additional evidence for each of the three theories.

III. Follow-Up to Reading

- When all students have completed the reading, the teacher uses the structured overview to guide a whole-class discussion of the key points in the chapter. As evidence for each theory is discussed, she encourages students to add this information to their overviews, to be used for later review.

FIGURE 10.5 *Semantic Feature Analysis Chart*

	Magma	Fossils	Mid-Ocean Ridges	Movement of Earth's Crust	Plate Boundaries	Alfred Wegener	Earthquakes	Earth's Mantle	Floating
Continental Drift									
Sea Floor Spreading									
Plate Tectonics Theory									

■ The teacher then distributes a semantic feature analysis chart (Figure 10.5) and reviews directions for its completion. The students work in small groups to fill in the chart, discussing the reasons for their choices. The groups then compare their solutions with the rest of the class.

Writing activities are one of the most effective ways of enhancing content area learning. Informational *learning logs* are becoming an integral part of the curriculum in many content area classes. They are among the most frequently recommended strategies for helping students learn English as a second language (Alvermann & Phelps, 2002). Many formats are possible. The students in this class keep learning logs that are used in various ways. One section is devoted to new vocabulary. For this particular chapter, they were asked to select three new terms, enter them in their logs, and develop them. Figure 10.6 shows a page from one student's log.

Students also make regular log entries consisting of their reactions to classes, specific activities, and reading. They are encouraged to record what they have learned, what is new or interesting, and what they like or dislike about the work they do, as well as to write questions about material that they find confusing or do not understand. The teacher collects the logs periodically and writes responses to each student. Figure 10.7 shows excerpts from one learning log.

Teacher's Role at the Refinement Stage

The format of our sample lesson illustrates how a content area DRTA may be designed and implemented to maximize student learning from texts. This approach is strongly teacher-directed and is called for even at the refinement stage when

FIGURE 10.6   *Vocabulary Page from Student's Learning Log*

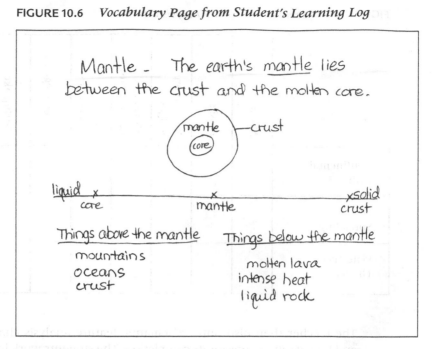

FIGURE 10.7   *Excerpt from Learning Log*

April 2:   I already knew the names of all the continents but I never thought about them moving. I liked the puzzle. It really showed how the continents could fit together. But I don't understand how anything as huge as a continent could move that much.

April 3:   There are mountain ranges and deep trenches like canyons under the ocean. I learned that the continents and the land under the ocean are on *plates* that can move because they kind of float on the earth's mantle.

    The experiment was neat. The pieces of styrofoam could drift on the pasty stuff, but not on the desk. So if the huge plates of earth can drift, they must be on something pretty liquid.

April 4:   After I read the chapter I decided I agree with the plate tectonics theory. There is a lot of evidence, like the fossils on the coasts match, like they used to be together.

    At first I expected the chapter to be boring, but it was pretty interesting. I liked working on the chart in groups. We had some arguments about the answers. It is easier and more fun to work together.

extensive concept building is necessary. As students proceed through the refinement stage, they will be expected to do more and more of the actual text processing and study independently once background concepts have been established. The teacher's role shifts from leading them through the entire DRTA to preparing them (in terms of concepts, vocabulary, and suggested approaches) to complete the reading and follow-up components independently. This shift can be successfully accomplished as students acquire proficiency in the use of study strategies.

Independent Study Strategies

During the basic literacy stage, most students are introduced to the use of textbooks and to the differences between studying and reading. Their teachers lead them through some basic study techniques such as use of reference tools, previewing, and summarizing. For the most part, these strategies are taught through demonstration, without much analysis. For example, previewing is introduced as a generally useful strategy for approaching content area texts. At the basic literacy stage, the teacher demonstrates each step and leads students through their application. The teacher makes the decisions about when and how students should apply the technique. Similarly, summarizing is begun as a group activity, led by the teacher and designed to give students an awareness of what the process involves. If these sorts of experiences have been provided, students entering the refinement stage will be able to analyze the requirements of a task, decide independently which strategy or approach will be most appropriate to the situation, and execute it (Baker & Brown, 1984). In the case of previewing, for example, students would assess the material to see whether it would lend itself to the use of that strategy. They would also consider their purposes for reading the assignment. Based on these observations, they might decide to use all, none, or some of the steps. Summarizing would be an analytical process at this stage. Students would independently scrutinize the text to distinguish major points from less important details and state them in their own words. When these competencies have been acquired, students can truly be called "strategic" readers.

The remainder of this chapter will describe a model through which teachers can help their refinement stage students to become strategic readers. The knowledge that students must have about their own reading strategies and learning processes will be described, along with a format students can use for self-assessment. A plan that teachers can use to foster these competencies will also be developed.

Competencies of the Strategic Reader

The competencies that enable students to process texts independently have their roots in the content area DRTAs led by their teachers over an extended period of time. The reading/study competencies that characterize strategic readers parallel the components of the DRTA. In preparation for reading, strategic readers preview the text, activate prior knowledge, and set purposes. During reading, they monitor their understanding, access prior knowledge, and relate the new to the known. As a follow-up to reading, they organize and study the material for further understanding and recall. Let us examine in detail how strategic readers process text.

Preparing for Reading: Setting Purposes

Until they become strategic, most readers plunge into an assignment without considering the dimensions of the task and doggedly plow through until it is done. In the words of one high school guidance counselor, "These kids do their homework, but they don't study." Previewing text is the first step in establishing purposes for reading. It leads to the formulation of questions that will help access prior knowledge and guide the reading. Strategic readers ask the following kinds of questions before reading:

- In general, what kind of information is in this chapter, and how is it organized?
- What am I expected to get out of this assignment (by myself, by my teacher)?
- What do I have to do to accomplish this? How should I approach the assignment? (Will I need to remember details? Should I take notes?)
- What do I already know about the topic? What do I need to learn?
- Can I read quickly for general understanding, or will I have to read slowly and carefully?

Good to review

Students formulate responses to these questions by analyzing both the assignment and the text. They consider the title, read the chapter introduction and summary, examine any boldface print, inspect visual aids, and look for any cues about the structure and content of the chapter. It should be apparent that previous experience with teacher-led preparation for reading contributes to students' eventual independent use of previewing strategies.

The results of previewing, even for very competent students, vary greatly from one situation to another. If the content of the reading is extremely unfamiliar or the writing style is obscure, a strategic student may conclude that the organization of the content is not discernible, that the reading is going to be difficult and must be accomplished slowly and carefully, and that the teacher or other students may have to be called on for help. There may be a lack of prior knowledge that the student is unable to compensate for. Although such conclusions may discourage students, the fact that they were drawn reflects awareness and strategic thinking about the difficulty of the task at hand. The student who has engaged in this process is more apt to gain something from the reading than the nonstrategic student, who is likely to read through the text accepting his lack of comprehension as inevitable.

Reading

Having previewed the material and established purposes, the student approaches the reading, anticipating both the content and requirements of the task. As the reading is undertaken, the reader decides on an appropriate reading rate. Because there are many misconceptions regarding reading rates, a few observations about this topic might be in order. Students at the refinement stage (particularly in the high school and college years) are confronted with greater and greater quantities of materials to be read and processed. They (and sometimes their parents and teachers) are convinced that if they could just increase the speed at which they read, they would become more efficient and effective students. This is an oversimplification. First of all, reading rate is contingent on the purpose for reading and the nature of the material. Narrative material that is being read for pleasure, for example, can be read at a more rapid rate than technical directions that must be followed or an informational text on which the reader will be tested (Roe, Stoodt, & Burns, 1998). Second, while it is true that readers who process all text at a very slow rate can learn strategies to speed up their reading, there are limits to the benefit of this sort of training. It is recognized that most informational texts cannot be processed *with comprehension* at rates greater than 250 words per minute. Narrative materials that contain familiar language and content can be read at a considerably higher rate, probably 400 to 600 words per minute. The absolute outer boundary is 800 words per minute. The reader who claims to be exceeding these rates is actually skimming; comprehension will be less than complete (ibid).

Strategic readers vary their rate according to their purposes and the kind of material they are reading. Their primary concern is extracting meaning, and their rate of reading is consistent with this goal. They read as efficiently as possible; even if a text is extremely difficult, they do not slow down to the point of reading word by word, since meaning will be lost. On the other hand, they do not speed up to the point where significant understandings might be missed.

Strategic readers actively monitor their comprehension. (In fact, such monitoring is the basis for selecting and varying reading rate.) General, ongoing monitoring involves the reader's awareness of whether or not meaning is being gained from text. Two metacognitive strategies should occur during reading. First, strategic readers constantly attempt to relate the new material to what is already known. Second, they detect ambiguities and inconsistencies in the text and recognize lapses in their own concentration as they are reading. When they realize that comprehension has broken down, they select from a repertoire of strategies to remediate their absence of understanding. For example, they may decide to continue reading with the expectation that subsequent sections of the text will clear up their confusion. Or they may decide to reread a portion of the text more slowly and carefully. They may look up the definitions of unknown words that appear to be crucial to understanding of the passage. They may even seek help from another student or from the teacher before proceeding (Glazer & Brown, 1993; Moore et al., 2003). Like the prereading phase, the reading itself involves a high level of awareness and independent decision making.

Follow-Up to Reading: Organizing and Studying

Relieved to have finished the reading, the nonstrategic reader closes her book, considering the assignment completed. In contrast, the strategic student engages in follow-up activities designed to organize the material for study and recall. In content area classes, students are characteristically required to demonstrate understanding, which in turn requires retrieval of information. In our discussion of comprehension (Chapter 5) we pointed out that the ability of the reader to organize and classify new information strongly influences how well it will be understood and remembered. If information is to be remembered and used, it must be integrated with the reader's prior knowledge and incorporated into a schema. Activities that help students accomplish this include: reflection and self-recitation, note taking, summarizing, outlining, and semantic mapping.

A logical way to begin the study is to reflect on what has been read. Readers may ask themselves, "What are some important things I learned from this chapter?" "How did this section relate to the preceding chapters?" More focused questions about topics that were covered might follow. "What did I learn about ____?" Paraphrasing helps the reader discover blind spots in understanding sections that should be reread or reviewed (Cooter & Flynt, 1996). Strategic students assume responsibility for self-assessment. Unlike their less successful counterparts, they do not leave this process up to external agents such as teachers and tests.

Following reflection and self-recitation, students can pursue several alternative activities to help them organize and retain the information. One of these is note taking. In order to make notes on the reading, students must identify key ideas and supporting details. Their decisions will be reflected visually in their notes. The act of taking notes facilitates memory, and the finished notes provide an efficient inventory of information for later review. Regardless of the specific format of the notes, the effectiveness of the technique depends on the student's ability to perceive the organization of the material.

Some students find it useful to write their own summaries of subsections of text. Although summarizing is an excellent way to pull together and distill information, it is a difficult, abstract task that usually requires direct teaching and a great deal of guided practice.

Years ago, formal outlining was considered to be an essential study skill. Students were directed to arrange ideas in hierarchical order, using various forms of numerals and letters to indicate the place of each item in the hierarchy. Rules of structure were rigidly adhered to (for example, "you can't include a point A unless you also have a point B"). Informal outlining may be of value to students; however, structure of the outline should be determined by the content, not vice versa. More recently, semantic mapping has largely replaced outlining as an effective way to represent content organization and show the relationships among ideas from the text. It is not only more flexible than the outline, but it makes relationships more apparent.

Teaching Metacognitive Processes

Most successful students do not become strategic simply by chance, or even entirely by their own efforts. They have been exposed to systematic modeling and the direct teaching of strategies by teachers who understand the processes involved in effective study. Following is a plan that content area teachers can use to teach virtually any metacognitive strategy (adapted from Vacca & Vacca, 2002). It includes four parts: *assessment, modeling, guided application,* and *independent application*. Each of these will be described separately; however, it should be borne in mind that they are likely to overlap somewhat in real instructional situations. To illustrate the application of the plan, we will describe how Jean Haskell, a seventh-grade social studies teacher, worked with her students on comprehension.

Assessment

A general self-assessment of study strategies often provides valuable information to both teachers and students. We have designed a questionnaire to be used for this purpose (Appendix A). The questionnaire has been used successfully with middle school and high school students. Students are led to reflect on their own metacognitive behaviors before, during, and after reading. The data generated can be used by teachers and students to pinpoint instructional needs.

There are several ways the teacher can make use of the completed self-assessments. The data can be used to identify strengths and weaknesses of individuals or the entire class, and the teacher could devise instruction for study strategies accordingly. Another idea is to have students share their responses and discuss common concerns. These exchanges establish a general awareness of the problem-solving behaviors that successful students use to cope with texts. The next step would be to identify areas that need to be worked on and plan simulations to assess the need for modeling strategies.

Self-assessment of strategies leads students to develop an awareness of the need for instruction in specific reading and study strategies. When the teacher is ready to focus on a specific study strategy, she can refer back to the appropriate part of the self-assessment to show the relationship between the strategy and the relevant phase of the study/reading process. For example, instead of presenting semantic mapping as a technique students are required to learn, the teacher would refer to students' self-assessments of what they do after reading and point out that they seem to need more strategies to help them organize and remember what they have read. Semantic mapping is another strategy they will be able to add to their repertoire and use for this purpose.

After a general self-assessment has identified instructional needs, the teacher must assess students' proficiency in using the particular strategy that is going to be taught. First the teacher should ask students whether they are familiar with the strategy and (if they are) how they use it. If they claim to have some experience with the strategy, the teacher will set up a simulation through which she can observe their application of the procedure.

In Ms. Haskell's seventh-grade classroom, she noticed that her students were not monitoring comprehension adequately, judging by their self-assessment responses. Many reported that they generally did not expect to understand textbooks and were unsure of how to identify the parts that caused them difficulty or how to remedy their lack of understanding. She decided to more directly assess students' ability to monitor their comprehension as they read. She constructed a passage that contained several contradictions, ambiguities, and other confusing elements. Students were asked to read the passage silently, placing a check mark at any point where they encountered difficulty understanding what they were reading. Many of them stated that the passage didn't make sense; however, they did not consistently identify the problematic parts of the passage.

Modeling

Virtually all the research on effective teaching underscores the absolute necessity of modeling procedures that students are expected to learn (Brown et al., 1996). No amount of explanation can compensate for the absence of a good demonstration of the expected learning outcome. In order to acquire proficiency at virtually any task or skill, it is necessary to have a clear notion of "how experts do it." Modeling may take many different forms, depending on what strategy is being demonstrated. However, it always involves performing an operation and describing how it is performed. These two features, a part of all effective modeling activities, show students *how* a strategy is employed. It is also important, however, to make sure students understand *why* the strategy is worth learning. Refinement stage students are naturally interested in and capable of understanding the general psychology of learning as it applies to them. Once they have an understanding of how and why a strategy is used, they are ready for guided practice.

To model the process of comprehension monitoring, Ms. Haskell read the assessment passage orally, stopping at various points to think aloud, revealing her thought processes with observations such as, "I'm getting confused. This seems to conflict with what the writer said in the first paragraph. I think I'll go back and reread that part," and "I'm not sure what the writer means by this. If I read on, maybe the writer will explain it." When she had completed the passage, the following dialogue ensued:

Ms. H.: How would you describe what I was just doing?

Student 1: You were thinking out loud while you were reading.

Student 2: You stopped whenever you came to something you didn't understand and thought about it.

Student 3: You read part of it over again.

Ms. H.: Yes, I was doing all those things. This is called *comprehension monitoring*. I was trying to keep track of my understanding all the time I was reading. There are several things good readers do to monitor their comprehension. Let's go through each step together.

Ms. Haskell referred the students to a wall chart of reader behaviors for comprehension monitoring, which she had made in preparation for the lesson (see Figure 10.8). She discussed each of the reader behaviors and related them to her demonstration. Although the students were able to appreciate the value of comprehension monitoring, they expressed doubt that they could do it on their own. The teacher then explained that she would show them a three-step process that would help them begin to monitor their comprehension.

The students were instructed to turn to the beginning of the next chapter in their social studies text. Ms. Haskell led them in a brief survey and overview of the chapter, encouraging them to predict what major points would be covered. She asked the students to read the first paragraph silently. She listed the three steps she was about to model on the board: *Summarize, Question, Predict*. She then demon-

FIGURE 10.8 *How Good Readers Monitor Their Comprehension*

1. They are aware of their level of understanding at all times.
2. They identify the points at which their understanding breaks down.
3. They decide what to do when they don't understand (Reread? Keep going? Ask someone for help?)
4. They take action.
5. They ask themselves whether their strategy worked.
6. They predict what will come next.

strated each one. First, she summarized the main idea of the paragraph in her own words. She asked the students if they agreed that her summary represented what the text said. She also explained that if they had difficulty coming up with a summary, they would have to go back and reread, to clarify. Next, she made up a question that she felt would test readers' understanding of the passage. Rather than have the students answer the question, she explained that making up a question helps readers identify what they should remember. To demonstrate the last step, prediction, she told the students what she thought might come next in the text.

Guided Application

Students' first attempts at using a new strategy are led by the teacher; the procedure is executed step by step, with the whole group participating. Each step is discussed. Thinking aloud is encouraged by the teacher, who asks students not only what they would do next, but also to explain why. Several trials by the group may be necessary before they are ready to try using the strategy on their own. Their first attempts at independent application need to be closely monitored. Immediately following their first independent applications, they should receive feedback and evaluation of their efforts from peers and/or the teacher.

One reason why so many students fail to acquire skill in the use of strategies is that they are not given sufficient opportunities to practice with guidance. Too often teachers omit the guided practice step in the teaching sequence, expecting their students to independently apply a technique immediately after seeing it modeled. We have noted that many students who are interviewed at our university literacy center are able to describe study strategies they have been taught but do not use them successfully. Perhaps this is because the strategies have been presented as recipes, without enough guided practice to lead to functional application.

After modeling the three-step process for comprehension monitoring, Ms. Haskell had the students read the next paragraph of their text silently. She asked them to summarize it in their own words and asked volunteers to share their responses. She then had them formulate and share questions about the content. Then they made predictions and discussed them. Next, she had the students work in pairs.

After reading each paragraph, they took turns demonstrating the three-step process. In subsequent practice sessions, she increased the length of passages read and invited students to work collaboratively.

Independent Application

Practice makes perfect! Even after students have acquired enough proficiency to be able to use a strategy independently, the teacher continues to play an important role. First, she must provide opportunities for students to use strategies that have been taught. She may include note taking as part of an assignment, for example, and require students to pass in their notes. In addition, the teacher must continue to give periodic feedback on students' use of the strategy, if they are to maintain and refine its application.

When the seventh-grade students had had adequate practice working together, Ms. Haskell assigned a section of the text and asked students to read it and jot down a summary statement, a question, and a prediction. When they had completed this work independently, she assigned them to small groups to compare and critique their responses. At the end of the activity, she collected the written responses and analyzed them to assess students' ability to apply the three-step comprehension monitoring process. From this point on she systematically promoted the use of comprehension monitoring strategies.

The activities that Ms. Haskell chose for guided and independent practice are representative. There are many other options for teaching comprehension monitoring. In this example, comprehension monitoring was used to demonstrate real instructional applications of the recommended general teaching format. This same format can be used to design effective instructional sequences for other study strategies including previewing texts, questioning techniques, webbing key ideas, and note taking. The goal is to create independent learners.

■ CASE STUDIES

We will visit Kim, John, and Theresa for the last time when they are seventh-graders, in middle school. They are no longer in self-contained classrooms; they move from teacher to teacher for different subjects. Students in their school are grouped heterogeneously, although there is special help available and a limited gifted and talented program.

■ Kim

When Kim began seventh grade, she was entering the basic literacy stage. She was a fluent reader of materials that did not extend beyond her linguistic and experiential background. She enjoyed independent reading; her favorite author was Judy Blume. Sharing her ideas about books with her teacher and peers was a pleasurable activity for Kim.

In the two years since the beginning of fifth grade, Kim had continued to develop as a writer. She was now writing longer pieces and had explored more genres. Her spelling and mechanical skills were still considerably below those of the majority of her classmates; she continued to require much help with editing.

Through her fifth-grade year, Kim had access to taped texts or to adults who could read content area texts to her. Beginning in sixth grade, when she entered middle school, she was required to read her textbook assignments independently. She found this very difficult and required special help with assignments related to the reading. Although Kim put forth a lot of effort, she received mediocre grades in content area subjects. By the time she entered seventh grade, she had a low self-concept as a learner.

Before reading on, consider Kim's situation and characteristics and speculate as to what sort of instructional program you would recommend for her. Then read on to compare your ideas with ours.

Kim's Instructional Program

Like other seventh-graders, Kim needs to continue to engage in self-selected reading and related activities. Voluntary reading should make up a significant portion of her reading program. As in earlier grades, Kim will be able to participate fully in this part of the program without special help. In addition to sharing through conferences, she can keep a response/dialogue journal in which she records her personal reactions to readings and corresponds with the teacher. Ideally, Kim should continue to have opportunities to write on self-selected topics in the context of a "writing workshop." In addition, at this level she will undoubtedly be required to do more teacher-directed writing across the curriculum. Kim will be able to complete such assignments, provided adequate preparations are given; however, expectations for her work must take into account her developmental level.

Kim will be able to participate in teacher-directed study of literature in her language arts class if the literature assigned is carefully chosen. Kim would probably do best working with a group of students of similar interests and literacy level when reading longer works, such as novels. She could successfully participate in whole-class study of shorter works such as poems and stories when there is more extensive teacher guidance and when material is more likely to be shared through reading aloud. The most important factor in the management of this portion of Kim's instruction is her teacher's awareness of the need to select and assign literature that is not beyond Kim's experience in terms of vocabulary and syntax. If these conditions are met, Kim can be a functional, participating member of the language arts class.

The most difficult area of instruction to plan for Kim will be her work in content areas requiring extensive reading. Kim needs to be placed with teachers who recognize the value of concept building and who devote adequate time to developing background experiences for reading. Kim will benefit from "hands-on" activities like those described earlier in our discussions of vocabulary/concept building and effective reading of texts. These kinds of activities used in preparation for reading will increase the likelihood that Kim will grasp key ideas presented in the text.

Independent reading of the text will be problematic for Kim. There are several alternative approaches teachers could pursue to accommodate the needs of students like Kim. One possibility would be to provide differentiated assignments. While some students read the text, others are assigned alternative readings on the same topic, with the understanding that all information will be shared with the larger group after reading. This results in the pooling of information from several sources, some of which are less complex and easier to read than the text. Nevertheless, students' contributions are valued equally. This approach—providing alternative readings dealing with the same topics—can be used in most content areas. The teacher can collect material from magazines, newspapers (including those designed for less able readers), trade books, and photocopied sections of other texts, for example. A structured overview can serve as a guide for organizing the information. After readings have been completed, students can fill in the overview with information they have gained through reading. Students who have read different sources may work collaboratively to pool their information and complete their overviews. For students like Kim, who are unable to read their textbooks independently, such a collaborative approach exposes them to the content of the lessons and helps them assimilate the key ideas.

On those occasions when the teacher wants to lead the whole class through a text for the purpose of introducing a reading strategy such as reciprocal questioning, Kim would be able to participate because there is such a high degree of teacher guidance and because text is read together in very small units.

The successful management of Kim's content area reading depends on careful analysis of the reading demands of the task. Assignments or lessons that require her to read large portions of content area textbooks independently should be avoided. When alternative assignments are provided for Kim and students like her, it is important that they be legitimately related to the content being studied and that her contributions be acknowledged as valuable.

■ John

When he reached seventh grade, John had entered the refinement stage of reading. He enjoyed reading but still did most of his independent reading at school. His favorite author was Scott O'Dell, and he listed *Island of the Blue Dolphins* as his favorite book. He took responsibility for record keeping and kept his reading log and response/dialogue journal up to date. His responses to reading (in conferences or in the dialogue journal) were spontaneous and often original. He enjoyed having exchanges about books with his friends and was an enthusiastic participant in teacher-led discussions and peer literature groups.

By seventh grade, John's interest in writing on self-selected topics was waning. He seemed more responsive to teacher-directed writing activities that focused on developing techniques for crafting different types of writing. As both a writer and a reader, he was interested in the effects that could be produced by the skillful writer. The reading tasks that John liked least and found most difficult were those that involved content area texts. Like many of his peers, John did not yet make much independent use of strategies when reading informational texts, even though he was a fluent reader. When asked to describe his approach to textbook assignments, John reported that he just read them through to get them done.

Before reading on, speculate about an appropriate instructional program for John. What elements should be included? What would you emphasize? When you have formulated some recommendations, read on to compare them with our suggestions.

John's Instructional Program

Voluntary reading remains an important contributor to John's continued literacy growth. One purpose of communicating with John through a dialogue journal would be to increase his awareness of authors' techniques, styles, and ways of affecting readers. Conversations with refinement stage readers focus less on general reactions to books and more on how authors achieve certain effects. John is capable of discussing how an author develops a character convincingly, how suspense is achieved, why flashbacks are used, and predictable characteristics of individual authors' works, for example. This will lead to evaluation of how successful an author is at achieving intended effects and will have carryover into John's writing. Stressing reading–writing connections at this stage will help John become more proficient at both reading and writing. He will be helped to read from the perspective of a writer and to write from the perspective of a reader. The ability to use both of these perspectives simultaneously is one hallmark of skilled reading.

Another component of John's program will be teacher-directed reading. This will provide breadth of exposure; John will be led to sample authors and works that he would be unlikely to select on his own. John's teacher should make choices of assigned readings based on her knowledge of her students and of appropriate literature. Through assigned readings, John will have opportunities to participate in group discussions based on common reading experiences. These exchanges will provide another vehicle for comparing authors' techniques and styles, analyzing characters, and making reading–writing connections.

John will continue to benefit from a structured program of vocabulary development. He could maintain a vocabulary notebook, adding and developing several words each week derived from his independent and assigned reading. In addition, his teacher should provide direct instruction on strategies for approximating the meanings of unfamiliar words in context. Extensive vocabulary development will also take place in the various subject areas in which technical vocabulary is prevalent.

To help John and his classmates identify and understand the key concepts set forth in their texts, content area teachers should make frequent use of directed reading activities, building interest and background concepts, introducing vocabulary, and establishing purposes for reading. John's content area teachers must also provide direct instruction in reading and study strategies for dealing with informational materials. This instruction should ideally be based on the results of an assessment of students' approaches to texts. The general format for teaching study strategies described earlier in this chapter should be followed. Expectations for independent application should be preceded by abundant modeling and guided practice. Some of the strategies John should be taught to use include previewing, comprehension monitoring, summarizing, note taking, and semantic mapping. If John's interest in reading is sustained, and if he gains skill in processing informational texts, he will continue to advance within the refinement stage.

■ Theresa

Like some of her classmates, Theresa entered seventh grade as a refinement stage reader. However, she had been in this stage since fourth grade and was a highly accomplished reader and writer. Since fifth grade, she had continued to read and write widely for her own purposes, both in and outside of school. Her earlier interest in fantasy had led her to explore science fiction. The summer after her sixth-grade year, Theresa discovered Ursula LeGuin, who became her favorite author.

By seventh grade, Theresa had become aware of many reading–writing connections. She liked to imitate other authors' styles in her own writing, and her response/dialogue journal contained many observations about the techniques used by writers and the effects they achieved. Her compositions were characterized by vivid descriptions, precise vocabulary, the effective use of similes and metaphors, dialogue, and steadily improving character and plot development. Informational reports were well organized and thorough.

Theresa had been a participant in the middle-school gifted and talented program since she entered sixth grade. Through this program, she had opportunities to participate in a number of special projects, including an advanced math class.

Before reading on, consider Theresa's advanced literacy development and speculate as to what you would include in her literacy instruction. Then compare your plan with our recommendations.

Theresa's Instructional Program

Theresa's instructional program should include the same basic components that were recommended for John: voluntary reading and sharing, teacher-directed reading of literature, writing, and content area reading and study. Within each of these areas we could expect differences between John and Theresa in their level of involvement and response. Her self-selected reading, for example, will be more extensive than John's because she is such an avid reader. Her choices of books will be more sophisticated and will very likely include a wider range of authors. Her responses to reading through conferences and dialogue journals will be more analytical. Her teacher can serve as a valuable resource, ensuring that she continues to extend her literacy experiences. The teacher can suggest new authors and recommend challenging books. She can stimulate Theresa's thinking with thought-provoking questions that require her to reflect, think critically, and support her conclusions. The individualized part of her reading program can be implemented within the context of the whole-class voluntary reading component.

Theresa will be able to participate along with John and her other classmates in the teacher-directed study of literature. She will undoubtedly be a major contributor to class discussions and group activities; however, she does not need a separate curriculum.

In content area reading, Theresa's instructional program will be very similar to John's. Directed reading activities, particularly the preparation for reading, will continue to help her deal with the content of text reading by building and elaborating background concepts, introducing technical vocabulary, and setting purposes for reading. Because of her extensive literacy experiences, Theresa is likely to have little trouble reading the required material and performing follow-up activities. Like other students, Theresa will profit from direct instruction in reading/study strategies. However, she will probably require less repeated modeling and guided practice in implementing strategies than most of her classmates. By the end of seventh grade, Theresa can be expected to use basic study strategies (such as previewing, summarizing, taking notes, and semantic mapping) independently and efficiently, whereas most of her classmates will require more guidance.

Throughout her remaining middle school and high school years, Theresa will continue to be an outstandingly successful student, provided she is engaged in a relevant and challenging curriculum. She will need a flexible curriculum within which she can go beyond the basic requirements and extend her knowledge and interests. She will be capable, if motivated, of great independence and self-direction; these qualities should be capitalized on.

Summary

As students progress during the refinement stage, they become truly strategic readers, provided that they receive direct instruction in reading processes and strategies and that they continue to have many and varied reading experiences. Reading instruction shifts significantly at this stage because of school structures and curriculum requirements. Since upper-level schools tend to be departmentalized, the reading program assumes different characteristics. The three major components of the reading program—voluntary reading, teacher-directed reading of literature, and reading/study of informational texts—are most often handled by different teachers. Responsibility for students' reading growth is shared.

The goal of refinement stage instruction is to produce readers who are strategic, who are motivated, and who are on their way to becoming lifelong readers. The refinement stage of reading has no termination point; throughout our lives, the practice of literacy contributes to all aspects of our evolution as individuals.

BIBLIOGRAPHY

Alvermann, D. E. , & Phelps, S. F. (2002). *Content reading and literacy* (3rd ed.). Boston: Allyn and Bacon.

Baker, L., & Brown, A. L. (1984). Metacognitive skills and reading. In P. D. Pearson (Ed.), *Handbook of reading research*. New York: Longman.

Brown, R., Pressley, M., Van Meter, P., & Schuder, T. (1996). A quasi-experimental validation of transactional strategies with low achieving second grade readers. *Journal of Educational Psychology, 88,* 18–37.

Cooter, R. B., & Flynt, E. S. (1996). *Teaching reading in the content areas.* Englewood Cliffs, NJ: Prentice-Hall.

Fielding, L. G., & Pearson, P. D. (1994). Reading comprehension: What works. *Educational Leadership, 51,* 62–68.

Glazer, S. M., & Brown, C. S. (1993). *Portfolios and beyond: Collaborative assessment in reading and writing.* Norwood, MA: Christopher-Gordon.

McKenna, M. C., & Robinson, R. D. (2002) *Teaching through text: Reading and writing in the content areas* (3rd ed.). Boston: Allyn and Bacon.

Moore, D. W., Moore, S. A., Cunningham, P. M., & Cunningham, J. W. (2003). *Developing readers and writers in the content areas, K–12.* Boston: Allyn and Bacon.

Richardson, J. D., & Morgan, R. F. (2003). *Reading to learn in the content areas* (4th ed.). Belmont, CA: Wadsworth.

Roe, B. D., Stoodt, B. D., & Burns, P. C. (1998). *Secondary school reading instruction: The content areas* (6th ed.). Boston: Houghton Mifflin.

Rupley, W. H., Logan, J. W., & Nichols, W. D. (1999). Vocabulary instruction in a balanced reading program. *The Reading Teacher, 52,* 336–346.

Stauffer, R. (1969). *Teaching reading as a thinking process.* New York: Harper & Row.

Vacca, R., & Vacca, J. (2002). *Content area reading* (7th ed.). Boston: Allyn and Bacon.

Assessment

*A*ssessment has two distinct but related purposes. The first is to document general achievement, which is accomplished through standardized testing. Standardized tests are designed by experts and are independent of curriculum and instruction. The audience for this type of assessment is usually outside of the classroom and consists of parents; administrators; and the larger community, which has come to include politicians at all levels of government. This audience views standardized tests as measures of student achievement and teacher accountability. Assessment of student learning at the end of a year, a term, or a unit of instruction is referred to as *summative evaluation*. Standardized achievement tests fall into this category; informal teacher-made tests can also be used for purposes of summative evaluation.

The second purpose of assessment is to monitor the ongoing learning processes of students in order to plan effective instruction. This can be accomplished through observations of students engaged in learning activities or through collections of their work over a period of time. The primary audience for this type of assessment, which is referred to as *formative evaluation*, is teachers and learners. Formative evaluation tends to be informal, ongoing, and tailored to individual contexts. It is designed by teachers to inform classroom decisions, and it is closely aligned to curriculum and instruction. Formative evaluation has become recognized as an appropriate and essential component of literacy instruction (Graves, Juel, & Graves, 2001; Valencia, Hiebert, & Afflerbach, 1994).

The validity and usefulness of assessment practices depend on several conditions:

- A sound knowledge of the literacy acquisition process is a prerequisite for effective assessment. Without such a knowledge base, valid interpretation and use of assessment tools is unlikely.
- There should be a close match in instructional goals (what is being taught, or what we educators want students to learn) and assessment procedures (what is being evaluated). One of the major problems with the general state of reading assessment in the schools is that this match is often absent. If we view reading as an active constructive process, but the instruments we use to assess it are based on a model of reading as a collection of specific skills, there is clearly a mismatch.
- We must recognize that tests provide a very limited sample of behavior. Since no test can evaluate the full range of student reading capabilities, the results must always be treated with caution. Thus, instructional decision making should never be based on the results of a single test or observation in isolation (Graves, Juel, & Graves, 2001; Harp, 1996).
- Assessment should be an integral, continuous part of the instructional process. Sound instruction is always based on some form of assessment of students' competencies, interests, and needs. Daily classroom literacy activities provide a rich source of information that the teacher can use for assessment purposes. Ongoing observation of children while they are engaged in real reading tasks provides more valuable assessment information than any single test does.

In Part IV, we will provide the background that classroom teachers need to understand the differences between formal and informal assessment. Examples of assessment tools will be provided, along with discussions of their strengths, limitations, and appropriate use. We will consider the growing use of standards in assessment as well as the implications of high stakes testing. In spite of the increasing investment in such assessments, we will devote considerable space to informal assessment approaches, which we believe are of great value to teachers in their efforts to provide effective literacy instruction.

BIBLIOGRAPHY

Graves, M., Juel, C., & Graves, B. (2001). *Teaching reading in the 21st century* (2nd ed.). Boston: Allyn and Bacon.

Harp, William. (1996). *Handbook of literacy assessment and evaluation.* Norwood, MA: Christopher Gordon.

Valencia, S. W., Heibert, E. H., & Afflerbach, P. P. (Eds.). (1994). *Authentic reading assessment.* Newark, DE: International Reading Association.

11 Assessment

■ *Overview*

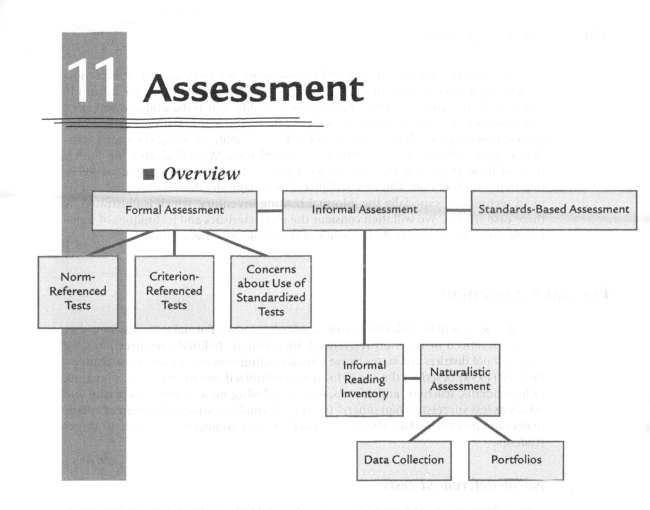

The American educational system and the government policy makers behind it are preoccupied with evaluation; there is constant pressure to prove that students are learning. Performance on tests has traditionally been the accepted evidence for measuring learning outcomes. Students are subjected to national tests, state-mandated competency tests, system-wide achievement tests, and, in many class-rooms, tests that accompany commercial materials or are designed by teachers. The move toward greater accountability through testing in literacy, as in other curricular areas, has been fueled by the publication of numerous national reports that are critical of school practices and student achievement and attitudes. Statistics on illiteracy and aliteracy have brought to the public's attention the fact that great numbers of students leave school with inadequate reading and writing skills and an aversion to literate pursuits. State departments of education and professional organizations have focused on learning standards and benchmarks of achievement at various grade levels. This trend will undoubtedly continue to affect assessment practices.

Faced with a barrage of tests and requirements for assessment, teachers must acquire some background information about the kinds of tests that are currently being used, the characteristics and purposes of different tests, and the intended interpretation and use of results, as well as other means of assessing learning outcomes. This chapter will first focus on formal assessment, including the characteristics of norm-referenced and criterion-referenced tests. We will discuss the limitations of these tests, how they can be used more effectively, and current trends in improving their design. Then we will give similar consideration to informal assessment techniques, especially the informal reading inventory, which is illustrated by three case studies. We will then consider the characteristics and techniques of naturalistic assessment and finally the issues of standards-based assessment.

Formal Assessment

Formal assessment includes the use of standardized tests. Formal tests may be either norm-referenced or criterion-referenced. Increasingly, political pressures have led many school districts and states to use formal reading tests as a means of assessment. Weaver (1994) describes the use of formal standardized assessments: ". . . they rank order students, teachers, and schools, thereby labeling some as more successful and others as less successful than others" (p. 216). Formal assessments have great appeal to decision makers because they can be used to make comparisons among groups of students.

Norm-Referenced Tests

Norm-referenced tests represent the most common kind of formal, standardized tests. They are machine-scorable instruments that assess reading performance based on a single administration. Their purpose is to compare the achievement of local groups of students with the achievement of a larger sample of students of the same age or grade level. Since the results of these tests are intended to be used for making such comparisons, norm-referenced tests are standardized. They are developed by test experts and have carefully specified procedures for administration and scoring to ensure uniformity. Norms are derived by testing large samples from populations that include various demographic characteristics (ethnic, socioeconomic, geographic). Once norm scores have been established, they serve as a basis for comparing the test performance of individuals or groups with the test performance of the members of the norming sample. These comparisons are used by school personnel to determine whether their students are performing above or below the level of the norming sample. It is extremely important that the norming sample be representative of the group of students being tested; otherwise, these comparisons are of questionable value. It should be noted that norm-referenced tests are not designed to provide the basis for instructional decisions about individual students. Their use should be limited to making group comparisons.

The scores from the norming sample are distributed along a *normal*, or bell-shaped, curve. Scores from any large sample tend to cluster symmetrically. The high point of the curve is the *mean*, or average of all scores. The distance of each score from the mean is described in terms of *standard deviation* above or below the mean (see Figure 11.1). A bell-shaped curve is divided into six standard deviations, three below and three above the mean. You will notice that the majority of scores (about 68 percent) fall within one standard deviation above or below the mean. Standard deviations provide a rough index for interpreting students' performance on a standardized test. For example, suppose the mean score of a standardized test is 500, and each standard deviation is 150 points. A student who scores 650 on the test would be one standard deviation above the mean and would be considered to have done well.

Test results are commonly reported in percentile scores and standard scores, such as stanines (defined below), both of which can be interpreted by using the bell-shaped curve.

FIGURE 11.1   *The Bell Curve*

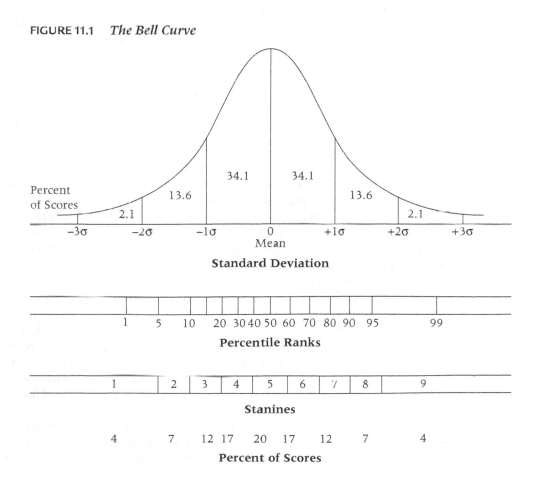

Standard Deviation

Percentile Ranks

Stanines

Percent of Scores

Percentiles indicate what percentage of the population scores below an individual. They show the student's relative position in a group. If a student's raw score on the hypothetical test mentioned above is 500, he would rank in the 50th percentile: 50 percent of the group scored lower than he did. Percentile scores provide information that may help teachers interpret relative performance within a grade level (see Figure 11.1).

Stanine scores are determined by means of a standard, nine-point scale. Raw scores are converted to stanine score levels from 1 (low) to 9 (high). A stanine score of 5 is the exact average. In other words, the scale divides the norm population into nine groups, "standard nines" (stanines). Figure 11.1 shows the relationship of standard deviations, percentiles, and stanines to the bell curve.

Another way in which test results are reported is in *grade equivalency scores*. These represent attempts to report reading progress as it relates to average student performance at various grade levels. These scores can be very misleading, however. If a student receives a grade equivalency score of 5.2, she is presumed to have the reading skill of a typical student in the second month of fifth grade. This is not necessarily true. Suppose our student is in first grade. The score suggests that she is reading well above the expected level for her grade; however, it is very unlikely that she could read "fifth-grade level" material with the same understanding as a fifth-grader. Grade-level equivalency scores, then, are not really equivalent. Another problem with this concept is that reading proficiency does not develop in equal increments from month to month, as this type of reporting implies. Almost twenty years ago, the International Reading Association passed a resolution proposing that schools abandon the practice of reporting students' test results in grade equivalency scores and cautioned teachers against the misuse of such scores.

Two very important characteristics of any standardized test are its validity and its reliability. *Validity* refers to the extent to which a test measures what it is designed to measure. There are several ways to determine the validity of an instrument. First, the test should have *construct validity*; in other words, there must be a clear relationship between the test items and a larger theoretical construct such as the process of reading. *Content validity* refers to how well and completely the test represents the domain that is being assessed (i.e., reading). Are the test items appropriate, and are there enough of them to adequately assess the reading process? *Predictive validity* is an indicator of how well the test will predict future performance.

Reliability refers to the dependability or consistency of the test. If a test is reliable, similar results will be obtained if it is administered more than once. The reliability of a test is expressed as a *correlation coefficient*, which can be found in the examiner's manual. The highest possible correlation would be a perfect one, represented by the coefficient +1.0. This means there is a perfect one-to-one correspondence between the results of two administrations of the same test. A reliability coefficient of .85 or better is considered to be acceptable; a correlation coefficient of less than .70 would indicate the test is not reliable.

The concept of *standard error of measurement* (*S.E.M.*) is closely related to reliability. It estimates the accuracy of test results for a given individual. If a person were to take the same test many times, her scores would be expected to vary slightly within a certain range. This range is represented by the standard error of measurement. For example, an IQ test may have an S.E.M. of 10 points. If a person scores 100, we could say that her true score lies between 95 and 105.

Criterion-Referenced Tests

The major premise behind *criterion-referenced tests* is that the attainment of particular skills should be assessed in relation to specific instructional objectives. The results of these tests are used quite differently from the results of norm-referenced tests. Students who have taken a criterion-referenced test are not compared with groups of students of the same age or grade; rather, they are compared with themselves in terms of the attainment of a specific set of predetermined objectives. Test items reflect objectives that are stated in behavioral terms. Expected mastery levels are specified. Testing reveals whether a student can perform the behavior specified in each objective at an acceptable level. If so, the student has "mastered" the objective. If not, it is assumed that the student needs additional work with that objective. Traditionally, criterion-referenced tests focused on discrete subskills of reading. They have recently evolved into standards-based assessment methods, which typically focus on broader objectives (usually called outcomes) and may include performance indicators other than tests.

Information about each standardized test, including a description of the norming population and the validation process, reliability coefficients, and the standard error of measurement, can be found in the examiner's manual. An excellent reference for educators to consult when they are considering which tests to use is *Tests in Print V: An Index to Tests, Test Reviews, and the Literature on Specific Tests*, published by the Buros Institute of Mental Measurements (1999), which gives thorough reviews of all educational and psychological tests currently on the market.

Concerns about the Use of Standardized Tests

Most of the current concerns about reading tests stem from the fact that assessment practices have not kept pace with the growth in our knowledge of the reading process and changes in instructional methods. The most commonly used reading tests do not give us the most important and relevant information about students' reading. Standardized test performance does not reflect students' ability to utilize reading, writing, and thinking in real-life situations, including school. Teachers need to know how students conceptualize the reading act, what strategies are used by the reader, and how the reader comprehends different kinds of texts (Weaver, 1994). In other words, standardized reading tests do not reflect the current definition of skilled reading—an active, constructive process that is fluent, strategic, and motivated.

In the words of Constance Weaver, "The purpose of standardized tests, by their very nature, is to rank order students, teachers, and students, thereby labeling some as more successful and others as less successful. Standardized test scores have little to do with promoting good education" (1994, p. 216). Standardized tests are commonly viewed as "objective," because they are scored the same way for all students. This impression is false, however, since the construction of tests is subjective. Tests are influenced by the background and cultural orientation of the test makers. Therefore they inevitably discriminate against students who do not share this background. (Even tests designed to be "culture-free" have this flaw.)

The mastery view of reading derives from behavioral psychology and assumes that skilled reading is the result of mastery of a hierarchy of discrete skills. Most reading assessments reflect this view, particularly if they are designed to be used for diagnostic purposes; they test isolated skills and report the reader's performance on each (sight vocabulary, phonics analysis, literal comprehension, and so forth).

This sort of information is of little value to teachers who view reading as a holistic act, involving the integration of many proficiencies that interact in various ways, depending on the reader's background and the text. These teachers are interested in the ways readers use strategies in real reading contexts, not in their ability to manipulate skills in isolation.

Another problem with reading tests is that they do not acknowledge the role of prior knowledge in reading comprehension. The strategic reader uses prior knowledge to construct meaning from the text, assesses the requirements of the task at hand, and proceeds accordingly. These competencies cannot be used (and therefore cannot be assessed) when tests consist of short, incomplete passages on many topics. The nature of the tasks on standardized tests negates thoughtful reading. First, the reading has only one very limited purpose: to correctly answer the questions that follow the passage. Second, the passages are so short that the reader's awareness of text structure as an aid for organizing information cannot be used. Moreover, the test passages cover many unrelated topics; the reader has no opportunity to assimilate ideas and make connections. Finally, the usual multiple-choice format requires the reader to select right answers. There is no opportunity for the reader to elaborate or to justify an alternative viewpoint. These conditions, which are inherent in most standardized tests, result in an extremely artificial reading situation that bears little resemblance to the circumstances of real-life reading situations.

Another concern with standardized tests is the preponderance of literal and low-level inferential questions used to measure reading comprehension. One of the characteristics of an expert reader is the ability to synthesize information from different parts of the text and across texts to draw conclusions and generate thoughtful interpretations. Readers have no opportunity to do this when test passages are short and unrelated and when test questions are restrictive.

Still another general concern about standardized reading tests is that they do not assess the growth and development of the positive reading attitudes and habits that characterize motivated readers. It is widely recognized that developing competent readers is only a part of the mission of literacy educators. Their larger goal must be to help students discover how reading can contribute to every aspect of their lives. Tests focus on reading competencies and ignore attitudinal and motivational factors, which should be a primary concern of literacy program planners.

Recognizing that standardized tests will continue to be widely used, there has been a concerted effort on the part of some literacy researchers and test developers to improve reading tests by making them more consistent with current theory and research. For example, some state assessments now include reading selections representative of the materials students use in classrooms: entire stories, informational articles, and poems. Some tests attempt to assess students' background knowledge of concepts central to understanding of the reading selection. Others include open-ended questions (students generate a response, rather than picking a multiple-choice answer) and questions about students' reading strategies.

Despite all of the concerns about the use of standardized tests, they are likely to continue to be widely used for large group comparisons. They are increasingly used for purposes of accountability. Educational decision makers see these tests as the most practical way to determine how their school population compares to other school populations across the nation. They also believe that standardized tests will indicate whether an entire school population is increasing or decreasing in general reading achievement.

Teachers need to understand and be able to explain what the standardized test scores of their students mean. If teachers are fully aware of the limitations of standardized tests and of the incongruity between the tests' content and the goals of reading instruction, they will be less intimidated by standardized test scores and better able to put them in proper perspective and to advocate for other effective forms of assessment.

Informal Assessment

Changes in our understanding of literacy acquisition and how it is best fostered have led us to question the appropriateness and value of commonly used formal measures of assessment. Most of the literacy tests in current use do not test the growth of real reading and writing proficiency. Today's teachers must choose or design assessment procedures that reflect their philosophies and instructional approaches. Informal assessments may consist of tests or of structured observations and collection of data from actual instructional contexts. We will consider several kinds of informal assessments, including tests and observations that are designed to provide useful information about students' reading performance and processes.

The Informal Reading Inventory

Informal tests differ from formal tests in that they have not been normed on large populations. Normed, standardized tests have an aura of authority because of their perceived objectivity. By comparison, informal assessments and teacher observations are often considered to be subjective and therefore less trustworthy and reliable means for planning instruction and assessing student progress. The result of these assumptions is that teachers are often reluctant to use their own knowledge of literacy acquisition, combined with their daily observations of children's performance, to assess student progress and to judge the effectiveness of their programs.

The *informal reading inventory,* or IRI, is an example of an assessment tool that is more structured than random observations and that allows the teacher to observe

reading in progress. A typical IRI consists of a series of oral and silent reading passages that increase in difficulty. Most IRIs also contain "graded" lists of words. These
are used to estimate how well students recognize words in isolation and to determine which passage would make a good starting point for the reading in context.

There are three types of IRI that differ slightly in construction and use. Some
basal reader programs provide IRIs that consist of reading selections taken directly
from the series. These inventories are designed to assist teachers in placing children
in texts at the appropriate level. While they may be helpful in matching children to
texts, they often do not provide more general information about students' reading.

A second type of IRI is teacher-made. The teacher selects passages (usually
from basal texts) representative of different readability levels and constructs questions to accompany each selection. This may be a time-consuming task. The teacher
must select representative reading passages ranging from 100 to 200 words in
length. Care must be taken to formulate comprehension questions that go beyond
the literal level and that are not too long and complicated.

The third type of IRI follows the same format as the basal and teacher-made
inventories, but is standardized and designed to be used more generically. Such IRIs
are generally constructed and analyzed by reading professionals and are more carefully designed than the other types. Passages and comprehension questions are assessed by field testing and are revised or replaced if necessary. Since standardized
IRIs have been subjected to thorough evaluation, they usually have greater validity
and reliability than the other two types of IRI.

The IRI is a diagnostic instrument that is administered individually. The
teacher selects a word list from the test booklet that he feels the student will be able
to read without difficulty and asks the student to read the words. Using the examiner's booklet, the teacher notes whether each word is recognized instantly, analyzed, or not recognized at all. This part of the assessment is discontinued at the
point at which the child no longer recognizes most words in a list easily. Based on
the results of the word recognition test, the teacher selects a passage in the inventory that the child is likely to read comfortably. Starting at this level, the child reads
several passages. After each passage is read, comprehension is assessed through
questions and discussions. Some passages are read orally to assess how well the student identifies words in context. The teacher follows along, noting the child's reading behaviors. Other passages are read silently to assess silent reading comprehension. Reading is discontinued when the student exhibits great difficulty in reading
and comprehending a passage. The information obtained by administering the IRI is
used to estimate the student's stage of reading development and to plan appropriate
instructional goals.

Like other assessment tools, the IRI has limitations. One major criticism is that
it provides a very limited sampling of reading. The reading selections are typically
short and incomplete and therefore do not have the structural and topical integrity
of whole texts. Informational selections predominate, since they fit more easily into
the test format. Because they are topical, they may be focused and brief but include
many facts that provide a basis for assessing literal recall. Narrative material, on the
other hand, has a story structure that is usually impossible to reduce to a short passage. The few narrative passages that do appear in IRIs are often incomplete excerpts

from stories. The fact that IRIs are weighted toward informational materials tends to give a distorted impression of reading performance, since most of young children's "real-life" reading consists of stories.

Another criticism of IRIs is their failure to adequately account for prior knowledge. The typical IRI format includes setting a purpose for reading each selection; however, prior knowledge is neither assessed nor developed. It is not unusual for a reader to perform unevenly on different passages that are at or near the same formulized readability level. For example, one inventory contains two passages that are at the fourth-grade reading level according to the formula (see Chapter 5). One passage is about skunks; the other is about uses of the newspaper. Younger children in particular tend to show much lower comprehension of the newspaper selection. The examiner may conclude that fourth-grade reading level material is too difficult for the child, when the results may actually reflect the child's lack of experience with newspapers.

This sort of situation leads to serious questioning of the role of readability formulae in the construction and interpretation of IRIs. We now know that readability is not simply a matter of the length of sentences and number of multisyllable words in a passage. The ability to read a selection also depends on a complex interaction among factors in the reader and factors in the text (as discussed in Chapter 5). Therefore, it is not logical to use IRIs to establish the precise reading level of a child (second-reader level, third-reader level, and so forth) determined by ability to read materials designated as a certain level according to a formula. In actual fact, once students have attained minimal independence in reading, they are capable of reading materials that span a band of readability levels. Their ability to read materials within this band will be influenced by the aforementioned factors, particularly interest and prior knowledge.

Another frequent criticism of the informal reading inventory is that teachers' interpretations of the same test results may differ. A great deal of the interpretation is left up to the examiner; hence it is imperative that users have considerable knowledge of the literacy acquisition process as well as familiarity with the IRI. Unlike standardized tests, which give specific directions for administration and scoring, IRIs require teachers to make structured observations covering a range of behaviors that cannot always be specified or anticipated. Therefore, written directions are generally insufficient; in-service training in using the IRI is recommended.

These criticisms may appear to support the impression that the IRI is an imprecise assessment tool and therefore of limited value. It must be remembered, however, that the purpose of the IRI is not to yield absolute scores or measure the attainment of discrete skills. Properly used, an IRI provides more significant information about reading. It provides insight into the child's reading process and allows the skilled teacher to make *tentative* decisions about the student's reading proficiency and needs. Specific examples illustrating this process will be given later in this chapter.

Specific directions for administering an informal reading inventory will vary from one IRI to another. For this reason, we will present a general description of the steps in administering most IRIs. Examples have been taken from the latest revision of an IRI we developed, *The Informal Assessment of Elementary Reading* (O'Donnell & Wood, 2001), which is included in Appendix B. Before an IRI is used, the teacher should become thoroughly familiar with its format. Most IRIs consist of a test booklet for the student containing the word lists and passages to be read and two recording booklets (for word lists and passages) to be used by the examiner.

Word Identification Lists: Administration and Scoring

The usefulness of word identification lists is limited. Reading words in isolation should not be used to judge reading competency. The results are appropriately used only to estimate the extent of a student's sight vocabulary and to determine at what level to begin the passage reading.

Assessment begins by having students read the lists of words in isolation. As each word is read, the examiner notes in her recording booklet whether the word was read accurately and without undue hesitation (in which case it is considered a "sight word"), analyzed, or not recognized at all. Figure 11.2 shows a teacher's recording of one student's responses to the first list of words (initial stage). Every time the student read a word "at sight," the teacher entered a plus sign (+) in the Sight column. The minus signs (–) in the Sight column indicate that the student read the word quickly but inaccurately. When this occurred, the teacher said, "Would you try that one again?" When the second attempt was correct, a plus sign was entered in the Analysis column (as with words 2 and 7). When the child was unable to pronounce the word correctly on the second try, a minus sign was placed in the Analysis column (words 14 and 18). The child was able to pronounce word 3 correctly on the first try but took a few seconds to analyze it ("bet, bet-ter"). This

FIGURE 11.2   *Scoring of Initial Reading Word List*

	Sight	Analysis		Sight	Analysis
1. with	+		11. did	+	
2. me	–	+	12. no	+	
3. better		+	13. red	+	
4. he	+		14. they	–	–
5. we	+		15. at	+	
6. my	+		16. on	+	
7. away	–	+	17. one	+	
8. can	+		18. some	–	–
9. like	+		19. have	+	
10. are	+		20. do	+	
			Scores	75%	90%

was indicated by leaving the Sight column blank and placing a plus sign in the Analysis column.

A score is computed by assigning a 5 percent value to each plus sign. Thus, to determine the sight score, count five points for each word marked with a plus sign. To determine the analysis score, begin with the total sight score and add five more points for each plus sign in the Analysis column. In the example shown in Figure 11.2, the student recognized 15 words at sight, receiving a sight score of 75 percent. Beginning with the words read accurately at sight (75 percent), an additional five points were added for every word that was read correctly when analyzed (three), resulting in an analysis score of 90 percent.

The word recognition test should be discontinued when the student's sight score falls below 75 percent on a given word list. The examiner uses the list results to determine which passage to have the student read first. It is advisable to select a passage that is at least one level below the level of the word list in which 75 percent of the words were read at sight. For example, a student received the following scores on a word recognition test:

Level	Sight	Analysis
2	100%	100%
3	80%	95%
4	60%	75%

The examiner had the student begin reading passages at the second level, where it was relatively certain that he would be successful.

Reading Passages: Administration

Most IRIs rank the difficulty of the reading passages according to traditional readability formulas. The problems with this are recognized; nevertheless, it is still a common feature. There is usually an oral and silent reading passage at each level. Because our IRI (Appendix B) is designed to identify the student's reading stage (and behaviors) rather than assign an arbitrary reading level related to grade, the passages are organized differently. There are three passages for initial stage reading, three for the transitional stage, two for the basic literacy stage, and one for the refinement stage. Successive passages gradually progress in length and complexity. With the exception of the first very simple passage (which is always read orally because beginning readers always read out loud), we recommend that all passages labeled initial and transitional be read silently first, followed by oral readings at the examiner's discretion. This makes the reading situation as authentic as possible (see the discussion of oral and silent reading in Chapter 4). Passages labeled basic literacy and refinement are only read silently; since readers in these stages are fluent, there is no longer a need to assess their word identification strategies.

Before each reading from an IRI, the teacher helps the student access prior knowledge and anticipate the content of the passage. Using the test booklet, the student reads the passage silently. Then, the teacher assesses comprehension by asking a series of questions (listed in the examiner's booklet) and evaluating the student's responses. In most IRIs, the examiner is instructed to compute a comprehension score by assigning a specified number of points (or partial credit, where deemed appropriate) for each acceptable response. A score of 70 percent or better is usually considered adequate for a given level. In order to make assessment of content more authentic, our IRI uses a different format. First, readers are asked to give a general recap of the reading selection. If it is narrative, they are asked to retell the story; if it is informational, they are asked to summarize the passage. In addition, several prompts or questions are provided, which the examiner may use to better gauge the reader's comprehension of the passage. Comprehension is not numerically scored; rather, it is estimated more generally and designated poor, average, good, or excellent. After the silent reading and comprehension check, the teacher may ask the student to read the passage orally as she follows along in the examiner's booklet, noting reading behaviors. (Many teachers prefer to tape record this part of the assessment so that they can make notations later from the tape.)

If teachers are going to share diagnostic data from an IRI, standardization of notations is advisable. Commonly used notations are shown in Figure 11.3, and a teacher's use of these notations to document a student's reading of an IRI passage is shown in Figure 11.4.

FIGURE 11.3   *Notations Used in IRI Assessment*

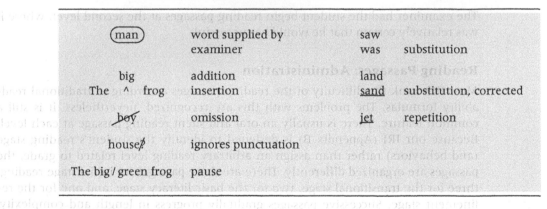

FIGURE 11.4   *Oral Reading of IRI Passage, as Documented by Examiner*

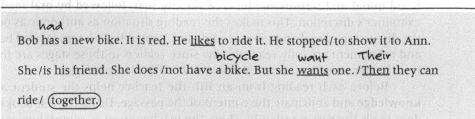

Figure 11.4 shows that the student made the following substitutions: *had* for *has*, *bicycle* for *bike*, *want* for *wants* (corrected), and *their* for *then* (corrected). *Likes* was repeated, there were several pauses, and the period after *friend* was ignored. The student paused for several seconds after *ride;* the teacher supplied *together.*

Regardless of the comprehension score for the oral reading passage, the silent reading selection at the same level should always be administered. When comprehension of the silent reading passage drops below 70 percent, testing is discontinued.

Reading Passages: Interpretation

The purpose of having students read passages orally is to gain insight into their use of word identification strategies. For this reason, the teacher makes a detailed record of oral reading behaviors, as already described. Once this information is collected, the teacher's task is to interpret this data and use it to evolve a profile of the child's use of reading strategies. One widely accepted criterion for adequate reading at a given level is recognition of 95 percent of the words in context. To help the teacher determine whether this criterion has been met, most inventories specify the number of errors a reader can make on a passage before word identification drops below 95 percent. What, then, constitutes an "error"?

The term *error* has largely been replaced by the term *miscue*. It has been found that children's reading mistakes are not random; they are based on the reader's attempts to use the cues in print to puzzle out the written language code. Thus, the term *miscues*, introduced by Kenneth Goodman and Yetta Goodman, is appropriate, since it reflects what is occurring during reading.

A miscue is defined as a deviation from an expected response (Goodman & Burke, 1972). Some miscues indicate that the reader is making sense of the writer's intended message whereas others do not. In this sense, some miscues are more acceptable than others. The quality of the miscue can be determined by asking, "Does the miscue alter or limit the reader's understanding of the text?" If it does not, it should not be counted as a word recognition error. For example, suppose a child reads the sentence "The hermit lived in an old *shack*" as "The hermit lived in an old *shanty*." According to traditional scoring, *shanty* is a substitution and therefore would be counted as an error. However, the nature of the substitution is such that the reader's understanding of the text is not significantly limited or altered. The miscue indicates that the child is reading for meaning rather than for precise word identification. The reader was unaware of the miscue because it sounded right, fit the context, and made sense. The initial letters (graphophonemic cues) and the constraints of word order (syntactic cues) and meaning (semantic cues) were probably used. Miscues of this type show that the reader is using information from all the major cueing systems to identify the words.

In contrast, other miscues reveal more serious problems. Suppose a student read, "The hermit lived in an old *shake*." In this instance, the reader's understanding of the text is clearly limited by the miscue, which would therefore be counted as an error. The reader has relied largely on graphophonemic cues and is clearly not focused on the meaning of the message. If the reader realizes that the sentence as it was read does not make sense, returns to the word *shack,* and corrects the miscue, then it would not be counted as an error. Such behavior would show that the reader is self-monitoring text comprehension, which is characteristic of skilled reading (unless, of course, there are so many self-corrections that reading is not fluent and comprehension is impaired by the interruptions).

Novice teachers have many questions about classifying miscues, and about which ones "count." For example, what about common mispronunciations (*why* for *while*), dialect differences (*ax* for *ask*), and constructions that reflect lack of English proficiency (*at school* for *to school*)? The teacher who is familiar with a student's speech patterns will usually be able to tell what the meaning of the word in question is to the student. Mispronunciations, in and of themselves, are not necessarily important. The question to ask is, "Will the meaning of the sentence be altered *for the reader* by the miscue?" Teachers should keep in mind that the purpose of the IRI is to establish a general estimate of reading competency, and within this, to determine reading strategies that are effective or ineffective for the reader.

In summary, then, miscues that alter the meaning of the text are counted as errors in determining whether the child can read 95 percent of the words in context. However, there are other reading behaviors that are also indicative of the student's ability to read the passage. Excessive pauses, repetitions of words or phrases, and ignoring punctuation are all signs that the reading material is difficult for the child, regardless of the number of substitution miscues. All these factors should be taken into account in deciding whether to advance to the next level. For example, if a student self-corrects substitution miscues but pauses frequently to analyze words and repeats many words, oral reading should be discontinued.

Another aspect of the diagnosis involves analyzing the student's responses to the comprehension questions that follow each passage. In doing this, teachers have traditionally focused on obtaining a numerical score by determining the degree of correctness of the child's answers. The object was to establish whether the child scored above or below the 70 percent criterion, which was assumed to represent adequate comprehension at that level. Often no attention was paid to the kinds of questions asked or to the reasons for the student responses. The focus was on the product rather than the process of comprehension.

The comprehension assessment sections of the inventory can be modified to yield more relevant information. Instead of concentrating on what the student is able to remember, the examiner should be concerned with the thought processes the student uses in interpreting the text. The questioning procedure should vary, depending on whether the passage is narrative or expository. For a narrative, the examiner could begin by asking the student to retell the story, noting whether the most significant features are included in the retelling. This procedure offers the potential of assessing both the product and the process of comprehension. Literal recall is revealed by the ability to provide facts, details, and essential components of the passage in sequence. Comprehension processes are revealed through inferences made, interpretation of the story, ability to summarize, and comments that link story elements to personal experiences. Story retelling, then, provides a holistic assessment of comprehension of a narrative piece (Morrow, 1996). Assessment of comprehension of an informational passage should begin before the student reads the passage. The examiner should ask questions to determine the extent of the student's prior knowledge of the topic. If the student appears to lack background, it is necessary to provide basic information through discussion. Following the reading of the passage, the examiner can begin questioning by asking the student, "What did you learn that you didn't already know?" or "Did you learn something new?" Responses will reveal whether the student is able to distinguish between new (for her) information and prior knowledge.

Retelling of a story or assessment of what was learned should be followed by questions that require the reader to go beyond the text. Quite often the suggested comprehension questions in commercial IRIs are predominantly textually explicit. The teacher should examine each suggested question to determine what is required of the reader in generating a response. If "Right There" questions predominate, the examiner should replace or supplement them with "Think and Search" or "On My Own" questions. (See Chapter 7 for discussion of the cognitive levels these types of questions represent.)

It should be clear by this point that determining the adequacy of a student's comprehension involves more than computing the percentage of "right" answers. Since comprehension is determined by the interaction of factors in the reader and in the text, as well as by instructional practices, judgments about students' understanding must be broad-based. The inventory should be discontinued at the point where the examiner has enough information to do two things: first, to estimate the child's stage of reading development and, second, to construct a profile of strengths and weaknesses, both in word recognition in context and in comprehension.

Traditional Use of the IRI

The original intent of the IRI was to establish reading levels that could be used by teachers to place students in materials of appropriate difficulty (Betts, 1946). The most prevalent use of the inventory is still to establish four reading levels for a student: independent, instructional, frustration, and capacity. When the child is reading at his *independent* level, the reading is "comfortable"; no teacher guidance is required. Ninety-nine percent of the words are identified in context correctly, and the reader responds appropriately to 90 percent of the comprehension questions following the passage. If graded word lists are used, the reader recognizes 90 percent of the words at sight. The reader's *instructional* level can be defined as the level at which some teacher guidance is required. The student correctly identifies 95 percent of the words in context and has a comprehension score of 75 percent. On the equivalent list of words in isolation, 75 percent of the words are identified at sight. If pronounced signs of reading difficulty are observed, the reader has reached his *frustration* level. Less than 90 percent of the words in context are correctly identified, and the comprehension score may be 50 percent or less. The sight score on the test of recognition of words in isolation is less than 70 percent.

To determine *capacity* level, the examiner reads passages (above the student's frustration level) aloud to the student and asks the accompanying comprehension questions. The highest-level passage for which the student can answer 75 percent of the comprehension questions is considered his capacity level; that is, the level at which the student can understand and therefore has the potential to read (Searfoss & Readance, 1994).

The primary concern of most teachers is to determine the child's instructional level. Teachers often assume the independent level to be one level below and the frustration level to be one level above the instructional level. They generally use this information to place children in homogeneous reading groups or to assign reading selections of appropriate difficulty.

Some criteria for estimating a child's reading competency are clearly necessary for teachers to provide effective guidance and instruction. Similarly, standards for estimating the difficulty of reading materials are useful. (See our discussion of leveled texts in Chapter 3.) It must be remembered, however, that every reading act involves a complex interaction between reader and text; therefore, rigid application of very precise criteria is misleading. The assumption that one can pinpoint a child's "reading level" through percentages of words recognized and comprehension scores fails to take into account variations in performance due to differences in the content and structure of texts. By the same token, the idea that the readability or difficulty level of material can be determined by charting the number of syllables and length of sentences and that this level is constant for all readers is equally flawed, since it does not account for the influence of the reader's prior knowledge, interest, and status as a reader. Therefore, it is not possible to establish a precise reading competency level that will determine a child's success in reading a given piece of material at the corresponding readability level. The focus of assessment with the IRI should not be on establishing a precise reading level, but rather on the estimation of an approximate band of competency. Such bands are, in fact, what the stages of reading development are intended to describe. For example, a transitional stage reader will be able to read, with differing degrees of success, materials that are typically read by second-, third-, and fourth-graders. The child's success with a specific piece of material will depend on prior knowledge of that topic, interest, and type of material, among other factors.

Three case studies will be used to illustrate the application of this process. The IRI used in each case was *The Informal Assessment of Elementary Reading* (Appendix B). We developed this inventory to conform to contemporary views about the construction and use of IRIs. It is organized according to stages of reading progress rather than by discrete, graded reading levels, and consists of seven lists of words in isolation and nine reading selections. These correspond approximately to the major stages of reading development. There are two word lists and three reading selections that are typical of material encountered by initial stage readers, two lists and three passages for transitional stage readers, two word lists and two passages for basic literacy stage readers, and one word list and one reading selection for refinement stage readers. A significant difference between our inventory and most other inventories is that the examiner uses the instrument to estimate the student's stage of reading progress rather than to derive a specific reading instructional level.

■ CASE STUDIES

▪ Wendell

Wendell is 7 years old and has just entered second grade. His performance on the test of word recognition in isolation is summarized below:

List	Sight	Analysis
1. Initial	85%	100%
2. Initial	70%	80%
3. Transitional	50%	65%

The examiner decided to have Wendell begin reading in context with the passage designated "Selection 1, Initial," since it was anticipated that he would be able to read the selection without difficulty. The passage is about a boy who got a new bike and showed it to a friend. Before reading, the examiner discussed Wendell's experiences with his bike, and stated, "This story is about a boy who wanted to show his new bike to a friend. Read the story out loud to find out what happened." The examiner made the notations shown in Figure 11.5 as Wendell read. There were no substitution miscues and very few indications of difficulty. The word *friend* was repeated, seemingly to verify the pronunciation, and there were three noticeable pauses.

Three comprehension questions were asked after reading:

- How did Bob feel about his bike?
- How do you know?
- How did Ann feel when she saw his bike?

Wendell's responses reflected good comprehension of the simple passage. The examiner then had Wendell read a slightly more difficult passage for initial stage readers. He began by asking Wendell, "Do you like frogs? Have you ever caught

FIGURE 11.5   *Wendell's Reading of Selection 1 (Initial Stage)*

Bob had / a new red bike. He liked to ride it. One day he stopped to show it to

his / <u>friend</u> Ann. She liked his bike. "I wish I had a bike," she said. "Then we could

ride / together."

<u>2 miscues = 95% word recognition in context</u>

one or touched one? What do you think a frog would do if you put it in a box? In this story, two children played with some frogs. Read it silently, to yourself, to find out what happened." Wendell's responses to the comprehension questions were as follows:

Examiner: Tell me in your own words what happened in the story.

Wendell: Some kids played with some frogs and one of the frogs jumped in his lunch box. Then when he was at school it jumped out.

Examiner: How did one of the frogs fool the children?

Wendell: It got in his lunch box.

Examiner: Did the children see it?

Wendell: I don't know.

Examiner: What do you think happened when the frog got to school?

Wendell: It jumped out.

Examiner: What do you think would be a good name for this story?

Wendell: The Frogs.

Wendell's responses suggest a minimal level of understanding of the passage. His retelling was brief and lacked precise details. He called the school bag a lunch box and missed the fact that the children didn't know the frog was in the school bag. He did not elaborate about what happened when the frog jumped out at school. The title Wendell suggested, while not inappropriate, did not pinpoint the topic. Wendell's overall performance indicates that his comprehension is limited at this level.

Wendell then read the paragraph orally with the results shown in Figure 11.6. Clearly the reading was becoming difficult for him. There were four significant

FIGURE 11.6   *Wendell's Reading of Selection 2 (Initial Stage)*

I met Tim/on the way to school. He had a/big box. There were/three frogs/inside.

We (stopped) to play / with them. I picked one up. So did Tim. We did not/see [packed above stopped]

the other one/jump out of the box/and hop/into my school bag. I (grabbed) my

bag. We ran / all the way to school. When I got to school, the frog/jumped out of

my bag./Everyone laughed. [screamed above laughed]

4 miscues = 95% word recognition in context

miscues. Two words were supplied by the examiner (*stopped, grabbed*). Wendell paused for several seconds before *stopped,* and when he came to *grabbed,* he said, "I don't know that word." In both instances the teacher told him the word. There were two substitutions that altered the meaning of the passage (*packed* for *picked* and *screamed* for *laughed*). Four miscues put Wendell barely at the criterion level of 95 percent recognition of words in context. Moreover, the numerous pauses and repetitions made his reading slow and laborious. The examiner concluded from these data that he had sufficient information about his oral reading and that it was not necessary to have him attempt more difficult oral reading passages.

Before finishing the assessment, the examiner invited Wendell to read another passage, slightly more difficult than "The Frogs," but this time silently. In preparation, he asked Wendell, "Did you ever have a day when everything seemed to go wrong? What happened? Did you ever think about running away from home? In this story, a little girl has a very bad day. Read this story to yourself to find out what happened to her." Wendell read the story in Figure 11.7 silently.

> *Examiner:* Tell me in your own words what happened in the story.
>
> *Wendell:* Nothing went right. The girl's mother was mad at her and her brother was calling her names. So she decided to leave. But when she went out it was raining, and her cookies got all wet. So she came back home.
>
> *Examiner:* What were some of the other things that happened to Mary on her bad day?
>
> *Wendell:* Well, I think everyone was mean to her.
>
> *Examiner:* Do you remember anything else?
>
> *Wendell:* (Pause) No.
>
> *Examiner:* Why did Mary feel better when she got home again?
>
> *Wendell:* (Pause) Maybe she got some cookies that weren't wet.

FIGURE 11.7   *Selection 3 (Initial Stage) Read by Wendell*

It was a cold rainy day. Everything went wrong. Mary spilled milk on her new pants.

Her mother yelled at her. Her little brother pulled the eyes out of her teddy bear.

Her sister called her a stupid brat. Mary was so mad that she decided to run away.

She put some cookies in a bag and went outside. She walked in the rain for a long

time. She tried to eat her cookies but they got all wet. Finally Mary went home.

Her mother gave her a big hug. She began to feel better.

Wendell's responses to the silent reading passage reflect the same patterns observed in his comprehension of the oral reading selection. He captured the gist of the story but missed specific details. At this point, testing was discontinued, since the examiner felt he had sufficient information to estimate Wendell's stage of reading, profile some of his strengths and weaknesses, and begin to plan appropriate instruction.

Stage of Reading

The examiner concluded that Wendell is in the initial stage of reading progress. Wendell's ability to identify words in context was satisfactory on the least difficult passage. However, as the passages increased slightly in length and complexity, so did the occurrence of meaning-altering miscues and other indications of reading difficulty. Wendell was barely able to recognize 95 percent of the words in context on the last passage read orally. This, coupled with the fact that his comprehension was limited, led the examiner to conclude that Wendell is still an initial reader.

Strengths and Weaknesses

In determining Wendell's strengths and weaknesses, the examiner compared his reading behaviors with the major goals of the initial stage of reading (see Chapter 2):

- *Understanding that reading is a meaning-making process:* In spite of the effort Wendell is expending on word identification, he does apparently read for meaning. In every instance he was able to derive the general idea of the passage. Moreover, only one of his miscues led to an unlikely sentence ("I *packed* one up").
- *Acquisition of sight vocabulary:* Wendell has certainly begun to develop a sight vocabulary. He was able to identify many words at sight on the lists of words in isolation and he read the beginning selection with ease. However, his sight vocabulary is not yet adequate for him to cope with materials beyond the initial stage of reading, as evidenced by his performance on the last oral reading passage he attempted.
- *Balanced use of word identification strategies (graphophonemic, syntactic, and semantic cues):* Wendell does evidently make use of all three cueing systems most of the time. In reading the passages he managed to identify the majority of the words accurately, in spite of his somewhat limited sight vocabulary; he undoubtedly "figured out" many parts of the texts by using his awareness of context and knowledge of letter–sound relationships. He still lacks precision with this process, however. He was unable to even attempt two words (*stopped* and *grabbed*). He appeared to be ignoring semantic cues when he substituted *packed* for *picked* and to be disregarding graphophonic cues when he read *screamed* for *laughed*.
- *Sees himself as a reader and writer:* This cannot be assessed through the IRI; ongoing classroom observations will inform his teacher about his self-concept as a reader and writer.

Planning Appropriate Instruction

Based on his analysis of the data from the IRI, the examiner designed an instructional program for Wendell that reflected his stage of reading progress: late initial. The program he planned included many opportunities to read highly predictable materials, both with a model and independently. Repeated reading of favorite books was encouraged to promote growth of sight vocabulary and increased fluency. When Wendell read orally, the teacher encouraged him to examine his use of word identification strategies by asking questions that focused his attention on the meaning or on the graphophonemic cues. To promote comprehension, the teacher helped Wendell anticipate what he was going to read about and provided frequent opportunities for him to retell stories and share his interpretations and reactions. A variety of reading and writing activities was used to accomplish these objectives, all of them designed to enhance Wendell's progress as an initial reader.

Bobby

Bobby, a 9-year-old, read the second of the three passages for initial readers from the IRI in the manner noted in Figure 11.8. Bobby differs significantly from Wendell in that he makes many miscues that are not meaningful. His principal strategy for identifying unfamiliar words is to sound them out, letter by letter, which often results in distorted pronunciations or nonwords. His skill at word identification is severely limited by overreliance on graphophonemic cues. He does not make sufficient use of semantic and syntactic cues; his word identification strategies are not used in a balanced way. Predictably, Bobby's comprehension is very poor because he does not anticipate meaning and because he focuses on individual words.

Clearly, Bobby is an initial reader. Beyond this designation of stage, however, it is not important to specify exact instructional level. The pattern of his reading behaviors is far more important. They provide compelling evidence that he does not see reading as a meaning-getting process. His teacher must help him acquire a

FIGURE 11.8 ***Bobby's Reading of Selection 2 (Initial Stage)***

me-et s-chol h-ab b-ox They where
I/met Tim/on the/way to school. / He had a/big/box. / There were/<u>three</u>/frogs

stop
in/side. / We stopped to/play/with them. I (picked) /one up. / So did/Tim. /

over jumped hope
We/did not see the/other one/jump/out of the/box and hop/in/to my (school) /

run Went
bag. I (grabbed) my/bag. We ran all the/way to/school. When I got/to school,

jump lo-logged
the/frog/jumped out/of my/bag. / / (Everyone) laughed.

greater repertoire of strategies for word identification. He needs to read (both with and without a model) a variety of well-written, highly predictable stories that will help him to predict content and to use all cueing systems. When Bobby reads aloud, his teacher should help him to monitor his use of context by asking such questions as "Does that make sense?" In addition, he would profit from cloze exercises (generated from his reading) that require him to make use of syntactic and semantic cues, as well as minimal graphophonemic cues. For example: We played baseball in the f_____.

▪ Rosa

Rosa is 12 years old. Her family came to this country when she was 6; her first language is Spanish. Although she is fluent in conversational English, she still struggles with the academic English needed in content area classes. During her assessment, she read every list of words in isolation without difficulty. Her oral reading in context was fluent and virtually error-free. However, she had difficulty comprehending some of the reading passages intended for transitional and basic literacy readers. Figure 11.9 shows the selection that she read silently. A transcript of the dialogue with the examiner follows:

> *Examiner:* Tell me what you learned from this passage, Rosa. What was it about?
>
> *Rosa:* Ah, about elephants, but not the ones in zoos.
>
> *Examiner:* Why are the elephants disappearing?
>
> *Rosa:* People are killing them? I don't know.

FIGURE 11.9   *Transitional Stage Passage Read by Rosa*

Save the Elephants

Elephants live in the wild in some parts of the world. There used to be many wild elephants. But people are moving onto land where elephants have always lived. People are building homes and towns. The elephants don't have enough land to live on or food to eat. Many of them are dying.

Another reason wild elephants are disappearing is that hunters are killing them for their ivory tusks. They sell the tusks to people who make them into expensive combs and jewelry. Things that are made from ivory are sold all over the world.

Some people are trying to save the elephants. They are making special parks for elephants to live in. They are also passing laws to keep people from killing too many elephants. They are asking everyone not to buy things that are made of ivory.

Examiner: Why are people killing them? Can you explain that?

Rosa: Hunters like to kill big animals, and sometimes they put the heads up on their walls.

Examiner: That's true. Is there any special part of the elephants that the hunters want?

Rosa: I don't know, just their heads, I guess.

Examiner: Hunters are a problem for the elephants—that's true. Did you read about any other problems that make it hard for the elephants to live?

Rosa: No—I can't remember anything else.

Examiner: In your opinion, what do you think people could do to help save the elephants?

Rosa: Well, we could make laws that you can't hunt them.

Examiner: OK—Anything else?

Rosa: No, I can't think of anything else.

In spite of her facility with word identification, Rosa does not comprehend much of what she reads. What are the possible explanations of this pattern? The teacher must consider the factors within readers that affect comprehension: experience, interest/motivation, fluency, and metacognitive status. In Rosa's case, lack of fluency can be ruled out on the basis of her oral reading performance. The teacher needs to obtain more information about the remaining three factors, which can only be accomplished by talking with Rosa about her comprehension processes. The teacher might begin by assessing further Rosa's background knowledge of the topics she reads about. For example, what does she know about elephants in the wild? Is she familiar with the terms *tusks* and *ivory?* Is she familiar with the concept of endangered species? Does she know some of the common reasons why some species are threatened with extinction? The purpose here is to determine whether she has a broad schema into which the new information about elephants can fit. It is very likely that absence of adequate prior knowledge will turn out to be at least part of Rosa's problem. She may be lacking in technical English vocabulary that is necessary for understanding the material. If this turns out to be the case, then the building of concepts before reading (described in Chapter 4) will be a particularly important component of instruction.

Another area the teacher needs to explore is Rosa's motivation, interest, and degree of attention to her reading. Unmotivated reading (for whatever reason) is characterized by lack of attention, and therefore a lack of comprehension. The teacher might question Rosa along the following lines: Did you find this selection interesting or not? Did you have trouble concentrating on it? Do you often have trouble concentrating? Do you find your mind wandering to other things when you're reading? If lack of motivation and concentration appears to be a problem for Rosa, there are two basic ways to help her: first, provide interesting and relevant material for Rosa to read, and second, when she must read teacher-assigned material, help her to establish clear purposes for reading and encourage her to check frequently to see whether these purposes are being attained.

This leads into the last reader-based comprehension factor, the metacognitive status of the student. To explore this last area, the teacher must attempt to find out what strategies Rosa is aware of using before, during, and after reading. Some questions she might ask Rosa are: "Do you usually try to predict what the writer is going to say before you start reading?" "As you're reading along, if you find you don't understand something, what do you do?" "What if you don't know the meaning of a word?" "When you finish reading, do you ever think back over what you have read?" Most students who have reading profiles like Rosa's, regardless of whether they are ESL learners, lack metacognitive strategies. These strategies can be directly taught and practiced; their development should be an integral part of the reading program. For example, the teacher can model comprehension monitoring by reading through a passage with students, stopping frequently to summarize in her own words what has been read. Students can then be guided in practicing this process themselves. For more examples of instructional strategies that help students become strategic readers, see Chapters 7 and 8.

Effective Use of IRIs

The preceding examples illustrate how the IRI can be used most productively to detect important patterns of reading behaviors rather than to pinpoint instructional levels. In order for informal reading inventories to become more viable tools for helping teachers assess reading and plan instruction, they must replicate, as nearly as possible, real reading situations. Before the reading of each passage is undertaken, the student's prior knowledge must be explored and, if necessary, developed. The reading selections must be reasonably representative of real, complete texts and must include both narrative and expository writing. Comprehension assessment must go beyond the recall of literal details and glib interpretations. It must include opportunities for retelling (narrative) and summarizing (expository), as well as exploration of students' interpretive abilities and use of reading strategies. An IRI that meets these criteria provides the teacher with the framework for a highly structured observation of reading.

Naturalistic Assessment

Regardless of the quality of an assessment tool, it provides a limited sample of reading behaviors under relatively artificial conditions. Valid, useful assessment must include cumulative observations of students as they function in real learning contexts. This is often referred to as *naturalistic assessment*, or, in Yetta Goodman's less formal language, "kid-watching" (Goodman & Burke, 1972). It involves observing children's engagement in a variety of literacy activities and noting how they approach various tasks and perform in different situations. It is an ongoing form of assessment, occurring over an extended period of time; therefore, documentation and record keeping are an important part of the process.

Data Collection

Teachers who engage in naturalistic assessment of their students' reading often use several of the following forms of documentation: running records of oral reading, records of books completed, reading response/dialogue journals, anecdotal records from conferences, inventories of reading habits and attitudes, and periodically taped samples of oral reading.

Running Records

The *running record*, a tool for recording, scoring, and analyzing a student's precise reading behaviors, has become popular with primary-grade teachers as a result of the growing use of the Reading Recovery program (Clay, 1993). Reading Recovery is an early intervention program used with first-graders who are having difficulty learning to read. It provides children with daily one-to-one instruction with highly trained tutors. The tutors make frequent use of running records for ongoing assessment. When making a running record, the teacher records miscues while the student reads orally. The running record differs from the IRI in that any reading selection from the classroom may be used. Selections are at least 100 words in length. As the student reads, the teacher writes on a blank piece of paper, recording each correctly read word with a check mark and writing in each miscue, adding SC to the word if the miscue is self-corrected. Figure 11.10 shows a sample from a running record. Looking at a running record, it is evident that the immediate information gleaned is primarily quantitative. You can see how many words were read accurately and how many miscues were made, but the context of the miscues is not apparent. Miscues can later be analyzed according to the probable sources of information or cues used by the reader. The teacher categorizes each miscue as M (meaning), S (structure or syntax), or V (visual, including letters and chunks, and the child's connections of these with sounds) (Fountas & Pinnell, 1996).

Most teachers use the running record in two ways. First, it is a way to establish the appropriateness of a book for an individual student. Clay (1993) maintains that if a beginning reader misses more than 1 out of 10 words in a text, it is too difficult

FIGURE 11.10 *Sample from a Running Record*

Text
Once upon a time there were three pigs who lived in a pen on a farm.

Student's Reading
"Once upon a time the — there — were three big — no, pig, I mean pigs who lived in a p-pen — in a farm.

Running Record

<pre>
        the sc   big sc   in
v v v v there v v pigs v v v v v-v on v v.
</pre>

to support the development and practice of word identification strategies. The second common use of the running record is to monitor students' reading progress. Teachers observe whether a student's oral reading shows attention to meaning and whether accuracy at a given level (of text) is increasing.

While running records are unquestionably useful for these purposes, it is important not to rely on them as the sole (or even primary) means of assessment. As they have gained in popularity and widespread usage, they have sometimes been overused. For example, there are instances where schools have required teachers to collect running records periodically on all children, including those who are progressing well or are in the upper elementary grades and already fluent. This makes large demands on teachers' time, with little information of value gained. The problem is compounded if teachers do not analyze the readers' miscues to determine their strategies, but rather sum up errors and focus on numerical scores for word identification. This practice may be the result of lack of time or of incomplete knowledge about the reading process and how to analyze the running records for information about the readers' strategy use.

An inherent limitation of the running record as an assessment tool is that it is designed to evaluate the reader's accuracy and proficiency at word identification, and does not address comprehension (except as it is used as a strategy for decoding). If teachers rely too much on running records for reading assessment, they downplay

The teacher observes reading in a real learning context.

the importance of comprehension—an indisputably crucial ingredient of reading competency. Balanced assessment may well include running records for beginning readers or struggling older initial or transitional stage readers, but it must also include assessment of comprehension through retelling, focused questions at various levels, and oral and written responses to reading.

Records of Books Completed. Keeping a record of books they have read gives students a sense of tangible achievement and documents for the teacher what they have accomplished. When either teachers or students look at what has been read over a period of time, they can observe the evolution of reading tastes, noting changes in the students' preferences for types of books, authors, and difficulty levels. This record provides cumulative evidence of progress and reading growth. Examples of reading records can be found in Chapter 4.

Reading Response/Dialogue Journals. Older students are often encouraged to carry on a written dialogue with their teachers about the books they read. These writings, when kept over a period of time, reveal growth in students' insights about the literature they read. Students typically move from plot summaries and expressions of personal opinion ("I really liked this book") to increasingly sophisticated observations about character development, plausibility of action, larger themes, and authors' techniques. This evolution is at least partially contingent on the teacher's responses to students' observations. A teacher who extends students' thinking through written questions and remarks can see evidence of the effectiveness of these interventions in the dialogue journal. The documentation of individual students' growth in responses to literature can most easily be obtained through written reactions to reading. Examples of response/dialogue journal entries can be found in Chapters 4 and 9.

Anecdotal Records from Conferences. Brief written notes that teachers make during reading conferences can be kept and referred to later for gauging student progress. Teachers often keep such records in a special notebook, in which they have several pages devoted to each child. Whenever they confer with a child, they jot down the date and any significant information about the student's response to the book read. These notes provide a safeguard against the limitations of memory. Observations about the reading and responses of individual children, when kept over a period of time, accumulate to form a helpful informal record of literacy growth.

Figure 11.11 shows a page of the conference record of a middle school student. Looking over this record, Deanne's teacher can see Deanne's increasing willingness to select challenging books and can document her ability to comprehend, appreciate, and analyze various elements of these books.

Inventories of Reading Habits and Attitudes. Inventories can be designed to assess changes in students' reading habits and attitudes. Claims are often made about the noticeable increase in students' enthusiasm about reading when they are exposed to literature-based programs that incorporate self-selection. If these claims are to be

FIGURE 11.11 *Sample Conference Record Page*

Name: Deanne

Date	Title/Author	Comments
16.3.84	James and the Giant Peach Roald Dahl	Clear understanding of author's intentions. Able to outline specific chapters.
22.3.84	The Shrinking of Treehorn Heide	Identifies well with characters-Relates to how she would feel.
2.4.84	Freckle Juice Judy Blume	Speaks freely. Is choosing books below her capabilities - introduce her to new authors. Has good strategies for word attack.
19.4.84	When the Wind Blows Raymond Briggs	Understanding of cause & effect→ in relation to both overall theme and characters. Enjoyed style of writing → Will read 'Gentleman Jim.'
4.5.84	A Taste of Blackberries D. Buchannan-Smith	'I just felt so bad Mrs. S. - I just wanted to cry for him and I did' ... → Deanne doesn't want to read sad books again!
2.6.84	Taylor's Troubles L. Tarling	Selecting more wisely → extending herself. Monitors story development well. High level of comprehension.
8.6.84	Sparrow Story at the King's Command J. Crabtree	- loved it! Oral reading fluent.
26.6.84	Five Time Dizzy N. Wheatley	Clear expression. Able to justify statements made with text extracts.

Reproduced with permission from David Hornsby, Deborah Sukarna, and Jo-Ann Parry: *READ ON: A Conference Approach to Reading* (Portsmouth, NH: Heinemann, 1986), p. 133.

taken seriously, they must be documented. Attitude inventories are useful for this purpose. They are best designed by individual teachers, based on the age and characteristics of their classes. Questions usually address students' reading preferences (favorite books or authors, for example), views of themselves as good or poor readers, and reading habits (when they read, how often). Some of the responses, at least, should yield quantifiable data. For example, choices of response may include "not at all, a little, a lot," "always, sometimes, never," or rating scales. The inventory is administered at least twice, once at the beginning of the school year, or when a significant program change is undertaken, and once later in the year. Increases in positive (or negative) responses are noted. Figure 11.12 is an excerpt from an attitude inventory used with fourth-graders.

Samples of Oral Reading and of Writing

To provide a general holistic perspective on reading progress, initial and transitional stage students can periodically record on tape their reading of short selections. Listening to the tapes often provides dramatic evidence of their progress in word identification, fluency, and expression. Such growth is not nearly as apparent on a day-to-day basis and is not demonstrated through any sort of written test. Taped reading samples provide very convincing evidence of beginning reading progress for children and parents, as well as teachers. If taping is not an option, teachers may photocopy a page from a book that the student can read with ease. Doing this every few months provides a continuous record of growth.

Writing is also most appropriately assessed naturalistically. Folders containing children's drafts, revisions, and edited copies of pieces; lists of topics and genres chosen; and checklists of editing skills (under development or fully acquired) can be maintained throughout the school year.

These forms of documentation provide assessment of learning over time; unlike other forms of assessment *they are useful and relevant to the learners themselves.* Many additional assessment tools and record-keeping forms have been compiled in such books as *Practical Aspects of Authentic Assessment: Putting the Pieces Together* by B. C. Hill and C. Ruptic (1994) and *Developmental Continuums: A Framework for Literacy*

FIGURE 11.12   *Sample Inventory of Reading Habits and Attitudes*

1. How well do you like to read?   not at all   a little   a lot

2. Do you have a favorite author?   yes   no
   If you do, who is it? _____

3. How would you rate yourself as a reader?   poor   fair   good   very good

4. How would you describe a good reader?

   _____

   _____

5. How much time do you spend reading for fun when you are not in school?
   none   1–2 hours per week   more than 2 hours per week

Instruction and Assessment K–8 by B. C. Hill (2001). Children can look back over their accomplishments, see their progress, and establish new goals. They become active participants in the process of assessment.

Portfolios

In the past, common practices for documenting and reporting children's progress to parents have included sharing standardized test scores, sending home report cards, and holding occasional parent–teacher conferences in which the parent and the teacher share their impressions of the child's progress. Standardized test scores and grades are viewed by parents as concrete evidence of their children's progress and achievement and therefore assume more importance than they deserve. Teachers may realize that test scores and grades provide very limited information about an individual student's actual growth in reading and writing competencies. They may be collecting other kinds of important information through naturalistic assessment procedures. How can all pertinent assessment data be efficiently organized and meaningfully presented?

Many teachers address this problem by developing individual literacy *portfolios* for their students. The most rudimentary form of portfolio is simply a collection of student work. This type of portfolio is often referred to as a *working portfolio*, and unless it is well organized and monitored, it may be of limited value as an assessment tool. From this working portfolio, samples representative of the student's best work may be selected and put in a more permanent "showcase" portfolio, which ideally can be expanded each year, eventually becoming the student's personal record of academic growth.

Formats for portfolios vary widely. Teachers have found that children take more pride in development and ownership of portfolios if they are professional-looking, yet personalized (Cockrum & Castillo, 1994). Traditionally, portfolios have consisted of sturdy folders, accordion files, or binders of various types, which children personalize by decorating the covers. Most recently, some schools are experimenting with the use of computers to store portfolios on CDs.

The contents of portfolios are more problematic than the format. Without a clear organizational plan, the portfolio can become an all-inclusive storage bin for literacy products. If portfolios become unwieldy and their maintenance becomes unmanageable and excessively time-consuming, teachers and students tend to abandon them. What is needed is a clear rationale for the aspects of literacy development that are most important to document. The stage model of literacy development provides a starting point for deciding specifically what will be collected.

Generally, the kinds of material collected include informal assessments, notes from teacher observations, records of work completed, periodic samples of student work, and student reflections on their work. The teacher keeps her assessment data in a file; the records and examples of student work go in the portfolio.

In the school attended by our case study students Kim, John, and Theresa, portfolios are maintained at every grade level. To illustrate how the stages of reading can be used to structure portfolios, we will describe the contents of John's portfolios as he progressed through the grades, highlighting grades K, 1, 2, 5, and 7, the grades included in the case studies in previous chapters. In kindergarten, John was an emergent reader. His teacher documented his progress in terms of the goals appropriate to that stage. Below we list the goals followed by the documentation that went in the teacher's file and the materials that went into John's portfolio:

- *Seek out and enjoy experiences with books and print.*
  Teacher's file: Anecdotal notes. Example: "11/3, John chose looking at books in library corner at free-choice time. Third time this week!"

- *Become familiar with the language of literature and the patterns of stories.*

- *Understand and follow the sequence of stories read to him.*
  Teacher's file: Informal early literacy assessment (see Chapter 1).
  John's portfolio: Taped retellings, October and June.

- *Become aware of separate speech sounds in words.*
  Teacher's file: Informal early literacy assessments (see Chapter 1). Anecdotal notes. Example: "10/23 J. consistently provided rhymes like beginning sounds today working with nursery rhymes." "1/23 J. now using initial and ending sounds consistently in his writing."

- *Begin to acquire specific understandings about the nature and purpose of print.*
  Teacher's file: Anecdotal notes relating to print concepts (see Chapter 1) based on writing samples and shared reading activities. Example: "10/23, John consistently follows print left to right when his turn to point. But writing still randomly placed." "2/13, J. writing left to right, includes many consonants (accurately) in spelling/writing."
  Informal assessments of letter knowledge.
  John's portfolio: A writing sample every 2 months.

- *Experiment with reading and writing independently, through approximation.*

- *Sees himself as a developing reader and writer.*
  Teacher's file: Anecdotal notes from observations of John's independent interactions with books and writing. Example: "10/18, J. looks at familiar books, tells story in own words."
  John's portfolio: A writing sample every 2 months.

At the end of kindergarten, the teacher's file contained anecdotal notes, informal assessments, and a summary of his development in relation to emergent stage instructional goals. John's portfolio contained the audiotape of his story retellings and five writing samples.

When John entered first grade, he was an initial reader, according to his teacher's observations (see Chapter 2). Like his kindergarten teacher, John's first-grade teacher used the stage goals as the basis for structuring her file and his portfolio. In addition, she met with his parents in early October and went over the goals with them. She also asked them what their goals were for John's first-grade experience, and she showed them how their goals (that he learn to spell more conventionally and that he "keep up with the others" in reading) related to his stage of reading development. Below we list the goals followed by the documentation that went into the teacher's file and the materials that went into John's portfolio:

■ *Understand that reading is a meaning-making process.*

Teacher's file: Monthly running records, from November through June. (Teacher stapled the running record to a photocopy of the text John read along with a summary of her interpretation.) IRI administered in May.

John's portfolio: Audiotape of oral readings (November, March, June). Three written responses to books (January, March, May).

■ *Acquire sight vocabulary.*

Teacher's file: Record of word bank counts (Sept. 25: 5 , Oct. 20: 16, Nov. 21: 23), IRI.

John's portfolio: Record of word bank counts.

■ *Make balanced use of the cueing systems in written language (syntax, semantics, and graphophonemics) to identify words not known at sight.*

Teacher's file: Running records, IRI.

John's portfolio: Oral reading tape.

■ *Sees himself as reader and writer.*

Teacher's file: Anecdotal notes.

John's portfolio: Attitude inventory (April), oral reading tape, selected writing samples jointly chosen by John and his teacher to demonstrate his progress as a writer.

At the end of his first-grade year, John's teacher's file contained anecdotal notes, running records, the IRI, and the record of his word bank (sight-word collection). John's portfolio contained his oral reading tape, writing samples, the attitude inventory, and the record of his word bank. At the beginning of second grade, John was entering the transitional stage of reading development. Below are the instructional goals his teacher used as well as the relevant material that went in her file and John's portfolio:

■ *Increase fluency in reading and writing.*

Teacher's file: Running records, IRI, anecdotal notes from conferences.

John's portfolio: Audiotape of oral reading (November, March, June). List of books completed, six pieces of writing.

■ *Maintain motivation to read and write.*

Teacher's file: Anecdotal notes from conferences.

John's portfolio: List of books completed, attitude inventory for September and May, samples from reading response journal (January, April, and June), six pieces of writing with accompanying reflections on why they were chosen for portfolio.

■ *Focus on meaning in reading and writing.*

Teacher's file: Running records, IRI, anecdotal notes from conferences.

John's portfolio: List of books completed, samples from reading response journal, six pieces of writing and accompanying reflections.

At the end of John's second-grade year, his teacher's file contained monthly running records with summaries, anecdotal notes from conferences, and the IRI. John's portfolio contained the audiotape of oral readings, a list of books completed, three responses from his reading response journal (begun in January), six writing samples chosen to show his growth as a writer, several letters about his rationale for his choices, and the two attitude inventories.

John was in the basic literacy stage by the time he entered fifth grade. The material collected in his teacher's file and in his portfolio throughout the year documented his growth in relation to each instructional goal:

■ *Expand breadth of experience in reading and writing.*

Teacher's file: Anecdotal notes relating to literature discussions and reading response journal entries, list of books assigned for teacher-directed reading.

John's portfolio: List of books completed, classified by genre. List of published writing, classified by genre. Six writing pieces, accompanied by self-evaluations.

■ *Comprehend and write increasingly complex material.*

Teacher's file: Anecdotal notes relating to literature discussions, response journal entries, and writing conferences, IRI (November).

John's portfolio: List of books completed, photocopied monthly samples of responses to literature taken from response journal. Six writing pieces, accompanied by assessment rubrics and reflections.

■ *Extend meaning vocabulary.*

Teacher's file: Quarterly evaluations of John's vocabulary notebook. Six vocabulary quizzes requiring use of new words in sentences.

John's portfolio: Six sample pages photocopied from vocabulary notebook. Several examples of semantic maps and feature analysis charts from content areas.

■ *Develop awareness and use of study strategies.*

Teacher's file: Copy of John's self-assessment of study strategies (November), anecdotal notes relating to John's approaches to content area study (October, February, May).

John's portfolio: Self-assessment of study strategies. Two examples of structured overviews, filled in after reading about/studying a content area topic.

At the end of fifth grade, John's teacher's file contained anecdotal notes, his IRI, his self-assessment of study strategies, six vocabulary quizzes, and a list of assigned readings completed successfully. John's portfolio contained a list of all books completed (sorted by genre), a list of all published writing, excerpts from his reading response journal and vocabulary notebook, his self-assessment of study strategies, a semantic map, a feature analysis chart, a structured overview, and six completed pieces of writing accompanied by rubrics and reflections.

In seventh grade, John had different teachers for each content area. His language arts teacher structured portfolio assessment similarly to his earlier teachers. Since the goal of the refinement stage is to extend the goals undertaken at the basic literacy stage, using increasingly advanced and abstract materials, John's portfolio and his teacher's file contained very similar content in fifth grade and seventh grade. The seventh-grade samples, however, showed his increasing sophistication as a reader, writer, and student. There was increased emphasis on literature and teacher-directed writing.

Parents generally react very favorably to portfolios. They appreciate the opportunity to see actual products of their children's efforts in school and to have progress demonstrated and explained in terms that they can understand. Many teachers now include students in conferences with their parents; the students explain their portfolios themselves. Teachers and students in this situation become empowered to teach parents about different assessment techniques and to show parents authentic indicators of their child's progress. Parents, in turn, become more supportive as they see the ways in which real progress can be accomplished and documented.

Standards-Based Assessment

In recent years, educators and the public have become increasingly concerned about linking curriculum to outcomes (what students prove they know and can do). This has led to increased demand for standards in all subject areas including language arts. In response to this movement, the National Council of Teachers of English (NCTE) and the International Reading Association (IRA) joined together to develop a set of national standards for the English language arts. The authors of the standards define *English language arts* as reading, writing, listening, speaking, viewing, and visually representing. The new standards include specific goals and curricular recommendations relating to students for whom English is not the first language. This is appropriate, given the steadily increasing cultural and linguistic diversity of students in American classrooms. The standards are presented below:

IRA/NCTE Standards for the English Language Arts

1. Students read a wide range of print and nonprint texts to build an understanding of texts, of themselves, and of the cultures of the United States and the world; to acquire new information; to respond to the needs and demands of society and the workplace; and for personal fulfillment. Among these texts are fiction and nonfiction, classic and contemporary works.

2. Students read a wide range of literature from many periods in many genres to build an understanding of the many dimensions (e.g., philosophical, ethical, aesthetic) of human experience.

3. Students apply a wide range of strategies to comprehend, interpret, evaluate, and appreciate texts. They draw on their prior experience, their interactions with other readers and writers, their knowledge of word meaning and of other texts, their word identification strategies, and their understanding of textual features (e.g., sound–letter correspondence, sentence structure, context, graphics).
4. Students adjust their use of spoken, written, and visual language (e.g., conventions, style, vocabulary) to communicate effectively with a variety of audiences and for different purposes.
5. Students employ a wide range of strategies as they write and use different writing process elements appropriately to communicate with different audiences for a variety of purposes.
6. Students apply knowledge of language structure, language conventions (e.g., spelling and punctuation), media techniques, figurative language, and genre to create, critique, and discuss print and nonprint texts.
7. Students conduct research on issues and interests by generating ideas and questions, and by posing problems. They gather, evaluate, and synthesize data from a variety of sources (e.g., print and nonprint texts, artifacts, people) to communicate their discoveries in ways that suit their purpose and audience.
8. Students use a variety of technological and informational resources (e.g., libraries, databases, computer networks, video) to gather and synthesize information and to create and communicate knowledge.
9. Students develop an understanding of and respect for diversity in language use, patterns, and dialects across cultures, ethnic groups, geographic regions, and social roles.
10. Students whose first language is not English make use of their first language to develop competency in the English language arts and to develop understanding of content across the curriculum.
11. Students participate as knowledgeable, reflective, creative, and critical members of a variety of literacy communities.
12. Students use spoken, written, and visual language to accomplish their own purposes (e.g., for learning, enjoyment, persuasion, and the exchange of information). (Farstrup & Meyers, 1996, p. 3)

The national standards are broad, general, and all-inclusive in terms of literacy development. Most states and many local school districts have developed or are currently developing their own sets of standards in all curricular areas. The local standards tend to be more specific. They frequently are accompanied by grade-specific "performance indicators" or "benchmarks" for assessing progress toward meeting the standards. For example, the following language arts standard from the *State of Maine Learning Results* is accompanied by grade-specific performance indicators:

Students will use the skills and strategies of the reading process to comprehend, interpret, evaluate, and appreciate what they have read. Students will be able to:

Elementary Grades Pre-K–2
1. Seek out and enjoy experiences with books and other print materials.
2. Demonstrate an understanding that reading is a way to gain information about the world.
3. Make and confirm predictions about what will be found in a text.

4. Recognize and use rereading as an aid to developing fluency and to understand appropriate material.
5. Figure out unknown words using a variety of strategies including rereading, context clues, and knowledge of word structures and letter–sound relationships.
6. Recognize and use clues within the text (sentence structure, word meanings), rereading, and other strategies as aids in developing fluency and comprehension.
7. Ask questions and give other responses after listening to presentations by the teacher or classmates.

Elementary Grades 3–4

1. Determine the meaning of unknown words by using a dictionary, glossary, or other reference sources.
2. Adjust reading speed to suit purpose and difficulty of the material.
3. Recognize when a text is primarily intended to persuade.
4. Select texts for enjoyment.
5. Read a variety of narrative and informational texts independently and fluently.

Middle Grades 5–8

1. Formulate questions to be answered while reading.
2. Reflect on what has been discovered and learned while reading, and formulate additional questions.
3. Identify specific devices an author uses to involve readers.
4. Use specific strategies (e.g., rereading, consultation) to clear up confusing parts of a text.
5. Understand stories and expository texts from the perspective of the social and cultural context in which they were created.
6. Identify accurately both the author's purpose and the author's point of view.
7. Summarize whole texts by selecting and summarizing important and representative passages.
8. Read for a wide variety of purposes (e.g., to gain knowledge, to aid in making decisions, to receive instructions, to follow an argument, to enjoy).
9. Explain orally and defend opinions formed while reading and viewing.
10. Adjust viewing and listening strategies in order to comprehend materials viewed and heard.
11. Generate and evaluate the notes they have taken from course-related reading, listening, and viewing. (*State of Maine Learning Results*, 1997, p. 13)

You will note that "Elementary Grades Pre-K–2" include emergent and initial readers, "Grades 3–4" represent mostly transitional stage readers, and "Grades 5–8" include basic literacy and refinement stage readers. Nearly all the performance indicators listed for grades 3–4 can be related to the transitional stage. Items 2 and 5 relate to fluency; items 1 and 3 relate to focus on meaning, and item 4 relates to motivation. Thus it is not difficult to use the performance indicators within the structure of a portfolio based on a developmental model of literacy acquisition, provided there is a reasonable degree of alignment.

While most educators agree that standards can lead to consistent expectations and improved instruction, there are several important issues and some pitfalls inherent in their use. First is the quality and appropriateness of the standards themselves. In the area of literacy they should be firmly based in our knowledge of the reading/writing processes, and they should be broad enough to accommodate differences among students and teaching strategies. On the other hand, if they are overly vague they are not useful.

Performance indicators and benchmarks developed on the local level often tend to become overly specific. When this happens, they tend to resemble "scope and skills" sequences of an earlier era—long lists of discrete skills to be mastered. Such lists push teachers toward isolated skill activities which may take valuable time away from reading/writing in context.

Another drawback to over-reliance on standards that are tied to grade or age levels is disregard for real differences in learning rate. Literacy learning is a continuous process that proceeds at different rates for different students. Our three case studies, Kim, John, and Theresa, exemplify this. Kim, for example, had very appropriate instruction in first grade, but would not have met standards designed for initial stage readers until considerably later. She should not be penalized for this, nor should her teacher. (However, if a large number of first-graders in her class were consistently unable to reach grade-appropriate standards, then the teaching methods and curriculum should be examined.)

Ideally the use of carefully developed standards can be integrated with assessment and instruction. One school system that has successfully woven these three elements together produced a *Literacy Guide* for teachers, parents, and administrators. In a concise, readable format, it illustrates how reading develops and how it is taught and assessed in their schools. The portion of this document that pertains to reading is reproduced in Appendix C (Gorham, Maine, School Department, 1997).

Summary

In the foreseeable future, standardized tests are likely to remain a dominant feature of schools' assessment programs, in spite of their serious limitations. Since they provide little, if any, useful information about the attainment of valid literacy objectives, knowledgeable teachers must create assessment programs that will generate data that can be used for designing and monitoring appropriate instruction.

Such programs should include both structured, focused observations (for example, administration of informal reading inventory or running records), ongoing observations of students' functioning in real reading and writing activities, and cumulative samples of their work. The increasing use of standards has added another dimension to assessment. These data provide the teacher with a sound basis for making informed decisions about instruction and for reporting pupil progress. Teachers must adopt and retain assessment procedures that are compatible with balanced literacy instruction. This is particularly important in an era when policy makers are imposing increased use of standardized tests. Teachers are leaders in the effort to maintain appropriate responsibility for literacy program design and implementation, and for meaningful student assessment.

BIBLIOGRAPHY

Betts, E. A. (1946). *Foundations of reading instruction.* New York: American Book Company.

Buros Institute of Mental Measurements. (1999). *Tests in print V: An index to tests, test reviews, and the literature on specific tests.* Lincoln, NE: University of Nebraska Press.

Clay, M. (1993). *An observation survey of early literacy achievement.* Auckland, New Zealand: Heinemann.

Cockrum, W., & Castillo, M. (1994). Whole language assessment and evaluation strategies. In B. Harp (Ed.), *Assessment and evaluation for student centered learning* (2nd ed., pp. 97–115). Norwood, MA: Christopher-Gordon.

Farstrup, A., & Myers, M. (1996). *Standards for the English language arts.* Urbana, IL: National Council of Teachers of English.

Fountas, I., & Pinnell, G. S. (1996). *Guided reading: Good first teaching for all children.* Portsmouth, NH: Heinemann.

Goodman, Y., & Burke, C. (1972). *Reading miscue inventory manual: Procedure for diagnosis and evaluation.* New York: Macmillan.

Gorham Literacy Committee. (1997). *Literacy guide for teachers, parents and administrators.* Gorham, ME: School Department.

Hill, B.C. (2001). *Developmental continuums: A framework for literacy instruction and assessment K–8.* Norwood, MA: Christopher-Gordon Publishers.

Hill, B. C., & Ruptic, C. (1994). *Practical aspects of authentic assessment: Putting the pieces together.* Norwood, MA: Christopher-Gordon Publishers.

Hornsby, D., Sukarna, D., & Parry, J. (1986). *Read on: A conference approach to reading.* Portsmouth, NH: Heinemann.

Morrow, L. (1997). *Literacy development in the early years* (3rd ed.) Boston: Allyn and Bacon.

O'Donnell, M., & Wood, M. (2001). *The informal assessment of elementary reading.* Gorham, ME: Reading Associates. (Copies of the assessment packet can be ordered from: The Gorham Book Cellar, University of Southern Maine, Gorham, ME 04038.)

Searfoss, L., & Readance, J. (1994). *Helping children learn to read.* Boston: Allyn and Bacon.

State of Maine: Learning results. (1997). Augusta, ME: Maine State Department of Education.

Weaver, C. (1994). *Reading process and practice* (2nd ed.). Portsmouth, NH: Heinemann.

Organizing and Managing Classroom Reading Instruction

*T*hroughout the preceding chapters the goal has been to help reading teachers build the knowledge base that is prerequisite to making sound instructional decisions. At this point the focus will shift to how this information can be used in classroom contexts to organize and implement effective reading instruction. The purpose of Part V is to highlight the management skills necessary to teach reading to whole classes of children with diverse experiences and abilities. First, this introduction describes recent trends in literacy instruction. Chapter 12 then examines the specific factors that teachers must consider as they design instruction. Chapters 13 and 14 present examples of management plans used by real teachers in different settings. Finally, Chapter 15 addresses instruction for children with special needs.

During the 1980s three significant trends in literacy instruction emerged in response to the cumulative body of research on how children actually learn to read and write:

- The move from basal-driven to literature-based reading instruction
- The shift from emphasis on product to emphasis on process
- The trend away from the view of the teacher as technician toward the view of the teacher as professional, or decision maker

These trends led to major changes in the organization and management of literacy instruction. Since 1995, these trends have been challenged by proponents of greater structure and consistency, as described in the Prologue to this text (National Reading Panel, 2000). Nevertheless, mainstream professional organizations such as the International Reading Association and the National Council of Teachers of English continue to reflect these trends in their publications and recommendations for practice. What we see in an effective classroom today is less of a "program" and more of a "workshop." Direct instruction is a component, but teacher and students also collaboratively explore and practice all facets of literacy (Cunningham & Allington, 1999).

The first trend, from basal-driven to literature-based instruction, has resulted in increased organizational flexibility as well as student engagement in authentic literacy experiences. In a traditional basal program, the reading instructional time is divided between teacher-directed reading groups and completion of workbook exercises or other seat work. The basal curriculum dictates the content of children's reading experiences and the allocation of time. In contrast, many literature-based programs have had no predetermined curricula, although many school districts now mandate that certain literacy content be covered at different grade levels. Most of this work, however, can be incorporated quite naturally in meaningful contexts. In today's literature-based program the teacher decides what kinds of literacy experiences will be made available to students and allocates time periods accordingly. This flexible format permits students to spend large blocks of time engaged in real reading and writing. The time formerly devoted to skill sheet completion is more likely to be spent, in a more current approach, on sharing, reacting to literature, and pursuing individual reading and writing projects. Even in schools that are using basals, the trend toward use of literature is unmistakable. The marketers of the basals themselves promote their incorporation of high-quality literature, and many teachers allow time for self-selected reading in addition to the basal work.

The practice of categorizing students on the basis of their perceived reading levels and grouping them accordingly has given way in many classrooms to more flexible and varied grouping patterns that are never permanent. Informal performance-based observations such as running records are used to assess the specific needs of individual students. In a literature-based classroom, students may come together to read and share the same book, focus on an identified need, explore a common interest, or work on a project together. When the task is completed, the group disbands (Cunningham & Allington, 1999).

Children are not labeled through such grouping, nor is their self-esteem affected by assignment to a group, as is often the case in the basal classroom with its static "ability level" groups. Another organizational feature of literature-based classrooms is the opportunity for frequent whole-class activities such as listening to a favorite story, sharing reactions and projects, and engaging in teacher-directed mini-lessons. Moreover, students in this type of class spend considerable time reading and writing independently, pursuing their individual tastes and interests. Perhaps the overriding benefit of the trend from basal to literature-based instruction is students' exposure to a greater quantity and broader range of reading experiences (Gambrell, 1999).

A second trend in reading instruction is a shift in emphasis from product-oriented instruction toward more process-oriented instruction. Product-oriented instruction has its roots in behavioral psychology (see Chapter 4). It is characterized by a focus on mastery and accuracy; objectives tend to be specific and narrow, and student outcomes are measured against performance criteria. Classroom management and instructional practices reflect these premises. Both instructional procedures and expectations are uniform for all students and are specified in great detail for the teacher. For example, a product-oriented objective for initial readers might be to recognize five sight words taken from a list of high-frequency words. The teacher might use several prescribed activities for teaching the words. As an outcome, students would be expected to read the words in isolation with 100 percent accuracy to demonstrate mastery.

In contrast, process-oriented instruction stems from cognitive psychology. Learning is seen as problem solving. Objectives tend to be broad, and student outcomes are not always expected to be uniform. Many alternatives are possible for accomplishing the same objectives. To return to the sight word example, a process-oriented objective for beginning readers would be to increase sight vocabulary by practicing reading predictable materials. All children would be expected to increase their sight vocabularies; however, it would not be assumed that all children would learn the same words or that they would acquire reading vocabulary at the same rate. The product-oriented teacher would be most concerned with their mastery of that skill. Instruction would be focused on teaching the skill and would be short-term and highly teacher-directed. More than likely, practice of the skill would not be related to a real reading experience. The focus of the process-oriented teacher would be quite different. She would be most concerned with facilitating the process by which students acquire a sight vocabulary. They would be given many opportunities to work out the pronunciation of unknown words using such strategies as prediction, use of context, and graphophonemic cues. As they read along with the teacher or reread familiar texts over an extended period of time, they would encounter these words repeatedly. This would eventually lead to their recognition of the words at sight.

Organization and management plans reflect underlying beliefs about teaching and learning. In the product-oriented classroom, the teacher is viewed as a dispenser of a predetermined body of information. All aspects of instructional planning and classroom management are directed toward the attainment of this goal. All learning activities are orchestrated by the teacher, who decides what to teach, to whom, and at what rate, according to the prescribed curriculum content.

The shift from product- to process-oriented instruction has resulted in another trend: a significant change in the teacher's role. When the instructional emphasis is on a product, the teacher is seen largely as a technician who implements a program designed by someone else. Teachers who have shifted to process-oriented instruction have a thorough knowledge of literacy acquisition that enables them to make sound instructional decisions. They do not have to depend on the rigid prescriptions of teachers' manuals; they assume control over the literacy curriculum. In this, more professional role, teachers assume greater responsibility for the design and implementation of instruction.

These trends in literacy instruction—from basal readers to literature, from product to process, and from teacher as technician to teacher as decision maker—all have their origins in research on learning and literacy acquisition, or constructivist theory. They provide a general focus for updating and improving literacy instruction. Part V will be devoted to specific aspects of organizing and managing classroom reading instruction that acknowledge these trends as well as the more recent emphasis on direct teaching and standards.

BIBLIOGRAPHY

Cunningham, P., & Allington, R. (1999). *Classrooms that work*. New York: Longman.

Gambrell, L. B. (1996). Creating classroom cultures that foster reading motivation. *The Reading Teacher, 501*(1), 14–25.

National Reading Panel. (2000). *Report of the National Reading Panel: Teaching children to read*. Bethesda, MD: National Institute of Child Health and Human Development.

12 Organization and Management

■ *Overview*

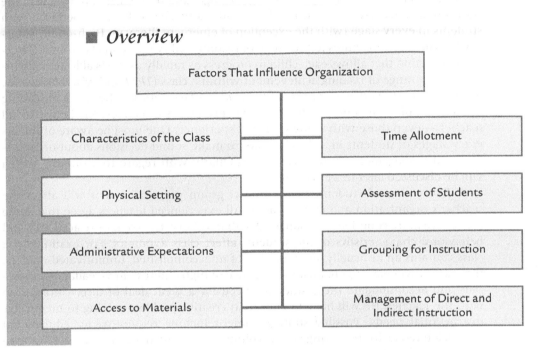

Factors That Influence Organization

Characteristics of the Class

Physical Setting

Administrative Expectations

Access to Materials

Time Allotment

Assessment of Students

Grouping for Instruction

Management of Direct and Indirect Instruction

Classroom environment

*P*revious chapters have focused on the content of literacy learning and reading instruction. Without good classroom organization and management, even reading instruction that is sound in content may be ineffective. Teachers must know not only what to teach, but also how to organize and manage the classroom in ways that maximize learning. In order to design a workable organizational plan the teacher must consider several factors, including the intrinsic "givens" of characteristics of the class, physical setting, administrative expectations, and materials; and the professional "chosens" of time allotment, ongoing assessment, and grouping for instruction. Let us examine these factors separately.

Factors That Influence Organization

Characteristics of the Class

Regardless of the grade he is teaching, a teacher can expect to find a wide range of literacy development among the children in his classroom. In a typical first grade, the majority of children will be initial stage readers; however, there will certainly be some children who are still at the emergent stage, and others who are well into the transitional stage. By the fourth or fifth grade, a teacher is likely to be faced with students in every stage (with the exception of emergent literacy). High-quality literacy instruction contributes to the range of reading ability found in classrooms. Literacy instruction that allows each child to progress as rapidly as she is able actually increases the range of reading achievement within a class (*The Longitudinal Evaluation of School Change and Performance (LESCP) in Title I Schools*, 2001). The range of reading capabilities of their students undoubtedly presents the greatest challenge to all teachers—even those with many years of experience. One must be aware of the literacy stages of students in a class in order to make sound decisions about organization and management of instruction, particularly with regard to grouping, which will be discussed later in this chapter.

Every class of students has a distinct group personality that will affect the teacher's organization and management. All experienced teachers agree that some classes are more cohesive and manageable than others. The composite academic and behavioral characteristics of the students affect class dynamics. For example, if a class contains an unusually large number of unaccomplished, unmotivated readers, the teacher will have to obtain an abundance of high-interest, low-readability materials and accommodate these students' need for a great deal of direct interaction with the teacher. He will have to engage in creative problem solving to meet their instructional needs. Possible strategies might include requesting an educational technician (ed tech), recruiting parent volunteers, or restructuring the use of time to facilitate many short, teacher-led activities for those who need them. Other problems that may have impact on a teacher's organization and management are more social in nature. Personality conflicts may exist among students in the class, for example, requiring the teacher to structure groupings carefully and to provide time for extra encouragement and support for those who need it.

Regardless of the makeup of the class, experienced teachers have found two conditions that contribute greatly to the smooth operation of the reading program irrespective of the specific methods or materials used. The first condition is the provision of a curriculum that is interesting to the children and developmentally appropriate. Students who are interested in what they are doing and who feel successful are likely to remain productively engaged in learning activities. Examples of this type of curriculum management have been described in our case studies of Kim, John, and Theresa.

The second condition is a high degree of structure and predictability with routines and procedural expectations well established. For example, students know what records have to be kept, how to sign up for a reading conference, what activi-

Students who are interested in and feel successful at their work will likely remain productively engaged.

ties they are expected to complete during the course of an hour (or a week), and where to find the materials they need. The school day is structured in a predictable way, as well. Students know when and how often reading and writing workshops will occur.

Physical Setting

The physical layout of the school and classroom will inevitably affect organization and management plans. Creative teachers, however, find innovative ways to use space and materials and do not allow physical constraints to diminish or eliminate the important components of their instructional programs.

The physical arrangement of the classroom should be conducive to literacy learning. Regardless of the type and amount of furniture (desks, tables, shelves, dividers, bulletin boards), it must be arranged flexibly enough to accommodate various working arrangements. For example, there should be areas that are designed for independent work and foster concentration on reading or writing. There must also be provision for large- and small-group instruction through flexible arrangement of tables and desks, or carpeted areas where children can gather. In addition, space must be <u>available for collaborative group</u> work and sharing. Novice teachers find it helpful to visit the classrooms of colleagues whose classroom facilities are similar to their own, to glean good ideas for physical classroom arrangements.

Administrative Expectations

In some schools there are administrative requirements to include certain commercial programs, materials, and grouping practices. As described in Chapter 11, the adoption of local standards and assessments further constrains teachers' decisions. Sometimes these expectations may be inconsistent with the teacher's philosophy or with what she perceives to be current thinking about how children acquire literacy. Successful teachers "<u>work around</u>" such constraints, finding ways to modify and consolidate the required exercises, leaving time for the reading and writing experiences that the teacher knows are essential elements of an effective literacy program. When teachers have a sound knowledge base and are able to articulate the rationale for their instructional decisions, administrators are more likely to relinquish their control over the reading curriculum as they gain confidence in their teachers' ability to plan and implement effective approaches to literacy and particularly as they observe the academic progress and positive attitudes of students.

Access to Materials

In any classroom, it is essential for students to have access to a variety of appropriate reading fare. Ideally, the classroom library should contain books from many genres and of varying levels of difficulty. The collection should include books of recognized literary merit and books that are known to be particularly popular with children of a certain age. There may be a special need for books that acknowledge the culture and language of novice English language learners. <u>Excellent lists of suggested titles</u> for <u>different grade levels are available</u> from <u>professional organizations such as the</u> International Reading Association and the National Council of Teachers of English. Websites of publishers of children's books (Scholastic, for example) are also excellent resources. Teachers must become thoroughly familiar with the literature appropriate to the ages of the children they teach, for they not only select books for the classroom, but also recommend titles to different children. They must decide when and whether to require individuals or groups of children to read certain books. As teachers' knowledge and appreciation of children's literature increases, their students tend to respond more and more positively to their reading experiences.

Time Allotment

Provision of adequate time for reading instruction and practice is a key element of any effective organizational plan. It is important to set aside extended blocks of time every day for <u>reading and writing, ranging from 1½ to 2 hours, in most cases</u>. The time of day at which this is scheduled is not as important as the regularity of scheduling. Students come to expect that they will devote a certain amount of time every day to reading and writing and related activities.

Even more important than time allotted to reading is the students' *engaged time,* the time during which the students are actually reading. Although the amount of engaged time depends, to some extent, on the amount of allocated time, the skill of the teacher in managing the class is also a major determinant. During the first few weeks of the school year, effective teachers establish routines for making transitions between activities, distributing materials, obtaining help when the teacher is busy, and handing in completed work. Well-established routines help to prevent discipline problems; when they do arise, skilled teachers handle them quickly and consistently. Effective routines help eliminate wasted time and thus give students more opportunities to practice reading.

The editors of the book *Preventing Reading Difficulties in Young Children* (1998) describe the classrooms of teachers in effective schools. These teachers create a literacy environment in which children have access to a variety of reading and writing materials. The teachers also attempt to make clear the purpose of every reading/ writing activity. They realize that their time-on-task rates are very good predictors of the achievement gains of their students. They make sure children understand how to do each task, and know what to do when they finish a task. In classrooms taught by these teachers, more of the precious time available for learning is spent on activities with real academic focus. Libraries and other media are integrated and used to their full potential (Snow, Burns, & Griffin, 1998).

In allotting reading time, how does the teacher decide how much is enough? Allington and McGill-Franzen (1989) studied how the volume of reading done by students was associated with gains in their reading. They found that the average higher-achieving student read approximately three times as much each week as the lower-achieving students. These differences did not include time spent on out-of-school voluntary reading. The 1998 NAEP *Reading Report Card for the Nation and the States* (U.S. Department of Education, 1998) reported compelling correlational evidence on the positive effects of extensive reading practice on reading achievement. Correlational studies such as the NAEP report do not provide evidence of a causal connection between quantities of reading and gains in reading, yet the results are highly suggestive. While it appears the volume of print processed is conducive to gains in reading competency, other factors must be considered. Brisk pacing is effective only when the material is at an appropriate level of difficulty for the students who experience success in their reading. Effective teachers move students along as quickly as possible, but they do not sacrifice comprehension (Allington, 1995; Anderson et al., 1985).

Teachers, then, must be aware of allocated time, engaged time, and the pacing of reading instruction. It is up to them as effective managers to ensure that sufficient time is available for students' reading and that this time is used as productively and appropriately as possible.

Assessment of Students

In a classroom with a literature-based, process-oriented reading program, assessment of students is ongoing and observational. During the first few days of school, the teacher observes how students approach and perform reading tasks. From this the teacher forms tentative impressions of the capabilities of individual children. These impressions can be verified and modified later through more structured observations, such as an informal reading inventory or (in kindergarten or first grade) an assessment of print awareness. Teachers use the general and specific observational data to design and monitor appropriate reading and writing experiences. For example, a second-grade teacher may find that four children in her class are still clearly early initial stage readers. She plans to bring these children together for word identification strategy work and practice reading in very predictable enlarged books. Her assessments show that the remainder of the class has achieved varying degrees of fluency and independence. She plans to help them select books and read them independently; the teacher-directed activities for these students will focus on developing fluency and comprehension strategies. Assessment that leads to differentiated instruction is especially crucial in multi-age classrooms.

Assessment not only helps the teacher plan instruction, it is also necessary for documenting students' progress. Ongoing records and samples of children's work must be kept. The teacher generally keeps one or more folders for each student and collects various samples and records throughout the year. (See Chapter 11 for a more extensive discussion of this process.)

Grouping for Instruction

The types of groups that can be used in reading instruction include large groups (whole class), small groups, pairs, and individuals. Effective teachers make use of all these forms of grouping within their literacy programs. There are three major reasons for grouping students: to address common needs efficiently, to accommodate shared interests and experiences, and to ensure exposure to reading materials that are at an appropriate level of difficulty.

When a teacher determines that a number of students have a *common need* and will profit from the same instructional activity, he may decide that the most efficient way to address this need is to teach the entire group. This is the usual reason for whole-group instruction. When a first-grade teacher leads the whole class in discussion and practice of word identification strategies and when a fifth-grade teacher models use of question/answer relationships to the whole class, these teachers have decided that all or most of the students in their classes will benefit from the activities. Whole-group instruction, then, is generally based on the teacher's perception of common needs among children. However, small groups of students may also be brought together for a common purpose that is not shared with the rest of the class.

Another type of group may be based on the shared interests and experiences of students. Such groups, often initiated by children, provide opportunities for collaboration. Discussion groups for children who have read the same books, books by the same author, or books of the same genre would be examples of special interest groups. A number of children might come together to collaborate on a special project, a piece of writing, or a report.

Probably the most common purpose for grouping for reading instruction is to ensure that students are exposed to reading materials that are at an *appropriate difficulty level.* This is the form of grouping most often associated with use of the basal reader. Teachers constitute "ability groups" on the basis of results of an informal reading assessment or on the basis of the previous teacher's recommendation or a list of basal readers already completed.

Problems with Ability Grouping

While the matching of readers with appropriate materials may be a legitimate rationale for grouping, there are many pitfalls associated with ability grouping. For example, research has shown that there tend to be qualitative differences in instruction between "high" and "low" ability groups. Children in lower groups do relatively more reading aloud and less silent reading. Teachers correct a higher proportion of their miscues and are likely to furnish clues about pronunciation rather than meaning. Moreover, low-group children are asked more simple factual questions and fewer questions that require reasoning (Johnson, 1999; Wheelock, 1992).

Another potential problem associated with ability grouping is inflexibility. Once a child is classified and assigned to a group, it is unlikely that she will be reassigned. Since groups are formed at the beginning of the school year partly, at least, on the basis of children's standing during the previous year, it is unusual for them to be reclassified. "Once a bluebird, always a bluebird" is unfortunately often true.

Perhaps the most serious drawback of ability grouping is the effect it can have on children's perceptions of themselves as readers and writers. Regardless of what the groups are called or how tactfully the teacher refers to them, low-group students view themselves as poor readers, and high-group students often see themselves as superior to other students. Teachers tend to have low expectations for students who have been classified as low-ability; their expectations often become a self-fulfilling prophecy (Allington, 1995).

Because of the many problems that arise from ability grouping, some teachers have largely eliminated this practice. In classrooms where children are no longer grouped on the basis of ability, the basal reader is usually not the primary vehicle for teaching reading. Even if ability grouping is retained, however, many of the problems associated with such grouping can be alleviated, if not eliminated. Teachers who are aware of the research on grouping can make a concerted effort to provide the same quality of instruction for their less able and more able readers. Specifically, they can help students focus on meaning making, avoid undue or premature emphasis on accuracy of word identification, provide a proper balance between oral and silent reading, and ask questions that engage the students in higher-level thinking.

It is also recommended that teachers explore other options for grouping, such as whole-class instruction, collaborative special interest groups, and work with partners. While grouping for developmentally appropriate instruction (with or without use of the basal reader) is certainly a valid practice, it should not be the sole method of grouping for all reading activities. Children need the experience of working with all their classmates in various combinations and of having their contributions valued (Johnson, 1999; Wheelock, 1992).

Individualized Instruction

Sometimes it is beneficial for students to work individually rather than in groups of any type. The term *individualized,* when applied to reading, often causes confusion since it has been applied to very divergent instructional practices. To some, individualized instruction means that each student moves through a prescribed set of materials at his own pace. This use of the term is generally found in the context of a skill-based model of instruction (see Chapter 4). Many reading kits, skill books, and computer software programs are designed to be used by students working independently at their own pace.

More often, "individualized reading" means student self-selection of reading materials, as well as self-pacing. The purpose of including this component in a reading program is to give students opportunities to choose books they want to read, which increases motivation and enjoyment of reading and builds overall reading competency. As we have stated many times, individualized or self-selected reading is an important component of effective reading programs at every stage of development.

Management of Direct and Indirect Instruction

Instruction can be defined as the design and manipulation of experiences by the teacher to help students achieve desired curricular outcomes. Instruction may be direct or indirect. When using *direct instruction,* the teacher assumes a very active, dominant role. Explanation by the teacher provides the information students are presumed to need to achieve desired outcomes. In contrast, *indirect instruction* depends more on a structured environment than on teacher direction and explanation. Activities are designed in such a way that students are led to discover outcomes (Weaver, 1994).

Both direct and indirect instruction have important places in literacy instruction. The choice of one or the other is based on the nature of the desired outcomes. Suppose, for example, a teacher wants his students to become aware of question/answer relationships (QAR) so they can develop strategies for responding to questions asked about their reading (see Chapter 7). This competency is not likely to be acquired spontaneously; it must be demonstrated and explained as well as practiced. Direct instruction by the teacher is clearly called for.

Suppose, on the other hand, that a teacher's objective is to help a group of immature readers increase their fluency. This is a relatively long-term goal. Moreover, fluency cannot be directly taught by the teacher; it must grow from the students' reading experiences. Indirect instruction would be the most appropriate choice for achieving the desired outcome. The teacher would structure the environment in a way that would promote reading practice. For example, sustained silent reading time (SSR) would be scheduled daily. The students might be assigned to practice assisted reading with tapes. The physical arrangement, as well as the atmosphere of the classroom, would invite reading (see Chapter 4). While the attainment of fluency does not involve direct instruction, the teacher can deliberately and systematically set up an environment and structured activities that will lead students to reach this goal.

The teacher, as decision maker, must decide what blend of direct and indirect instruction will be most appropriate for the students. Generally speaking, accomplished readers (for their grade level) who have had extensive literacy experiences need less direct instruction than their less accomplished classmates. Many good readers tend to gain insights and develop strategies on their own, whereas poor readers need to be led to insights and have strategies demonstrated in order to make gains in reading. All children, however, regardless of reading stage or grade level, will profit at times from both direct and indirect instruction.

This blend affects the classroom climate. A teacher who employs direct instruction much or all of the time is likely to create a classroom climate that is very restrictive, one in which children assume little responsibility for their own learning and feel undervalued as learners. Language arts instruction particularly lends itself to indirect instruction; nevertheless, if there is insufficient structure and accountability, the climate can become chaotic and less productive than it might be, and children may not get the information and support they need to progress to their full potential. There has recently been particular concern that students not from the "culture of power" (i.e., not white, middle-to-high-income Standard American English speakers) will be shortchanged by the tendency of white, middle-class teachers to teach by implication, and by the lack of sufficient direct instruction. Children who are used to explicit directions from the adults in their lives ("Put your folder away now") can be confused by directions that are implied or disguised as requests ("Would you like to put your folder away now?"). It is particularly important for these children to have important aspects of the system of printed language taught explicitly rather than left to them to figure out (Delpit, 1995). Balance and a keen sense of what individual children understand and need are essential. Language arts educators are increasingly aware of the need for an appropriate mix of teacher and student direction of literacy learning. Calkins (1995) identifies as most effective those classrooms that have both high teacher input and high student input within the language arts program. The goal is to create a climate in which individuals can flourish as well as participate as valued members of the group. This requires an environment that is predictable but flexible, stimulating but not chaotic, and disciplined but not restrictive.

Summary

Designing an effective organizational plan for teaching reading requires that the teacher consider many relevant factors, including characteristics of students in the class, physical setting, expectations of the administration, availability of materials and resources, and allocation of extended blocks of time for reading. The teacher must assess students' reading capabilities in order to plan instruction and document progress. She must also make ongoing decisions about grouping students for instruction, and provide a viable balance of direct and indirect instruction. To illustrate how to effectively manage classroom instruction, Chapters 13 and 14 present examples of two teachers' organizational plans. These teachers work in very different settings and their principals have different expectations of them; therefore, their plans are quite different. Both, however, are effective teachers.

BIBLIOGRAPHY

Allington, R. (1984). Content coverage and contextual reading in reading groups. *Journal of Reading Behavior, 16,* 85–96.

Allington, R. (1995). Literacy lessons in the elementary schools: Yesterday, today and tomorrow. In R. Allington & S. Walmsley (Eds.), *No quick fix: Rethinking literacy programs in America's elementary schools.* Newark, DE: International Reading Association.

Allington, R., & McGill-Franzen, A. (1989). School response to reading failure: Chapter 1 and special education students in grades 2, 4 and 8. *Elementary School Journal, 89,* 529–542.

Anderson, R. C., Hiebert, E., Scott, J., & Wilkinson, I. (Eds.). (1985). *Becoming a nation of readers.* Washington, DC: National Institute of Education.

Calkins, L. (1995). *The art of teaching writing.* Portsmouth, NH: Heinemann.

Delpit, L. (1995). *Other people's children.* New York: The New Press.

Duffy, G. G., & Roehler, L. R. (1989). *Improving classroom reading instruction* (2nd ed.). New York: Random House.

Johnson, G. (1999). Inclusive education: Fundamental instructional strategies and considerations. *Preventing School Failure, 43,* pp. 72–80.

National Assessment of Education Progress (NEAP) (1998). *Reading report card for the nation and the states.* Washington, DC: US Department of Education.

The Longitudinal Evaluation of School Change and Performance (LESCP) in Title I Schools (2001). Education Publications Center, U.S. Department of Education, P.O. Box 1398, Jessup, MD 20794-1398.

Snow, E. F., Burns, S. M., & Griffin, P. (Eds.). (1998). *Preventing reading difficulties in young children.* Washington, DC: National Academy Press.

Weaver, C. (1994). *Reading process and practice.* Portsmouth, NH: Heinemann.

Wheelock, A. (1992). *Crossing the tracks: How "untracking" can save America's schools.* New York: New Press.

13 Ms. Stein's First Grade

A Literature-Based Program

■ *Overview*

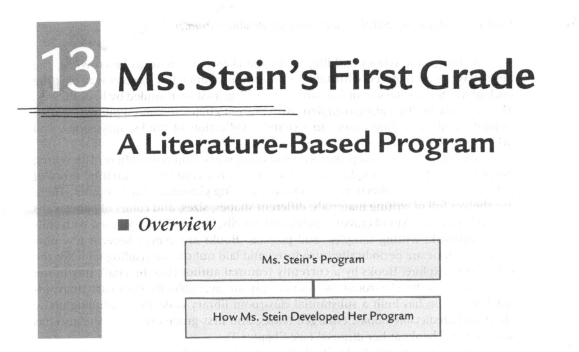

Ms. Stein's Program

How Ms. Stein Developed Her Program

*I*n this chapter, we will introduce you to Ms. Stein, a first-grade teacher who has organized and implemented a successful literature-based literacy program. She has recently eliminated the use of a basal reading program in her classroom.

First, we will take you into Ms. Stein's classroom and describe the teaching context she inherited and the program she has developed within this setting. Later in the chapter, we will examine her evolution as a teacher and look at some of the problems and issues she faced that are typically encountered by teachers who move away from the use of basal programs and commercially packaged materials.

Ms. Stein's Program

Ms. Stein teaches first grade in a large, urban elementary school. Her class size ranges from 22 to 28 children, and her students come from a variety of ethnic and socioeconomic backgrounds. The class includes ESL students, several of whom have recently immigrated to the United States. Collectively, they represent different languages and cultures, and there is a considerable range in their ability to understand and communicate in English.

The principal of Ms. Stein's school is cognizant of current trends in literacy instruction and supports and encourages teachers' efforts to design and implement reading programs that are responsive to students' needs. Approximately half the teachers in the building still make some use of a basal program that includes an anthology of children's literature and informational texts; however, Ms. Stein does not use this series.

Although the school building is old and classrooms tend to be crowded, the desks have been replaced with tables that can be arranged in various ways. At the back of Ms. Stein's classroom is a carpeted meeting area surrounded by bookshelves. This is a very inviting place complete with old soft chairs, oversized pillows, stuffed animals, and, most important, an extensive collection of books, magazines, and other reading materials.

Ms. Stein's classroom projects an informal, workshop atmosphere. The setting encourages children to explore and learn. One area contains an inviting array of plants, tropical fish, collections of rocks, magnifying glasses, and a computer. There are shelves full of writing materials; different shapes, sizes, and colors of paper; cans of markers; and boxes of crayons, pens, and pencils. The walls are covered with children's artwork, writing samples, and projects. Books are everywhere. A few new books at a time are periodically introduced and laid out on the reading table for the children to explore. Books by a currently featured author line the chalk tray in the library area. In this classroom, books not only are available, they also are unavoidable! Ms. Stein has built a substantial classroom library collection including many short and predictable books, enlarged books, and first-grade favorites. She also has some leveled books at her disposal (see Chapter 3).

During the first week of school, Ms. Stein made an informal assessment of her students to determine their literacy levels. She did a general screening of phonological awareness, alphabet recognition, understanding of major print concepts, and knowledge of story grammar and story language using the protocols for emergent readers described in Chapter 1. She administered the informal reading inventory to several children who had had many literacy experiences and were already reading some words. She determined that she had a range of students from the emergent stage to the late initial stage. Ms. Stein is particularly cognizant of the instructional goals and approaches for early readers described in Chapters 1 through 4.

The typical day in Ms. Stein's school begins at 8:30 when the first-graders come into their classrooms. After the morning routines are accomplished, the children gather on the carpet for reading time. Ms. Stein generally begins by soliciting a morning message as a language experience activity. The children are encouraged to tell about special events that are happening in their lives, at home, and in the world. The chilrden are directed to observe Ms. Stein as she transcribes exactly what they say, repeating each word as she records it and then inviting the children to read along with her after she completes writing each phrase or sentence. Follow-up activities usually include calling attention to certain letters and chunks and directing children to recurring sight words.

Next Ms. Stein reads aloud a familiar story or two in an interactive manner. She encourages the children to make <u>predictions</u> and <u>pauses</u> from time to time to elicit comments about events and characters. She often leads the children in several songs, poems, and chants as they follow the words on a chart propped up on the easel. This provides an opportunity for building phonemic awareness and reinforcing letter–sound correspondences. Next, she usually brings out an enlarged book. If it is new to the children, she reads it through for their enjoyment, stopping from time to time for them to comment on the story or predict what will happen next. If it is one the children have read before, she encourages them to chime in and read with her, as she follows the print with a pointer. Reading is followed by a variety of activities that draw children's attention to the print and to the content of the story (see the discussion of shared reading in Chapter 3). These whole-group activities typically last 30 to 40 minutes and expose the children to a large quantity of print. The activities also enable Ms. Stein to note individual and group responses. Can the children rhyme? Can they identify beginning sounds and link them with letters? Can they match speech to print? The answers to such questions guide her group instruction and individual coaching in later periods in the day.

Next she directs the children to a choice of independent reading activities such as following along with a taped story at the listening center, drawing and labeling their favorite part of the story, and "reading" familiar books (enlarged or small versions) independently or with friends. During this time, Ms. Stein works with groups of children according to needs she has identified. For example, she frequently gathers together the children who have not yet begun to read independently and records their dictated reactions to stories or events. She uses many of the techniques of the language experience approach (described in Chapter 3) to further develop their understandings about print. She guides these children in selecting appropriate independent follow-up activities and then moves on to another group. She brings together several more accomplished initial readers, who read a predictable book (from multiple copies) together, thus expanding their sight vocabularies and practicing word identification strategies. She often uses portions of big books and other materials the children have read to design cloze activities that lead students to use the various cueing systems and share their strategies (as described in Chapter 3). She encourages students to practice reading orally. She observes their progress in word identification. She confers periodically with the few children who are already fluent, independent readers about books they have completed on their own. From time to time she convenes groups of children for special purposes, such as discussing a book they have all read or comparing different books on the same topic (dinosaurs, for example) or by the same author. The period of time during which children are either working independently or meeting in a small group with Ms. Stein generally lasts about 45 minutes. The reading period ends with 10 or 15 minutes of whole-class sharing. The children gather in the carpeted area again, and Ms. Stein encourages volunteers to talk about books they have particularly enjoyed. Sometimes she introduces a new book, reading all or part of it to the children, or rereads a favorite story.

As the fall progresses, Ms. Stein tries to schedule some time at least once a week for "reading buddies" to interact. Children in her class who can read very familiar stories may go into the kindergarten room and read to emergent readers. Third graders are invited to come to her class and read books that they have practiced to her first-graders. Children in Ms. Stein's class become "reading buddies" and share their favorite stories as well. These experiences provide readers with an authentic audience and help develop their reading fluency (Peterson, 2001).

From 8:30 until 10:00 every morning, the children in Ms. Stein's room are engaged in reading and reading-related activities. Her organization of this time block is characterized by flexibility and variety in activities and grouping patterns, yet it has a consistent overall structure. The children quickly become comfortable with the established routines of whole-group reading followed by independent work and meetings with the teacher and finally whole-group sharing. The atmosphere is that of a workshop. Expectations are clear, and children are always engaged in purposeful activities that they can perform successfully. Within the time allotted for reading, children spend most of their time reading real texts, with varying degrees of assistance.

Literacy instruction does not end at 10:00, however. After their recess, the first-graders spend an hour or more in "writing workshop." Early in the year Ms. Stein models for her children how some first-graders write, using the different writing forms described by Sulzby (see Chapter 2). She emphasizes the process of "invented" or phonetic spelling, since it develops phonemic awareness and knowledge of letter–sound correspondences. The children use a variety of materials and media to draw and write about topics they have chosen; they work independently on drafts, share their drafts with each other and with the teacher, make changes and additions, and, with Ms. Stein's help, prepare their favorite pieces for classroom publication. Books the children have authored are added to the classroom library.

Not only do students read and write during the times allotted for "language arts," but Ms. Stein integrates literacy activities with virtually all areas of the curriculum. For example, when the class is studying animals, Ms. Stein encourages children to read stories about animals, examine informational books about animals, and keep logs of what they have learned. Children's literature frequently generates interest in topics that lead to exploration of other curriculum areas. In a class such as Ms. Stein's there are no sharp boundaries between traditional curriculum areas. The key is integration, which takes place naturally, if a range of children's literature is fully utilized.

How Ms. Stein Developed Her Program

Ms. Stein began teaching first grade three years ago. At that time, all the teachers in her school based their reading instruction on the basal reading series adopted by the district. During her second year of teaching, she enrolled in a graduate-level course entitled "Reading Development and Instruction" and attended two regional workshops, one on literature-based instruction and one on early reading–writing connections. These experiences inspired her to begin moving away from dependence on the basal system toward more literature-based instruction.

First she eliminated the use of the basal workbook entirely and became more selective about the skill sheets she assigned for seat work. Most of the children's independent work time was now devoted to extension activities based on the stories read. Children illustrated stories, read with partners, listened to tapes, and engaged in writing activities related to their reading. The children responded enthusiastically to this change.

Next Ms. Stein cut down on the amount of time devoted to basal reading groups and increased time spent on direct, whole-class instruction using big books and enlarged print versions of poems, chants, and songs. By spring of that year, Ms. Stein was convening the basal groups only three days per week. On the other two days, children engaged in self-selected reading, using familiar classroom favorites as well as new books from the school library.

Ms. Stein was pleased with the results of the changes she had made. Both she and her children were enjoying reading more. The children's increased ability to work independently and collaboratively was noticeable, and their progress in reading and writing was apparent, both from her observations and from the children's performance on the end-of-year standardized tests. Even her "high-risk" students were progressing well, and parents had begun requesting that their children be placed in her classroom.

Based on the positive results of her modifications, Ms. Stein decided for the coming school year to eliminate the use of basal readers entirely and base her instruction on authentic literacy experiences with a variety of texts. Although she was convinced that this decision was sound, she had many concerns about giving up the security of the basal structure and about organizing and implementing a totally literature-based program. During the summer she talked with several teachers she

A first-grader shares the writing activity she has completed.

had met at conferences and read several books they recommended, including *With a Light Touch* by Carol Avery (1996), *Foundations of Literacy* by Don Holdaway (1979), *Book Talk and Beyond* edited by Nancy Roser and Miriam Martinez (1995), The *Beginning Reader Handbook: Strategies for Success* by Gail Heald-Taylor (2001), and several books by Regie Routman. In these books she found clear explanations of the reading, writing, and thinking processes and specific suggestions for setting up a classroom environment that fosters these processes. She found Routman's books particularly useful since these are written by a teacher who successfully moved from basal instruction to totally literature-based instruction. Routman's book suggested solutions to many of the problems Ms. Stein had identified. How would she know how many books to buy and what titles to choose? How could she organize the classroom library and manage the flow of books? What other materials would be essential? How would she document students' progress? What about grouping? How should phonics instruction be managed?

Using the suggestions given by Routman and others, Ms. Stein developed plans for addressing these questions. She ordered a "core" first-grade library containing a range of books (including some multiple titles and leveled texts) appropriate for initial readers. (Such core libraries can be purchased from Scholastic, Inc.; Rigby Education; Richard C. Owen, Publishers; and The Wright Group.) She ordered as many other books as her budget would permit from a wholesale distributor, using Routman's bibliographies as well as her own familiarity with children's literature to guide her selections. She was able to begin the year with 100 books in her classroom library and to add to this collection during the year. She purchased several new big books and made others according to Routman's directions. Many of these were made with spaces for children to generate their own illustrations.

Ms. Stein obtained an easel (for big book readings) and several book storage/display units, including book spinners, plastic tubs, and shelves. She made sure she had an ample supply of materials for writing: felt-tip markers, pens, pencils, many sizes and varieties of paper, and materials for publishing.

The professional books Ms. Stein read suggested various plans for organizing and maintaining the classroom library. From these she developed a workable system for storing and keeping track of books. Each book contained a sign-out card, and children were taught specific procedures for signing out, taking home, and returning books. Students and parent aides helped to keep the classroom library in order, monitor the flow of books, and change displays of special collections.

Ms. Stein kept various records of children's reading, including anecdotal records, running records, and lists of books completed. She collected work samples periodically, developing a portfolio with each child (see Chapter 11). Knowing that her children would be required to take standardized tests, she followed Routman's advice about preparing children for them:

> We give instruction and practice in test-taking formats, typical questions, and ways to figure out an unknown answer. Neither we, nor the children, enjoy these procedures, but they are necessary in a culture that places so much emphasis on tests. (Routman, 1988, p. 209)

Ms. Stein eventually used every type of grouping described in Chapter 11. In her new program, the children spent considerably more of their reading time in whole-class, teacher-led activities and independent extension activities and proportionately less time in teacher-led ability groups. Small groups were formed to accomplish specific objectives (for guided reading of a book together, to work on strategies, or to pursue a special interest) and were dissolved when the objective was met.

Summary

Ms. Stein's program evolved gradually over a period of approximately three years. Like many teachers, she made a gradual transition from dependence on the basal system to literature-based instruction that did not involve the use of the basal reader. Her awareness of the need for change emanated from her involvement in professional development activities (reading, coursework, conferences) and from her careful observations of her students. Her expanded awareness of the literacy learning process made her much more conscious of her students' developing awareness of language, their emerging understanding of the relationship between speech and print, and the conditions that facilitated their learning and enhanced their motivation to read and write.

Ms. Stein's program will undoubtedly continue to evolve and change, as she learns from her experiences and sees the need to make improvements. There is no one recipe for the day-to-day organization and management of literacy instruction. Each teacher implements instruction according to her own teaching style, belief systems, level of experience, and characteristics of the class. In effective classrooms, we do find common features, however. Extensive time is spent on reading and writing for real communicative purposes. There is explicit teaching of strategies that the children can then apply independently. The children are given many opportunities to share their reading and writing. And the children's experiences, concerns, and interests form the content of the literacy curriculum.

BIBLIOGRAPHY

Avery, C. (1996). *With a light touch*. Portsmouth, NH: Heinemann.

Dragon, P. B. (2001). *Literacy from day one*. Portsmouth: Heinemann.

Heald-Taylor, G. (2001). *The beginning reader handbook: Strategies for success*. Portsmouth: Heinemann.

Holdaway, D. (1979). *Foundations of literacy*. Portsmouth, NH: Heinemann.

Meyer, R. J. (2002). *Phonics exposed: Understanding and resisting systematic direct intensive phonics instruction*. Mahwah, NJ: Lawrence Erlbaum Associates.

Peterson, B. (2001). *Literacy pathways: Selecting books to support new readers*. Portsmouth, NH: Heinemann.

Roser, N., & Martinez, M. (Eds.). (1995). *Book talk and beyond.* Newark, DE: International Reading Association.

Routman, R. (1988). *Transitions from literature to literacy.* Portsmouth, NH: Heinemann.

Routman, R. (1991). *Invitations.* Portsmouth, NH: Heinemann.

Routman, R. (1996). *Literacy at the crossroads.* Portsmouth, NH: Heinemann.

14 Mr. Gordon's Fourth Grade

Using Basal Readers

■ *Overview*

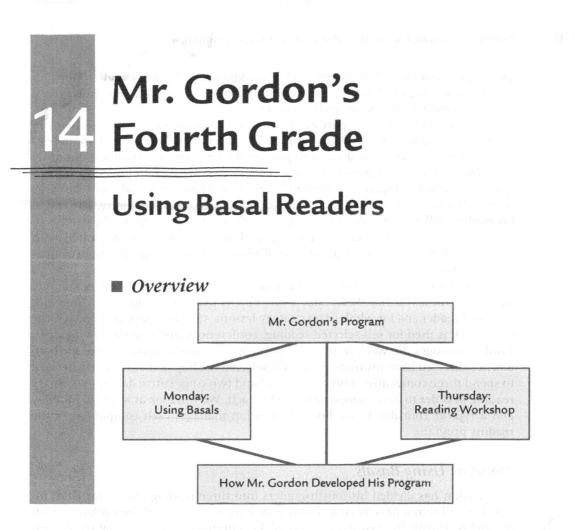

In this chapter you will meet a teacher whose reading instruction is based on the use of a commercial basal program. As we did with Ms. Stein, we will describe the context in which Mr. Gordon teaches, present his program, and relate how his program has evolved over the last few years.

Mr. Gordon's Program

Mr. Gordon is a fourth-grade teacher in a rural elementary school. The school's population is quite homogeneous in cultural and ethnic background but includes students from a range of socioeconomic levels. Class sizes are very manageable, ranging from 20 to 25 students. The school has no central library, and because of a restrictive budget the purchase of books for classroom libraries is limited. Recognizing the importance of varied reading opportunities for his students, Mr. Gordon makes extensive use of the regional public library, ensuring a frequently changing collection of high-quality books for his students. Teachers in Mr. Gordon's school are required to use a basal series with the accompanying workbooks, skill sheets, and end-of-unit mastery tests. Mr. Gordon uses the basal program as a major resource; however, it does not constitute his entire reading program.

There is adequate space in Mr. Gordon's classroom for students to work in large or small groups, move about comfortably, and display projects. The room contains movable individual desks as well as several tables and two computer stations.

Mr. Gordon has a particular interest in science, which is reflected in his frequently changing displays of interesting science-related materials and projects. Science books make up a substantial proportion of his classroom library. The rest of his reading collection consists mostly of books that have been donated by parents or acquired as book club bonuses. The walls of his classroom are decorated with posters. One bulletin board is devoted to displays of student writing with accompanying artwork.

Mr. Gordon devotes 1½ to 2 hours each morning to reading instruction. On Mondays, Tuesdays, and Wednesdays, this time is used for group instruction with the basal reader and for whole-class strategy lessons. On Thursdays and Fridays, the time block is used for self-selected reading, conferences, and related activities. Mr. Gordon arranges the week in this way because he wants to provide time for both teacher-directed basal instruction and self-selected reading of literature. He decided to spend three consecutive days on the basal and two consecutive days on voluntary reading in order to have more continuity for each. We will look at a typical Monday and a typical Thursday to see how Mr. Gordon manages each component of the reading program.

Monday: Using Basals

Mr. Gordon has divided his fourth-graders into three reading groups for basal instruction. Children have been assigned to groups on the basis of their relative reading ability. During the first week of school, he administered an informal reading inventory included with the basal series to establish reading groups by matching students to the basal texts. His class was typical in that all students did not fit perfectly into one of the three groups. He had two students who were considerably less accomplished than any others in the class; they were still in the initial reading stage. He also had two students who were refinement stage readers and were considerably more skilled and experienced readers than their classmates. While Mr. Gordon realized that ideally he should have two additional groups for these children, he felt he could not effectively work with more than three groups. Therefore, he included these four children in the most appropriate ability groups and made an effort to meet their special needs in other ways. A Title I tutor came into the classroom two days a week to assist the two initial readers, and the individualized reading periods on Thursdays and Fridays gave Mr. Gordon the opportunity to work more closely with all four of the special needs students, recommending materials that would be particularly appropriate to their reading levels and interests.

Mr. Gordon's work with the three basal reading groups is typically organized as shown in Figure 14.1.

The reading instruction period often begins with a whole-class strategy lesson. Mr. Gordon bases these lessons on his perception of the strategies that fourth-

FIGURE 14.1 *Mr. Gordon's Management Plan for Reading Groups*

Time	Group A	Group B	Group C
10–20 min.	Orientation to day's reading activities and/or strategy lesson		
30 min.	Teacher-directed reading	Assigned independent work	Voluntary reading, journal writing
30 min.	Assigned independent work	Voluntary reading, journal writing	Teacher-directed reading
30 min.	Voluntary reading, journal writing	Teacher-directed reading	Assigned independent work

graders need in order to read more effectively. The content of the strategy lessons is derived from two sources: his observations of his students' reading behaviors and the skill lessons included in the basal. In many cases he has replaced isolated skill activities with related strategy lessons, thus adding to his students' repertoire of usable strategies, as well as greatly reducing the amount of time given to skill instruction in the separate reading groups. For example, his basal program prescribes numerous lessons involving the use of the dictionary, such as locating specific words, determining accented syllables, and using a pronunciation key. Mr. Gordon wanted his students to be able to use the dictionary as a functional reference tool for finding the meanings of unknown words. He had his students jot down words from their literature reading that they didn't know the meaning of. During a strategy lesson, he demonstrated the use of guide words and locating the unknown word on the dictionary page. He provided guided practice by leading the group through the process of finding several words. Independent practice took place during students' assigned independent work time. Mr. Gordon gave each group several unknown words in context and asked them to find the words in the dictionary and write down the most appropriate definitions. He encouraged collaboration. He followed a similar format in all his strategy lessons, which included summarizing, using context to determine word meanings, generating story maps, comprehension monitoring, and question/answer relationships.

Following the mini-lesson and before beginning group work, Mr. Gordon orients his students to the morning's reading activities, reminding each group of its schedule and briefly outlining reading and independent work to be accomplished. He then begins his work with groups.

Each group, in turn, meets with Mr. Gordon around a table at the front of the room for a teacher-directed reading activity using a basal selection. If the group is ready to begin a new story, he prepares students for reading by discussing the general topic and type of story, introducing key concepts and vocabulary, and leading students to predict the content of the story. Students read at least part of the story (silently) during their directed reading time. This enables Mr. Gordon to make sure everyone in the group gets involved in the reading, and he is right there to help anyone who has a question or encounters some problem with the reading. Students read large portions of text without interruption. The least-accomplished readers often complete a whole story during their allotted instructional time, since their stories are relatively short. The other two groups, who are dealing with longer selections, usually complete their reading independently when they return to their seats. If a group has completed a story independently, the following day's lesson begins with a discussion of the story. Mr. Gordon follows many of the recommendations described in Chapter 7 that help students elaborate their understanding of the text. They establish the story line, discuss their interpretations of the selection, and compare the story theme, characters, and structure to other stories they have read.

The last five minutes of the teacher-directed reading time is devoted to a brief sharing of what has been read so far. Mr. Gordon assigns independent follow-up work to be done once the reading of the story is completed. Sometimes he uses a suggested activity from the basal or the accompanying workbook. (He selects only those that he feels are congruent with his goals for his students.) At other times or in addition, he assigns a follow-up activity he has designed himself. These often involve writing about the story.

During a significant portion of the time that they are not working with Mr. Gordon, his students are engaged in assigned independent activities. These include completing the reading of an unfinished story, doing workbook activities or writing assignments, and completing practice activities related to the day's strategy lesson. Mr. Gordon occasionally suggests that certain activities be completed in pairs or small, collaborative groups.

Most students in Mr. Gordon's class look forward to completion of their assigned independent work so they can move on to voluntary reading and journal writing. The voluntary reading that children do on Monday, Tuesday, and Wednesday is usually a continuation of reading in a book they selected for the more extended SSR time on Thursday and Friday. No formal sharing or follow-up is undertaken until the end of the week.

Each student is expected to make a journal entry on Monday, Tuesday, and Wednesday. No topics are suggested; students are free to respond to their reading in any way they wish. On Wednesday, Mr. Gordon collects the journals. He reads student entries and writes brief responses before giving them back to their owners. These dialogue journals constitute a written conversation between Mr. Gordon and each of his students.

Mr. Gordon not only fulfills the requirements of his district by using the basal program, he also has addressed the major criticisms educators voice today concerning the inflexible use of basals (Shannon & Goodman, 1994). If we were to follow one student from any group through the 1½-hour period devoted to reading instruction, we would find that the majority of the student's time is given to sustained reading and writing.

Thursday: Reading Workshop

On the last two days of the week, Mr. Gordon's reading instruction time is structured quite differently. He orchestrates a reading workshop in which students select their own books, and he works primarily with individuals, rather than groups. The reading workshop is usually structured as shown in Figure 14.2.

FIGURE 14.2 *Mr. Gordon's Management Plan for Individualized Reading*

Time	Activity
15–20 min.	Whole class: Strategies for individualized reading, literature talks
40–45 min.	SSR and conferences
10 min.	Reading records
20 min.	Whole class: Sharing

Mr. Gordon generally begins the reading period by giving a brief talk about one or two books, or about an author. He solicits comments from students who have read the books. In this way he brings a variety of books and authors to the students' attention and stimulates their interest. While he has the whole class together, he often models strategies for individualized reading, such as making appropriate choices, writing reactions to books, and keeping records up to date. At the beginning of the year, he often spent this time going over expected procedures and anticipating problems and questions his students might raise. (What do you do if you finish your book during SSR? What do you do if you can't figure out a word? Do you have to finish every book you start?)

The major portion of the reading period is devoted to sustained silent reading. Students are responsible for selecting a book before the beginning of SSR. Most of them have gotten into the habit of exchanging or selecting books when they first come into the classroom in the morning. This is one of several guidelines Mr. Gordon has established to ensure the smooth operation of SSR. He allows students to find a comfortable place to read; however, it is understood that everyone is expected to stay in one place and read. Interruptions of other readers, or of Mr. Gordon while he is reading or conferring, are not allowed.

During the first 10 to 15 minutes of SSR, Mr. Gordon reads too, conveying to students that he values reading. He spends the remainder of SSR time holding brief conferences with individual students. Since there are only two SSR periods per week, he is unable to meet with every student every week. He has devised a system for them to sign up for a conference when they have completed a book. He manages to see every student once every two weeks, at least, structuring his conferences as described in Chapter 4.

Following SSR, all students bring their reading records up to date. They list their book title and the number of pages read on their daily reading logs, which are clipped to the front of their reading folder. On the back cover of the folder is a form for listing completed books. Each time a student completes a book, she makes a more extensive entry in her response journal. This response can be written during SSR, immediately after the book is completed. The journal is kept in the reading folder and brought to individual conferences and sharing time for reference.

Mr. Gordon has a computer in his classroom. Students are invited to type their reactions into the computer reading file for other students to consult when they are choosing what to read. One student a day may do this during the last part of the

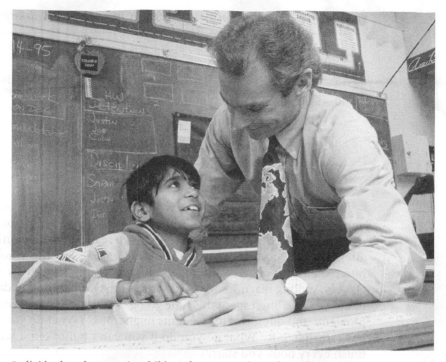

Individual conferences give children the opportunity to share their reading.

reading period, but others use recess time or other free time to record their entries. Book descriptions can be accessed by title, author, or category (adventure, mystery, biography). The fourth-graders are enthusiastic users of this computer file.

The reading period ends with approximately 20 minutes of whole-class sharing. The children gather in a circle on the large rug in the library area. Each student, in turn, tells what book he read that day and briefly highlights what was read. Mr. Gordon keeps this activity moving quickly and encourages students to "just tell us what's most important."

He alters the format of the individualized reading period once or twice a month to allow students a large block of time for creating and presenting follow-up projects (see Chapter 4) and for more in-depth sharing of what they have read and enjoyed. Mr. Gordon has found that these kinds of activities sustain motivation for reading and encourage creative contributions from every member of the class.

The teacher-directed and individualized reading instructional periods we have described do not constitute Mr. Gordon's entire literacy program. He devotes the first hour of the afternoon three or four days a week to writing workshop. His students write on a mix of self-selected and teacher-directed topics, confer with Mr. Gordon and with each other, and revise, edit, and publish their best pieces of writing.

Mr. Gordon systematically integrates reading and writing with content area study. In science, for example, he provides a variety of supplementary reading materials that range in difficulty. When using the textbook with the class, he acknowledges the components of the content area DRTA (see Chapter 10) and provides many direct experiences to build conceptual background for the text. His students maintain learning logs in science. They summarize their learning and address comments and questions to their teacher, who responds on a weekly basis. In Mr. Gordon's classroom, reading and writing are modeled and used in many different ways; they pervade the curriculum.

How Mr. Gordon Developed His Program

When Mr. Gordon began teaching, he felt insecure about designing reading instruction. His forte was science, he confidently developed an excellent program of science instruction for his fourth-graders. For his reading instructional program he depended, at first, entirely on the basal reader program he was required to use. Initially, he did a great deal of whole-class instruction and adhered very closely to the recommendations of the teacher's manual. He assigned nearly all the worksheets and skill activities and spent a large amount of time helping his less able readers to complete them. He noticed that his students loved science and looked forward to science lessons and activities, but disliked reading time and plodded through assignments without enthusiasm, for the most part.

During the summer following his first year of teaching, two significant things happened. First, Mr. Gordon spent several days with a friend who also taught fourth grade and who suggested he could improve his reading instruction by grouping students, using the basal program more selectively, and incorporating a 20-minute SSR period each day. Later in the summer, he attended a week-long in-service course entitled "Integrating Reading and Writing into the Science Curriculum." He discovered that a large body of children's literature could be effectively related to science topics. He became aware of the problems most children have in comprehending informational texts and learned some effective techniques for enhancing their understanding of unfamiliar concepts. He was introduced to the concept of writing to learn through the use of learning logs.

During the following school year, Mr. Gordon incorporated many of the new ideas he had gained over the summer. His reading program ran more smoothly and seemed more appropriate for the range of students in his class, once he devised a system for managing groups. He became more confident in his own judgments of which activities to include and which to eliminate or modify. His students enjoyed the daily SSR time, and he noticed an improvement in attitudes toward reading from the previous year.

Mr. Gordon found that the use of learning logs in science not only resulted in enhanced learning of science content by the children, but also enabled him to monitor individual students' understandings and misunderstandings. Of all the changes he made, incorporating children's literature into the science curriculum had perhaps the most significant impact on Mr. Gordon's teaching. The children loved the books he read aloud to them or made available for them to read independently to add to their science knowledge. Many of them selected these books to read during SSR, and a number of children began to write informational or narrative pieces that contained science information during writing workshop. Their enthusiasm led Mr. Gordon to recognize the power of good children's literature, systematically presented, to inspire children's reading and learning. He subsequently made a concerted effort to learn more about the most appropriate children's literature for fourth-graders and about effective ways to incorporate it into the reading program. He sought out colleagues who used literature extensively and solicited book lists and teaching suggestions from them. He attended relevant workshops on improving reading instruction. By the end of his third year of teaching, Mr. Gordon saw himself as an effective teacher of reading as well as science.

Mr. Gordon successfully reconciled the requirements of his school's administrators with his understanding of the kinds of literacy experiences that lead children to become motivated, skilled readers and writers. His modifications of the basal system allowed children to spend adequate time engaged in real reading and writing. Moreover, his program provided opportunities for student choice and self-direction, elements that are characteristically missing in basal instruction.

Summary

There is no one "right way" to organize for reading instruction. Planning and implementation will necessarily differ according to the teacher's knowledge base and experience, the characteristics of the children, and the constraints of the school context. Irrespective of the specific materials or approach used, however, virtually all effective management plans for reading instruction have certain common features. First, there is a balance between teacher-directed instruction and teacher-facilitated independent learning.

In addition, all effective programs provide opportunities for time, choice, and sharing. Children must have daily periods of uninterrupted classroom time for reading. A general guideline used by many schools is the following: At least half the time allotted for reading instruction must be devoted to the reading of children's literature. Much (if not all) of this literature should be self-selected by the students. Finally, daily opportunities for children to share their reading experiences in a variety of ways must be provided.

BIBLIOGRAPHY

Codell, E. R. (1999). *Educating Esme: Diary of a teacher's first year.* Chapel Hill NC: Algonquin Books.

Keane, N. J. (2001). *Book talks and beyond: Thematic learning activities for grades K–6.* Ft. Atkinson, WI: Upstart Books.

Shannon, P., & Goodman, K. (Eds.). (1994). *Basal readers: A second look.* Katonah, NY: Richard Owen.

15 Instructing Readers with Differences

What student traits contribute to their classroom learning needs?

▪ Overview

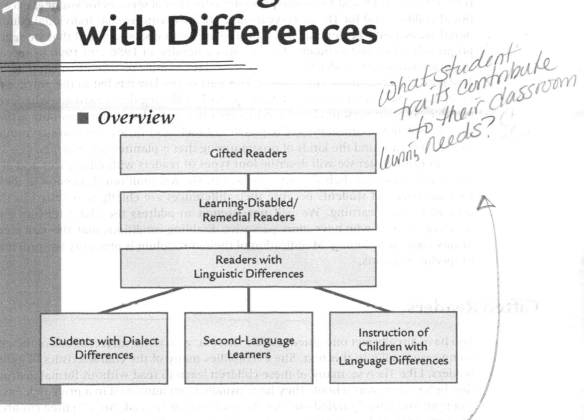

Gifted Readers

Learning-Disabled/
Remedial Readers

Readers with
Linguistic Differences

Students with Dialect
Differences

Second-Language
Learners

Instruction of
Children with
Language Differences

*E*very student has a <u>unique composite of general interests, experiences, and</u> personality traits as well as a specific language background. Because each child in a class is different from the others, all children could be said to have "special needs." One of the greatest challenges teachers face is designing literacy instruction that acknowledges and capitalizes on this diversity. This task is made easier by the fact that students in a class generally have similar, though not identical, needs. These children's differences can usually be accommodated through appropriate assessment, instructional management, and grouping. However, in almost any class teachers are likely to encounter a few students whose characteristics are so divergent from those of other children in the class that they require special attention. They may learn much more quickly or much more slowly than others. They may respond to instruction in atypical ways. Or they may have significantly different language backgrounds. These are the children we call "readers with differences," who are often labeled *gifted, learning-disabled, remedial,* or *LEP* (limited English proficient).

U.S. Public Law 94-142, The Education of the Handicapped Act, was passed in 1975. It mandates free, appropriate public education for all disabled children between the ages of 5 and 18. It also promotes educational services for younger exceptional children and for 18- to 21-year-olds. The law requires that individual educational plans (IEPs) be generated for all students with disabilities and that students' progress be reviewed annually. The law was amended in 1986 and 1990 to specify that each student with identified learning disabilities must receive instruction in the *least restrictive instructional environment.* This part of the law has led to the practice of inclusion, serving children with handicaps within the regular classroom, whenever possible. Support personnel and services are often provided in the classroom rather than in isolated circumstances. The practice of inclusion varies in schools according to available time and the kinds of programming that is planned for students.

In this chapter we will describe four types of readers with differences and discuss implications for their literacy instruction. We will limit our discussion to these four categories of students because their differences are chiefly manifested in the area of literacy learning. We will not attempt to address the characteristics and needs of children who have more pervasive disabling conditions that affect all areas of classroom functioning. Modification of their curriculum is primarily the province of special educators.

Gifted Readers

How would you monitor the progress/motivation of a gifted reader?

You have already met one gifted reader: Theresa, who is the subject of one of the ongoing case studies in this text. She exemplifies many of the characteristics of gifted readers. Like Theresa, many of these children learn to read without formal instruction before they start school. They have usually been immersed in a print-rich environment and have "puzzled out" for themselves how to read. Not all gifted children are early readers. However, those who are not yet reading independently when they enter school generally make rapid progress in reading once they do begin.

Ruddell (1998) points out that gifted readers usually have advanced language abilities in comparison with other children of their age. They tend to use language very creatively and have extensive vocabularies, which they use in innovative ways. This language ability mirrors their cognitive ability. They detect and verbalize relationships that often escape the notice of others. They grasp difficult ideas and solve problems—sometimes in unconventional ways.

How would you structure a lesson to tailor it to a gifted Reader

When considering how best to instruct gifted readers, some teachers mistakenly assume that because of their obvious capability these children will do very well and require no special attention. If appropriate instruction and guidance are not provided, gifted children sometimes become unmotivated, and their achievement sinks far below their potential. Another pitfall to avoid in working with the gifted is keeping them busy by giving them "more of the same," or insisting that they "cover all the skills" before going on to more advanced reading materials. In general, gifted learners require far less practice than their peers to become competent users of reading strategies (Heward, 2000). What, then, do gifted readers need?

Although PL 94-142 does not mandate programs for gifted students, the need for such programs has become more and more widely recognized; most states now have guidelines for gifted education. According to The National Association for Gifted Children, the most important principle in planning reading instruction for the gifted is to differentiate instruction and provide more challenging content, rather than simply to give more work. *Differentiated instruction* most often takes the form of enrichment activities that encourage the learner to explore in greater depth a topic or type of literature that is of particular interest to her. Joseph S. Renzulli, a well-known leader in the field of gifted education, recommends a model that includes three stages of learning: (1) *exploratory learning*, which might involve experiencing a certain kind of reading or collecting information about a problem or topic, for example; (2) *higher-level thinking,* that is, expanding upon the topic, interpreting, comparing, drawing conclusions; and (3) *application to a real-life purpose*, creating a real product for a real audience (Renzulli, 1998). Smith and Luckasson (1995) have offered the following suggestions for challenging gifted students in the area of literacy:

1. Encourage your students to become independent learners who pursue topics of high personal interest.
2. Initiate small group cooperative learning activities to develop social interchange skills and tolerance for the thinking of others.
3. Enrich units of study with guest speakers, field trips, demonstrations, and interest centers.
4. Watch for signs of boredom and provide intellectual stimulation through cooperative learning, problem-solving, and discussions involving interpretative, applicative, and transactive thinking.
5. Create a psychologically safe classroom environment where novel ideas can be discussed and accepted.
6. Develop instructional interactions and activities that use questions to generate application of higher-level thinking skills.
7. Teach and foster the use of independent library and research skills.

While these curricular suggestions are certainly well suited to the needs and capabilities of gifted students, we feel that they are also appropriate for learners of all ability levels. In the area of reading, virtually all the recommendations for gifted students seem to be appropriate for other children as well.

What student would not benefit from these suggestions? The recommended practices should be an integral part of any effective classroom reading program. The difference between instruction for gifted students and instruction for less accomplished readers is really a matter of degree. Adapting literacy instruction to the needs and capabilities of gifted students involves adjusting expectations and tailoring pacing and content to the interests and abilities of the students.

This point of view is reflected in our recommendations for Theresa's instructional program as we follow her passage through the stages of reading development. If you look back through her case study, you will notice that her instructional goals were always consistent with her identified stage of reading development.

Since she passed through the stages much more rapidly than most of her class-mates, however, recommendations for her instruction were always influenced by consideration of her chronological age and social needs. For example, when Theresa was in fourth grade, she was in the refinement stage, and her instruction was guided by the instructional goals that would become appropriate to most of her classmates in sixth or seventh grade. However, she was not expected to engage in activities designed for seventh-graders. Socially and emotionally, she was a fourth-grader, so the instructional goals were translated into activities appropriate to her age and situation.

Learning-Disabled/Remedial Readers

Experienced teachers, as well as beginners, report that their greatest challenge is trying to help students who are having difficulty learning to read and write. Although they expend great amounts of time and effort providing sound instruction and special help, these children do not respond at the same rate or in the same way as their peers. These struggling readers are given extensive formal tests and then are assigned various labels: *learning-disabled* (LD), *dyslexic, remedial readers, neurologically handicapped.* Such labels attempt to classify according to a presumed cause; however, they are not particularly helpful to the teacher, whose concern is designing and implementing appropriate instruction.

The labels that are applied to children with learning difficulties tend to overlap because of the lack of consensus regarding definitions and their application. For example, students who enter our university's reading clinic manifesting similar reading behaviors often have been assigned different labels. Some have been receiving Title I instruction (for remedial readers) while others have been in their school's resource room (for students with learning disabilities).

The first term that was used to describe reading problems was *dyslexia,* which appeared in the literature around 1886 (Searfoss, Readance, & Readance, 2000). Literally the term means inability to read. One definition used by educators is "a condition manifested by difficulty with learning to read and write efficiently despite the presence of normal intelligence, adequate educational opportunities, and normal psychiatric makeup" (Galaburda, 1986, p. 192). Children with major sensory deficits or with mental or emotional impairment are excluded from this definition. The term *learning disability* is more widely used today; it includes children who have reading and writing problems. There are many definitions of the term and ongoing debate about the nature of the condition. Most definitions are based on the assumption that learning disabilities are caused by neurological dysfunction, although there is seldom direct evidence of neurological damage in students so identified (Rhodes & Dudley-Marling, 1996).

In determining which students get LD services, most school personnel consider the discrepancy between the student's apparent ability, often measured by an IQ test, and his achievement in reading and writing. If there is a considerable discrepancy, the student is likely to be labeled LD. If there is less discrepancy, the child is more likely to be designated a remedial reader or slow learner. Theoretically, children designated as LD are assumed to have an <u>intrinsic impairment or disorder involving the central nervous system.</u> Poor readers who have been deprived of literacy experiences, who have emotional problems, or who have been taught inappropriately are not supposed to be classified as LD. The problems of learning-disabled students are supposedly qualitatively different from other learning problems. In other words, learning disabilities involving reading are assumed to reflect a unique syndrome of poor reading that is different from "ordinary" poor reading. To test this assumption, Spear-Swerling & Sternberg (1998) analyzed two groups of students with reading problems. One group was classified as "learning disabled" and the other was labeled as "students with reading problems." They found no discernable differences in the reading problems experienced by the two groups. They recommended that both groups receive high quality reading instruction delivered by teachers with an understanding of literacy.

Since there is such a lack of consensus as to what actually constitutes a learning disability and who may be classified as learning-disabled, it seems unproductive to spend time and effort determining whether children who are having difficulty with reading should be labeled LD. <u>Our concern should not be what to call these students, but rather what to do about them.</u> Children who are failing in school need our help. Our first priority should be to provide literacy instruction that will help these children to succeed.

Until recently, the prevalent form of instruction for unaccomplished readers was reductionist in nature. That is, it was widely believed that the reading process could be best learned by these children if it was broken down into smaller parts, or subtasks. Emphasis on skills was the focus of these instructional programs. Behavioral approaches to literacy instruction sometimes subjected LD and remedial readers to years of drill and practice, reading exercises devoid of meaning or real communication purposes. In addition, such programs focus on students' perceived deficits. The more poorly students did in these programs, the more intensively teachers applied them (Allington, 2001; Rhodes & Dudley-Marling, 1998). Too often, remedial instruction of this nature has led to repeated cycles of failure. Students come to believe that something is wrong with them, that they are not able to learn to read like "normal people."

More recently our attitudes and views on what readers in trouble need are changing. More and more educators are coming to realize that success for these children often depends on "revaluing" them (and leading them to revalue themselves) as readers. All children can learn language. All children have strengths and strategies as language users that can be used as the bases for learning to read and write, even when the rate at which some children progress is extremely slow. <u>Instructional programs must help them regain confidence in their own ability to learn</u> to interact <u>successfully with written language.</u> This is best accomplished through <u>meaning-based approaches</u> to reading and writing, because these approaches acknowledge the developmental nature of literacy learning. Moreover, they <u>focus on children's strengths rather than on weaknesses</u> or deficits. They draw on and build on what the student knows, and learning is always placed in meaningful contexts. We advocate balanced approaches to written language instruction for all children; however, we feel they are particularly valuable for slow learners, LD students, and remedial readers. The difference is that these children need more individual coaching, direct teaching, and practice that is tailored to their own demonstrated needs.

Our recommendations for Kim, whose case study you have followed throughout this text, exemplify the kind of instructional program that supports and nurtures success in students who are "behind" their classmates. Is Kim learning-disabled? Is she a remedial reader? Or is she simply developmentally slower than her classmates? We have not attempted to classify her, since instructional recommendations would be essentially the same in any case. Both expectations and instructional goals for Kim were determined by her stage of reading progress, rather than by her grade level. Kim's teachers accepted her "difference" but had (and conveyed to her) confidence in her ability to eventually become a successful reader and writer. In the early grades, her teachers continued to immerse her in print experiences and engage her in activities that would develop her understanding of the relationship between speech and print, long after her classmates had begun to read independently. As she progressed through the grades, she had access to special help, which was always related to her stage of reading progress. She was always provided with a quantity of reading material that was of interest to her and that she was able to read easily. Gradually she mastered the alphabetic code and developed fluency without becoming discouraged or losing interest in reading.

Reading aloud sustains motivation for all students.

Kim's teachers, like Theresa's, based some of their instructional decisions on her social needs. Whenever possible, she was encouraged to participate in group activities and to respond appropriately at her own level. SSR and writing workshop are examples of activities in which she participated fully. In the later grades, she took part in content area work, but often with modified expectations or special help. What learners like Kim need most is an instructional climate that accepts and supports their efforts, that validates them as learners and as contributing members of the class, and that provides them with literacy experiences that "fit" their stage of reading progress.

Readers with Linguistic Differences

In the majority of American schools there are significant numbers of students who are "linguistically different." Some of them speak nonstandard or regional dialects of English; for others, English is their second language. McLaughlin & McLeod (1996) comment on how linguistic and cultural diversity is impacting our schools:

> The linguistic and cultural diversity among students in American schools is greater now than at any time since the early decades of the last century. If students were distributed evenly across the nation's classrooms, every class of 30 students would include about 10 students from ethnic or racial minority groups. Of these 10, about 6 would be from language minority families (homes in which languages other than English are spoken); 2–4 of these students would have limited English proficiency, of whom 2 would be from immigrant families. Of the 6 language minority students in the class, 4 would speak Spanish as their native language, and 1 would speak an Asian language. The other language minority student would speak any one of more than a hundred languages. (p. 1)

It is our responsibility as teachers to help all children, regardless of their backgrounds, to become proficient users of oral and written English in order that they can succeed in school and in the larger society beyond. We will discuss two groups of linguistically different children: those who speak nonstandard English dialects and those whose native language is something other than English.

Students with Dialect Differences

The language that children learn at home is influenced by a variety of factors, including geographic location, ethnic origin, social–cultural setting, and educational level of their parents. Language is also affected by the context in which it is used. We choose different ways of speaking depending on where we are and whom we are talking to. Dialects differ in three respects: in the way words are pronounced, in sentence structure or syntax, and in special meanings attached to words. Study of dialect differences has shown that although they differ from standard English, all dialects are equally consistent, rule-governed, and sophisticated. In other words, no dialect of English is superior or inferior to any other, from a linguistic point of view (Pinker, 1994; Ruddell, 1998). However, it is an inescapable fact that Standard American English is the language of power in this country. The educational, political, and economic gatekeepers of our society judge individuals and include or exclude them on the basis of their ability to communicate in oral and written standard English. For this reason, proficiency in the standard dialect is a goal for all students. This goal must be accomplished, however, without devaluing the dialects that children bring with them from home.

Dialect variations are not necessarily impediments to learning to read and write. Standard English should be viewed as an alternative dialect, appropriate and necessary for use in school and certain work environments; it should not be considered a replacement for a child's nonstandard dialect. The books that are read to children and that they learn to read themselves are not transcriptions of speech. It is not necessary to talk like a book in order to read one. In regard to pronunciation differences, for example, Gumperz and Hernandez-Chavez (1972) report that urban black children who failed to distinguish orally between such word pairs as *jar* and *jaw, toe* and *tore, six* and *sick* were nevertheless able to distinguish between them in their written forms when reading them in context. Provided children are familiar with the language patterns of books and the structure of stories, they will be able to predict meaning and thus will learn to read the standard dialect that is somewhat different from their spoken dialect. Some students who speak non-mainstream dialects will become truly *bidialectical;* in other words, they will be able to shift easily between non-mainstream and mainstream English. Other students' language will remain predominantly non-mainstream. The difference is caused by a variety of factors including attitude toward each dialect form and its speakers, peers, and community, and presence or absence of academic and economic opportunities (Ruddell, 1998).

Teachers who are predominantly speakers of standard English must objectively examine their own attitudes about non-mainstream dialects and their speakers. Keep in mind that dialect differences are surface language differences in pronunciation and grammatical features. These differences will be evident in speaking and oral reading but do not indicate lack of ability to communicate effectively. Teachers who consistently offer a wide variety of meaning-based language and literacy opportunities while at the same time working with students on the eventual mastery of the standard dialect will observe progressive growth and development in all dialects.

Second-Language Learners

Children in our schools whose native language is not English are referred to as *ESL* (English-as-a-Second-Language) students. Prior to 1974, there was no clear mandate for schools to provide any special services for non–English-speaking students. According to a 1974 U.S. Supreme Court decision (*Lau* v. *Nichols*), this situation violated students' civil rights, since they did not, in fact, have equal access to education.

The Bilingual Education Act of 1978 mandated schools to provide non-English speakers with bilingual education, using the child's native language, as well as English, as a medium of instruction until he or she is sufficiently proficient in English to function without the native language support. This legislation has not been easy for schools to implement and has led to considerable controversy. Many proponents of bilingual education argue for continued native language instruction, not only for purposes of academic support but also to ensure that the students preserve their cultural heritage. Others insist that American schools have the obligation to transmit "American culture" and that it is appropriate for all students to receive all instruction in English. The issues surrounding bilingual education go beyond pedagogy; they include sociological and political concerns as well.

In order to make sound instructional decisions for ESL learners, teachers need to understand the relationship between learning a first or native language and learning a second language. A few children are truly bilingual when they enter school. They have developed two languages simultaneously as preschoolers, and they are equally fluent in both. In terms of language learning, at least, they are at a distinct advantage. No special adaptations of instruction are necessary. Most ESL children, in contrast, are much more proficient in their native language than in English.

Native-language learning provides a linguistic basis for second-language learning. In the process of acquiring a language, children learn a great deal about the way all languages work. This is true of literacy learning as well as oral language learning. Adult education teachers report that immigrants who are literate in their native language have an easier time learning to read and write in English than those who are not literate in their own language. Similarly, it has been found that ESL children who are taught first to read in their native language achieve better results learning to read English than their peers who learn to read only in English, their second language (Hudelson, 1994; Snow, 1990). Since reading is a process of constructing meaning from text, it is not surprising that students are best able to construct meaning in a language they speak fluently, rather than in a language they do not know well. More language cues (particularly syntactic and semantic) are available to them (Goodman, Goodman, & Flores, 1979; Weaver, 1994). Readers are then able to transfer their knowledge of reading strategies and processes to their attempts to read and write the new language, English.

For these reasons, some school districts have adopted the practice of teaching ESL children whose English is not yet proficient to read in their native language before attempting to teach them to read English. Unfortunately, for most ESL children this option is not available. In urban settings, classrooms often include children who represent many different language groups. In addition to these factors, many school communities subscribe to the belief that English is the only appropriate language for instruction in an American school; indeed some states have banned use of languages other than English by teachers. In any case, ESL children are often placed in classrooms where the teacher does not speak their native language and is not a bilingual/ESL specialist. How can such teachers best meet the literacy needs of their ESL students as well as of the children who speak nonstandard dialects?

Instruction of Children with Language Differences

A major feature of effective literacy programs for children with language differences is that teachers consistently focus on helping students to construct meaning from print rather than on correcting or improving their speech. Their oral language will approach standard English over a period of time as a result of constant modeling by the teacher and other standard English users and through daily opportunities to practice using English for real communication purposes. The meaningless pronunciation drills of yesteryear are out! The goal during the early phases of instruction should be vocabulary and concept development within meaningful oral and written contexts. Understanding of what another has said or written is far more important than accurate pronunciation (Au, 2002; Carey, 1997).

Instructional recommendations for English-speaking emergent and initial stage readers are equally appropriate for second-language learners and children with nonstandard dialects. For example, it is recommended that all early stage readers be engaged frequently in listening to stories read aloud and in discussing, retelling, and reenacting them (see Chapters 1, 2, and 3). Listening to stories read by the teacher can provide a particularly powerful stimulus for the language development of children with language divergences (Carey, 1997; Wood, 2001). They learn vocabulary, develop concepts, increase oral fluency, and gain a sense of the story structures used in the western European tradition. (Stories that come from their own cultures may be structured differently.) Retelling activities are, if anything, even more important for these children than for those who are proficient in standard English. Rather than asking specific questions about the story, it is important to encourage ESL students to tell everything they remember about the story. This gives the opportunity for more oral language production. Teachers who speak the native language of their children or who have a translator in the classroom often accept native-language retelling of a story read in English, translating the child's retelling back into English.

The language experience approach (LEA) (see Chapter 3) is another example of an instructional technique that works well with all initial readers but is particularly appropriate for students with language divergences. Dictated language experience "stories" are based on children's actual experiences and are therefore familiar in content and easy for the ESL student to understand. In fact, for some English language learners who come from cultures that are very different from ours, dictated language experiences may provide the only material that is culturally familiar to them. Dictation helps them connect their experiences to the text they will read, and therefore it is widely advocated as a starting point for initial ESL readers (Rigg, 1989). Moreover, the language patterns of dictations conform closely to the students' oral language patterns, adding still more to the predictability of the text.

Another advantage to using the LEA is the opportunity it provides for generating narratives. Everyone has stories to tell that are of great personal importance. Storytelling is a universal process of the human mind that crosses all cultures and individuals. Stories help us make sense of the world (Witherell & Noddings, 1991). Students' stories may focus on everyday occurrences, or they may recount major events such as escaping persecution or war, living in a refugee camp, experiencing a drive-by shooting, or participating in a family or community ceremony. In the words of Searfoss and Readance, "When individuals share their stories, they come to understand each other better and appreciate each other more in terms of both how they are alike and how they are different" (1994, p. 373).

In early-grade classrooms ESL children benefit from heterogeneous grouping for language experience instruction. The dictations of their English-speaking peers provide language that is understood by the ESL children. The activities used in the language experience approach enable ESL children to work collaboratively in a community of beginning readers and writers.

Although LEA is an effective approach to use with children who have language differences, it is limited to child-generated texts and is therefore not sufficient to provide the literacy experiences necessary to become successful readers. Students must also be exposed to texts written by professional authors. Like other beginning readers, ESL students do best with highly predictable stories and books that are already familiar to them from being read aloud. Predictability may take the form of repetition of events, rhyme and rhythm, or repeated language patterns. Shared book experiences with predictable books expose students to well-crafted stories and the language of literature. For children with language divergences, it is particularly important to read the same books, poems, and chants again and again to help them internalize both language and content. The techniques of using shared reading are described in detail in Chapter 3. A special adaptation used by teachers who speak the native language of their ESL students is to precede the reading of the story by telling it in the students' native language so that they will understand the gist of the story.

Do the stages of reading development apply to students with language differences? We would answer that in general they do. However, the amount of time and experience needed by these students to progress through the early stages is likely to be greater, particularly for ESL students.

Native English-speaking initial readers are already familiar with most of the ideas and meanings of words that they encounter in early reading experiences. The language itself is familiar; only the printed form is new. Their task is essentially to learn to match the printed form of language to the spoken form that they already know. The ESL child, in contrast, must learn to match the printed form of language to a spoken form that is unfamiliar, and both forms must be acquired simultaneously. This is a far greater challenge and requires more time to accomplish, even under the best of conditions.

Like other children, ESL students pass through a transitional stage, during which their fluency and ability to read independently increase as a result of many reading experiences. As they near the end of this stage, however, their apparent fluency may mask their continuing need for concept development. This phenomenon relates to the difference between first- and second-language learning. As children acquire a second language, conversational fluency develops first. They become able to carry on conversations with other children on the playground and outside of school, for example. Acquiring the academic language used in the classroom for giving directions or explaining and discussing ideas takes longer. Similarly, as they begin to acquire literacy, they become fluent first with familiar, narrative materials, which make up most of the reading fare at the initial and transitional stages. This does not necessarily indicate the kind of reading competence that is required to deal successfully with the abstractions and new concepts typical of content area study. Thus, as ESL students move into the basic literacy stage, it is essential that they continue to have many direct and vicarious experiences (with accompanying language use) to build concepts in preparation for reading or study. Once again, this is not a matter of providing *different* instruction for these students. Rather, it is a matter of seeing that their instruction consists of those practices that are recognized as best for all students.

The teacher's attitude about language differences will largely determine whether children with language divergences feel comfortable and accepted. Language arts instruction should acknowledge how language is used, rather than prescribing how it should be used. Flexible language users recognize that the ability to use standard oral and written English is important; however, they do not regard their own dialects or native languages as inferior. We can help promote flexible language use by valuing and capitalizing on the linguistic and cultural diversity represented in the classroom. Such diversity affords all children the opportunities to learn about other languages and cultures. Children can celebrate holidays from other cultures, learn songs from other countries, share the customs of different ethnic groups, and prepare and eat ethnic foods. Teachers can make an effort to obtain and share books from other cultures that have been translated into English. *The Reading Teacher*, a professional journal published by the International Reading Association, periodically contains reviews of children's books from other countries and provides lists of multiethnic literature for children and adolescents.

Summary

We have described gifted readers, disabled readers, and language-divergent readers as "readers with differences." These groups of learners are often referred to as children with special needs. Although these learners are obviously very different from each other and from their other classmates, their instructional needs are similar in many ways. Major differences occur in expectations, pacing, and materials used. However, all these children pass through the stages of reading progress, and all profit from the same types of instruction, tailored to their stages of development. All learners, including readers with differences, learn language from immersion in a language-rich environment and from using language for real communicative purposes. All learners acquire literacy most effectively and naturally in programs of instruction that focus primarily on meaning. All children, regardless of differences, thrive in learning environments that are secure and supportive, where they are valued members of a community of readers and writers. When working with readers with differences, we must remember that although rates of development differ, the conditions for literacy learning are the same for all children.

BIBLIOGRAPHY

Allington, R. (2001). *What really matters for struggling readers*. Boston, MA: Allyn and Bacon.

Au, K. H. (2002). Multicultual factors and the effective instruction for students of diverse backgrounds. In A. E. Farsturp, & J. Samuels (Eds.), *What research has to say about reading instruction* (pp. 392–414). Newark, DE: International Reading Association.

Au, K. (1993). *Literacy instruction in multicultural settings*. New York: Harcourt Brace Jovanovich.

Carey, S. (1997). *Second language learners*. York, ME: Steinhouse.

Galaburda, A. M. (1986). Responses to "The many faces of dyslexia." *Annals of Dyslexia, 36,* 192–195.

Goodman, K., Goodman, Y., & Flores, B. (1979). *Reading in the bilingual classroom: Literacy and biliteracy*. Rosalyn, VA: National Clearinghouse for Bilingual Education.

Gumperz, J. J., & Hermandez-Chavez, E. (1972). Bilingualism, bidialectalism, and classroom instruction. In C. Cazden, V. John, & D. Hymes (Eds.), *Functions of language in the classroom*. New York: Teachers College Press.

Hadaway, N. L., Vardell, S. M., & Young, T.A. (2001). *Literature-based instruction with English language learners*. New York: Longman.

Heward, W. I. (2000). *Exceptional children: An introduction to special education* (6th ed.). Columbus, OH: Charles Merrill.

Hudelson, S. (1994). Working with second language learners. In L. Searfoss & J. Readance (Eds.), *Helping children learn to read* (pp. 363–391). Boston: Allyn and Bacon.

McLaughlin, B. & McLeod, B. (1996). Educating all our students: Improving education for children from culturally and linguistically diverse backgrounds. *Final Report of the National Center for Research on Cultural Diversity and Second Language Learning* (Vol. I, June) University of California at Santa Cruz.

Pinker, S. (1994). *The language instinct*. New York: W. Morrow.

Renzulli, J. S. (1998). *Talent development: A practical plan for total school improvement*. Mansfield, CT: Creative Learning Center Press.

Rhodes, L., & Dudley-Marling, C. (1996). *Readers and writers with a difference*. Portsmouth NH: Heinemann.

Rigg, P. (1989). Language experience approach: Reading naturally. In P. Rigg & V. Allen (Eds.), *When they don't speak English: Integrating the ESL student into the regular classroom* (pp. 65–76). Urbana, IL: National Council of Teachers of English.

Rosier, P., & Holm, W. (1979). *The Rock Point experience: An experiment in bilingual education*. Washington, DC: Center for Applied Linguistics.

Ruddell, R. (1998). *Teaching children to read and write: Becoming an influential teacher*. Boston: Allyn and Bacon.

Searfoss, L., Readance, J., & Readence, M. H. M. (2000). *Helping children learn to read*. Boston: Allyn and Bacon.

Searfoss, L., & Readance, J. (1994). *Helping children learn to read*. Boston: Allyn and Bacon.

Smith, D., & Luckasson, R. (1995). *Introduction to special education: Teaching in an age of challenge*. Boston: Allyn and Bacon.

Snow, C. E. (1990). Rationales for native language intruction: Evidence from research. In A. M. Padilla, H. H. Fairchild, & C. M. Valadez (Eds.), *Bilingual education: Issues and strategies* (pp. 60–74). Thousand Oaks, CA: Sage.

Spear-Swerling, L., & Sternberg, R. J. (1998). Curing our epidemic of learning disabilities. *Phi Delta Kappan, 79*(5), pp. 397–401.

Weaver, C. (1994). *Reading process and practice* (3rd ed.). Portsmouth, NH: Heinemann.

Witherell, C., & Noddings, N. (1991). *Stories lives tell: Narrative and dialogue in education*. New York: Teachers College Press.

Wood, M. (2001). Project Story Boost: Read-alouds for students at risk. *The Reading Teacher, 55,* 76–83.

Informal Assessment of Study Strategies

Directions: The purpose of this questionnaire is to find out how you use certain strategies when you read and study your text. There are no correct answers. You are simply to rate yourself on each item. For some questions, you will be asked to write an explanation.

Before Reading

1. Do you look over the chapter to see what will be covered and how it's organized?

   Yes   Sometimes   No

2. Do you think about what you already know about the topic?

   Yes   Sometimes   No

3. Do you think about what you will learn from the reading?

   Yes   Sometimes   No

4. Do you know what you are expected to learn from the assignment?

   Yes   Sometimes   No

5. Do you know how the teacher will ask you to demonstrate what you have learned (answer questions in class, take a test, write a paper, etc.)?

   Yes   Sometimes   No

6. Do you plan what you will have to do to complete the assignment successfully (read carefully, take notes, write summaries, etc.)?

   Yes   Sometimes   No

7. Is there anything else you usually do before you read?

During Reading

8. Do you consciously read different kinds of materials at different rates (speeds)?

   Yes   Sometimes   No

   Please comment on how you decide what rate to use.

9. Are you aware of which parts of the text you understand, and which parts are confusing to you?

   Yes   Sometimes   No

10. When you realize you're having problems understanding the reading, what do you do?

11. Do you generally expect to understand what you read?

    Yes   Sometimes   No

12. As you read, do you take time to examine study aids such as maps, graphs, and charts?

    Yes   Sometimes   No

After Reading

13. After you finish reading, do you think about what you have learned?

    Yes   Sometimes   No

14. Do you go back over the material and take notes?

    Yes   Sometimes   No

15. Can you pick out the important ideas that should be included in your notes?

    Yes   Sometimes   No

16. Can you put them in your own words?

    Yes   Sometimes   No

17. How do you review for tests?

18. Do you find your notes helpful when you review and prepare for tests?

    Yes   Sometimes   No

19. What are some other things that cause you difficulty when you are studying texts?

APPENDIX B

Examiner's Manual

Informal Assessment of Elementary Reading
FORM A (1997 Edition)

Word Recognition Test

The *Word Recognition Test* consists of seven word lists of increasing levels of difficulty. The words were derived from studies of words that occur frequently in reading materials used in different grade levels. However, there are no word lists that are indigenous to specific grade levels. The word lists are simply estimates of occurrence and should only be used to establish a placement level for beginning the informal reading inventory. A 75 percent accuracy score in the sight column should be used to determine the stage in which it would be appropriate to have the student begin reading.

List 1 (Initial)

	Sight	Analysis			Sight	Analysis
1. with			11. did			
2. me			12. no			
3. better			13. red			
4. he			14. they			
5. we			15. at			
6. my			16. on			
7. away			17. one			
8. can			18. some			
9. like			19. have			
10. are			20. do			
			Scores			

List 2 (Initial)

	Sight	*Analysis*
1. old	_____	_____
2. took	_____	_____
3. water	_____	_____
4. way	_____	_____
5. many	_____	_____
6. again	_____	_____
7. know	_____	_____
8. over	_____	_____
9. other	_____	_____
10. next	_____	_____
11. please	_____	_____
12. off	_____	_____
13. night	_____	_____
14. be	_____	_____
15. time	_____	_____
16. work	_____	_____
17. thing	_____	_____
18. when	_____	_____
19. their	_____	_____
20. would	_____	_____
Scores	_____	_____

List 3 (Transitional)

	Sight	*Analysis*
1. still	_____	_____
2. uncle	_____	_____
3. need	_____	_____
4. begins	_____	_____
5. end	_____	_____
6. bounced	_____	_____
7. front	_____	_____
8. learned	_____	_____
9. remember	_____	_____
10. thought	_____	_____
11. biggest	_____	_____
12. turned	_____	_____
13. post	_____	_____
14. bake	_____	_____
15. happened	_____	_____
16. wires	_____	_____
17. pull	_____	_____
18. fence	_____	_____
19. blow	_____	_____
20. judge	_____	_____
Scores	_____	_____

List 4 (Transitional)

	Sight	Analysis
1. sale		
2. batting		
3. whether		
4. finally		
5. cheered		
6. taste		
7. recreation		
8. thirsty		
9. harbor		
10. built		
11. company		
12. agree		
13. speak		
14. flat		
15. asleep		
16. clearing		
17. brass		
18. fruit		
19. whole		
20. already		
Scores		

List 5 (Basic Literacy)

	Sight	Analysis
1. pedal		
2. hobo		
3. introduce		
4. lame		
5. ruin		
6. teeming		
7. unequal		
8. shanty		
9. mount		
10. bacon		
11. breathe		
12. chicf		
13. racket		
14. gown		
15. ablaze		
16. manner		
17. crew		
18. forge		
19. distress		
20. exact		
Scores		

List 6 (Basic Literacy)

	Sight	Analysis
1. terror	_____	_____
2. ambulance	_____	_____
3. molasses	_____	_____
4. welcome	_____	_____
5. twine	_____	_____
6. barrel	_____	_____
7. gurgle	_____	_____
8. lime	_____	_____
9. exclaim	_____	_____
10. provoke	_____	_____
11. furrow	_____	_____
12. butternut	_____	_____
13. snuggle	_____	_____
14. roost	_____	_____
15. injure	_____	_____
16. physical	_____	_____
17. oath	_____	_____
18. accomplish	_____	_____
19. cylinder	_____	_____
20. committee	_____	_____
Scores	_____	_____

List 7 (Refinement)

	Sight	Analysis
1. novel	_____	_____
2. wallop	_____	_____
3. tango	_____	_____
4. scribe	_____	_____
5. unwise	_____	_____
6. memorial	_____	_____
7. irate	_____	_____
8. recipe	_____	_____
9. girder	_____	_____
10. partial	_____	_____
11. extensive	_____	_____
12. abandon	_____	_____
13. jumbled	_____	_____
14. spoil	_____	_____
15. herring	_____	_____
16. cooperation	_____	_____
17. portable	_____	_____
18. casual	_____	_____
19. divert	_____	_____
20. appreciate	_____	_____
Scores	_____	_____

Passage Reading

Structure of the Assessment. The reading passages gradually increase in difficulty. Recognizing that a reader's ability to process a text depends on more than vocabulary and sentence length, we have included different kinds of passages, including personal narratives, fictional narratives, and informational pieces. An attempt has been made to use whole texts or passages that have structural integrity, given the constraints of the testing situation.

Suggestions are given for the examiner to assess and (if necessary) provide prior knowledge that is essential to understanding each passage. Whether a given passage is to be read orally or silently is designated. It is suggested that all passages, with the exception of Selection 1, be read silently first. It is then up to the examiner to decide which passages to have the student reread orally, for purposes of miscue analysis. Following each of the first six passages, there is a checklist for recording and classifying miscues.

Each selection is followed by suggested comprehension questions. First, the reader is asked to retell what s/he remembers from the passage to establish recall of the basic story line or information included. Subsequent questions are designed to elicit elaboration, interpretation, and application. On the basis of the reader's responses, the examiner makes a general estimate of the student's comprehension, ranging from poor to excellent. No numerical score is given.

Interpretation of Results. The examiner is not attempting to establish definite instructional levels; rather the purpose is to estimate the student's stage of reading development so that appropriate materials and instructional activities may be provided. The reader's stage is determined by noting the highest level at which the reader can identify most of the words in context, make sense of the text, and demonstrate reasonable understanding of the passage through discussion. *The Informal Assessment of Elementary Reading* provides a structure for the observation of individual students' reading behaviors. Interpretations must be verified through day-to-day interactions with students.

Emergent Literacy

This familiar nursery rhyme may be used to assess the child's ability to match speech to print, assuming s/he is not yet able to read independently.

Begin by asking the child whether s/he has heard the rhyme "Humpty Dumpty." Read the rhyme aloud to the child. Next, suggest reading together. Follow the print with your finger, pointing to each word as it is spoken. Then ask the child to "read" it alone.

Things to note:

- Does the child repeat the entire rhyme?
- Does the child follow each line of print from left to right?
- Does the child point to each word as it is being spoken?

Humpty Dumpty sat on a wall.

Humpty Dumpty had a great fall.

All the king's horses and all the king's men

Couldn't put Humpty together again.

Observations:

SELECTION 1 (Initial)   Oral reading only

Prereading Discussion. Do you have a bike? How would you feel if you got a new bike? This story is about a boy who wanted to show his new bike to a friend. Read the story out loud to find out what happened.

Bob had a new red bike. He liked to ride it. One day he stopped to show it to his friend Ann. She liked his bike. "I wish I had a bike," she said. "Then we could ride together."

- How did Bob feel about his bike?
- How do you know?
- How did Ann feel when she saw his bike?

Word Identification in Context	*Deviations from Text*	
2 Miscues = 95% word identification	*Meaning altered*	*Meaning not altered*
Number of Miscues ___	___ words given	___ self-corrections
	___ substitutions	___ substitutions
	___ omissions	___ omissions
	___ additions	___ additions

Comprehension _____   (poor, acceptable, good, excellent)

SELECTION 2 (Initial)   Silent reading, followed by oral rereading

Prereading Discussion. Do you like frogs? Have you ever caught one or touched one? What do you think a frog would do if you put it in a box? In this story, two children played with some frogs. Read it to find out what happened.

I met Tim on the way to school. He had a big box. There were three frogs inside. We stopped to play with them. I picked one up. So did Tim. We did not see the other one jump out of the box and hop into my school bag. I grabbed my bag. We ran all the way to school. When I got to school, the frog jumped out of my bag. Everyone laughed.

Tell me in your own words what happened in the story. (Note whether story events are retold in sequence and how much detail is included.) Additional questions may be used to further assess comprehension. (If story retelling was complete and detailed, these questions would not be necessary.)

- How did one of the frogs fool the children?
- What do you think happened when the frog got to school?
- What would be a good name (title) for this story?

Request an oral rereading of the story and record miscues.

Word Identification in Context

4 Miscues = 95% word identification
Number of Miscues ___

Deviations from Text

Meaning altered	*Meaning not altered*
___ words given	___ self-corrections
___ substitutions	___ substitutions
___ omissions	___ omissions
___ additions	___ additions

Comprehension _____ (poor, acceptable, good, excellent)

TION 3 (Initial)   Silent reading, followed by oral rereading

Discussion. Did you ever have a day when everything seemed to go
ˑhappened? Did you ever think about running away from home? In
ˑrl has a very bad day. Read to find out what happened to her.

ˑy day. Everything went wrong. Mary spilled
ˑts. Her mother yelled at her. Her little
ˑut of her teddy bear. Her sister
ˑy was so mad that she decided
ˑkies in a bag and went outside.
a long time. She tried to eat her
wet. Finally Mary went home. He
ˑg hug. She began to feel better.

Tell me in your own words what happened in the story.

Optional questions:
- Why did Mary decide to run away?
- Why do you think she changed her mind and decided to go home?
- What would be a good name (title) for this story?

Request an oral rereading of the story and record miscues.

Word Identification in Context	*Deviations from Text*	
5 Miscues = 95% word identification	*Meaning altered*	*Meaning not altered*
Number of Miscues ___	___ words given	___ self-corrections
	___ substitutions	___ substitutions
	___ omissions	___ omissions
	___ additions	___ additions

Comprehension _____   (poor, acceptable, good, excellent)

SELECTION 4 (Transitional)   Silent reading, followed by oral rereading

Prereading Discussion. Read the title of the selection with the student and speculate about what the selection will be about. Find out if the student knows anything about woodchucks. If not, provide background information. (Woodchucks, which are also called groundhogs, are brown furry animals that are about the size of a cat. They live underground in fields, and are known for raiding vegetable gardens.) It may be helpful to compare the woodchuck to animals that are familiar to the student.

The Woodchuck Family

In the middle of a large field there was a hole that ran dow
to a hidden room underground. A family of woodchucks
dug it out early in the fall. Deep in the safe dark hole w
five new babies. They were all snuggled together. The
sleeping on a soft bed of dried hay. When they were f
all the babies wanted to do was sleep. Their eyes w
closed, and they didn't move around at all. But af
hours their eyes opened. With their small black
sniffed all around. They were all hungry. Moth
gathered her babies close to her. They drank

- What do you think it was like inside the woodchuck's hole? Describe it.
- What do you think the word "snuggled" means? (Reread, "They were all snuggled together.")
- Why do you think the babies wanted to do nothing but sleep at first?

Request an oral rereading of the story and record miscues.

Word Identification in Context	*Deviations from Text*	
6 Miscues = 95% word identification	*Meaning altered*	*Meaning not altered*
Number of Miscues ___	___ words given	___ self-corrections
	___ substitutions	___ substitutions
	___ omissions	___ omissions
	___ additions	___ additions
Comprehension _____	(poor, acceptable, good, excellent)	

SELECTION 5 (Transitional)   Silent reading, followed by oral rereading

Prereading Discussion. Find out what the student knows about elephants and where they live. (Focus on their natural habitats.) Read the title together. What do you think this selection will be about? Read it to find out if you are right.

Save the Elephants

Elephants live in the wild in some parts of the world. There used to be many wild elephants. But people are moving onto land where elephants have always lived. People are building homes and towns. The elephants don't have enough land to live on or food to eat. Many of them are dying. Another reason wild elephants are disappearing is that hunters are killing them for their ivory tusks. They sell the tusks to people who make them into expensive combs and jewelry. Things that are made from ivory are sold all over the world. Some people are trying to save the elephants. They are making special parks for elephants to live in. They are also passing laws to keep people from killing too many elephants. They are asking everyone not to buy things that are made of ivory.

- Why are wild elephants disappearing? Explain.
- Why do you think it will be difficult to get hunters to stop killing elephants?
- In your opinion, what would be the best way to save the elephants?

Request an oral rereading of the story and record miscues.

Word Identification in Context	*Deviations from Text*	
7 Miscues = 95% word identification	*Meaning altered*	*Meaning not altered*
Number of Miscues ___	___ words given	___ self-corrections
	___ substitutions	___ substitutions
	___ omissions	___ omissions
	___ additions	___ additions

Comprehension _____   (poor, acceptable, good, excellent)

SELECTION 6 (Transitional)   Silent reading, followed by oral rereading

Prereading Discussion. Find out if the student is familiar with the story of the lion and the mouse. For students who have heard the story before: Have the student retell what he/she remembers about the story. Ask the student to read this version to see if it is the same as the one he/she knows. Ask students who have not heard the story before: Do you think it would be possible for a mouse to help a lion? Discuss briefly. Read this story to find out about a mouse who did help a lion.

The Lion and the Mouse

Once upon a time a big lion was asleep under a tree. A little mouse came by and started playing with his tail. The lion woke up and grabbed the mouse with his paw. "How dare you play with my tail?" he roared. "I am going to eat you up."

"Oh please, Lion, don't eat me," begged the mouse. "If you will let me go, I will help you some day."

The lion laughed. "How could a little mouse help me? That is such a funny idea that I will let you go." And the mouse ran away.

A few days later, some hunters left a net under a tree to catch the lion. The lion got caught in the net. He could not get free. He roared and roared. The mouse heard him roar and ran to see what was wrong. "Lie still," said the mouse. "I will help you." He chewed on the net with his sharp little teeth. He chewed and chewed. He chewed a big hole in the net and the lion got free. "You see?" said the little mouse. "I did help you."

- Tell me in your own words what happened in the story.
- How do you think the lion's feelings about the mouse changed?
- Do you think the mouse would make a good friend?
- What lesson could you learn from this story?

Request an oral rereading of the story and record miscues.

Word Identification in Context	Deviations from Text	
9 Miscues = 95% word identification	*Meaning altered*	*Meaning not altered*
Number of Miscues ___	___ words given	___ self-corrections
	___ substitutions	___ substitutions
	___ omissions	___ omissions
	___ additions	___ additions
Comprehension _____	(poor, acceptable, good, excellent)	

SELECTION 7 (Basic Literacy)   Silent reading

Prereading Discussion. Ask whether the student has ever heard of Jackie Robinson. (He was the first black to play on a major league baseball team.) Ask, "Do you think it was hard for him to be the first black player in the major leagues?" Explain. Find out what the student knows about prejudice, particularly against blacks. (Most children have heard of Martin Luther King, Jr. and can discuss how he fought against this prejudice.)

Jackie Robinson

In 1946, the game of baseball was over 100 years old. But there were no black players on any major league teams. Branch Rickey, manager of the Brooklyn Dodgers, wanted to change this. He started looking for a black player to lead the way. The man had to be special. He had to be a very good player. He had to be brave. Many fans would call him names and boo him. Other players might refuse to play with him.

Rickey finally found his man. Jackie Robinson had been a sports star in high school and college. He was playing on an all-black team when he agreed to play for the Dodgers.

Robinson's problems began right away. Some teams didn't want to play the Dodgers if Robinson played. But the head of the league said they had to. Robinson couldn't believe how much some of the fans and other players hated him. They called him "black boy," and worse names. He wanted to fight, but he had promised not to. He fought back by staying cool and playing hard.

In his first game he scored the winning run. He played well all season, but it was very tough. A turning point came when a runner from another team smashed into Robinson's leg with his sharp spiked shoes—a dirty play. Robinson's whole team ran onto the field, ready to fight. They showed they were behind him. He was part of the team.

Robinson played for many years. He was so good that when he retired, he was voted into the Baseball Hall of Fame. He showed everyone he was a hero.

■ Describe what happened when Jackie Robinson joined the Dodgers.
■ Why did Jackie Robinson have to be so special?
■ Why do you think people treated him so badly?
■ What can we learn from Jackie Robinson?

Comprehension _____ (poor, acceptable, good, excellent)

SELECTION 8 (Basic Literacy)   Silent reading

Prereading Discussion. Find out what the student knows about icebergs. Discuss what they are and where they are found. Read the title together. Why do you think the authors called this "Floating Mountains?" What do you think the writers will say about icebergs?

Floating Mountains

In 1912, the Titanic, loaded with passengers, set off on its first trip across the Atlantic. The Titanic was built in a new way. Its builders said it could not possibly sink. But the Titanic struck an iceberg and sank. More than 1500 people lost their lives.

Icebergs are a great danger to ships because only a small part of the iceberg can be seen above the water. In fact, there is nine times as much ice under the water as above the water. So ships must not get too close to an iceberg. The Titanic got too close. The part of the iceberg that was under the water ripped open the bottom of the ship and made it sink.

Where do icebergs come from? In the coldest parts of the world, the land is covered with ice that moves slowly toward the sea. Ocean waves break off huge pieces of this ice. The pieces that float away from land are called icebergs. Icebergs that stay in the coldest parts of the ocean can float around for 50 or even 100 years. The icebergs that float into warmer parts of the ocean only last a few years.

Icebergs come in all sizes. Many are 20 or 30 feet long. But others are as big as mountains. They can be 80 miles long. To get an idea of how big these giants are, think of a 50-story skyscraper. An iceberg can be just as tall. It may reach 500 feet into the sky. Such icebergs really are floating mountains.

The ice mountains cannot be destroyed. The Coast Guard has tried bombing them, firing torpedoes at them, and shooting at them with their largest guns. But the icebergs do not sink. Since they cannot be destroyed, the Coast Guard does the next best thing. It uses planes to keep track of them. The planes use radar to help locate the icebergs. They report where the icebergs are. And ships are warned by radio.

Floating mountains of ice are among nature's most beautiful sights. But don't get too close to them. They can be deadly.

■ What did you learn from this selection?
■ Why do some icebergs last much longer than others?
■ What are some things ships can do to avoid hitting an iceberg?
■ The authors describe icebergs as "beautiful . . . but deadly." Explain what they mean.

Comprehension _____ (poor, acceptable, good, excellent)

SELECTION 9 (Refinement)   Silent reading

Prereading Discussion. Involve the student in a discussion of what he or she thinks life will be like in the future. How is it likely to be different from life today? Ask the following questions: Have you ever moved to a new home? Do you have friends or relatives who have moved recently? How does moving make people feel? Discuss the student's observations and feelings about such a major change.

Explain that change is occurring in our world at a faster and faster rate. Sometimes people feel they can't keep up with it. This feeling has been called *future shock* by author Alvin Toffler. You are going to read a summary of some of Toffler's ideas about future shock. What do you think might be included?

Are You Headed for Future Shock?

In his book *Future Shock*, Alvin Toffler describes a very different world in the near future from the one we know today. In fact, he says, parts of that world are already here. He warns us to be prepared for the future, so that we are not "shocked" by it.

The new world Toffler describes is one in which life will be even faster than it is today. Much more importance will be placed on getting things done in a hurry. Everything will be more temporary, from your car to relationships with other people. You will move from place to place more than your parents did in their lifetimes. More significance will be placed on newness. If it isn't fresh from the factory, it will be old and not so valuable. And there will be a much wider variety of things made and available in the future.

In the world Toffler foresees, everything will be new, temporary, and varied. The rate of speed at which things will change will grow faster and faster. According to Toffler, this will produce future shock, the dizzy feeling that things are changing too fast. Future shock is the disturbing feeling that the future has arrived before you are prepared for it.

We can see examples of future shock in today's world. Our relationships with things are more temporary now than ever before. We throw away bottles, towels, wrappers, paper bags, newspapers, rugs, radios, televisions, bikes, cars. Almost everything our society produces and buys is designed to be used up quickly. More people rent apartments now than in the past. One can use an apartment for a short while and then move away. Just like paper bags, apartments are designed to be temporary. People move today more than before.

If your parents work for a large company or for the government, you know that a transfer means the entire family must move to a new place. Sometimes you do not even have time to make new friends before you move again. Toffler says this will happen more and more as time goes on. We will have to get used to temporary bottles and cars and apartments. We will also have to get used to temporary friends. A symptom of future shock is the feeling that making new friends is useless, because you will not be around long enough to enjoy them. Or maybe your new friend will move and you will be left behind. It is an empty feeling. Future shock can bring confusion about who you are and where you are going. It can produce irritability, nervousness, and even violence. When you have had too much future shock, you become apathetic. You just sit back and let things happen, whether they are good or bad. You become numb to emotions, people, and things around you.

Future shock is a serious threat. What can you do about it? Toffler suggests some strategies for survival. First, he suggests that students study themselves and the future in school. Future shock can be avoided by starting now to prepare for the future. The future must be managed by us, or else the future will manage us. If we act individually to slow down the pace of our lives, we shall begin to manage our present and our future. If everyone does this, perhaps our society can be brought back under our control and slowed down. That means doing fewer things, but doing them better. It means hanging onto the jacket or the car you were going to get rid of, if only for one more year. It also means making efforts to keep your friendships more lasting. Remembering to send cards and letters to friends, especially on birthdays, holidays, and special occasions, will help keep your friendships going. These are only a few things that each of us can do.

Some people today are working against future shock. They make decisions to settle in one place for a long period of time, sometimes for a lifetime. They buy quality clothing and furniture that will last. Some big companies are not asking their employees to transfer to new locations as often as they did in the 1970s and 1980s. All of this is partly because it is more expensive to live today than it was ten or twenty years ago. People are also beginning to realize how important it is to hold onto the friends and possessions they love.

Personal efforts are necessary to bring future shock under control in our society. But individual efforts are not enough. It is the responsibility of all generations—including yours—to make government and industries work for the best interests of all of the people.

We must decide what is most important to us. Do we want a world without pollution, which would provide a better life for the animals, plants, and people of this planet? Or do we prefer the conveniences and luxuries that pollution-producing industries and transportation provide us? Is there a way we can have the benefits of both?

Nuclear energy and nuclear war are two other important issues we must face. Can nuclear energy be made safe enough for our use? Can nuclear weapons be manufactured and used in a way that will protect us, rather than threaten our existence? These and other issues pose a tremendous challenge for us and our world today and in the future. What will be your response to the challenge?*

- Tell me as much as you can about what the author said in this selection.
- Which of his ideas were new or unexpected for you? (Additional questions may be used to further assess comprehension. However, if these points have already been covered in the student's "retelling," further questions are not necessary.)
- How does future shock affect people? Have you seen any examples of these effects on yourself or other people?
- The author raises these questions: Do we want a world without pollution, or would we rather have the conveniences and luxuries that cannot be provided without pollution? Is it possible to have both? How would you respond?

Comprehension _____ (poor, acceptable, good, excellent)

*From John Jay Bonstingl, *Introduction to the Social Sciences*, pp. 527–529. Copyright © 1985 by Allyn and Bacon. Reprinted with permission.

Gorham (ME) Schools' Literacy Guide

Following is one school district's Literacy Guide for teachers and parents. It is based on adaptations of the ideas presented in *Becoming a Reader*.

Literacy Guide

A description of the developmental stages of literacy with instructional approaches

Gorham Literacy Committee

Copyright by
Gorham School Department
1997

Literacy Guide

Compiled by the Gorham Literacy Committee

Stephanie McLaughlin and Debbie Loveitt, Cochairs

Peter Blackstone

Colleen Fleming

Cheryl Madden

Jane Milliard

Patrick O'Shea

Derek Pierce

Susan Sedenka

Lona Tassey

Priscilla Waters

Sharon Wescott

Resources for this booklet include:

Becoming a Reader by O'Donnell, Wood

Standards for the English Language Arts, a project of IRA & NCTE

Report of the California Reading Task Force

State of Maine Learning Results

Gorham Literacy Curriculum Guide

Introduction

Reading and writing are wonderfully rich and complex human activities. They provoke reflection, introspection, and imaginative thinking and allow us to create and explore new ideas.

This document is meant to help teachers recognize the characteristics students exhibit as they pass through the stages of reading. Instructional approaches are listed to accompany each of the developmental stages of reading. Also included are the State of Maine Learning Performance Indicators for the areas which pertain to reading performance at specific grade levels.

Literacy acquisition is a continuous process and proceeds at differing rates for individual students.

Emergent: *Letters have sounds/Words have meaning*

Goals for the Emergent Reader:
- Seek out and enjoy experiences with books and print
- Become familiar with the language of literature and the patterns of stories
- Understand and follow the sequence of stories read to them
- See themselves as developing readers and writers
- Begin to acquire specific understandings about the nature, purposes, & function of print

The Reader

- Is interested in print
- Has oral language facility
- Begins to understand the nature and purpose of print
    - print is meaningful
    - print is recorded language
    - reading progresses from left to right, top to bottom (in English)
    - printed language is divided into words
    - each written word represents one spoken word
    - words are made up of letters
    - letters represent speech sounds
- Becomes familiar with various children's authors/stories
- Begins to gain familiarity with basic story structures
    - beginning, middle, end
    - introduction, setting, problem, resolution
    - repetitive (The Gingerbread Man)
    - cumulative (The Old Lady Who Swallowed the Fly)
    - patterns: days of week, numbers, ABC, rhyme
    - nursery rhymes and folk/fairy tales
- Expands language development and increase spoken vocabulary
- Discusses books and own writing
- Begins to explore written language
- Begins to recognize word family patterns
    - cat, fat, sat (phonemic awareness)

Emergent: *Letters have sounds/Words have meaning*

State Performance Indicators (By end of grade 2 students will be able to:)
- Distinguish between and make observations about formal and informal uses of English.
- Recognize characteristic sounds and rhythms of language, including the relationship between sounds and letters.
- Make valid observations about the use of words and visual symbols.
- Tell about experiences and discoveries, both orally and in writing.
- Respond to stories orally and in writing.
- Respond to remarks or statements orally and in writing.
- Dictate or write stories or essays which convey basic ideas, have sequences that make sense, and show evidence of a beginning, middle, and ending.
- Understand the main idea of simple expository information.
- Develop a search strategy which uses appropriate and available resources.
- Formulate questions to ask when gathering information.
- Record and share information gathered.

The Teacher

Reads aloud daily from a variety of genres (to small & large groups)

Has a variety of printed material available, including predictable books

Uses shared reading approach daily

Uses language experience approach

Allows opportunities for children to write

Provides many opportunities for students to retell stories
- puppets, story boards, story aprons, drawing, etc.

Provides time for show and tell and other speaking opportunities

Provides a well-stocked classroom library to facilitate self-selection

Provides opportunities for children to listen to stories

Models webbing and other word classification strategies

Models word identification strategies
- syntactic, semantic, and graphophonemic

Uses environmental print

Initial—*Write to read and read to write*

Goals for the Initial Reader:
- View reading and writing as meaning-making processes
- Develop sight vocabulary
- Use syntactic (language patterns), semantic (meanings), and graphophonemic cues to figure out words and construct meaning from text
- See themselves as readers and writers
- Become familiar with a wide variety of age-appropriate texts

The Reader

<u>Begins to explore reading independently</u>

Uses good reading strategies: (reads to the end of sentence, rereads sentence, guesses what word would fit, uses sounds of letters and blends, uses picture clues, knows if word makes sense, and evidences self-correcting monitoring.)

Listens to and discusses a wide variety of literature

• Retells stories in sequence

Understands story language

Can present simple reports and book talks

Responds to literature in a variety of ways including: oral discussion, drawing, writing, book adaptations

Begins to understand sentence structure, capitalization, and punctuation

Uses writing process (prewriting, drafting, revision, simple editing, final product)

Initial—*Write to read and read to write*

State Performance Indicators (By end of grade 2 students will be able to:)
- Distinguish between and make observations about formal and informal uses of English.
- Recognize characteristic sounds and rhythms of language, including the relationship between sounds and letters.
- Make valid observations about the use of words and visual symbols.
- Tell about experiences and discoveries, both orally and in writing.
- Respond to stories orally and in writing.
- Respond to remarks or statements orally and in writing.
- Dictate or write stories or essays which convey basic ideas, have sequences that make sense, and show evidence of a beginning, middle, and ending.
- Understand the main idea of simple expository information.
- Develop a search strategy which uses appropriate and available resources.
- Formulate questions to ask when gathering information.
- Record and share information gathered.

The Teacher

Immerses students in children's literature and a print-rich environment

Uses shared reading

Uses the language experience approach

Uses cloze and sequencing activities from shared reading

Uses follow-up activities focusing on sight vocabulary, story retelling, word identification strategies

Promotes writing process

Reads aloud daily

Uses repeated reading activities

Promotes listening to stories on tape

Creates paired reading opportunities

Promotes home reading

Promotes story patterns using predictable materials

Models use of word identification strategies

Builds phonemic awareness

Transitional—*The reader in exploration*

Goals for the Transitional Reader:
- Expand sight vocabulary and begin to develop fluency
- Expand awareness of sound/symbol correspondence
- Begin to recognize word structures (compound words, root words, prefixes, suffixes, etc.)
- Locate information to support an idea
- Rely on semantic, syntactic, and phonetic cues when reading
- When summarizing a story support it with more detail
- Develop comprehension at all levels (literal, inferential, and evaluative)

The Reader

Recognizes many words on sight in different contexts

Applies different strategies for different purposes (reading for information, reading for enjoyment)

Begins independent selection of appropriate reading materials

Reads a variety of genres

Identifies details in a story through literal questions asked by a teacher

Begins to infer or make associations between characters and their action

Actively listens, asks appropriate questions and comments (audience skills)

Develops a personal point of view about a book, a discussion, or a viewing

Begins to have awareness of basic story elements—character traits, setting, actions that lead to conclusions and involve a problem

Becomes more fluent as an oral reader

Engages in more silent reading practice without subvocalizing

Develops ability to respond to various levels of questioning enabling students to extract essential information from texts

Continues developing phonetic skills and decoding strategies

Recognizes word structure

Expands sound/symbol correspondence in context (digraphs, blends, diphthongs)

Expresses orally and in writing personal connections from reading

Continues to use good reader strategies (see Initial)

Transitional—*The reader in exploration*

State Performance Indicators (By end of 4th grade students will be able to:)
- dentify and evaluate how language use varies according to personal situations and settings (e.g., school, home, and community).
- Identify the social context of conversations and its effect on how language is used.
- Identify the use of nonverbal cues in conversations.
- Make observations about the use of language and graphic symbols encountered in various real-life situations.
- Investigate the languages of other cultures and compare/contrast them to English.
- Make observations about specific uses and idioms of language.
- Use information contained in chapter and section headings, topic sentences, and summary sentences to construct the main ideas.
- Use various informational parts of a text (index, table of contents, glossary, and appendices).
- Read for a variety of purposes (e.g., to answer specific questions, to form an opinion, to skim for information).
- Summarize informational texts (e.g., identify the main idea or concept and the supporting detail).
- Recognize when a text is primarily intended to instruct or persuade.
- Understand common technical terms used in instructional and informational texts.
- Recognize when and how new information in a text connects to prior knowledge.
- Use print and non-print resources (such as encyclopedias, dictionaries, people, indexes) to gather information in connection on research topics.
- Present information obtained from research in a way that combines various forms of information (e.g., maps, charts, photos).
- Distinguish between facts encountered in documents, narratives, and other sources and the generalizations or interpretations a person draws concerning those facts.

The Teacher

Exposes children to rich examples of literature

Demonstrates appreciation for literature by reading aloud

Reviews print concepts (i.e., punctuation, paragraphing, text organization)

Sets purpose for reading; provides opportunities to retell

Provides opportunities for immersion with print

Leads activities such as word banks, word walls, wonder words

Engages in repeated rereadings of text

Teaches study skills, text previewing strategies

Leads Directed Reading Thinking Activities; teaches audience skills

Encourages self-selected reading; teaches 5-finger rule

Provides opportunities to practice literacy (time, choice, sharing)

Models comprehension check by think-aloud activities

Provides opportunities to locate information to support ideas

Provides opportunities for oral and presentation sharing

Basic—*Reading becomes useful to the reader*

Goals for the Basic Reader:
- Expand breadth of experience in reading and writing
- Comprehend increasingly complex reading and writing
- Extend meaning vocabulary
- Develop awareness and use of strategies for reading, writing, and studying
- Automatically rely on semantic, syntactic, and phonetic cues when reading
- Further strengthen comprehension at all levels (literal, inferential, and evaluative)

The Reader

Can set a purpose for reading

Can automatically access prior knowledge during reading

Has internalized and independently uses the three cueing systems

Reads a variety of materials independently with fluency

Makes meaning of new vocabulary derived from literature and content reading

Has an extensive sight vocabulary

Will give oral reports and public speaking addresses, and learn to debate

Can predict and confirm expectations and outcomes from a text

Distinguishes between fact and opinion

Understands author's intent

Uses graphic organizers such as semantic mapping to help comprehension

Is aware of characterization in text

Can recall details

Recognizes story elements such as plot, conflict, theme

Recognizes a topic's main idea

Can synthesize information gathered from skimming

Able to link story problems to their solutions or resolutions

Able to compare and contrast genres, story lines, and authors' styles

Can gather relevant information from content reading

Uses a variety of genres to promote discussion and understanding within subject areas

Continues to work on summarizing

Building note taking skills, begin outlining in preparation for a report

Able to ask questions to seek new information in content areas

Can preview text with the intent of information gathering

Basic—*Reading becomes useful to the reader*

State Performance Indicators (By end of 8th grade students should be able to:)
- Form conclusions regarding formal, informal, and other varieties of language use, based on experience.
- Understand factors that commonly affect language change and use.
- Consult pertinent information sources on language use (e.g., a dictionary, a thesaurus, a handbook on style).
- Use knowledge of the fundamental parts of speech when writing and speaking.
- Demonstrate an understanding of the concept of propaganda.
- Seek appropriate assistance when attempting to comprehend a challenging text.
- Identify information that is personally useful.
- Identify both the author's purpose and the author's point of view when reading expository information.
- Identify different ways in which informational texts are organized.
- Produce and support generalizations acquired from informational text.
- Describe new knowledge presented in informational texts and how it can be used.
- Identify common technical terms used in informational texts.
- Use the various parts of a text (index, table of contents, glossary) to locate specific information.

The Teacher

Models book talks, literature discussion groups, literature activities, and projects

Models comprehension strategies and metacognitive connection making

Builds methods in discourse and debate

Offers opportunities to react to a variety of texts

Models thinking strategies on all three comprehension levels

Models literary terms (character, plot, foreshadowing, etc.)

Develops environment in which questioning is seen as a way to stimulate learning

Models inquiry approaches

Builds phoneme awareness through English mini-lessons in the writing process and vocabulary development work

Displays different formal language structures of tests to student (comparisons and contrasts of stories, poems, books, newspapers)

Facilitates spelling and vocabulary development as part of literacy program

Builds understanding of parts/affixes, homophones, etc.

Models these practices (book talks, use of compulsories) in developing skills for report writing and delivery, use of Socratic method in teaching of debate abilities

Directs students' attention to refining decoding strategies (use of running records, IRIs)

Reviews study skills, text previewing strategies

Refinement—*Perfecting reading skills*

Goals for the Refinement Reader:
■ At this stage the goal is to refine the goals addressed for basic readers using increasingly more sophisticated material and more complex analysis of that material

The Reader

When researching, student selects topic and appropriate texts, surveys, scans, extracts and analyzes necessary information

Reads automatically for any variety of purposes and can adapt to level of difficulty of text

Connects texts to own life and society

Understand subtexts

Recognizes and critiques themes and patterns in texts

Makes sense of difficult words in context

Evaluates and critiques tone and style in texts

Draws on prior knowledge and experience in conceptualizing and synthesizing

Applies advanced summarizing and visualizing

Understands formal language structures of a variety of genres

Adjusts strategies to meet challenges of a particular text

Refinement—*Perfecting reading skills*

State Performance Indicators (By end of 12th grade students should be able to:)
- Demonstrate an understanding of the relationship among perception, thought, and language.
- Demonstrate an understanding of how language considerations and representations involving gender affect communication.
- Compare the ways various social, occupational, and cultural groups use language, and comment on the impact of language use on the way people are viewed and treated.
- Compare form, meaning, and value of different kinds of symbol systems (e.g., religious symbols, holiday symbols, the symbolism of particular type of architecture).
- Demonstrate understanding of the history of and changes in the English language by explaining examples.
- Use dictionaries, handbooks, and other language-related resources to evaluate the accuracy of their use of English.
- Demonstrate an understanding of the political implications of different forms of language.
- Identify propaganda techniques used by writers and speakers.
- Scan a passage to determine whether a text contains relevant information.
- Distinguish between apparent fact and opinion in nonfiction texts.
- Use discussions with peers as a way of understanding information.
- Identify complex structures in informational texts and the relationships between the concepts and details in those structures using texts from various disciplines.
- Analyze and synthesize the concepts and details in informational texts.
- Explain how new information from a text changes personal knowledge.

The Teacher

Incorporates all Basic Stage approaches

Provides opportunities for self-selected reading and sharing

Utilizes the writing process to develop reading and thinking in all content areas

Chooses high-quality, level-appropriate literature and content readings to model teacher-guided strategies that promote critical thinking and comprehension
- Directed Reading–Thinking Activity
- Question/Answer/Relationships
- Reciprocal Teaching
- Analogies
- Text Preview Guides

Helps potentially "frustrating" texts become more reader-friendly

Encourages integration of content-related literature (all genres) to enrich students' knowledge base

Facilitates development of research skills

Developmental Stages of Literacy
(O'Donnell/Wood)

Emergent

- Has oral language facility
- Shows interest in print

Initial

- Reads some words
- Has developed some specific print concepts
- Matches some speech sounds with letters

Transitional

- Recognizes many words at sight
- Successfully applies word identification strategies
- Reads independently

Basic

- Reads a variety of materials independently
- Has an extensive sight vocabulary (reads fluently)

Refinement

- Has acquired functional literacy
- Reads for a variety of purposes

Author Index

Subject Index